THE MAASAI OF MATAPATO

First published in 1988, *The Maasai of Matapato* has become a classic of ethnography. This detailed study of the Maasai of the Matapato region of Kenya builds up a full and engaging picture of the rituals and ideals of life amongst the Maasai. It deals with the cultural phenomenon of age organization, and looks particularly at three central questions: how men and women are controlled by age organization for the majority of their lives; how men and women develop age-sets and turn them into ongoing concerns; and how age-sets are connected to the management of households, particularly the control of women, children and cattle. Spencer examines the age system, marriage and family to consider how the Maasai's social values and relationships are expressed in, and shaped by, concepts of age.

In his new preface, Paul Spencer looks back at how he came to write this important work, its continuing relevance today, and how the Maasai have been affected by global developments since the book's first publication.

Paul Spencer is Honorary Director of the International African Institute and Emeritus Professor of African Anthropology at the School of Oriental and African Studies in the UK. He is a world authority on the peoples of East Africa and author of *The Samburu* (1965, 2004), and *Time, Space and the Unknown* (2004).

ROUTLEDGE CLASSIC ETHNOGRAPHIES bring together key anthropology texts which have proved formative in the development of the discipline. Originally published between the 1930s and the 1980s, these titles have had a major impact on the way in which anthropology, and most particularly ethnography, is conducted, taught, and studied.

Each book contains the text and illustrations from the original edition, as well as a new preface by a leading anthropologist explaining the book's contribution to the development of anthropology and its continuing relevance in the twenty-first century.

ABORIGINAL WOMAN
Sacred and profane
Phyllis M. Kaberry

WOMEN OF THE GRASSFIELDS
A study of the economic position of women
in Bamenda, British Cameroons
Phyllis M. Kaberry

STONE AGE ECONOMICS
Marshall Sahlins

THE MAASAI OF MATAPATO
A study of rituals of rebellion
Paul Spencer

THE SAMBURU
A study of gerontocracy
Paul Spencer

HUNGER AND WORK IN A SAVAGE TRIBE
A functional study of nutrition among the southern Bantu
Audrey Richards

CUSTOM AND POLITICS IN URBAN AFRICA
A study of Hausa migrants in Yoruba towns
Abner Cohen

THE MAASAI OF MATAPATO

A study of rituals of rebellion

Paul Spencer

Routledge
Taylor & Francis Group

LONDON AND NEW YORK

First published 1988
by Manchester University Press

This edition first published 2004 by Routledge
11 New Fetter Lane, London EC4P 4EE

Simultaneously published in the USA and Canada
by Routledge
29 West 35th Street, New York, NY 10001

Routledge is an imprint of the Taylor & Francis Group

Printed and bound in Great Britain by
TJ International Ltd, Padstow, Cornwall

British Library Cataloguing in Publication Data
A catalogue record for this book is available from the British Library

Library of Congress Cataloging in Publication Data
Spencer, Paul, 1932–
The Maasai of Matapato : a study of rituals of rebellion / Paul Spencer ;
[with a new preface by Paul Spencer].
p. cm.
"First published 1988 by Manchester University Press" – T.p. verso.
Includes bibliographical references and index.
ISBN 0–415–31723–1 (pbk.)
1. Masai (African people) – Social life and customs. 2. Masai (African
people) – Rites and ceremonies. 3. Age groups – Kenya – Matapatu.
4. Matapatu (Kenya) – Social life and customs. I. Title.
DT433.545.M33S64 2004
306'.089'965 – dc21   2003046979

ISBN 0–415–31723–1

To Aidan and Idun

CONTENTS

Maps

Tables

Figures

PREFACE TO NEW EDITION

The Maasai of Matapato was first published in 1988, and this new edition by Routledge is linked to the reissue of my earlier book on *The Samburu* (1965) and to the publication of a new volume that elaborates on the Maasai more generally. In this sequence of research, the Samburu of Kenya were the most northern group of pastoralists in the Maa-speaking region with an age organization that was more rudimentary and clear-cut than among the Maasai proper, but also a more elaborate system of clanship. Although I did not realize it at the time, the Samburu were an ideal society for an anthropological novice and a very practical starting point for a later career in Maasai studies.

The path leading me from the Samburu to the Matapato Maasai was not straightforward as my longer-term commitments lay elsewhere. After leaving school, my national service had provided a rudimentary training in electronic systems and circuitry in order to undertake repair work. I then took a degree in engineering at Cambridge, which made me aware that we have to cope with the complexities of this world through crude working models. However, technological progress appeared to be racing ahead of industrial relations, and it was the latter that aroused my curiosity. At that time, social anthropology suggested a useful way into this subject, and as I turned to study it, my intrigue grew. This led me to spend three years in East Africa, focusing on the Samburu for a doctorate at Oxford. It was an unrepeatable experience, and I regarded it as a fundamental way of broadening my understanding that would lead me to some kind of employment in industrial relations. At the age of 30, with the Samburu behind me, I joined the staff of the Tavistock Institute of Human Relations in London, where an industrial project was earmarked for my next piece of research. But with problems of funding, I came no nearer to any industrial complex than conducting a series of interviews on garage forecourts. This was followed by work with operational research colleagues on aspects of planning in local and central government, the national health service, and a period of secondment to the Royal Commission on Local Government. The frustrations of this medley of experience were interspersed with illuminating patches that generated their own enthusiasm. But after nine years and now in mid-career, I felt that I had achieved my only really worthwhile piece of research among the Samburu. *The Samburu* had by now been published as my first book and it was time to move back to the academic world, if they would accept me with such a piecemeal package of experience. The Introduction to the present work picks up the story from this point.

Above all, with my opportunities for a career slipping away, I had acquired a sense of ageing – a topic that was to become my speciality. It may be no coincidence that the elders in the present volume are given an altogether bumpier ride than those in the pages of *The Samburu*. My first work had focused on the stark opposition between *moran* (warriors) and elders. This was clearly relevant in Matapato also, although with a distinct shift towards rivalries between age-sets that persisted throughout elderhood.

Among my various writings on Maa-speaking peoples and some of their neighbours, I would single out the present work on the Matapato as the fullest statement of an age system. The relevance of this topic should be stressed. Age systems have been reported in most parts of the world, ranging from Ancient Greece, to China, the Plains Indians, and scattered parts of Africa. The universal pattern, however, has been for this phenomenon to dwindle to insignificance in the historical process of development and urbanization, when alternative principles that foster social differentiation and inequality become dominant. The only significant cluster of age-based societies that still remains lies in the hinterland of East Africa, where the development of the market system has an altogether shallower history than in West Africa, for instance. This is reflected in striking differences between the two regions in relation to the impact of world religions and the status of women through their trading networks, which are altogether more developed in the west. Thus the Maasai and their age-based neighbours – ranging from northern Tanzania to southern Ethiopia and eastern Uganda – provide a diminishing opportunity to understand a fundamental alternative to society as we find it elsewhere. It was the need to study this phenomenon while the opportunity remains that determined my choice to focus my next study on the traditional system of the Maasai.

The Maasai of Matapato was originally conceived as the first part of a larger volume, leading to a second part entitled 'Models of the Maasai', and then to an extensive survey of variation among the Maasai as an appendix. In the event, it became clear that the Matapato section was quite long enough to form a book in its own right, and I reshaped it to this end, leading to its publication.

'Models of the Maasai' considered other aspects of the Maasai peoples, with special reference to a fundamental shift in emphasis from north to south. The Matapato were situated towards the centre of this range, provid-ing a useful intermediate point from which to view this wider pattern. It was from this perspective that the third volume in the present series took shape, coining the title *Time, Space, and the Unknown* (2004). Besides the regional pattern of variation, this work examines facets of the Maasai sense of existence and of being Maasai; and beyond this world-view lies a whole realm of cosmology that cannot be known, but is dimly perceived and explains the power of the elders' curse. At some distance from Matapato lives their Prophet, who can penetrate this uncertain realm, protecting them from sorcery. In this outline of beliefs, the Samburu are strikingly different, with less concern for sorcery and the power of Prophets, and a more vivid cosmology that throws further light on Maasai beliefs. In this way, the final volume of this series leads back to the first, just as the regional pattern among the Maasai may be extended to the Samburu in the far north and suggests certain historical inferences. In this series of three successive volumes, I regard *The Maasai of Matapato* as the central ethnographic statement, albeit inspired by *The Samburu*, and leading on to *Time, Space, and the Unknown* as an elaboration of the wider scene.

On returning to the academic fold, it was ironic that my research interest turned back from contemporary issues – satisfied that I had little more to offer – to the study of traditional African societies, just at a time when social anthropology was poised to shift its attention to problems of development and urbanization in a multicultural world. Analysis of recent development among the Maasai or Samburu is significantly absent from these three volumes. This is not to deny the complexity or the urgency of this topic, nor the extent to which it can throw further light on the individuality of traditional societies and their ability to cope with change. But it draws attention to two divergent priorities in research. The literature on pastoralism in East Africa reveals a striking contrast between the vivid individuality that characterizes each tribal group and the monotonous uniformity of the relentless process of development, leading to the erosion of rich traditions. While development is an urgent and humane issue, the variety of cultures is a dwindling asset that can teach us much about the fundamentals of humanity itself, as I have argued above. This led me in two diverging directions. Among the Maasai, I chose the Matapato because they were one of the remoter parts least affected by change, and their central position and intermediate size seemed to offer a representative sample for studying the traditional system, although not the process of development. I deliberately chose to focus on their traditional way of life, as they presented it, before it was drained of colour, and this no doubt dulled my perception of the drab nuances of globalization and development that were creeping in and formed the inescapable background to my research.

At the same time, especially for my teaching at the School of Oriental and African Studies, I needed to be aware of the process of development. Fieldwork among the Chamus of Lake Baringo, who were a hybrid of indigenous, Samburu, and Maasai cultures, and my reading of the literature on East African pastoralism led to a further volume. This was *The Pastoral*

Continuum (1998), which sought to trace the emergence of development out of traditional societies and a historical process that has been much broader than social change in any single tribal group. Operating at a more global level, this entailed a separate line of enquiry from my fieldwork among the Maasai, who unlike the Chamus had little sense of their own history. The absence of anything original to write on development among the Maasai is an admission that I have failed to find any unique feature there that does not appear to be altogether more general.

Nor am I alone in finding the problem of social change among the Maasai elusive, for pronouncements on this topic are notoriously misleading. Official reports from time to time have pointed to the imminence of change and the end of the age system and moranhood; and then these claims have been contradicted subsequently. Official education policies have been notoriously ineffective. Grazing schemes have been introduced in some parts and then they appear to have broken down at the most critical point. The title *The Last of the Ma(a)sai* was coined for a book in 1901 and then again in 1987; and two other writers claim to have witnessed the final *eunoto* ceremony in a dwindling tradition (or so they were told). Yet the Maasai have retained a distinct identity, and these ceremonies have continued to be performed as a central feature of moranhood about every seven years. Clearly, there must always have been some change among the Maasai, and there must eventually be a final *eunoto* ceremony and an end to the notion of 'Maasai' in any recognizable sense. However, these pronouncements have underestimated Maasai resilience in responding to the inevitability of change, and this is a phenomenon that deserves attention. In the present volume, minor changes and shifts in custom are relevant in so far as they illuminate the ability of the custodians of the traditional system – the elders – to adapt to change, as must always have been the case.

There remains the unpublished survey that was originally intended as an appendix to the present volume. This was based on visits to nine other Maasai communities in addition to the Matapato, exploring confusions in the literature and local variations that emerged in the course of my enquiry. This is essentially archival material for the specialist on Maasai practices. I would invite any readers who are interested in a copy of this survey to contact me, whether it is for their personal collection or to delve into the wider pattern for themselves and perhaps suggest alternative ways of analysing it, especially if they have further material of their own on the Maasai.

In addition to those that I have already thanked in *The Maasai of Matapato*, I would like to add the Publications Committee of the International African Institute for permission to republish this work. No changes have been made to the original text, apart from correcting some obvious errors.

When I submitted my proposal for a further book on the Maasai to Routledge, Julene Knox was the commissioning editor for anthropology and religion, and I must express my special gratitude to her for the idea that the new work should extend to a trilogy, including this reissue of *The Maasai of Matapato*. This suggestion made good sense in terms of a coherent package, as I have tried to show. However, it went far beyond my more limited vision of trying to reduce my debt to the Maasai with just one further volume that has been intermittently emerging for over two decades. It gives me hope that I may at last turn to Masiani's life-story, to which I aspired (p. 3), and the Maasai can then have the final word.

Paul Spencer
2003

Bibliography

Amin, M. and Willetts, D., 1987, *The Last of the Maasai*, Nairobi: Westlands Sundreys.

Hinde, H. and Hinde, S.L., 1901, *The Last of the Ma(a)sai*, London: Heinemann.

Spencer, P., 1965, *The Samburu: a study of gerontocracy*, London: Routledge and Kegan Paul (reprinted 2004, London: Routledge).

—— 1988, *The Maasai of Matapato: a study of rituals of rebellion*, Manchester: Manchester University Press, on behalf of the International African Institute.

—— 1998, *The Pastoral Continuum: the marginalization of tradition in East Africa*, Oxford: Clarendon.

—— 2004, *Time, Space, and the Unknown: Maasai configurations of power and providence*, London: Routledge.

PREFACE AND ACKNOWLEDGEMENTS

The research on which this volume is based was undertaken between July 1976 and September 1977. I would like to take this opportunity of expressing my gratitude to four bodies whose support was essential. The School of Oriental and African Studies, as my employers, gave me leave of absence from teaching to undertake the field work, a loan to purchase a landrover, and the milieu in which to translate my field experience into publishable form. The research was based on sponsorship by the Social Science Research Council, and they provided a grant that covered my basic expenses. The Office of the President in Kenya gave me research clearance which proved invaluable while working close to the border with Tanzania during a sensitive period. This clearance was linked to a Research Associateship at the Institute of African Studies, University of Nairobi, whose academic hospitality during periods in Nairobi was an important counterpart to time spent in the field.

Working principally among married Maasai elders, a strategic component of this research was to accompany my own family into the field. To the extent that we were as much a domestic curiosity to them as they were to us, there was a basis for a rapport out of which understanding developed. The experience of sharing this opportunity with Rosalind, Aidan and Benet is a memory that we treasure. At the same time, I have to thank them for all their help, and for putting up with the discomforts and frustrations of an existence that constantly revolved around my own preoccupation rather than theirs. Quite apart from my own thanks to them for their companionship and contribution to this work at many levels, this is an opportunity to acknowledge the help and support that we received as a family from many people during our time in Kenya.

In Nairobi and on a visit to Lamu, we were given generous hospitality by Jim Allen, whose enthusiasm for research arising from his position at the Institute of African Studies extended to pastoralists such as the Maasai. His shrewd advice undoubtedly saved time on a number of issues and gave orientation for our work with the Institute. In Nairobi also we benefited from the kind hospitality of Roy Shaffer and his family, whose interest in our work arose out of their lifelong involvement with the Maasai. Through the British Institute in East Africa, we had further loans of equipment and also friendly help from Margaret Sharman, and from Neville Chittick and David Phillipson.

Our research in Matapato arose out of a visit to Diana Witts, a friend who was developing the mission at Meto and was devoted to helping the local population, especially during the serious drought while we were there. What had originally been intended as a brief visit to test our camping equipment in the Maasai area was quickly converted into a base for our research proper when it became clear that Meto provided an ideal location, remote and in the heart of Maasailand, but still accessible. Camping about four miles from the mission, we were close neighbours and benefited from Diana's ready help and enthusiasm, and through her from our friendship with Derek and Pat Wilks, and with Max Nicolaison at Loitokitok. From Meto we travelled to other parts of the Maasai area in the course of our work, but we constantly returned to Meto, adding to our indebtedness to the mission there.

Our deepest gratitude is clearly to the Maasai themselves, and so far as this volume is concerned to those of Matapato. Chief David Ole Kisipan gave us his blessing and some friendly advice. We deliberately avoided Swahili or English-speaking assistants so that Rosalind could learn Maasai and I could convert my rusty Samburu dialect into a more presentable form. I employed Kinai Ole Chieni to this end during the first few months, and my initial grasp of what later proved to be key issues arose out of our long discussions together. Our closest and most endearing companion was Ndooki Ole Musei, who joined us as camp assistant and travelled with us throughout our work, helping Rosalind to grasp the language. Towards the end, when I revisited other parts of Maasai alone, Lemaya Ole Parmaya accompanied me as camp assistant with a flair for clarifying issues that I had not quite grasped.

With these companions, there was no sharp dividing line between our team of helpers and the Matapato from whom we were seeking to learn, and our indebtedness extends to all those Maasai that we knew at Meto and elsewhere. We were driven by their infectious and insistent enthusiasm for their system, as they explained, elaborated, and reiterated any point, until they were satisfied that we had grasped it. On almost any issue, they could cite case examples that clarified Maasai practice, often from the Meto area itself and involving people whom we knew. It was such examples coupled with our own experience that formed the basis for further discussion. These examples provide the core of this volume, although the need to retain confidentiality has necessarily led to changing the names of the actors. But this does not lessen our debt both to my informants and to all those whose Maasai-ness led to their doings being recorded here. The engaging aspects of many of these examples is the enchantment of our memories of the area.

During the long period of writing up this work, my approach has benefited from discussions with many colleagues, both in seminars and informally. Among these I must record my special thanks to Richard Waller, whose unrivalled grasp of Maasai history and generous advice over the years has added a further dimension and confidence to my own work. This was capped by his extensive comments on the penultimate version of this volume before it went to press, providing a final check on a wide range of issues and (characteristically) further insights.

Finally there remains my thanks to those involved on behalf of the International African Institute with the production of this work, notably Elizabeth Dunstan, and also to Lotte Hughes for checking the proofs. This volume is the outcome of all this help and encouragement and it is to be hoped that it goes some way towards fulfilling my general obligation.

NOTE ON MAASAI TERMS

Tucker and Mpaayei's grammar (1955) played an essential role in my original learning of the Maasai language; and more recently Mol's dictionary (1978) has provided a useful supplement. With these source books available, I have not attempted here to elaborate on linguistic aspects. However, the context of a variety of Maasai vernacular meanings is often lost in such works, and it has been useful to incorporate these at appropriate points in the text (in parenthesis as far as possible). They are systematically listed in the index at the end of the volume.

Because this is not intended as a linguistic work, I have tried to simplify the spelling for easier reading. Terms in general use in Kenya, such as *moran* and *manyata*, have been coined in their most popular form. Similarly, popular spelling has been adopted for the names of places, tribal sections and age-sets, omitting their gender prefixes. Tonal marks have been omitted. The use of hyphens is confined to terms such as verbs where it is useful to separate the root from its prefix. The spelling *ch* should invariably be pronounced as in *change*; *nk* represents a sound between NK as in *thinker* and NG as in *finger*; *ng* is used for the velar nasal sound as in *thing*, and not as in *finger*. Thus the term *Loonkidongi* pronounces the K implosively and does not pronounce the G at all. In other respects, I have tried to follow Tucker and Mpaayei's system for indicating Matapato usage.

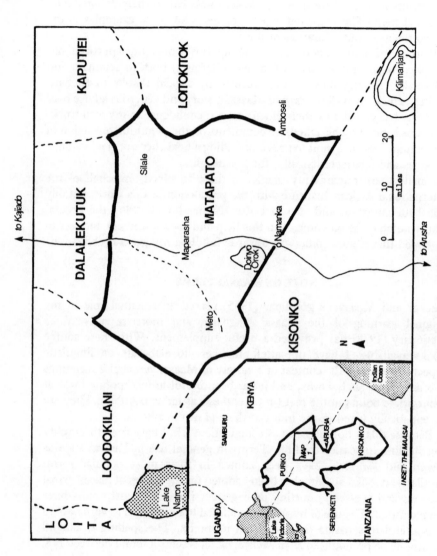

Map 1   The Matapato and their neighbours

INTRODUCTION

The Maasai are widely known as an East African phenomenon, associated with their domination of the plains between Lake Victoria and the coast in the nineteenth century. Their reputation clings, and with it a popular fascination in the persistence of their society and identity which marks them off from their neighbours. The present study owes much to my earlier work among the Samburu, where I first learned the Maasai language and culture, and became aware of the significance of age organisation in East Africa. At that time, my original intention had actually been to work among the Maasai themselves. However, with two other anthropologists already established in the area, it seemed more sensible to turn instead to the Samburu further north, who shared a tradition of common origin with the Maasai. This switch to a simpler, more rudimentary culture about whom, unlike the Maasai, virtually nothing had been written was an unexpected stroke of good fortune. The Samburu were an ideal society for a novice anthropologist in a way that the Maasai were not, and this clarified the topic for research. With peace broadly established in the area, one could no longer account for the stability of their age system, with its emphasis on warriorhood, by reference to past intertribal warfare. It seemed necessary to examine the links between the age system and other aspects of Samburu society, notably problems associated with extensive polygyny and the implications of this for young men. It was an unashamedly functionalist study, but with the persistence of tradition against all the odds and the general absence of any basic models of age organisation, no alternative approach readily suggested itself as a working premise.

In the present volume there is no need to repeat all the arguments pieced together in its predecessor, *The Samburu: a study of gerontocracy* (1965). These apply broadly to the Maasai, but the two societies have some striking differences and themes examined here are rather different. It is tempting to regard the Samburu with their simpler age system, weaker diviners, stronger clans, and situated in the far north, as closer to some proto-Maasai ancestral group. Such a group seems to have existed before the Maasai migrated southwards to build up their formidable reputation and more complex institutions in their present area. This possibility is beyond the scope of the present volume, but it accurately reflects the history of my own understanding. The Samburu model provided an initial approximation for the Maasai and had its uses as an ideal type. My approach had been moulded by the Samburu, and from that starting point, I had to rely on the Maasai themselves to redirect me.

After completing my work on the Samburu, my interests led in other directions. I only returned to the problems of age organisation in East Africa and the continuing need for further research among the pastoral Maasai after a break of nine years, when I was appointed as a member of staff at the School of Oriental and African Studies in London. It then became apparent that the existing literature on the Maasai overlooked the possibility of variation between the sixteen or so tribal sections. Writers had tended to note that the Maasai do this or that, rather than noting, for instance, that the Purko Maasai do this or the Kisonko Maasai do that. This in itself could account for many of the contradictions between different sources. There were, for instance, at least seven incompatable versions of the major events leading up to the formation of a new age-set, eleven versions of their system of clanship, and so on.[1] In certain other respects there were glaring gaps. There was nothing of substance on their system of kinship, and no clear indication of the ways in which the age organisation was linked with the family, which had been a critical feature of my earlier study. There were surprisingly few case examples to relate custom to the give and take of daily life, apart from Gulliver's striking study of the agricultural Arusha (1963), and even his rich material lent itself to an alternative interpretation (Spencer 1976). Of particular interest was the evidence that many Maasai men married earlier than the Samburu, reducing the age gap between father and son. This could increase the scope for competition between generations and have relevance for the age organisation beyond the family, especially as there was also evidence of greater competition for wives.[2] If some basic model could be established, then the variation between tribal sections promised to be a research asset rather than a liability, since the model could be tested by examining possible correlations within the broad pattern of variation.

In August 1976, now as a family team with Rosalind and our sons, Aidan and Benet, playing a crucial role in my fieldwork and exactly twenty years after first proposing to study the Maasai, I actually found myself for the first time setting foot inside the Maasai area. Our starting point was clearly to take just one Maasai tribal section and to examine the connections between the age organisation and other facets of their existence. The need to base our research on a traditional area led us first to the Matapato Maasai who have probably had less close administration than any other tribal section, less contact with recent change, and virtually no tourism. Apart from a fast main road for traffic speeding non-stop through their area, the Matapato are remote, wholly surrounded by other Maasai, and typical in so many ways as to be almost uniquely unremarkable. Within Matapato we selected an area that lay at the end of an impermanent motor track stopping at the border with Tanzania: Meto. Here was a scattered cluster of villages coping with the worst drought they had experienced in at least fifteen years, and many claimed it was even worse than the notorious drought of 1961. This in no way diminished their faith in the indigenous system as the only practical adaptation to their problem. Drought prevailed throughout the wider region and they could only rely on the local mission station and on government aid up to a point. Beyond this they had to cope on their own as they knew best.

It is characters known or remembered at Meto who figure prominently in this study, their identities suitably disguised. One of them, whom I will call Masiani, was our first host, and while we camped by his village his son for a time became my research assistant. As an informant, Masiani was not particularly well informed. He was becoming deaf and had a casual disregard for the niceties of Matapato convention coupled with a lack of interest in the underlying system. However, as a raconteur who could hold an audience with tall stories of his own past, he was outstanding. Hopefully, the recorded text of his life story will be published elsewhere, providing an extended case example as well as a character study. In the present volume, this story is fragmented and interspersed with other illustrations in the trend of the argument. It is especially relevant to the developing relationship between father and son. Masiani was caught up in the problems at both ends of this relationship, first as a truculent boy and later when I knew him as a domineering patriarch. In the intervening years, as a warrior who never quite settled down to a docile elderhood, he was the centre of various local disputes and at one point of a major crisis between Matapato and their closest allies, the Loodokilani Maasai. Yet as a warm and generous member of his age-set, who was heavily dependent on the companionship of his age mates and always finally deferred to their judgment, he retained his place in the local community and the respect due to a man of his age. One can clearly discern in his life story the inherent tension between the two principal institutions of the Maasai: the independent family under the authority of a self-seeking patriarch and the age-set of peers that demands selfless loyalty. Masiani with his erratic ways was a product of Matapato society and not a quirk. Nor, it should be stressed, is this a purely Matapato phenomenon. In a recent autobiography by Tepilit Ole Saitoti (1986), the author is manifestly outlining his own experience as a Serenket Maasai whose chequered career led him through the modern educational system to attain professional status. But the subsidiary theme that gives his account a moving timbre is his deep attachment to the family dominated by his overbearing father. Saitoti's dilemma as a Maasai suspended between two cultures appears to be matched by his father's dilemma as an ageing patriarch who finds himself strangely isolated as his sons reach towards a degree of independence, rebelling against his regime, and yet clinging to the principles on which it is based and deeply loyal to him as a person. It is this second dilemma, concerning the indigenous career structure of Maasai manhood and the succession of generations, that is a major theme in the present volume.

In Matapato, the complexity of the system called for an altogether wider range of examples than could be collected from first-hand experience in only a year of fieldwork, especially during the earlier months of severe drought. As opportunities arose, I collected some first-hand data, as in Chapter 9 on the *eunoto* ceremony. However, beyond these it was necessary to rely on the memories and integrity of perceptive informants and to accept that this had its dangers. It also had its advantages, for gossip and discussion are as much a part of the ritual process among the Maasai as the nodal events when they briefly collect together to perform their ceremonies. Gossip revealed a perspective on these events that was at least meaningful to the tellers, and formed a basis for further discussion and further examples. To the extent that these second-hand examples are often anecdotal rather than profound, they are at least Matapato anecdotes. What they may lack in accurate reporting, they gain in presenting the elders' view of themselves. They are the stuff of folklore in the form that it is reiterated and handed on. They are the type of precedent cited in debate and this gives them a dynamic role within the system. For the Matapato, they *are* the system.

After an initial five months at Meto, we began to visit some of the other tribal sections among the Kenya Maasai: Loitokitok because they were the Kenya representatives of the important Kisonko group to the south; Purko because they were the dominant section of the north; Loita because they were historically important; and Uasinkishu because they were an outlying section with links outside Maasai society. Increasingly, it became clear that I should extend this survey to the Loonkidongi dynasty of diviners and Prophets who mostly lived on the boundaries between the major tribal sections. By accident rather than design, I was able to work briefly with some Tanzanian Kisonko who were temporarily resident on the Kenya side of the border in Meto, and with Siria Maasai whom we met on the way to Uasinkishu. It was the Loitokitok and Purko who in particular opened up my understanding, and I paid them further visits. But we constantly had to return to Matapato and Meto, using this comparative data to explore the new themes and check on old ones. The comparative dimension will (hopefully) be explored in a sequel to this volume, *Models of the Maasai*, and reveal a pattern of variation from north to south, with the Samburu appropriately located in the far north, and the Matapato Maasai slightly south of centre.[3]

The present volume concerns the dynamics of the age system in Matapato, which provides the central institution for political action. Like other Maasai, the Matapato are unconcerned with this pattern of variation beyond their borders or its historical significance. They share a pride in their past, but have no developed sense of their own history or of the changing opportunities of the contemporary scene. It is not that they are unaware of development or unconcerned, but they are absorbed in the continuous process of change generated within their own social system. Men of all ages, and ultimately women too, have aspirations geared to this system beside which outside opportunities are perceived as irrelevant and even unrealistic. Their perception of time is primarily linked to their age organisation with its own internal processes of change entailing a periodic cycle of about fifteen years, which is the interval between successive age-sets. To an outsider, the endless recurrence of this cycle may appear static as compared with the dialectics of change in Kenya. For the individual passing through this system in the course of his life, it entails a succession of radical transitions with its own inner dialectic, and the unfolding of a shared experience. Unlike modern change and development, the process here is basically predictable in outline, although in detail it is a matter of endless speculation and uncertainty: it is always a live issue. This is a study of a society as a process in time relative to the individual, concerning cyclical change, ageing, and the dynamics of community life. This is somewhat different from the cyclical change in Highland Burma inferred by Leach (1954), which takes place over too extended a period to be perceived by the people themselves. In the Matapato instance, it is a thoroughly self-conscious process; and it provides an endless topic of anticipation and concern.

Central to this concern is the process whereby each successive age-group of *moran* (or warriors) establish their warrior villages (*manyat*, s. *manyata*). This is achieved through a ritualised form of rebellion directed against their fathers. It is the first stage of an extended rite of transition separating them from the villages ruled by the elders and culminating years later when they are themselves incorporated into elderhood. The elders at times lose a degree of control over the younger men, but it is they who control the system and perpetuate it, domesticating the moran by stages, and ultimately controlling them. In the final resort, elderhood lies at the heart of the system and it grows out of moranhood and the manyata experience. Wars and warrior-villages are no longer strictly relevant for this society, but moran and manyat have survived attempts by successive Kenya administrations to abolish them and I have resisted the temptation to translate or respell these widely known terms.

'Rituals of rebellion' is a term coined by Max Gluckman (1963) in his attempt to refine the work of Frazer (1922), which had also inspired Freud's excursion into anthropology (1950). Matapato provides an exceptionally useful context in which to examine this widespread phenomenon of ritualised protest in a variety of guises, and I have borrowed Gluckman's term here. Other anthropological usages associated with age organisation should be noted. Matapato youths, who have been initiated during a given period to become moran, comprise an *age-group*. When eventually they are promoted to elderhood, each pair of successive age-groups throughout Maasai join together to form a single Maasai-wide *age-set*. *Age mates* are members of the same age-group (or age-set according to context). For the casual reader, the distinction between age-groups and age-sets need not be constantly borne in mind. If these terms are regarded as interchangeable, then little will be lost – and even the Maasai themselves tend to be rather loose in their usage of terms associated with each level. For the careful reader, the terms are used consistently with this distinction in mind. An *age grade* is a stage through which males progress, such as boyhood, and then moranhood, and eventually elderhood; and these may be sub-divided into junior and senior moranhood, and so on. By analogy, if one were to envisage the age organisation as a procession up a ladder, then each climber would represent age mates (of the same age-group or age-set), and each rung would represent the age grade to which they currently belong, with its own privileges and constraints. This volume is largely concerned with this upward procession. Boys climb onto the bottom rung on initiation to join their age mates, and they work their way together upwards by fits and starts, with jostling in the queue at some levels and unoccupied rungs elsewhere. Nevertheless, with its cyclical pattern, the sequence is wholly predictable; so that about fifteen years later when everyone has moved to a higher rung, there would be jostling and gaps – and rituals of rebellion – at the same points on the ladder.

Power in Matapato is only granted to those prepared to bid for it, and ritualised forms of rebellion is a theme that recurs throughout this work. Even before they build their manyat, initiates can only become moran in a full sense when they have asserted their right to this status coveted by their predecessors. A similar process occurs when they approach middle-age and achieve the fullness of elderhood. And then fifteen years later still, they find themselves nudged into retirement, forced onto the wobbly upper rungs of the ladder, as it were.

The aim here is to go beyond a purely formal account of the Matapato age organisation. The richness of ceremony and its associated beliefs forms the background of an unfolding emotional experience, which perhaps accounts for its tenacity and certainly is expressed vividly by the Matapato themselves. It is a male experience, expressed by men as an all male institution. Yet intriguingly as they mature, each transition is grounded in the transformation of their relations with women – and through women. Women are dominated by men – even mothers by their own sons – and they too respond to their subservient position in a ritualised form of protest that temporarily wrests the initiative from the elders. There is more to this than simply an institutionalised safety valve. Lévi-Strauss's (1969) notion of the role of women in maintaining the alliance between rival clans has its structural counterpart in the age organisation. It is women who are the guardians of the most sensitive aspect of an age organisation that holds them in subservience; and Gluckman's claim that the system is strengthened through rituals of rebellion has an unexpected twist. The perpetuation of the age system depends as much on women as on men. Both moran and especially women through their rituals of rebellion are shown to play key roles in defending the system from the danger of power corrupted by older men; and for the Matapato themselves, their performances are regarded as high-lights in their culture. This, then is not just a study of a system dominated by elders and seen from their point of view. It is a study of a fraught triangle: the relationship between older men, younger men, and women.

NOTES

1 Conflicting accounts of the succession of ceremonies prior to the formation of an age-set are given by Merker (1910:61–2), Leakey (1930:188–9 cf. Mpaayei 1954:50–51, 53), Whitehouse (1933:146–7), Fosbrooke (1948:27), Jacobs (1965:255–62), Sankan (1971:26), Hamilton (nd.:183–8). Conflicting accounts of clan segmentation are given by Hollis (1905:260), Merker (1910:16–7, 99) Hobley (1910:124–5), Leakey (1930:206), Fox (1930:457–8), Fosbrooke (1948:40–1), Mpaayei (1954:3, 29–30), Jacobs (1965:196), Sankan (1971:1–3), Hamilton (nd.:iv-vi). Cf. Mol 1978:43, 50.

2 Spencer 1976:169; and Spencer 1980:124–5, 139–40.

3 The provisional title for the sequel to this volume, *Models of the Maasai*, is referred to here simply as *Models*. For a fuller account of the strategy and itinerary of our research among the Maasai, see Spencer 1978a.

CHAPTER 1

THE PASTORAL ENTERPRISE[1]

THE TWO ASPECTS OF MATAPATO PASTORALISM

Dominating the pastoral livelihood of the Matapato Maasai is the striking contrast between the wetter months especially in the spring and the long dry season that extends throughout the summer into the autumn. The wet season is also erratic and this gives rise to a further contrast between the good years when the rain is adequate and the cattle are in fine condition, and the bad years, or worse a series of bad years, when the rains fail. The Matapato then face the dismal prospect of entering a new dry season with their cattle already emaciated and their land a dehydrated wilderness.

The symbiotic balance between humans and stock has to be viewed over time. The steady growth of the herds at a rate of perhaps 5%, 10% even on occasion 15% a year is offset by the toll of a serious drought compounded with illness, with sharp losses of 30% or 50%, and sometimes even 80% after a prolonged drought. Growth increases the pressure on the land and their own vulnerability to the next drought or epidemic. As each drought unfolds, it gets progressively worse, and the stock owner is increasingly aware that it could become worse than anything he has ever experienced, ultimately threatening survival itself as occurred in the 1890's. In this sawtooth profile of fortune, it is the sudden disaster that tends to be widely reported rather than the prolonged growth during the benign periods. To appreciate the attractions of their pastoralism, one has to accept that the stock economy is predominantly benign for most of the time. If a competent stock owner can cope with crises as they occur, the growth of his herd at other times is reasonably assured. The problem of drought is never quite resolved, but as Matapato view their mode of adaptation to their ecological niche, the benefits for those who survive and thrive are preferable to any alternative. The human population are cushioned from the worst effects of these droughts by the fluctuations in their herds and presumably by the selective adaptation of the Maasai physically to this way of life. The survival rates of the very old and very young are almost certainly affected. But the most active sector of the population, having survived to adulthood, appear to have enough resilience to weather quite severe droughts.

Flocks of sheep and goats complement the herds of cattle and play a vital role in this pattern of survival. Cattle provide more food for the effort required, making the cow a more valuable beast; and social values are geared towards cattle almost to the exclusion of small stock. However, small stock breed at a faster rate, and can be slaughtered and replaced more easily. During the dry season, therefore, when milk from the herd becomes scarce, there is a greater reliance on the flock for meat and goat-milk. Equally important, by not relying too heavily on cattle for milk production at this time, their calves have a better chance of survival. By tending his flock carefully, the stock owner is both feeding his family *and* protecting his herd. If his herd collapses, it is small stock that offer him a way back to self-sufficiency and the possibility again of building up his herd.

Corresponding to the good and bad times in their pastoralism, the Matapato recognise two distinct moods, relaxation and tension. These are not unlike the popular contrast between the restrained behaviour expected of the elders and a certain wilfulness associated with younger men, the moran. Regardless of age and status, however, all men are expected to respond in similar ways when handling their cattle depending on the occasion, and to take precipitate action when the herd is at risk. Any situation that involves cattle is brittle. Cattle may show impatience at a water-point, for instance, mixing with another herd, and one man may raise his herding stick to separate them, prompting another to attack him in defence of his own cattle. Any breach of Matapato precedence would be punished, but there is also a general sympathy expressed in the popular saying that normal etiquette does not apply where cattle are concerned: 'cattle have their own law.' Men committed to their herds are expected to react impulsively, and they should all avoid provoking one another and keep their herds carefully apart. There are two moods, two sets of expectation, and the coolness of the elders is that they at least should be adept in avoiding confrontation.

The more relaxed mood in their pastoralism is also more typical, with an established routine delegated largely to herdboys, freeing the stock owner to pursue his other affairs locally. His visiting and gossiping are by no means irrelevant for his herd. What he sees and what he hears extend his grasp of the changing opportunities for grazing and migration, and help to anticipate crises. The moods of tension and relaxation are never far from one another. At any moment in a relaxed period, a cow may stray or there may be a threat from a lion and an immediate call for swift action. Or during the hardship of a drought, there may be no immediate crisis, but just a need for vigilance. One has, in fact, a combination of qualities often noted among East African pastoralists reflecting the extremes of their ecological niche. The reward of constant vigilance against the risks is a way of life that has been envied by neighbours of the Maasai in the past, and still retains its hold on them. It is a way of life that is only open to those who succeed.

THE STOCK OWNER AND HIS POSSESSIONS

An example illustrating the hazards of the stock economy concerns the change in fortune of Masiani and his senior son, Kinai, who shared the same village in Meto (Map 2). While Masiani still held authority over Kinai, he allowed him to manage his own affairs and to migrate separately.

Case 1.

By October 1976, Masiani and his son Kinai had both lost substantial numbers of cattle due to the prolonged outbreak of East Coast Fever followed by a severe drought. Masiani's herd had been reduced by more than half to ninety cattle, and Kinai's herd was reduced to twenty-five. Then rain was seen to fall about fifteen miles to the north. Masiani on impulse decided to drive his herd to this spot. Kinai chose not to migrate arguing that one isolated cloudburst would not affect the grazing, and his cattle could survive a while longer where they were. During the next four weeks, Kinai lost five more cattle reducing his herd to twenty. Over the same period, news filtered back that his father's cattle were suffering heavy losses. Matapato from all directions had been attracted by this single shower, and the grazing and water supplies simply were not adequate for the large number of stock now concentrated there. By the time that the full extent of his miscalculation became clear to Masiani, his cattle were too weak to be driven elsewhere. After two months when further rain at last fell, his herd of ninety cattle had dwindled to about twenty-five, and for the first time in his life, Kinai was almost as wealthy as his father. Both men had good reputations for their skill and devotion to cattle, and subsequently none of his sons were prepared to criticise Masiani for having made the fatal decision to move in the first place. As they pointed out: 'There is no such thing as skill during a drought. Only God prevails.' Yet this could well reflect the loyalty expected of sons. They had tried to persuade Masiani not to migrate, and then not to stay there when it was clear that he had miscalculated. It is arguable that Masiani had at first been hasty in his judgment, and then stubborn in his refusal to admit sooner that he would face continuing losses if he remained in this overgrazed and underwatered area.

The sequel to this episode is equally revealing. Seven months later, the rains had been adequate and Masiani's herd had recovered considerably. He had now moved to an area where he owned a well, a number of his cattle had calved, and he had in addition begged back some other cattle owed to him. Kinai on the other hand faced severe difficulties. His senior and favourite wife, exhausted after months of hunger and a series of increasingly difficult pregnancies, had died in childbirth. In his grief, he had begun to drink heavily and to neglect his family and herd. Others then tried to persuade him to rejoin his father, hoping that his influence would break Kinai's drinking habits and help him overcome his grief, but Kinai had resisted. Now, as a new dry season was setting in, his surviving wife had nine children to look after, and was herself in the final stages of pregnancy and becoming weak. Kinai was forced to admit that they could no longer cope, and he migrated to rejoin his father, accepting his ultimate dependence on him.

A feature of the drought of 1976 was the diversity of the response in the Meto area. Some elders chose to disperse their families and stock to offset disaster in any one spot. Others summoned their dependants elsewhere to bring them together, arguing that they alone had the experience to ensure survival. Others took their families beyond the boundaries of Matapato to the foothills of Kilimanjaro. And others appeared to do very little, apart from sending some of their best stock with a herdsman to another area. The national press at this time showed pictures of Maasai driving their starving cattle in search of grass along the highway verges to within the city boundaries of Nairobi itself, their route strewn with abandoned carcases. The notion that there is no skill in such unpredictable circumstances was generally expressed only in retrospect. Prospectively, each elder sought to steer the best course as he saw fit, and the survival of his family and of the remnant of his herd was his highest priority.

In this situation of risk and enterprise, it is the family that forms the principal unit of pastoral management under the exclusive authority of its senior male. Merker (1904:333) expressed this aptly: 'The polygynous household of the Masai may be compared to a joint stock company . . . The father of the family is the chief shareholder . . .' It is useful to bear this analogy with a family business in mind, for it evokes a sense of independence and enterprise in a challenging economy; and indeed the parallel between pastoralism and rudimentary capitalism has been noted by various writers.[2] In Matapato, there is even an incipient form of labour exploitation whereby the wealthy may take on the impoverished as herdsmen, offering them little more than food as payment and the very occasional animal to build up herds of their own. Where the herdsman is dependable and this develops into a stable relationship, and especially if the stock owner has no sons, he can offer one of his daughters to the herdsman in return for his continuing services. In such circumstances with no marriage payments, the herdsman has no claim over his children, and the employer would marry off the daughters and adopt the sons as his own heirs. The ultimate status of the herdsman depends on the herd he builds up for himself as the means to negotiate an independent marriage.

Family loyalties and a shared concern for the herd pervades Matapato society, and the experience and discretion of the father as family head is

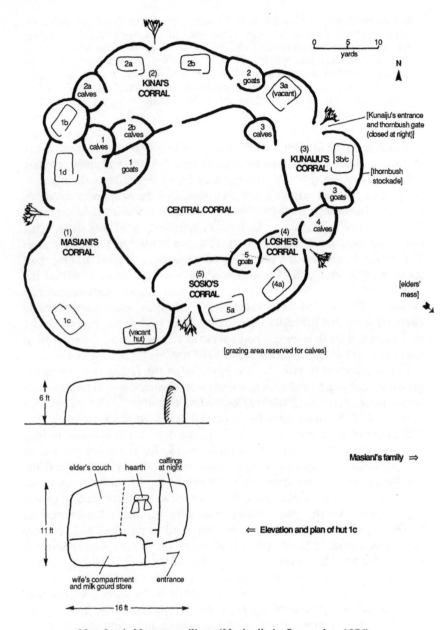

Map 2 A Matapato village (Masiani's in September 1976)

In a Matapato village, each stock-owner has his own entrance and corral *(emboo)* for his stock at night. Each wife has her own hut in this area, with successive wives placed alternately on the right-hand and the left-hand sides of the entrance. In Masiani's village in 1976, for instance, Sosio had only one wife and her hut (5a) was to the right of his entrance; Kinai had two wives, with the senior to the right (2a), and the junior to the left (2b). Each new wife is placed in a hut by her husband's entrance, and those wives senior to her on the same side move their huts round, the most senior wives being furthest from the entrance. In this way, Masiani's most junior wives (1c and 1d) were closest to his entrance on either side, sharing the responsibility for closing the gate at night and opening it up for visitors; and his senior wife (1a), who was absent as a manyata-mother, could be expected to move into the vacant hut on the far right when the manyata disbanded (Chapter 9).

Before she has her own hut, a new bride lives in the hut of the wife preceding her, or with her mother-in-law in the case of a man's first wife, and this senior woman should help and advise her. Kunaiju's most recent wife (3c), for instance, would

normally have dwelt at first with her co-wife on the right (3a); however as this wife had run away, the bride was obliged to live with her only other predecessor (3b on the left). She was expected in due course to move into the spare hut vacated by 3a. Apart from these rules, all co-wives are free to form other special friendships with one another, regardless of their relative positions in their husband's homestead.

In the course of nomadism, temporary improvisation very common. Squatting is common, and with the consent of the village elders, immigrants may move into huts that happen to be vacant, rearranging the thornbush fence to suit their needs, and not normally building new huts. Thus during the 1976 drought, Loshe left his tick-ridden corral after he had lost nearly all his cattle, and the vacant homestead was occupied by a succession of impoverished migrants who lost further cattle and moved on. Then Sosio lost his only surviving cow and moved away; and Masiani himself left in search of grazing elsewhere (Case 1). Increasingly, the village became too small to remain viable and in July 1977 the other families, including Masiani's sons, dispersed to join other villages and it was abandoned.

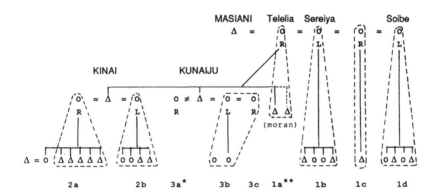

fundamental. Elsewhere, Merker went further in suggesting that the
father is the 'overlord' (*Oberhaupt*, 1904:30). This is conveyed in two
Maasai expressions. The first is the notion of an elder's 'possessions'
(*imaali*) which extends from his stock to his wives and children and even to
his married sons. The second expression refers to his authority to 'decide'
or more generally to 'rule' (*a-itore*). God 'decides' in all matters where
chance prevails: God 'rules' as Providence. The elders 'decide' in managing local community affairs. The moran 'decide' in handling their own
manyata affairs. In domestic family matters, it is the family head who
'decides', with the power to deploy his dependants and stock as he sees fit
to ensure their welfare. There may be a certain backhanded criticism
among his wives of his arbitrary style, but there is a pervasive faith in his
wisdom and experience in handling stock; and his right to 'decide' is
unquestioned.

The family head's decisive role is well illustrated in the figurative use of
other Maasai terms. Men emphasise the dependence of women in general,
even their own mothers, by referring to them as 'children' (*inkera*). The
verb 'to herd, tend, look after' (*a-irrita*) implies the deft use of a herding
stick to keep the herd firmly under control, and it is in this sense that he is
expected 'to look after' his family. To suggest that an elder 'does not look
after his children' (*me-irrita inkera*) is to criticise him for sparing the rod,
allowing his wives especially to get out of control, rather as a negligent
herdsman lets his cattle stray. Both the herd and the family have to be
mastered as a condition for success and even survival. Again, the verb
a-ibok applied to herds is 'to corral' them at night in the village, and also
'to contain' them in a tidy group, as at the water point. Extended to
women, it applies to the elder's ability 'to confine' his wives effectively to
the environs of the village, apart from short journeys for wood and longer
journeys for water. He seeks to curb any streak of adulterous independence which may drive young untamed wives to break loose.

Women's existence centres on the village. At night when the cattle
return, it is the women who must milk them and assume responsibility for
them until they are milked again next morning and leave to graze. The
separation of calves from their dams and of different kinds of stock in the
village is the women's task. If a cow is about to calve, it is the wife who
should get up at intervals throughout the night to check that the birth is
progressing smoothly. If a visitor calls at night to be let into the village, it
is the wife who should get up to open the thorn barricade that blocks the
entrance. In polygynous families, this task devolves on the two junior
wives, whose huts are next to the husband's gateway. In a sense, women
and herds are both penned in for the night, while men are freer to visit
elsewhere. Women are not accustomed to being outside the village at night
while the cattle are inside. It is implied that God's protection extends

outwards from the villages as cattle go out to graze in the morning and then contracts again onto the villages as they return in the evening. When women say they are afraid of the dark alone, they refer to the very real dangers of the bush at night. There is also the notion, however, instilled into them since childhood, that they are deserting their post and will be suspected of having some adulterous liaison. Outside after dark, they should have a good reason and a male escort.

VILLAGE, LOCAL COMMUNITY AND TRIBAL SECTION

The economic ideal is for each family to tend their stock independently, migrate independently, and be self-sufficient for their daily needs. Inevitably there is a limit to this. Smaller families are less viable and even larger families need to disperse into smaller units to extend their grazing, and to spread the risk. Any stock owner may need help to cope with an unexpected crisis. He needs to belong to a local network of interaction for reciprocal aid and for the exchange of relevant information.

Within this network, each village has a pragmatic rather than a moral unity. At night it is a stockade against intruders. During the day, with the herds dispersed and visitors coming and going, it tends to merge into the wider local community. Over the months with families migrating typically perhaps twice a year, its composition changes. Newcomers move into empty huts and establish homesteads, and then quite often move on while others stay indefinitely. While they are together, villagers share meat prepared in the elders' mess, search together for any lost animal before it gets too dark, and lend children temporarily for herding. Reciprocity of this sort would extend to any Maasai – even a non-Matapatoi – who happens to be present.

Villages typically contain about five independent families. Many are smaller, but no family should live alone. Apart from the practical difficulties especially at night, an elder who choses to live alone is assumed to covet his possessions – his wives and his stock – betraying a streak of meanness and wielding an arbitrary power. The knowledge that each stock owner shares residence reassures the local community that they are represented in the village as a moderating influence, as well as a protection against the unexpected.

The local community (*enkutoto*) is harder to define. It consists of a local concentration in the network of interaction that cultivates a shared concern for opinions and events. It has no boundary, but there is a collective rapport and a sense of identity that the village normally lacks. It is the local community that has the moral authority to resolve the sorts of issue discussed in this volume. Collectively, the local elders of an age-set, of a clan or of the community at large assume the responsibility to resolve

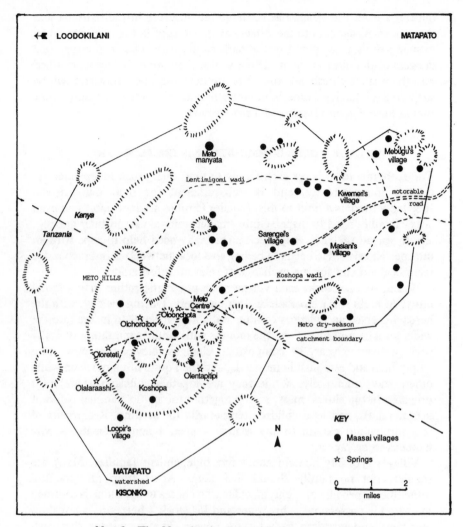

Map 3 The Meto local community (September 1976)

The Meto dry season catchment area and the ownership of water

In Matapato during the wetter months of the year, water is generally accessible by digging at points along the riverbeds. In the dry season, this reduces to the permanent springs in the hills, and natural catchment areas emerge of those villages centred on each cluster of springs.

Any stock-owner may develop a water point from a spring, using his ingenuity to create a series of small reservoirs and channels to feed into a cattle trough, or any other arrangement that serves this purpose. It then becomes his possession and is inherited by his principal heir. As owner, he oversees a rota for its use. Any man wishing to enter this rota should first seek his permission, and he will suggest an appropriate time of day when the point is likely to be available. All users should help keep it in repair, and no-one who has observed these rules should be refused permission. Anyone migrating with their cattle through the area has a right of immediate access to water stock without permission or delay - just once.

If the owner migrates elsewhere, he may entrust his water point to the care of a friend, preferably a clansman to ensure that the rights of his family will always be respected. Or he may simply abandon it, and anyone who cares may bring it back into use. Either way, the point becomes jointly shared when the first owner returns, each man having sole ownership and responsibility on alternate days (*ilkekuno*). The arrangement is ideally suited to the Maasai practice of taking cattle to water every other day, each joint owner managing a separate rota. In one instance at Meto, a permanent water point (Olalaraashi) was actually jointly owned by a Matapato and a Kisonko Maasai; the Matapato watered their stock by agreement on one day, Kisonko on the next, and so on. It was an arrangement that overrode any temporary tension between them along their border.

There is no further elaboration beyond two joint owners. If, for instance, a water point falls into disrepair and is retrieved and developed further by a third elder, he has no claim to part ownership until it is quite certain after some years that one of the original owners has no intention of reclaiming his rights. This appears to have occurred at two Meto water points. One of these (Oloonchota) had been annexed by a powerful diviner and he was unlikely to be challenged; regarding the other water point (Olchoroibor), it seemed unlikely that the original owner would reclaim his rights after a lapse of many years, but no-one was prepared to rule out the possibility altogether.

During the height of a drought, stock-owners may drive their cattle to water only once every three days, but again there is no elaboration of the rota system. Even the original owner may then be obliged to approach his own partner for permission to enter his rota on every sixth day until conditions improve.

There is no claim to private ownership of pasture, apart from an area reserved for calves near each village. Problems relating to grazing are treated as a joint community issue in which the elders of the locality assume trusteeship.

relevant issues. The metaphor of herding even works its way into their style of debating when the speakers ply their sticks to marshal together the strands and counterstrands of their arguments as though these were cattle to be manoeuvred. Any recent immigrant from another part of Matapato has the right to participate in this decision-making. The relevance of migration between localities is that it keeps alive the sense that in their decisions they all represent the interests and unity of Matapato as a whole, legitimising any minor reinterpretation of custom. The relevance of those families that tend to remain in the locality is that their presence provides a local knowledge and a sense of continuity.

Each local community has its determining characteristics. In the Meto area (Map 3), there is the natural concentration of permanent water points, the ridge of hills along the boundary with Kisonko, the *manyata* (warrior village) of the moran associated with the area, and largely stemming from these in 1976, the nascent Meto Centre.

It is the local community that provides an arena for most issues although it lacks the precise definition of the independent family, or of the stockaded village, or of Matapato as a tribal section with its claim of jurisdiction over a defined territory. Matapato as a whole provides the mandate for the local community to act in what they see as the public interest within the broad Matapato tradition. They are all Matapato. While the unity of Matapato is only manifested in the major ceremonies associated with the age organisation, the principle of its territorial integrity is reaffirmed by the strong preference for internal migration and marriage. Very broadly, Matapato emerges as a viable pastoral entity that is large enough to reproduce itself and normally to accommodate its herds, even when the rains fail over a wide area.

Beyond Matapato is the premise of Maasai as a federation of tribal sections. Most families never move or marry out of their own tribal section, but there is broad approval of those that have gone further afield within the Maasai milieu. Distant marriages cement the ideal of a more powerful union to which Matapato belong. Critical situations may drive some families across the boundaries between tribal sections and rein-vigorate the pan-Maasai principle. In the 1976 drought, some Meto families had migrated beyond the boundaries of Matapato. A few years earlier, it had been Kisonko from Tanzania who had migrated for similar reasons into Meto. Immigrants from another tribal section must first seek the permission of the local elders, explaining their intentions in the longer term. If their stock are healthy, permission can hardly be refused even if the drought extends here also. For in these extreme circumstances especially, the claim that all their land is Maasai is supreme, and no part – even areas demarcated as official grazing schemes – can claim exclusive rights.

Dominating the unity of Maasai is their shared age organisation which is discussed more fully in later chapters. Tribal sections are also cross-cut by a system of clanship, loosely associated with traditions of common patrilineal descent. In the problems with which this volume is concerned, clans are a somewhat subordinate theme, but they do have a significance almost by default where there are no closer kinsmen. When a man migrates to a new area or to another tribal section where he is a stranger, then he first searches for clansmen to whom he can turn for support. As Figure 1 indicates, the precise profile of the system of clanship and the level of exogamy vary between tribal sections. Where differences exist, however, there also tend to be recognised links between sub-clans. Thus, a Matapatoi of Laitayok clan who migrates northwards to Purko should have little difficulty in finding distant kinsmen of his sub-clan, even though in Purko this segment would be affiliated to a different parent clan and a different profile of clanship.

Moieties	Clans	Sub-clans	Comments
Lorokiteng (Black Ox)	Laiser	5	Sub-clans intermarry except Parkeneti with Partimaro. Loonkidongi dynasty of diviners are a sub-clan.
	Lukumai	none	Clan exogamy. Sparse in Matapato, with no sub-clans.
	Laitayok	17	Sub-clans tend to be small and most intermarry. Absent among northern Maasai; numerous in south.
Loodomongi (Red Oxen)	Molelian	8	Clan exogamy. Mamasita are a sub-clan in Matapato, although recognised as a separate clan in Kisonko.
	Makesen	4	Clan exogamy.
	Tarosero	5	Clan exogamy.

Figure 1 Maasai clans in Matapato

CONCLUSION: MAASAI PASTORALISM OVER A PERIOD OF CHANGE

The economic significance of Matapato pastoralism today should be viewed historically within a broader context. Altogether, one may identify five sectors relevant to the Maasai economy. Three of these correspond closely to the distinctive roles of elders, moran and wives. And two others

– foraging and the cash economy – have had an important bearing on the survival of the Maasai as a culture. These five sectors may be regarded as separate modes of production in as much as they entail different types of activity, concepts of ownership, and relations of production. In other words, this is to suggest that the notion of a 'pastoral mode of production' is elusive because there is not just one mode. This raises the question of the hierarchy of dominance in the articulation between these modes within the total economy.

In the past, peaceful husbandry controlled by the elders was complemented by stock-raiding undertaken by the moran. Raiding added a further arbitrary element to the twists of fortune to which the herds were subject. It made the wealthy a little less secure and offered hope for the less fortunate. With a measure of luck and nerve, an impoverished moran could transform his prospects. The balance between husbandry and predation appears to have shifted with the prevailing political conditions. The elders had more to gain from conditions of peace and security from raiders and sought to limit the excesses of the moran at such times. However, in periods of turmoil, and especially when drought and epidemic had altered the population pressures between various areas, military opportunism was inescapable; and for a time the initiative slipped away from the older men to the moran. This is reflected in a certain contradiction between early accounts, in which von Höhnel (1894 (I):132), for instance, illustrates the elders' complete control over the moran; MacDonald (1897:69) a partial control; Jackson (1930:291) a loss of control; and Thomson (1885:169–71) each of these. Without doubt, the assertiveness of the moran was vital in protecting Maasai territories and herds and this is still seen as their legitimate role. As Maasai population and stock increased, so the moran also played a leading role in their outward expansion to secure new pastures and water points, especially southwards. However, the role of the moran in actually increasing Maasai herds beyond this seems to have been symbolic rather than profound. Peaceful husbandry was almost certainly more productive than raiding, and it is the protective role of the moran within this sector that appears to have been more important. A moderately wealthy elder with 100 head of cattle and an annual increase of only 5% would add five cattle to his herd in one year. Judging from the general comments of Matapato, this would probably have been altogether greater than the net haul of a typical moran in his entire career as a stock-raider. Added to this, as the Maasai increased their military dominance of the area, so the most critical warfare became internecine, and the war-gains of a more successful tribal section were offset by the losses of another with no overall increase in their herds. In the final analysis, even where there were spectacular hauls, each raider was expected to hand over his share to his father and to regard it as an indirect investment toward his own future elderhood which he would eventually inherit. In terms of property relations, predation fed into husbandry as the dominant sector. To this extent, the imposed peace in the area has affected the balance of the traditional economy, but not its foundation. Predation appears even in the past to have been a means towards husbandry as an end.

Within the traditional economy, women are still tied down to the domestic sphere and the village in a way that men are not, collecting firewood, fetching water, and milking the cattle. In effect, women take over immediate responsibility for the herds at night, while males retain overall responsibility and especially when the herds are grazing away from the village in the daytime. This gives the women a subordinate role within the husbandry sector of the economy. However, there is also a belief that it would be unpropitious for men to undertake the women's tasks, and in extreme circumstances this can provide a weapon for women to defend their basic rights. They can threaten to humiliate the elders by withdrawing their labour (Chapter 11). To this extent at least, the women's sphere has a certain autonomy, and forms a separate economic sector in its own right, subordinate and yet not wholly subdued.

For the less fortunate in earlier times, there was foraging for subsistence by hunting, gathering, or offering their services in a variety of ways to their pastoral neighbours. Exploiting the lowest niche for survival in the area, they were generally despised by the Maasai and regarded as separate; they were *dorobo*. Nevertheless some pastoralists as individuals or even as groups were forced into this niche by misfortune for at least a period, and some tribal sections are thought to have had earlier associations with *dorobo* (eg. Siria, Serenket and Olgirgirri Laitayok). Today, with declining opportunities for hunting, the foraging sector has transferred to the margins of the Kenya economy, in the various townships in the Maasai region and especially in Nairobi. This is the direction followed more recently by emigrants who for one reason or another have been squeezed out of the Maasai pastoral economy.

This account of Matapato pastoralism has omitted any reference to their involvement in the modern economy. The description of the Meto area (Map 3), for instance, did not elaborate on the status of the Meto 'Centre' itself, with its mission station, primary school, shoplets, piped water, and fringe settlement hovering between two cultures. Case 1, which focused on the response of a family to severe drought, omitted the fact that Masiani's second son, Kunaiju, joined a working party to extend the motor track westwards towards Loodokilani in exchange for some famine relief food and payment from aid agencies. The possibility of this work influenced some stock owners not to leave the area. This account has also omitted any reference to the sale of the hides of the starved animals to local traders and of the purchase of grain-meal and other foods with the income. Beyond the local economy, no mention has been made of the 400% profit that some traders appeared to be making on their transactions during the drought, nor of the number of Matapato employed and unemployed outside the District, especially in Nairobi.

For those who remain as Maasai, modern conditions have altered the balance between the various precolonial sectors of the economy. The elders, supported by successive administrations hold the upper hand and predation has been reduced from an organised wet-season activity when cattle were in their prime to pilfering goats in the dry-season when moran are hungry. Warfare and epidemics are held in check, stock sales bring in money which buys veterinary medicines and a few other luxuries, and the population grows. This raises the inevitable question: have the Maasai been relegated to a dependent fringe of Kenya as a whole, protected by modern police, veterinary and other medicines, and subservient to the cash economy as a new sector that dominates all others? If so, then this wider dependence of the Maasai should be reflected in this volume.

Inevitably, the wider issues impinge on Matapato society. Yet within these boundaries, there remains their self-reliant mode of husbandry and their pronounced sense of identity and their inviolate presumption of their own traditions. At the local level, it is the Matapato themselves who have to cope with drought. In Case 1, where each stock owner had to decide for himself in a situation of crisis and take responsibility for the consequences of his decisions, modern innovations were a part of his environment that had been imposed. They were as relevant as a change in the climate. They affected his choices but not his freedom to choose. Those who could not survive either did not survive or they were absorbed as dependants of the system outside the stock economy, just as in the past they would be absorbed into the niche exploited by *dorobo*. It is not that Maasai shun cash, medicines, or alternative foods, but they have no control over their availability or exchange values, and they cannot afford to depend on them. So long as they retain the freedom to choose and a commitment to pastoralism, then this by their own assertion has an overriding autonomy. The political umbrella and economic dominance of the national sector is a recognised fact that lies beyond the scope of their community life or the force of Maasai tradition. They would be seriously affected by a total collapse of the national economy, but their way of life would surely survive, as it has survived earlier disasters.

The extent to which the process of accommodating new opportunities incorporates these into the Maasai system was well illustrated in an area of Loitokitok where Maasai have adopted agriculture. This is a general phenomenon in various border areas that is widely regarded as a sign of the breakdown of the Maasai system. Significantly, however, the division of holdings between each owner and his wives followed exactly the principle involved in dividing a cattle herd. There was no concession to the fact that their holdings, unlike their herds, have no prospect of growth to accommodate the growth of their families. The owners I met were living elsewhere with their herds, which they felt required their undivided skills and attention. They left the actual farming to non-Maasai as share-croppers, as though they were herdsmen employed to look after cattle rather than land. Certain parcels of land had been given to Kikuyu as bridewealth for Kikuyu wives, as though it were expendable and replaceable like cattle. Seen from the outside, these new holdings were nibbling irreversibly at the boundaries of Maasai territory. For the Maasai, new agricultural land was treated as a gratuitous extension to their herds, reflecting a different accommodation to reality. It is a situation that is also reflected in David Western's study of the eco-system of the area. Western (1973:139) found that in trading surplus cattle, the Loitokitok Maasai generally failed to take advantages of the wet seasons when their cattle would be in prime condition and fetch better prices. They tended to wait instead until the need for money was immediate, optimistically hoping that they could survive the dry season without depleting their herds. As a result, for every cow per unit of rainfall sold in the area during the rains, nearly fourteen were sold during the dry season; whereas the commercial ideal would be to reverse this bias, selling off cattle when they were fat rather than emaciated. Once again, pastoral values intruded. Money was treated like slaughter stock, to be converted from their herds when the need was immediate rather than when the time was opportune.

There is, I suggest, a more fundamental reason why Maasai generally have not extended their opportunism as pastoralists to the opportunities of the market economy in Kenya. This is the importance of time as a utility in a truly capitalist system. Such a concept is quite incompatible with the Maasai perception of time and career progression created by their age system. This system provides an unfolding life experience for the individual male with its own fascination and rewards, both in youth and in middle age. It is not that the Maasai lack a desire for independent acquisition. On the contrary, their economy might usefully be described as one of rudimentary capitalism, just as their pastoralism is essentially a family enterprise (Paine 1971, Spencer 1984). However, it is part of a closed system linked to the age organisation which protects the individual male on the one hand and limits his freedom for unrestrained competition on the other. A model of family enterprise and (arguably) of rudimentary capitalism provides the economic backcloth against which to assess the dynamics of what has proved to be a highly resilient alternative to the market economy.

NOTES

1 The gist of the first two sections of this chapter has been further developed for East African pastoralists generally in Spencer 1984.
2 Barth 1964, Paine 1971, Lewis 1975:437, Spencer 1984. See also Native Labour Commission 1913:196 for evidence that the employment of herdsmen predated modern capitalism among the Maasai.

CHAPTER 2

INVESTMENT IN MARRIAGE

In the symbiotic balance between humans and stock, the growth of the family is as important as the growth of the herd, and marriage may be viewed as an aspect of the family enterprise. Women are exchanged for cattle in a system where the accumulation of wives is an essential investment and daughters are a commodity for exchange. Among some other East African pastoralists where bridewealth payments deplete the family herd, the general competition for wives is translated into direct rivalry between close agnates for cattle.[1] This particular source of rivalry is bypassed among the Maasai where marriage payments only accrue over an extended period with a slow commitment to the marriage itself. The emphasis shifts from the individual suitor's ability to dip into the family herd to his ability to persuade his future affines of his potential as a stock owner.

Negotiations over the transfer of a woman as a possession from her father who reared her to her husband who rules her are entirely in the hands of elders. Younger people do not understand such matters, it is held, and any notion that they should choose their own partners could only lead to mismatches and unstable marriages. Young elders are expected to accept the marriage broking of their seniors and to be grateful for their patronage and a wife. The power of older men lies partly in sustaining their reputation for wisdom in arranging suitable marriages, and partly in accruing wives for themselves.

Polygyny is an ideal and Table 1 shows the extent to which the Matapato achieve this in practice. The inevitable shortage of marriageable women is offset by delaying the age of first marriage of younger men as compared with girls who are married at puberty. In this way, the father may accrue wives much younger than himself, while his sons have to rely on him to initiate marriages on their behalf when he sees fit.

Age-set of males	Approximate age range	Number of wives							Total (% men)	Sample Base	Wives/ Male
		0	1	2	3	4	5	6			
Terito	56-70 years	7	35	30	17	9	1	1	100	138	1.96
Nyankusi	41-55 years	13	53	27	5	1	1		100	128	1.29
Meruturud	26-40 years	21	58	18	4				100	106	1.05
Ngorisho[R]	18-25 years	84	16						100	86	0.16

Source: Meto stratified sample, 1977.[2]

Table 1 The increase of polygyny with age

The developing relationship between fathers and sons is elaborated in later chapters. At this point, it is useful to outline the process of marriage negotiation by an elder who is old enough to combine the roles of negotiator and suitor in arranging his own marriages.

MARRIAGE NEGOTIATION AND THE MARRIAGE DEBT

Marriage in Matapato transforms a girl's whole existence. As a child, she avoids her father and, for instance, must leave the hut before he can enter. She bows her head submissively to all other elders to palm in greeting. She learns to associate elderhood with a mystical domain of power that resides in knowledge and knowing what is best. It is the elders, and especially her father, who determine her marriage to a man who is normally at least twice her age, and occasionally even four times or more. Her removal to a totally new and strange milieu is an awesome prospect to which she has been conditioned from her earliest years. She is offered no alternative other than to accept her obligation to honour her father's choice with his blessing or to risk his anger, which could have the effect of a curse.

She might be eight years old when a prospective husband first registers his suit with some small gift to her mother known as 'the anointment' (*esiret*): some butter, a bracelet, and nowadays tea and sugar. This transaction is a women's affair, and it is treated as a joke at the girl's expense. The suitor discreetly approaches one of the village wives to be his courier, perhaps a clan 'sister' or the wife of an age mate. In an unguarded moment, she calls over the girl and taking her by surprise, traces a smear of the butter from the bridge of her nose to her crown. Realising what has occurred, the girl is expected to rage. She snatches at leaves or grass or anything on hand to wipe off the butter, while the other women and even girls laugh at her. Then, more solemnly, the courier and another wife, wearing their ritual finery and carrying staves, process round the outside of the village as a delegation to the mother's hut to present her with the gifts. The tea is shared by everyone in celebration except the girl. There is a belief that if she has any part of this gift she will lose her reason. The episode is repeated with each successive suitor. The more bracelets the mother has, the greater her credit for having brought up daughters that are so highly sought after.

The gift of 'the anointment' is to the mother, but the signal is to the father. No direct request has been made to him, and the girl need not be promised until closer to her marriage when her breasts begin to develop. She is told the identity of each suitor, so that she can know to avoid him. Otherwise she is kept wholly ignorant of the progress of the negotiations, and even her mother is not consulted. The father is expected to survey the field, without either committing himself or seeming so aloof as to discourage promising suitors. There need be no loss of face at this stage. The polite refusal to an unwanted suitor is simply to hint that the girl has already been promised elsewhere or is still too young to consider. Alternatively, the father may encourage the suitor to offer him a gift also. The suitor should then respond while his suit is still 'hot'; to delay might be taken as a sign of indifference and spoil his chances. The suitor is now clearly the favourite (ol-kirotet) and this gift, including beer over which they discuss the suit further, is known by this term (en-kirotet). This normally leads to an agreement in principle, ending further speculation.

Once a particular suitor has been selected, he and the father become stock-friends, implying trust and mutual support. The father may solicit gifts of cattle building up a marriage debt before the actual marriage. In the spirit of this friendship, even the suitor can ask for an occasional gift, although this is rare. Neither side should presume too rashly at this stage that this will lead to a stable marriage. If the suit is called off, then the friendship is 'killed', and all these gifts and their natural increase must be repaid. If any animals have been given away or lost or slaughtered, they must be replaced and all expenses must be repaid apart from the 'anointment'. The father's most prudent course is to build up a rather modest debt which signifies his commitment to the match in principle only. If he goes further than this and begs more animals to fulfil other obligations, then with each request, he is losing the initiative. At some point he may be refused in the knowledge that he cannot afford to repay past gifts except with his daughter. He has in effect pawned her as a possession and has gambled on the successful outcome of her marriage. As the debt mounts, the most prudent course for the suitor is to ask some other accomplice in the father's village to keep a discreet watch on the cattle incurred in the debt and their calving. He then can have an accurate notion of what to demand in the event of a breach.

Occasionally, a reckless elder has been known to solicit gifts from two suitors for the same daughter, building up a double marriage debt. With luck, he may hope to build up his herds enough to repay one of these debts fully. However, if fortune turns against him, then he can only redeem himself with the promise of a second daughter. Generally, the worse a man's reputation for miscalculation, indebtedness and double dealing, the less demand there would be for his daughters. Suitors can resist his requests for further gifts, offering him altogether less than he asks, and he is in no position to bargain.

A father may ignore the field of suitors and offer his daughter to some other elder to cement a close friendship, building up only a nominal marriage debt. Or it may be that he has a daughter with no marriage prospects. No-one, for instance, would want to risk a debt for an untamed girl who is unlikely to settle down in marriage; although she might be accepted as an unconditional gift, for she could well be very fertile and bear perfectly normal children. As Matapato see it, there is no clear correlation between the characters of mothers and their children: 'It is not the womb that is bloody-minded' (me-mada enkuset), they say, and more expensive marriages are often childless.

Altogether, there is a randomness in this process of arranging marriage. A suitor who has bid for, say, six different girls simultaneously may find that he is offered none of them, or he may be offered all six. By the time that Masiani was in his fifties, he was comparatively wealthy and yet still had only one wife. He had suited a succession of girls, but they were all married to other men. Then, within a very short period, he successfully negotiated three wives for himself and one for his senior son, Kinai. As a family with five wives, their whole prospect was completely transformed.

Another elder living in the Meto area was a middle-aged bachelor. No-one suggested that he was in any way unsuitable, but just unlucky. As a young man, he had suited a number of girls from good families, but they had been given to other men. Eventually he reached an age when any bachelor was assumed for one reason or another to be slightly ineligible. From this point, his chances dwindled. It became generally assumed that in some indefinable way he too was ineligible. Elders became reluctant to risk their daughters on someone who seemed dogged by bad luck and might prove a bad risk.

Because of this randomness, there is no exact correspondence between wealth in cattle and wealth in wives, although a general trend is assumed. To account for the anomalies, Matapato emphasise the importance of a man's prospects in an economy where fortunes can fluctuate sharply. If a number of elders independently agree to confer their daughters on one man, it is argued, then this is a measure of their trust in his ability to build up his herds and to care for their daughters. This confidence in popular suitors reflects a general confidence in their marriage system as a strategy for coping with chance. Because choices are slanted towards the more dependable men, most men find themselves obliged to cultivate the qualities of dependability. These qualities entail a commitment to stock keeping on the one hand, and a sense of moral responsibility for dependants on the other. To be marriageable as an individual or as an extended family is to benefit from a good reputation for success in marriage. However, it is also to be under constraint in a system that confers wide-ranging powers on the husband. Equally, it places a constraint on the father-in-law in making a responsible choice, and justifying his claim for knowing what is best. An unsuccessful marriage and a revoked debt reflect on the soundness of his judgment. There is no accepted wisdom in the choice between, say, a relatively unknown young suitor who could prove to be quite unsuitable as a husband, and an older, richer, and respected suitor who could prove to be just as ill-matched for the bride and might die at any time, leaving her a vulnerable widow. The father has to weigh the reputations attached to suitors and to their extended families against the element of chance.

THE MARRIAGE VETO

If a suitor has offended any elder, there is a final hurdle that he may have to clear before he can marry. Certain elders hold the power to curse his fiancée's future children. They include members of her father's age-set or clan and of her mother's sub-clan, in fact, broadly those ineligible to marry her themselves. If the suitor has offended any of these men, then he may be threatened with this curse, intending no harm to the girl but knowing that plans for her marriage will stall until the suitor has made his peace. The formal compensation for a grievance of this sort is nine cattle, but an adversary is expected to accept just one cow, one blanket and smaller gifts as a gesture of good will with his blessing. A less compromising man may wait until all plans for the wedding are complete, and then pronounce his veto and refuse to accept a mere token. He does not enhance his own reputation, but the suitor cannot afford to spoil his own chances of a successful marriage by showing an unbecoming stubbornness. Any attempt to reduce the payment should be left to other elders, while he should be grateful that the marriage is allowed at all, even at a higher price.

THE REMOVAL OF THE BRIDE

A girl is not told of plans for her marriage until it is fully settled. Any thoughts she may have of running away to a lover are soon overtaken by events. The immediate and most significant step is her circumcision, which places her in a ritual limbo between girlhood and wifehood. In this ceremony, her father's power over her is a dominant feature, while the suitor's role is merely to provide an ox for the circumcision feast. He then goes to her mother's hut where she is recovering to see her taste some fat. This is their first formal encounter, and the girl signifies that she accepts her father's choice by the act of tasting. In her debilitated state she is hardly likely to refuse, but in any case she really has no alternative.

As an initiate a girl remains largely confined to the village by ritual prohibitions for weeks or even months. She is again warned that she could lose her reason if she violates these, and then no-one would want her as a wife. During the period following her initiation, she is ritually ready for marriage. It is now possible for any determined man to enter the village where she and her father are sleeping and force her marriage to him. The usurper and an accomplice wear black capes and carry bows without arrows. At the very least to force the marriage, they must succeed in driving an ox, a cow and her female calf through the father's gateway before others discover them and start to beat them. They have then performed the nub of the final marriage ceremony, and it would be highly unpropitious for the father to refuse them his daughter. Before running away, if they are still undiscovered, they may creep into the hut where the girl is asleep and leave a mud doll representing a baby and a cowhorn shell filled with butter beside her. This final touch would be regarded as an act of sorcery that would endanger the girl's life if the marriage does not proceed. Such an act is the kind of initiative expected of a reckless young man who is prepared to pay the consequences, and acting quite possibly with the connivance of the girl and even her mother. A forced marriage of this kind is a form of rebellion through ritual that provides a running theme through this work. The father is obliged to accept this fait accompli and complete the marriage; but he can demand an inflated payment of cattle in return for his final blessing, and become a demanding affine thereafter. Usurping a marriage is a vivid possibility in popular belief, but it is also a risky undertaking and apparently rare.

It is the groom who decides when to remove his bride, ending her ritual restrictions. Compared with her initiation ceremony, this removal is a muted affair. In the days leading up to it, the groom makes regular visits to discuss details with the girl's father and to provide her mother with ingredients for brewing beer. On the evening before her removal, the local elders gather in the mother's hut to drink the beer and discuss any issues relevant to the marriage. They shower advice on the bride in the deep recesses of the hut and on the groom, awkwardly perched just inside the doorway, with an age mate as his best man.

In the morning, the girl is smeared all over with sheep's fat. She is dressed up as a married woman adorned with her trousseau, and carries a stave and a gourd on her back with more fat (photograph Beckwith 1980:201-3). She and the hut itself are blessed by the assembled elders, and she leaves, normally in tears, following the groom and his best man in a slow procession. She must not glance back at her mother's hut; and her parents remain inside the hut and must not look after her. For several days, they should avoid the path she has taken until other feet have obscured her footprints as a visible reminder of her departure. Meanwhile, the girl has been thrust into a hostile world, protected by the layer of sheep's fat that is thought to be permeated with the final blessing of the elders and the goodness of her parents' home. It is said that for some time after arriving at her husband's village, she may refuse to wash in order to retain this protection. It is quite uncertain when she will next see her parents. Often it is a local marriage, and mother and daughter will continue to see one another as the occasion permits. At other times, the groom will lead her to a distant part of Matapato with no immediate prospect of seeing her parents; and if he comes from some other tribal section, there is a bleak possibility that she may never see her family again.

The journey to the husband's village should be uneventful. The best man leads the way, removing debris from her path and carrying her over any flowing water that might wash away the blessing. For most of the journey, she remains a lonely figure in an unfamiliar area, dragging her steps some distance behind the two men. The climax of this journey is her reception at her husband's village, when once more she is the butt of a joke, bringing her isolation to a head. She is left by herself outside this village, and is then greeted by the women, who come out to taunt her persistently until she breaks down in tears. They may tease her for being her husband's current favourite who will in her turn be discarded. They pretend to rummage through her belongings to discover a hidden store of tobacco and prove that already she has the secret habits of an old woman and has never been taught a full sense of respect. She is no longer a girl and now even girls come out to taunt her. These are jokes that point up some of the sombre realities of wifehood, and mark the most radical transition in her life with a totally new role and surrounded by new faces.

She is then left alone, and there follows a series of friendly approaches by those women who are closely related to her husband. Each in turn comes to confer (*a-imal*) a gift of respect to entice her to enter the village: ideally a cow, or a sheep or goat, or a lesser item according to the giver's means. Later the husband's full brothers and sons – those who should avoid her sexually – make similar gifts as a token of respect between them. In future the bride and donor address (*a-imal*) each other by a reciprocal term of respect making these welcoming gifts a memorable feature of her homecoming: '*pa-heifer*', '*pa-calf*', '*pa-goat*', and so on. In this mixed reception at her new home, the transition *girl/outsider* → *wife/insider* entails a display of *disrespect/hostility* → *respect/friendliness*, symbolised by the *taunting* → *gift giving*. For the girl, this mixed reception may entail an element of brain-washing, confusing her up to a point, degrading her for what she has been, but also promising her a future in her husband's home. For the other women, it may entail an outlet for their hostility towards the newcomer who has received so much attention, after which they can more readily accept her. Beyond this, the juxtaposition of taunting and gift-giving may also be felt to anticipate the ambiguities of the various relationships the bride will form in her new home.

She enters the village through her husband's entrance and is led to the hut of the preceding wife who is expected to befriend her (p. 13). Inside this hut, she is greeted by local members of her husband's age-set. They then choose a new name for her, endowing her in a sense with a new identity to match her new role.

THE CONSOLIDATION OF MARRIAGE

As the marriage stabilises, the debt is not simply written off, but continues cautiously to accrue. In the event of divorce, it may still be reclaimed in full.[3] In various ways this is treated as a trial marriage. The wife may be referred to as an *enkapiani*. This implies a trial wife who is not really her husband's possession or more strictly it refers to a woman who has run away to live with a lover. There is a broad expectation that the marriage will prove stable, but the way may not be smooth. A young wife has to weigh any desire to run back to her parents with a sense of having betrayed their trust if she does. To justify running back to them, she must have a genuine grievance, and her father has to bear in mind that undue harshness could drive her next time to run away to some other man and make a divorce even more likely. He in turn has to weigh his feelings on her behalf with the knowledge that a father's gratuitous sympathy for his runaway daughter is unworthy of a marriageable family. She should have been brought up not to run away. Her reception after running away will depend on the genuineness of her grievance.

When a woman runs away to another man, the husband retains considerable rights. Even if he has no strong desire to reclaim a difficult wife who has deserted him, he is still entitled to all the children she bears in her lover's home while the marriage debt remains. At a time of his own choosing, he may mount a raid with some close clansmen to snatch all the children by force. The lover has no claim. Torn between her lover and her children, and with the prospect of further raids if she has further children, any normal wife is expected to follow the children back. They are the only security on which she can always depend, and they bind her to her husband.

With the birth of children in her husband's home, a measure of stability is achieved, and divorce becomes expensive and unlikely. The debt implicitly is transformed into a marriage bond which continues to accumulate indefinitely. The wife's close kin still beg from her husband; and if he were to refuse a request for a cow, say, he would risk an involuntary curse on his children. No cow, it is held, is worth a human life. On the whole, a limit to this begging is set by the extent of local intermarriage and the concern for reputation. The popular view is that 'cattle are easy.' They are easier to come by than wives, easier to breed than children, and easier to cultivate than reputation. A worthy affine is always moderate. However, the right to beg remains and no husband can ever claim that the final marriage payment has been made.

LEADING THE WIFE WITH CATTLE

The ritual sequence of a bride's removal from her father's village to her husband's follows the classic stages of a rite of passage, with separation, transition and integration. However, there is a notable absence of any symbolic union between bride and groom, and the clear emphasis is on a transfer of control over the bride.

Some years after the birth of children but traditionally before any of them are initiated, a final ceremony is performed to complete the marriage. This is a re-enactment of the earlier removal of the bride. There is a similar blessing in her mother's hut and procession back to her husband's village, though without the taunting or gifts when she arrives. There is a general spirit of celebration and even pride on both sides which replaces the earlier embarrassment of the husband and the desolation of the bride. She has now firmly established herself and her family's reputation in her husband's homestead, and she commands respect, especially on this occasion. During this re-enactment, formal bridewealth is paid.[4] In this at least there is an expression of a marriage union: the legs of the cattle of this payment are tied to their necks, forcing them to lie down immobile, just as the marriage itself is now figuratively bound in a permanent knot. It can now be claimed to be a marriage for which the 'legs of the cows have been tied', and the wife has been 'led with cattle'. This proudly emphasises the mutual trust that has been built up and the marriageability of both parties in a society where many marriages do not survive the trial period. She is no longer a trial wife whose legitimate position is in question. Her husband may now speak of her warmly as his *e-sainoti*, a properly bestowed wife for whom he has had to beg (*a-sai*) and to pay bridewealth (*e-saiyeta*). She really *is* his possession.

THE WIFE'S ALLOTTED HERD

On her first morning in her husband's homestead, a bride should be allotted one bull and eight heifers by her husband. These, together with the gifts of respect from her new affines, make up her allotted herd from which her sons will build up herds of their own. She has no right to give away any of these cattle to anyone outside the family. Her husband retains far-reaching rights, however, and he may confiscate cattle back if she neglects her duties. His strategy is to manipulate the balance between the various allotted portions of his total herd to his best advantage. He himself retains a residual unallotted portion, the cattle-of-his-corral' (*eboo*) to which he has sole rights, although he may loan them as milch-cattle to those wives whose need is greatest. When he acquires an animal from elsewhere, he places it in his own residual herd. When an animal is to be slaughtered, given away or sold, he almost invariably takes it from one of his wives. If, for instance, a wife's close agnates come to beg a cow to add to the marriage debt, the husband is expected to take it from her allotted cattle since she cannot easily protest at his generosity or at their greed. However, he is fully entitled to take this cow from *any* of his wives, perhaps from one with a larger herd and fewer children. No word of explanation is necessary to his wives or this might give them a pretext for arguing with his decision. In giving away cattle, he may discriminate against a less favoured wife. The only condition is that he must never transfer cattle directly between wives or the loser would run back to her parental home. In this way, he is in a strong position to distribute his disfavours between wives and build up his own residual herd of cattle to allot to his next bride.

As elders view it, the power of the husband to dispose of animals as he sees fit is firmly linked to the integrity of his judgment. It is he who has the responsibility for balancing the needs of his dependants against all other considerations. If other elders were to question his basic rights in this matter, they could undermine their own control over their own wives.

Case 2.
When Terune lost all his cattle, his wife persuaded her brother to give her a milch-cow to feed her children. Shortly after this, Terune took away the cow and sold it. She then ran away with her children to her brother. At a meeting of the local elders to resolve the issue, Terune argued that the gift of the cow for his wife's allotted cattle automatically placed it within his own total herd over which he exercised complete discretion, and he needed the money to feed his family. For the sake of the children, his brother-in-law offered another milch-cow to accompany the woman on her return. But he made it quite clear to the elders that if this cow was also sold and his sister again ran away, then he would insist that she and her children should remain with him. This was widely regarded as an anomalous case in which the brother was praised for his concern and Terune was roundly criticised for his irresponsible lack of judgment. However, all the elders agreed that within Terune's sphere of responsibility, the cow had been his to sell, and that technically the further gift would still be *his* and not his wife's. At the same time, they warned him against any further provocation that could destroy his chances of recovery.

The dogma that the husband rules in these matters and that only he understands cattle management and the balance of domestic needs is repeated with weary resignation by the wives; but they do not doubt that his personal whims influence his decisions. The best guarantee for each wife is that her husband cannot afford unnecessary discord and that he is equally keen to see his sons adequately endowed through her allotted herd.

Case 3 (elaborates Case 1).
Kinai's senior and favourite wife had borne him five children and had built up a comparatively large allotted herd. His junior wife with four children had altogether fewer cattle, and these dwindled to just one ageing cow in the 1976 drought. So long as this cow lived, Kinai was not obliged to allocate her any further cattle, and she had to rely on cattle loaned from the senior wife to feed her children. This was God's will, he argued enthusiastically, and even this ageing animal could become the founder of a large herd [qv. Hollis 1905:288–9, and Saitoti 1986:23]. Then his senior wife died in childbirth. The care of all the children and all the cattle at night now devolved on his junior wife who was herself pregnant. She still had no right to further allotted cattle and she did not pin much hope on her ageing cow. However, she remained optimistic with regard to her two sons. God had given her these, and when they grew up to become devoted herdsmen, they would always provide for her.

Women are fully aware that it is husbands and not just God who indirectly favour certain wives with more cattle than others. Yet the future still holds hope, for God also favours them with children, and the reasonable hope of even the least favoured wife is not in conflict with her husband's interests. He retains his rights as a patriarch, but ideologically children are peculiarly within the women's domain, rather as cattle are in the men's. More realistically, it is a young son and not an ageing cow that is most likely to become the founder of a large herd.

CONCLUSION: THE COMMUNITY AND PROCESS OF MARRIAGE

In many respects, the process of marriage among the Maasai is comparable with that of the Samburu, and it has been unnecessary to elaborate here what has been described at greater length elsewhere.[5] Case examples and the principles underlying the Samburu marriage veto, the manipulation of the wife's allotted herd, and the resolution of divorce could be matched for the Matapato, and the ritual procedures are very similar.

There are also some striking differences. Among the Maasai, there is a prolonged marriage process with the slow build-up of the marriage debt years before initiation. Then there is the removal of the bride weeks after her initiation, and finally the payment of ritual bridewealth and the formal removal of the 'bride' years later when the marriage has taken on a permanent aspect. Marriage among the Samburu is altogether a more compact process, with no initial marriage debt, no prolonged period of betrothal, and no suggestion that it is at first in a sense a trial marriage. There is a single ritual climax: the girl is initiated, her formal bridewealth is driven into the village in the morning, and then she is removed by the groom on the second morning, corresponding ritually to the second removal of the Maasai wife years later.

This difference has to be seen in relation to the effective unit of local political action in the two societies. The Samburu live in a more arid area and are generally regarded as up-country cousins of the Maasai with an altogether simpler system in most respects and politically less developed. However, in comparison with Matapato and other Maasai, they have exceptionally strong clans. Clanship for the more nomadic Samburu is what local community is for the less nomadic Maasai, only more so. Stock owners are free to migrate independently, but they should move between localities where there are concentrations of their clan. In this way, the Samburu clan comprises a mobile network of transient but tight communities, and the principal arena of competition is between clans, which by definition are exogamous. A Samburu wedding is thus a brief coming together of two exclusive clans, bridging the tensions that normally divide them. Among the Maasai, the unit of political action is the local community as a whole, incorporating all clans and cross-cut by numerous affinal ties. Distant marriages may resemble those among the Samburu up to a point, but more usually the extended process of marriage is an aspect of the local community network extending throughout the tribal section. Altogether as compared with the Samburu, the slow development of affinal bonds is a cordial aspect of community life and there is less tension between clans and more trust over marriage itself. Among the Samburu, the mother's-brother is from another clan, and is avoided because of his curse. Among the Maasai, he is altogether a more popular figure, and it is the father's-brother who is in the more ambivalent position.

A particularly striking feature of Maasai marriage is their practice whereby an elder may bid for a number of suits simultaneously and end up with several wives or none. This contrasts with the more political nature of marriage diplomacy in Samburu where suitors can only negotiate for one marriage at a time, leading to a more even distribution of wives. The individual is more constrained by his clan and the range between the most polygynous elders and the least is altogether narrower than in Maasai. There is an individualistic streak among Maasai elders, leaving individuals to their own devices in matters of personal endeavour that concern their families and herds.

In the chapters that follow, the course of the life-cycle of the Matapato male is traced. This first covers the period when younger men have to cope with the arbitrary power of their seniors while they themselves are constrained by the age system. This then leads to their own elderhood when the element of enterprise and even competition becomes more pronounced.

1 Gulliver 1955:133–6, Rigby 1969:183; Spencer 1984:67

2 This table is based on the marriages of living men recorded in a number of Matapato (mostly Meto) genealogies that I collected. As there were too few older men in this sample for the purpose of this table, it was augmented by a further sample of ninety-four other Terito and forty-nine other Nyankusi elders living in the Meto area. Too few elders of the Dareto age-set survived for an adequate sample. The name Meruturud is used throughout this work for the most junior age-set of elders in preference to Seuri which was not recognised in the area in 1977. Similarly, the name Ngorisho for the right-hand age-group of moran was more widely recognised than Makaa.

3 In the past, it is said that divorce was impossible once the first child had drunk milk from the family herd. The contemporary situation is altogether more fluid and divorce is said to have become more prevalent. Where there are children, husbands today retain these and only reclaim part of the marriage debt. Problems with the repayment of the marriage debt is sometimes said to occur after an in-clan marriage (Figure 1). The father-in-law may argue that on divorce his daughter has reverted to being the husband's clan 'sister', and that the gifts of cattle are therefore no longer a marriage debt, but the normal traffic of give and take between clansmen and are not returnable. For a parallel among the Samburu where there is another expression of the reestablishment of 'brother'-'sister' relations at the termination of marriage on death, see Spencer 1973:108–9. The Matapato have no comparable custom at death.

4 The formal bridewealth (*inkishu enkaputi*) is quite distinct from the marriage debt (*inkishu osotua*). The bridewealth amounts to three heifers, an ox, a sheep and a pot of honey beer. If several children have been born by the time of this ceremony, the three heifers are reduced to two. If the wife dies first and is survived by any children, then only one heifer is paid. The ox and sheep are gifts of respect to the bride's father and mother respectively, whence the formal reciprocal terms of address: *pa-ox* and *pa-sheep*. From this point, the further payment of cattle and its implications for divorce appear quite similar to that described in more detail for the Samburu and need no repetition here.

5 For references to the Samburu on this section, see Spencer 1965:46–70, 193–206, 233–45; 1973:100–4; 1980:124–5, 134, 139.

Three other points may be noted in comparing Maasai marriage with Samburu, each bearing indirectly on the greater strains surrounding Samburu marriage.

(a) *The marriage veto.* Among the Samburu, with deeper rifts between clans and less formalised control over the moran, vetoing marriages seemed (impressionistically) more prevalent. On the other hand, I did not record any instances among the Samburu where brides were returned after marriage or where the veto was applied to all members of an age-set (Chapter 10).

(b) *The allotted herd.* A Maasai bride is only given a nominal allotted herd. A Samburu bride is allotted an altogether larger herd at first leading to more exploitation by her husband to rebuild his own residual herds for his next marriage. Samburu husbands must not, however, take cattle from the herd allotted to one wife to give away to the kinsmen of another, and this gives their wives rather more security than in Matapato.

(c) Forced marriages (olmomai).   The stronger element of trust that surrounds Maasai marriage is also reflected in the rareness of marriage by fait accompli whereby a thwarted suitor performs part of the wedding ritual after a girl's initiation, forcing his suit, and obliging her father to complete the ceremony and accept his new son-in-law (p. 30). Normally, this would only occur during the month or so before she is led away as a bride; but it is also possible if she has run back to her parents after marriage and her formal bridewealth has not yet been paid (Case 41). The dangers of a fait accompli marriage are no less great in Samburu, but with a general tension between clans, the possibility of a forced marriage is not regarded as remote, and they take fewer risks. A principal reason for the prompt payment of the bridewealth and removal of a bride after she has been initiated is to prevent men from other clans usurping the marriage by fait accompli (Spencer 1965:42–5).

CHAPTER 3

THE UNCERTAIN GIFT OF LIFE

There is a prevailing Maasai belief that women are innately dependent on men. They are held to be constricted in their outlook and abilities, and above all it is they who are responsible for bringing forth life and must be protected together with their children. In all matters associated with birth and infancy, there is an element of providence expressed as the prerogative of God. This belief extends to all living things. Lions are enemies in a formidable and ritualised sense, but to kill a lioness still suckling cubs and leave them as orphans would be heinous. A column of marching ants might be disturbed with impunity, but if they are carrying their eggs, then they should be left strictly alone, or misfortune would surely follow. In the past, warriors were warned to avoid killing women, because they might be pregnant. Two lives could be at stake, and to take life in embryonic form is a sin (*engooki*). They would be reminded of the persistent misfortune of some older men who were thought to have killed women as moran, not knowing that they were pregnant.

The notion of a foetus as a thing of God is also associated with a coercive form of foetal betrothal. A man may approach a pregnant woman and beg for her unborn 'daughter' with the gift of the anointment, by smearing butter across her womb. The child might of course be male or die young. However, the suitor has taken his chance, and if the child is born a girl and survives to the age of marriage, it is as if God has shown favour towards the suit, and it would be dangerous to offer her to any other man. If the child is a boy who survives, then again this is God's will and he and the suitor should become close 'stock friends', a term that also refers to the navel-string (s. *osotua*, pl. *isotuetin*).

Because of polygyny, the fertility of any one woman has no unique importance for an elder. If one wife remains childless, he is very likely to take on another; and with a certain sharing of sexual rights between age mates, even his own potency is not at issue. For a woman, on the other hand, her own fertility is uniquely important. It is her own children that give meaning and a sense of purpose to the drudgery of her daily routine. Matapato society offers no secure future for a woman with no surviving sons, and a totally barren woman faces an even bleaker prospect. A woman, therefore, prizes her own fertility and fears any threat to this above all else. Throughout her child-bearing years, her constant desire is for the next pregnancy. Periodically, this concern can build up to a collective hysteria as rumour spreads that fertility over an area is threatened. The elders may then have to perform a sacrificial festival to bless all the women in an attempt to restore confidence and stem the panic (Case 49).

THE PRIMACY OF THE UNBORN AND THE NEWLY BORN INFANT

When pregnancy is confirmed by the lapse of menses, a woman must safeguard her unborn child and avoid sexual intercourse, which is thought to cause miscarriage. The prevailing view that women are frivolous and easily seduced is coupled with a general recognition that it is babies they desire above all, and when they are pregnant they are highly responsible and will normally reject advances by frivolous men.

From about the fifth month of pregnancy, an expectant mother avoids fresh milk, and experiences a craving for certain foods, which her husband must satisfy. This is not because it is his wife who has this desire, but because it is this thing of God, growing in her womb that craves. If she is sick and has an aversion to food, then it is held to be the child within her that is ill and unhungry. This is recognised as a demanding period for the husband. He must either slaughter his own stock to satisfy his wife's craving or beg the craved cuts from other elders when they slaughter. There are well established cuts that are commonly craved, and an expectant father may invoke the authority of her unborn child in making his claim wherever a slaughter takes place. Sometimes, the craving may be for a cut particularly prized by the other elders, and the father may have too much respect for the slaughterer to put this request. Since the only alternative is to slaughter one of his own oxen for what may be an insubstantial part, it seems quite usual to persuade his wife that she is just being foolish in misinterpreting the true desires of her foetus. Yet others insist that pitting a human life against a mere ox in this way is itself a foolish risk. When such a craving is coupled with illness, it is less likely that he would be insensitive to the apparent demands of the unborn child. In one instance, a neglected junior wife had a strong desire to sleep under her husband's cloth during this phase in her pregnancy. No attempt was made to explain this since the ways of God and the whims of the unborn child are inscrutable. The husband simply bought himself a new cloth to replace the old and continued to sleep with his favourite wife.

Once the craving subsides, the foetus is said to have fully grown and to have lost its hunger. The mother continues to follow its demands, and from this point she is expected to eat sparingly and to avoid fat in order to slim herself and ease delivery.

The birth itself is in the hands of women who stay with the mother constantly for some days after the event. They prepare food, taking turns to fondle the baby, singing and sleeping in her hut, while her husband sleeps elsewhere. At this time above all, it is as if they have been blessed with a fragile life, and the whole village acquires a certain sanctity with one overriding priority. God has given them a life, and only God knows what the future holds. There is hope and yet uncertainty, and these mixed feelings are associated with the various restrictions placed on the mother at this time. It is a closely regulated period with a sequence of minor ceremonies and slaughterings to build up her strength over a period of perhaps six weeks. On this occasion her food is rigidly prescribed and she is allowed no special fancies.[1]

The notion that the infant is just a foetus (*olkibiroto*) persists for as long as it is fed wholly on the mother's milk. Its death would be regarded rather as a delayed miscarriage. After perhaps a month, milk from the herd is introduced into its diet, and from this point the 'foetus' becomes a 'person' (*oltungani*) with an independent personality and directly involved in the symbiotic relationship between family and herd. Once a woman's first surviving child reaches this point, divorce is quite anomalous, and in purely Matapato terms, this might be said to consummate her marriage.

The general confinement of women to the village, particularly at night, is emphasised during the months following childbirth. During this period, mother and infant are ritual dependants (*intomonok*). This term implies a certain pollution because they must not wash with water, and also a distinctive appearance because their hair becomes *olmasi*, ritual hair that must not be cut. This is the period when the child is most vulnerable. It is the weakness and dependency of people in this state that are emphasised, and their closeness to God.[2]

The nursing mother resumes routine domestic tasks within days of the birth, but the ritual restrictions continue to weigh heavily. She has almost constant bodily contact with her infant, carried on her back, sleeping under her cloth and suckling on demand. They must not sleep in any other village, or even be outside their own village after the cattle have returned home. The night outside is especially dangerous at this time. The mother's anxiety is heightened by conflicting advice and varying family traditions concerning the precise interpretation of these restrictions. When does night for instance actually begin? When the first cow enters the village or the last? If a cow strays outside the village during the morning milking, can the mother step outside herself to return it? If a visitor calls her to open the thorn gate at night to let him in, is she also letting the night outside into the village? Families and wives with a long history of infant deaths tend to extend the interpretation and the period of ritualised confinement. However, even mothers with well established families of their own show signs of anxiety if they are away from their village as the afternoon shadows begin to lengthen. When they hear the faint sound of the bells of cattle returning from grazing, they scurry home. Herdboys in these families are instructed always to detain some of the cattle outside the village each evening until it is quite certain that the mother with her infant is safely inside. The whole family is alert, focusing attention on the mother and child, and she is not allowed to forget her anxiety.

After a number of months, varying with family custom, the period of danger is assumed to be over. The restrictions are ended in a small women's ceremony in which the ritual hair is shaved, and the child is given a childhood ('mother's') name. For the parents who are locally known by a teknonym as 'father (or mother) of so-and-so', this draws respectful attention to their parenthood, and the first child's naming has a particular relevance. As the family grows, there is a tendency to identify the father with the name of his oldest son and the mother with her youngest or perhaps with some child that has established its personality within the village and becomes a favourite by popular acclaim. Through their children's names, the parents are endowed with status.

THE VULNERABILITY OF THE SMALL CHILD AND THE THREAT FROM PERSONS WITH 'EYES'

There are two interpretations of the healthy appearance of Maasai. The popular view is to note the excellence of their diet and way of life by normal African standards (Orr and Gilks 1931). The more sombre view is to accept that only the most robust children have a chance of survival and natural selection is a major factor in the level of health (Merker 1904:334). The true balance between these is hard to assess. The Matapato are reluctant to discuss family tragedies and they dispose of dead children unobtrusively. The general absence of congenital disabilities inevitably raises questions regarding the fate of defective babies.[3] It is held that any deformity could indicate some past sin dogging either parent, but God condoned this birth and God alone should choose the moment of death. As children are progressively exposed to the outside world, those that are maladapted are less likely to survive, but still a few may do so and even live to raise healthy families of their own. It is God's will, they say.

It is the helpless dependency of a child that is stressed. Because their survival is in balance, they belong to God, and also in a sense to all people. The future of Matapato, Maasai and humanity at large resides in children. Children are associated with a uniquely charmed world of their own, and there is a feeling of widespread philanthropy towards them. A child in distress raises anxieties that are shared by all. A child lost in the bush might be from any family, and once the alarm is raised everyone will scour the area for days if necessary. Some children have been found alive even after ten days. The interpretation of such a chance is similar to foetal betrothal. God has brought finder and found together, and if it is a lost girl that has been found by a male, then most aptly she should be given him in marriage. If it is a boy, they should become firm friends.

Because a child has this touch of God and may be snatched away, his (or her) requests are hard to refuse. A popular example is when a small child clutches at the cloth of a man who is beating his wife, as if to plead with him on her behalf. They might not be the child's own parents, but the man should stop at once. The innocent spontaneity of the child's act, the closeness to the mother and ultimately to all women, and the uncertain future, all combine to appeal to men's hearts.

The vulnerability of children is also closely associated with the belief in a threat from people with 'eyes' (*inkonyek*). Unlike ordinary men, those with 'eyes' can peer right into living things and 'see' what they have eaten, which women or cows are pregnant, the sex of the foetus, and so on. This gives rise to involuntary desires for food, for cattle and for children of their own. Such desires are natural in all people, but they are dangerous when they well up in those with 'eyes'. Their own families and herds are not harmed by these hidden desires, but others are at risk. They have 'poison in their eyes'. When they look at a fully grown person or a cow, then this might cause faintness or mild illness; but a small child or a calf could become seriously ill and even die. The effect of 'eyes' is virtually the only condition that is held to be beyond the scope of the Loonkidongi diviners to cure. It is believed that possessing 'eyes' can be inherited by either sex from either parent, and it does not necessarily imply malevolent intent. Those with 'eyes' merely have to give a blessing, spitting in the direction of any possible victim and the 'poison' has no effect. They would have little difficulty in living and marrying provided they are prepared to spit on every conceivable occasion.

There are also thought to be those with 'eyes' and bad hearts who pose a distinct threat to the community. In addition to malcontents, there are strangers passing through the area or migrating with their families who might wish to conceal their power. At any local celebration, a group of unknown visitors to the elders' meat feast should be welcomed with a display of hospitality, but the hosts may add a polite note of caution: 'Spit, those of you with "eyes". Spit, so that people here will not faint.'

It is because of this ability of those with 'eyes' to probe and to harm the very young that pregnant women are expected to keep their bodies well covered to protect the foetus, especially when there is a stranger in the vicinity. The mother and her new born infant as ritual dependants are especially vulnerable, and this is another reason for confining them to their own villages and avoiding gatherings where there may be strangers. Once they have shaved their ritual hair, the mother ceases to be vulnerable, but not her child whom she should hide in the folds of her cloth whenever she sees a stranger. Later when the child is old enough to walk, adults will warn of the possibility of people with 'eyes' to discourage any wandering off into the bush. It is said to be this terror as much as any other that impels children to run and hide behind their mothers' skirts when visitors approach. The Matapato stereotype of the stranger has a slightly nightmarish quality.[4]

Certain dangerous animals are sometimes said to have 'eyes'. When, for instance, an elephant or a buffalo chases a man who then stumbles over a hidden root, it is as if it had an uncanny power of 'seeing' the hidden object and deliberately chased its victim in that direction. The victim is almost portrayed as a child once again, stumbling his way to safety from a dangerous encounter in the bush with a powerful stranger.

There is a variation of this basic theme which is of special interest because it comes closer to a sociological interpretation by the Matapato themselves. According to some elders, there are certain abnormal people with 'eyes' who pose a general threat, but in Matapato these are rather few in number as compared with, say, the Kisonko Maasai to the south. The real danger to mothers and infants, they suggest, comes from normal Matapato who nurture grief for a child that died or a child that was never even conceived. When such people see a young mother and her child, both carrying their ritual hair, they have memories (*isiriri*) that sharpen their inner grief and their longing. Inwardly they want to cry. Whether or not involuntary tears come to their eyes and whether or not they consciously feel a pang of jealousy, the effect can be to endanger the mother and her infant. Those that have sad memories or unfulfilled desires should spit to annul the harm that might stem from their suppressed feelings. In this interpretation, it is not because of strangers with 'eyes' that the confined mother should avoid festive gatherings, but because there would be so many people gathered together who would be wistfully conscious of her good fortune, and the level of risk increases sharply.

It may be just coincidence that there is a phonetic similarity between the Maasai term for a dead child, *en-kiyo* (pl. *in-kiyotin*), and the term for tears, *il-kiyio* (s. *ol-kiyioi*). More certain and of relevance for later chapters is the association between weeping and anger on the one hand, and between spitting and bringing life through blessing on the other. Inner feelings are assumed to emanate from within the person and to affect his intimate social environment. The beliefs in 'eyes' are an expression of this.

ADOPTION

Altogether more sinister than the stranger with 'eyes' is the sorcerer whose stereotype is often no stranger, but a jealous brother or co-wife. This belief reflects the intensity of rivalries that can exist within a family. It also provides good reason for redistributing the occasional child between wives (and brothers) just as the balance of stock may be deployed to ensure an equitable spread. Economically, adoption makes sense for the viability of each household; and emotionally it may avert a situation that could provoke bitterness and jealousy. Children, after all, belong to everyone. After a child has been weaned, it may be adopted by an infertile woman in exchange for a heifer. She then becomes the child's mother in a very full sense and acquires a more secure position. The original mother who already has a number of children suffers the loss of this child in one sense; but in sharing the affliction of another, she avoids losing it or her other children through sorcery. In particular if a wife has twins, it is as if she has been endowed beyond her expectations, and would be blessed with many more children by handing on this piece of fortune to someone in greater need. She cements a friendship with an invaluable gift, and the adopted child will be especially cherished by its new mother. It is a moot point how far such a gift of a child is a spontaneous response to worthy Matapato ideals rather than a calculated move against bad feeling and possible misfortune. It is the warmth of the gesture that is emphasised when discussing individual adoptions, while the possibility of sorcery is only put forward when discussing the underlying principle.

Case 4.
Lolamala's senior wife had a number of children and was a close friend of his second wife who was barren. She therefore persuaded Lolamala to allow her to pass on her most recent baby daughter to the second wife. Shortly after the adoption, the girl died. Then the fertile wife bore twin boys, and persuaded her husband to allow her to give one of these to the barren woman; it was as if God intended there should be an adoption and had sent a blessing. The twins have grown up as half-brothers. When they became moran together, the junior wife stayed with Lolamala while the senior wife, following Matapato custom, accompanied his sons to the manyata (warrior village) at Meto where they were living at the time of my field work. In this way, the twins she bore were again living with her, though as her true son and her step-son.

Only a girl would be given for adoption to any kinsman outside the intimacy of the family. Boys are altogether too highly prized.[5] Also there is the possibility that if a boy were offered to a distant kinsman for adoption, then he could cause trouble by returning to claim a birthright in his original father's herd.

A father too may take the initiative in arranging the adoption of one of his children, and his wives should accept his decision. To argue could provoke anger between them over the child, and risk its life rather as a curse would. The following example illustrates the cavalier way in which an elder may handle such matters, and also the extent to which he may use adoption over time to balance the changing needs of a family without regard for generational anomalies.

Case 5

(a) In about 1943, Masiani's only wife, Telelia, had three children, while his younger brother who had always been very close and loyal to him had a wife but no children. Masiani therefore offered this brother his infant daughter. When the girl was about ten years old, her adoptive father died, her mother ran away, and she was left with a younger brother. The girl returned to live with Telelia, her true mother, although technically her foster-aunt, until her marriage. Her younger brother was also fostered and there was no question of adoption; he remained his father's heir with full rights in his father's herd, though under Masiani's protection.

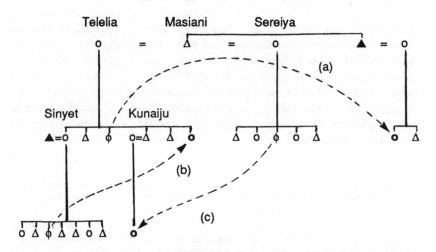

(*b*) By about 1958, all Telelia's daughters had married away and she still had no co-wife to help her look after her husband, three sons and foster nephew. Her oldest daughter, Sinyet, had a number of children and lent Telelia one of her daughters. Telelia became very attached to this girl and asked to adopt her formally. Sinyet was a widow who had always remained close to her parents and readily agreed. Her own daughter now became her adopted sister. Later, it was Masiani as this girl's adoptive father who arranged her marriage. By this time, he had acquired further wives and Telelia was no longer obliged to cope unaided.

(*c*) In about 1973, Masiani arranged for his son Kunaiju to marry a childless divorcee (Case 51). This bride brought trouble and the question now arose: was she barren and would she stay with Kunaiju? In order to stabilise the marriage, Masiani gave one of the daughters of his second wife, Sereiya, for Kunaiju and his new wife to adopt. In this way, Kunaiju's half-sister became his adopted daughter. Sereiya found herself in a distressing position. Masiani had arranged the transfer with hardly any explanation, and for the sake of the child, she wished to suppress any anger or grief. While Kunaiju's marriage lasted, she could see his wife maltreating and nearly starving the child. Kunaiju and every woman in the village grew to hate her. Sereiya could not directly interfere; at most, she could only ask Kunaiju as a friend to control his wife and protect the girl. Eventually, this woman left Kunaiju, and the child, minute for her age, was adopted by his next wife. The heifer in exchange for this child was still owed to Serieya and had to remain unpaid until Kunaiju could afford it.

Masiani's miscalculation in the final instance was typical of his impetuous style in managing his affairs (cf. Case 1). Other elders claimed they would have been more cautious on such a sensitive issue. However, no-one questioned the correctness of his intentions. He had a duty to manage his family as he saw best, and he had a right to dispose of his children in adoption just as he had right to marry off his daughters.

It is in this way that Matapato explain earlier reports that Maasai had exchanged children for food from non-Maasai at the height of the disastrous famine in the 1890's (cf. Waller 1976:534). They argue that through this exchange, parents were not just feeding themselves for the moment, but they were also giving their children a better chance to survive. Later some of their sons made their way back to Matapato, searching for their families to claim their rights: God, they said, had led them back . . .

CONCLUSION: THE CHILD AND THE DUAL ASPECT OF GOD

There is a unique gentleness in the Matapato view of the dependent young child. Infant mortality is high, and a child that survives is a gift of life that touches on the communitas of all mankind. This indulgence towards infancy does not extend to freedom of expression. To the extent that children become less dependent and are seen to develop minds of their own, they are relegated to the most junior position in a highly age-conscious society. They have to learn respect (enkanyit) and the moral debt they owe to their seniors. From this point, the gerontocratic premise begins to impose itself, bestowing privilege and the final word on the older generation. When a father wishes to enter his hut, and especially when he has guests, the children are curtly ordered to leave. Girls are taught to avoid elders and boys to accept the scorn of older males. What are at first no more than impatient gestures may become smacks and even the sting of a herding switch if at any time they seem to presume too much. There is little patience with a child in the wrong place.

The sharp ambivalence in this attitude towards children is well expressed in the Matapato belief in the father's power to invoke a blessing *or* a curse. A mother is assumed to have similar powers, but with her more protective role it is altogether less likely that she would threaten her curse against her own dependent children. In moments of exasperation, however, she could invoke the power of the father with the warning: 'Don't do that . . . or your father will curse you'. In practice, it is the blessing that is constantly uttered, whereas the curse is largely a rhetorical threat. These threats are generally seen at most as attempts to intimidate children into submission, since even in the heat of anger no reasonable father would want to undermine his own family and inflict misfortune. Some maintained, however, that in extreme situations the death curse really is intended. They argued that a really wicked child's death would teach other children more respect, and hinted darkly that various child deaths could be explained in this way (cf. Saitoti 1986:142). In a society where the lives of playmates and siblings are frequently cut short, each death lays bare for other children the awful contradiction between the aura of parental protection and the truth of their own fragile mortality. To the extent that there is the possibility of the father's curse, even if it is never intended as more than a threat, the fact of child deaths could be seen as a naked demonstration of the supreme authority of the senior generation. Beyond the protective care of parents, the morality of respect for age is seen in the final analysis as a life and death matter; and the mystical knowledge and power of the elders at large takes on a more formidable aspect.

This ambivalence towards children, then, may evoke an ambivalent response, and this seems to correspond to a dualistic perception of God, protective on the one hand and castigating on the other. God (*Enkai*) is everywhere, in the sky (*enkai*) and the rain (*enkai*), bringing grazing for the cattle and generally providing for the food chain of all living things. However, God is also in the hazards of the bush that threaten life, ranging from unexpected encounters with animals to diseases that take their toll and spread in an erratic course. It is God's judgment that is invoked in a curse and it is God's inscrutable will that is decisive. In this way, God, has a terrible as well as a benign aspect. While the Matapato emphasise that there is only one God, they sometimes address two Gods in prayer: the God above and the God below. Some suggested that a thunderstorm is a quarrel between these two, over the heads of mortals. One God wants to take the life of some person with the destructive power of lightning and the other wants to give protection. They finally resolve their dispute in a peaceful shower of rain. This cosmic view is dismissed by others as mere hearsay since there is only one unfathomable God. Nevertheless as an allegory, the symbolism of two aspects of an omnipotent God in conflict is evocative. It is an adult belief, but it presents an almost unmistakable reflection of the two aspects of parental power impressed on the growing child. It almost seems to evoke a stormy overhead quarrel between a castigating father and a protective mother which is resolved by the fertile spittle of the father's blessing once the fury has abated.[6] The Maasai, however, refuse to speculate. God is seen as a powerful moral force and appears to have many of the highly respected attributes associated with extreme age, only more so. But no-one can know God's age or shape or sex, they say. God is inscrutable, and only God knows.

NOTES

1 Following the birth of a boy, four feints are made at bleeding a heifer and then the blood is taken from an ox; and vice versa for a girl. A mixture of this blood and fresh milk *enkalipeta* is fed to the mother. Next day, a sheep may be killed if there is no fat available to feed her; this is *olkipuket*. Then she has unsweetened tea and cereal for two days. On the fourth day a fat goat is killed and named after the *loluai* tree (species?) whose bark is added to a soup to make her pee and settle her stomach. It is about this time that she is expected to resume her normal domestic duties and her husband may once again sleep in her hut. Further *loluai* soups may be prepared over the next two weeks until she feels fit again. Finally an ox is killed (*olkiteng lentomononi* or again *loluai*) for more soup and other cuts; and the infant will be encouraged to take small bits of the rib fat. This would be regarded as a village slaughter, primarily to feed the wife, and not as a ceremonial feast: see Chapter 14.

2 The term *en-tomononi* refers most commonly to a young mother whose hair reveals her ritual state, but it also applies to certain other ritualised roles including the infant itself. Apart from emphasising the weakness of her condition, informants offered no derivation of this term. In the related language Bari, however, a phonetically similar term, *tomunyan*, is translated as 'tenderness, feebleness, weakness' (Spagnolo 1960:300). In its male form, *ol-tomononi* may refer to a generally propitious elder with children, who is especially suitable for a prominent role in any ceremony.

3 I am grateful to David Turton for pointing to the significance of the general absence of congenital deformities in societies similar to the Maasai (personal communication). Extrapolation from data previously collected among the Samburu suggested that possibly one half of the children under 14 years were unlikely to survive to that age. (Spencer 1965:320 (Table B); 1974:421).

4 In various parts of Maasailand, a mother with ritual hair should paint chalk around her eyes when visiting other villages to protect herself against 'eyes'. In Matapato, this is adopted by initiates but not by young mothers. Hollis (1905:133) relates the story of Konyek (Eyes), the name of an uncannily observant and greedy ogre whose principal victim is a woman who has just given birth to twins. The twins (a freak of God) escape. This type of story, incidentally, is primarily intended for children, and seems almost calculated to increase their apprehensiveness of strangers, and to discourage them from wondering off into the bush. (See also Peristiany (1939:226) for a similar belief among the Kipsigis.)

5   The preference for boys is reflected in a variety of expressions in Matapato. 'Only a lucky man begets a boy, for a girl grows up and another man comes to take her away.' 'You don't get trouble through a boy.' 'A boy is like your tribal section: both are sweet.'

6   There is obviously a temptation to pursue a more erotic analogy in this stormy relationship that is resolved in an orgasmic shower, but further evidence is lacking. Hollis's suggestion that the 'black' God (below) is good and the red God (above) is malicious is cosmologically appealing (1905:264–5), and is certainly consistent with the general association of 'black' with rain and red with blood. However, any clear distinction of this kind was denied by all my informants, who were generally sceptical that anyone could possibly know. In Merker's version of this belief, both fortune *and* misfortune come from above (1904:198). In a very early paper on Samburu religion (Spencer 1959), I speculated on the possibility of the ambivalent view of God as a projection of a child's ambivalence towards its parents when faced with the fact of the death of a sibling or friend. While the evidence was insubstantial, unexpected confirmation came years later from the Matapato, who were altogether more explicit on the possibility of a parental curse in relation to child deaths.

CHAPTER 4

THE MATERNAL BOND AND THE PATERNAL YOKE IN CHILDHOOD

THE FATHER, THE HERDBOY AND THE WASTREL

A boy's upbringing is geared towards the unremitting care of stock. From the time he can barely walk, he may try his hand at herding, clutching an upraised stalk as he tumbles towards the smallest stock as if to round them up. When he is first left by himself in charge of calves near the village, he has to learn to master a situation that constantly tends to get out of hand, as the calves spread out in search of grazing. His father or his older brothers teach him to control the herd and to respond to any situation that may arise, developing an awareness of the opportunities and hazards of the bush. The more he can be trusted, the greater his responsibility. As he becomes more involved with mature stock further afield, he is left to interpret the broad directions given to him in the morning, and to make his own judgments during the day.

The skill of the herdboy is confined to this daily experience, and does not extend to decisions concerning migration or survival during a serious drought, which clearly demand the experience of an older man. Even so, this wider understanding grows out of the intimate knowledge of cattle, goats and sheep acquired during boyhood. In one respect, herdboys excel as the acknowledged experts. Their long hours of herding give them an encyclopaedic knowledge of each herd in their neighbourhood, and this has relevance for elders. When, for instance, a cautious suitor wishes to check the state of his marriage debt, then as an elder and prospective son-in-law, he cannot himself pry too closely. But he can ask a clansman or age mate living near his father-in-law to find out from his herdboy son which indebted cattle have been given away, or lost, or have produced calves. In the process of acting as discreet spies for their fathers, boys are drawn into the element of calculation even between stock friends. They assimilate the ethos of Matapato pastoralism in which the open cooperation of the stock economy conceals a covetousness recognised by all, and expressed in their beliefs in sorcery and people with 'eyes'.

The pace at which boys are increasingly involved in herding depends largely on the needs of the family. Inevitably, the father relies more heavily on his oldest son while his family are still relatively young. If this son responds well, then he may well become his father's favourite (*olkirotet*), a term which is used quite freely. The father is free to bestow his favours through gifts of stock on any son, especially one who is more devoted to the herd. For boys – even senior sons – differ in this respect, and some simply do not take to herding. A boy that squanders his opportunities is a wastrel, *olwishiwishi*, the repetition within this term stressing contempt for his laziness. A wastrel is a day-dreamer whose attention wanders from the herd, a good-for-nothing who plays with other herdboys while the cattle stray and return home hungry. He roams around and drifts through his boyhood aimlessly. He is not necessarily weak, unintelligent, unsociable, or mentally unstable – there are other terms for these – he is just uninterested in stock and lacks the will to succeed. There is no allowance for boys who may be late developers, for disinterest in the herd is wholly alien to their way of life. The Matapato cannot account for it. Sometimes a wastrel develops a cattle sense at a later age, but there can never be any certainty. Equally unaccountably, a grown man may become a wastrel for a period, these days turning to alcohol, and then recover; or he may lapse altogether. A wastrel, they say, is like a 'breeze of the sky/God' (*enkijepi e Nkai*): only God knows which way it will blow next.

When incidents are reported of slacking by herdboys and even of truancy from the herds as their initiation approaches, elders may show their contempt and dismiss all boys loosely as wastrels. This is not regarded as a deep-seated problem, since boys are boys, and it is essentially a family matter. Within the family, however, when a man is faced with his own son's shortcomings, there is less tolerance; and any hint that one of his own sons is actually a wastrel is regarded with disgust. It amounts to disloyalty. The development of the relationship between a wastrel and his father is intriguing. The father is seen by all his sons as a protective figure who takes the brunt of the pressures on the family. Every decision, from the management of the herd to the arrangement of marriages, devolves on his judgment and years of experience. He is to be respected and even loved, but also to be feared for his anger. When the son has lost stock while herding, even by sheer accident, he may be beaten severely to teach him and his brothers that care of the herd must be their first concern. At other times, if he is thought to be slacking, the father may lash out with his stick. The son should then run away as a sign of respect, concealing his own anger, and then persevere or risk a full beating. If he shows his anger by looking his father in the eye, he would be cursed.

Fathers and their sons are expected to reach a ready understanding that the herd is all important, and beatings should be rare reminders. The anomaly of the wastrel is that somehow, the father has lost this control and his son no longer responds like a well conditioned ox. He will take his beatings and run away, but he does not come to his senses.

Certain boys are regarded as wastrels from a comparatively early age. Just as stock owners have their favourite sons whom they encourage at every turn, so there are 'disfavourites' (ildinkin), who are beaten and even fined from their embryonic herds. My casual impression was that in certain cases from a rather early age, the relationship between a father and son was caught up in a vicious spiral. It was as if the essential rapport that the herdboy needed to help him gain confidence and enthusiasm was lacking, and each encounter merely discouraged him further. That some wastrels later take to cattle may be that with moranhood, as we shall see, they emerge from the direct control of their fathers and have an opportunity to break this spiral.

This does not explain why some elders also may lapse and become wastrels. Yet this too seems to reflect the underlying competition of the pastoral economy. In such instances, it is as if such men have lost their nerve and determination at a critical time, leading again to a vicious spiral as they progressively lose their stock and become paupers. There is sympathy for anyone who loses cattle in a drought, but not for those who are felt to have brought failure upon themselves: they become dorobo, scavengers.

The existence of wastrels is a matter of deep concern among the Maasai, and they suggest that all societies have their wastrels, as well as some of their own most responsible families. Yet in the literature on other East African pastoralists this topic is barely discussed, if at all. This suggests that the stereotype of the wastrel is basically a Maasai phenomenon. In other words, having wastrels is not the woeful lot of humanity at large, but a proneness that might be a product of the high aspirations of the Maasai themselves.

THE WIDOW AND THE GUARDIAN

The ambivalent regard for a stock owner within his own family is highlighted by his death. While he is alive, the arbitrary aspect of his authority is offset by the knowledge that in relation to outsiders his interests are his family's interests and his seniority by age within the wider society is their shield. He is revered for his clout, and his ability to fend off the incessant begging of others. His death leaves his wives unprotected, for neither they nor their sons can stand up to persistent requests from predatory seniors.

Widowhood is common: first wives are typically fifteen years younger than their husbands, and the chances of an early widowhood increase for each successive wife. If the father dies before any of his sons are initiated, then their future lies with his agnatic group – an extended family typically stemming from the generation before the oldest living members. Elders from this group select one of his brothers or some other worthy member of his generation to act as guardian and take responsibility for the household until the initiation of the oldest son. Meanwhile, he directs the orphan sons as herdboys, he arranges the marriages of the daughters, and he may sell or give away cattle from the herd as he sees fit. He may even beat the widow as he would his own wives for negligence or improper behaviour. If she feels she has been exploited, a widow has the same right as any wife to brew beer for the local elders, notably those from her husband's age-set and agnatic group. She invites them to drink this beer at a meeting in her hut and airs her grievance. In an extreme situation, she may may even ask for her guardian to be replaced. One of her own brothers could be appointed to this role if there is no other suitable elder.

Remarriage for a widow is an anomaly, and would not be contemplated if she has children. She retains an elders' couch in her hut and continues to fulfil her role as hostess to legitimate visitors. The guardian has no sexual rights over her and would avoid her if he is a full brother of her husband (p. 31). If he is less close, she may consort with him or with any other agnate of her husband's generation or member of his age-set. Through them she should continue to bear children in his name. It is to such men that she looks for support if necessary, and it is in her interest to cultivate their friendship. As they express it: 'she looks towards the corral' – from her hut for visitors. It is an expression that is also used of a loose woman who has been ostracised by her husband and made to live in a separate part of his village (qv. Case 26). His relationship with her is in fact quite similar to that of an aloof guardian, retaining an overall authority especially in relation to the management of her stock and the disposal of her daughters.

There are two views of the guardian, which neatly polarise the ambivalence towards a living father. The first appears to be especially popular among women and expresses their worst forebodings. According to this view, the guardian is a grasping insensitive elder who has all the worst characteristics of a father with his overbearing seniority, but without his fundamental interest in the future of the family. He uses the sons' labour and the daughters' marriage prospects to suit his own ends, and he exploits the cattle herd quite ruthlessly. According to some women, the widow keeps a tally of all the cattle taken from her herd and tells her sons as they grow up. When they become moran, these women expect them to confront the guardian and threaten to take full compensation by force.

Such a view is very close to Masiani's memory of his own childhood, which was quite possibly coloured by his mother's confidences when she was a widow. He portrayed his guardian uncle almost as if he were an ogre in some Maasai children's story: 'He was as big as that tree over there, each finger was as thick as my wrist. He was gigantic. And his nose – it was terrible!'

Case 6.

According to Masiani, when he was still an infant, his uncle killed his father by sorcery and then as guardian he systematically exploited their herd. At first Masiani and his younger brother were too small to understand what was happening and their mother was powerless. Later, when he understood, Masiani urged his uncle for an early circumcision so that he could take direct responsibility for his mother and cattle. He first asked him to pierce his ear-lobes: a task performed by each father as a significant step towards initiation. The guardian refused, and Masiani went to another uncle who performed the operation. When he returned home, the guardian beat him and broke his arm. Shortly after this, his guardian took away a calf from his mother's herd, and tied it up outside one of his own huts. Masiani went over, untied the calf and took it back to his mother's hut. The uncle returned to fetch the calf and Masiani threw a spear at him, missing him though piercing his blanket. At this point, other elders rushed to intervene. They insisted that Masiani should pay his uncle a heifer to annul any curse. But they also persuaded the uncle to arrange for his circumcision as soon as possible to prevent their relationship deteriorating further.

The elders generally maintain an alternative view of the guardian. They dismiss stories of ruthless exploitation as wives' tales, emphasising that the guardian is carefully selected as a worthy representative of a group of agnates. No selfish man who might tarnish their reputation would be given the task. In taking cattle from the herd, he would be fulfilling the dead man's obligations and would not exploit the widow more than his own wives. Violence in the heat of the moment, as occurred in the above example, is always possible, although it is felt to be inconceivable that a young man would deliberately set out to confront his guardian and risk his curse. A sensitive guardian is expected to realise that he has more to gain from the respect of his nephews and their need for his patronage than from the uncertain advantage of exploiting their herds when they are still young. Significantly, perhaps, Masiani belonged to a large and respected agnatic group from which other guardian uncles could have been found, yet his mother apparently did not complain. This guardian uncle appears to have treated Masiani little worse than Masiani himself subsequently treated his own sons, and he taught him to be a devoted herdsman. In Masiani's narrative, the uncle acquires a more human and trusted image after his initiation. That this story was widely known appears to have been as much a reflection of Masiani's own flamboyant reputation as of his uncle who was long dead.

The true nature of the guardian uncle may lie between these two views, with a tendency to exploit the dependent widow when she is most vulnerable and to show worthiness in full view of the agnatic group, when for instance her sons are marriageable and in need of wives. The exploited widow motif seems to reflect the predicament of any wife during the early years of her marriage until her oldest son is initiated and her position is finally secure. For her older sons this gives an added encouragement – from their mother – to involve themselves wholeheartedly in the herding regime, for it is their ability to take over the father's responsibilities that provides the family as a whole with an ultimate security.

At best, a guardian is a stop-gap for a widow until her sons are old enough to take charge. At worst, he is a bleak prospect if she has neither sons nor firm allies.

Case 7.

Soliak was widely criticised for neglecting her husband during his final illness and making no attempt to feed him adequately. After his death, she was handed over to the guardianship of one of his brothers who was his heir as she had no sons. She then tried to give away some of the cattle of her allotted herd to one of her three married daughters. The guardian responded by confiscating the entire herd. A meeting was promptly convened, and one of Soliak's sons-in-law called on her father's clansmen in particular to support her rights to the return of her allotted cattle. The guardian stated categorically that he was prepared to return enough cattle to feed her if she stayed with him, but no more. Alternatively, she was free to go elsewhere with no cattle at all. His own clansmen supported him, and no other elders, even Soliak's kinsmen, were prepared to argue her case. She then left the area to live with one of her daughters as a total dependant.

Among themselves, women maintain that guardians are unscrupulous in alienating stock, yet discussing the above case, it seemed that none of them was prepared to sympathise with Soliak. They too maintained that she had committed an outrage against her husband and bore the sin.

THE RITUAL PREPARATION OF THE CHILD

The ritual preparation of a child for initiation forms part of an extended sequence of personal ceremonies spanning a lifetime. This is summarised in Figure 2 as a flowchart that links one generation to the next: the mother should be 'led with cattle' and the father should celebrate his 'Great Ox' feast before any of their children are initiated. The sequence is based on the family domain and complements the series of larger ceremonies that regulate the Matapato age system. The significance of initiation is that it is a high-point in the sequence of personal ceremonies leading directly to marriage for girls and to entry into the age system for boys. This latter aspect is considered further in the next chapter.

A feature of the personal ceremonies up to initiation is that they virtually ignore gender differences, which are very marked in other

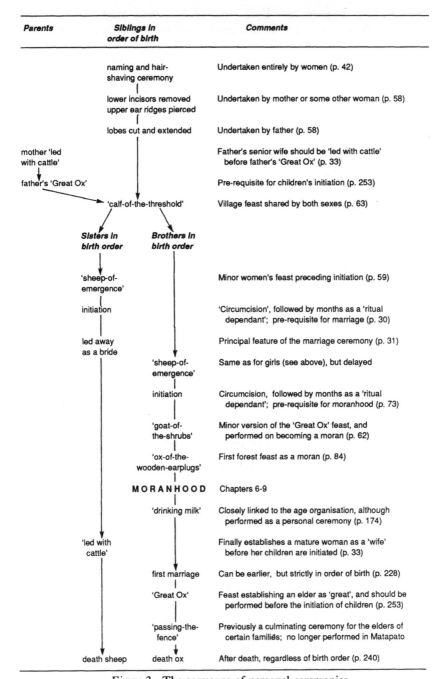

Parents	Siblings in order of birth	Comments
	naming and hair-shaving ceremony	Undertaken entirely by women (p. 42)
	lower incisors removed upper ear ridges pierced	Undertaken by mother or some other woman (p. 58)
	lobes cut and extended	Undertaken by father (p. 58)
mother 'led with cattle'		Father's senior wife should be 'led with cattle' before father's 'Great Ox' (p. 33)
father's 'Great Ox'		Pre-requisite for children's initiation (p. 253)
	'calf-of-the-threshold'	Village feast shared by both sexes (p. 63)
	Sisters in birth order Brothers in birth order	
	'sheep-of-emergence'	Minor women's feast preceding initiation (p. 59)
	initiation	'Circumcision', followed by months as a 'ritual dependant'; pre-requisite for marriage (p. 30)
	led away as a bride	Principal feature of the marriage ceremony (p. 31)
	'sheep-of-emergence'	Same as for girls (see above), but delayed
	initiation	Circumcision, followed by months as a 'ritual dependant'; pre-requisite for moranhood (p. 73)
	'goat-of-the-shrubs'	Minor version of the 'Great Ox' feast, and performed on becoming a moran (p. 62)
	'ox-of-the-wooden-earplugs'	First forest feast as a moran (p. 84)
	MORANHOOD	Chapters 6-9
	'drinking milk'	Closely linked to the age organisation, although performed as a personal ceremony (p. 174)
	'led with cattle'	Finally establishes a mature woman as a 'wife' before her children are initiated (p. 33)
	first marriage	Can be earlier, but strictly in order of birth (p. 228)
	'Great Ox'	Feast establishing an elder as 'great', and should be performed before the initiation of children (p. 253)
	'passing-the-fence'	Previously a culminating ceremony for the elders of certain families; no longer performed in Matapato
	death sheep death ox	After death, regardless of birth order (p. 240)

Figure 2 The sequence of personal ceremonies

respects from an early age. Each child in the family must pass through each stage in strict order of birth regardless of sex. In so far as gender has some relevance, it reflects a symbolic transfer of ritual responsibility for the child from the mother and the domestic domain to the father and the outside world (rather as responsibility for the herd is transferred from the mother's sphere to the father's when it is driven out to graze each morning). Children meanwhile, in ritual terms, are deprived of gender, as if to emphasise their dependency. Gender is only bestowed ritually after initiation when they acquire adult roles.

After the naming ceremony in infancy, the next steps in this sequence are a series of operations on the child's face, marking its progress to adulthood. The first are performed by the mother or some other adept woman. When the child is old enough to be left in charge of young stock near the village and adult teeth appear, the lower incisors are prised out. Shortly after this a small hole is pierced in the upper ridge of each ear so that small beaded earrings can be worn. Years later, when the child is old enough to herd cattle alone and to withstand the pain, the initiative passes to the father to cut larger holes in the earlobes for wearing larger ornaments. To lessen the chances of serious infection, the right lobe is cut in one wet season, and the left a year later. The lobes are then extended with larger and larger wooden earplugs. So long as the father keeps strictly to the order of birth, he may cut his daughter's lobes at the first signs of puberty. From this point, he would avoid her even more strictly than before. Cutting a son's lobes might be delayed until nearer his initiation to show his true mettle in standing up to pain. In this way, the notion is implanted in boys, but not girls, that circumcision is largely a test of manhood measured by their ability to surmount pain.[1] Sons eager to prove their worth and become moran may pester their fathers to cut their ear lobes as in Case 6. Fathers on the other hand may delay the cutting with vague promises in order to retain more control over their sons.

Shortly before initiation, the first of a number of feasts associated with stages of adulthood is held. This is the calf-of-the-threshold, and it has certain parallels with the final feast of the series for the male, which should be performed before any of his own children are initiated.[2] In other words, the series spans just one generation, and a father celebrates the Great Ox at about the time that his oldest child celebrates the calf-of-the-threshold. The celebrant in both feasts tastes the brisket-fat and is given a new name; and each occasion is highlighted by a ritual contest over the rib-fat by other participants. There is also an implicit opposition between the two feasts. The first is a mere calf, slaughtered in the threshold area of the mother's hut and associated with the ritual emergence of a child from primary dependence on her; it is occasionally called the calf-of-emergence.[3] The second must be a very fine ox slaughtered in the bush and followed by a solemn procession back to the village to mark the final stage of the father's domestication as an elder. They represent the first and last stages of an extended van Gennepian rite of transition with the passing of a generation in-between. It is a pattern that is repeated in the ceremonies associated with the age organisation, to be discussed presently.

The ritual emergence of the initiate is made yet more explicit in a small feast that precedes the initiation, when women of the village suffocate the sheep-of-emergence, again in the threshold area of the mother's hut. It is held that any man who eats this mutton will lose his reason. Even pregnant women stay away from this feast in case they are bearing a male who might be born an idiot.

The initiation takes place two days later and this is the principal event in a child's upbringing. Yet significantly, it is the father who is the key figure. The operation itself is only a brief prelude to the festivity and it is undertaken before the cattle leave the village in the early morning. At this point for the first time in this ceremonial sequence, there is a shift in practice by sex. A daughter is confined to her mother's hut for the operation attended only by women; while a son is circumcised more publicly outside the village by his father's entrance, before being taken to his mother's hut.

After the operation, attention switches to the father, conspicuous in his ceremonial regalia and sitting in his corral. He is first blessed by the other elders conferring on him a potent blessing and curse over his child. It is this occasion to which adults refer later when they emphasise their deep respect for their father, or for the guardian who held this role at their initiation. Accompanied by an age mate, the father (or guardian) must then sit placidly throughout the heat of the day, receiving the greetings of his guests, but not joining in the feasting. His public inaction in the yard, rather like a couvade, is vaguely linked to the private recuperation of the initiate a few feet away in the mother's hut.

The father's best opportunities to provide a memorable feast are at his Great Ox, when he also sits placidly with an age partner, and at the initiation of his children. If he is known to be generous and to have brewed quantities of beer for the occasion, expectations build up beforehand and many come from over a wide area. A spirit of reunion and revelry will be generated at the elders' meat feast in the middle of the day, capped by the women's dances in the early afternoon and then the dances of the moran. If he tries to stint the occasion or underestimates the number of guests, then gossip will be spread by hungry and thirsty elders about his meanness. In either outcome, it is the father's reputation that is closely linked to the spirit that is generated.

The father's sitting in state ends when the cattle return from grazing in the late afternoon. The initiate remains a secluded nonentity until the evening when the principal festivities have ended. The elders who still remain then come to the mother's hut to drink beer, and to praise a boy initiate for his courage, or to witness a girl initiate tasting fat in the presence of her suitor. By this act she publicly accepts her father's choice.

Following their initiations, boys band together, while girls remain largely confined to the area of their parents' village until they are led away as brides. In some other respects, the two sexes continue to be treated identically. The initiate and the mother once again become 'ritual dependants'. Their hair, which was shaved before the operation, becomes 'ritual hair' and must grow, they must not wash in water, or be outside the village while the cattle are inside. The father also must shave and then grow his hair, but restrictions on him largely end after his sitting in state at the initiation itself.

As ritual dependants, initiates are thought to be especially vulnerable to people with 'eyes'. To protect themselves, male initiates paint an intricate pattern of chalk round their own eyes when they visit neighbouring villages and band together to dance. Once again, a more penetrating insight was offered by some that went beyond the conventional notion of strangers with probing and damaging 'eyes'. It is the 'eyes' of many Matapato together, they suggested that brings the danger. When initiates collect together at a dance, they are not visibly weak and anxious, but exuberant and distinctively dressed, with blackened cloaks, scrolled earrings of brass and ornate feathered headdresses. Everyone gazes in their direction and gasps: 'Hai! Here come the initiates.' Those with sad memories of lost children, who might even now be dancing among them, feel involuntary pangs of yearning as they watch, and the initiates are exposed to their soulful gaze. Indeed, the pattern around their eyes is so striking and allusive that it can hardly fail to draw attention to the belief, arousing memories and fears.

Case 8.
Lepunian had recently migrated to Matapato from the Kisonko of Tanzania where he was in trouble with the local administration. To establish new friends in the Meto area and reaffirm old friendships across the border, he arranged to initiate a son and a daughter on the same day, pressing invitations on his age mates and clansmen over a wide area. In this border area, recovering from the 1976 drought, it became a successful festive occasion, with many Kisonko crossing over from Tanzania a few miles away to make this in some ways a Kisonko occasion. The lavishness of the meat feast was widely noted, and there were no discordant features in the celebration itself. At the afternoon dance, there were both Matapato and Kisonko moran, and also a delegation of Kisonko initiates who had come to greet their new age mate. With their elaborate chalk patterns round their eyes and distinctive headdresses and gear, they were the most striking feature of the occasion.

In the evening, some Matapato moran, who had escorted a party of girls back to their villages after the dance, reported fainting. At first just one of the girls in their party had fainted and then others followed. On the following day,

Matapato and Kisonko elders suspected each other of harbouring some person with 'eyes'. The initiates had been protected by their chalk, the moran were strong and mature, but the girls were still young and vulnerable. The incident was soon discounted. For the Kisonko, these had not been their own girls and it was a Matapato affair. For the Matapato, it was the Kisonko and not themselves who had a reputation for 'eyes', and this was a trivial incident that did not compare with the alarming epidemic of fainting in the area a year earlier (Case 49).

It may be significant that this episode occurred at a phase of the age cycle when the Kisonko still initiated their boys; whereas all male circumcisions in Matapato were suspended. The age cycle is the Matapato clock, and everyone was anticipating the new male initiations heralding a new age-group. The presence of the Kisonko initiates in a sense anticipated the next change in the Matapato age cycle. It is a matter of speculation how far the girls who fainted had anxieties aroused by the unfamiliar sight of these male initiates and this sense of anticipation. Nevertheless, the fact that they did faint suggests a possible association. Initiation is a watershed in a child's development that leads in quite different directions for the two sexes. Boys look forward eagerly to their future as moran, while girls face the apprehension of their arranged marriages. This is to suggest figuratively that perhaps on this occasion, it was the girls who gasped at the unfamiliar spectacle. Their own 'eyes', as it were, turned not on the initiates with wistful memories, but inwards with apprehension on themselves as their time ticked away.

CONCLUSION: INITIATION AS A FORM OF REBIRTH

Aspects of initiation bear an unmistakable resemblance to birth and infancy. The notion of a child emerging from the mother's hut before initiation is highly suggestive in a ceremony that, like birth, is entirely in the hands of women and indirectly associated with an operation on the genital region. The sheep killed before initiation (*olkipunieki*) and the one after birth (*olkipulet*) are both shared by women. Initiations for each sex are strictly in order of birth, and again entail certain risks to life associated with minor variations in family custom. There is also the parallel between infancy and the period following initiation in the beliefs concerning mother and child as ritual dependants and the threat from people with 'eyes'. Initiates must not have sexual relations of any kind; and girls, who previously were free to associate with moran, are now despised by them in their unwashed state. Like infants, they are dirty, smelly, and unsexed. Initiates must not touch knives or meat with their hands and this makes them heavily dependent on others to prepare their food. A simple request, normally for food, should not be refused for this would be like sending a small child away hungry. An initiate must not be involved in any fighting, and even enemies of the Maasai shared the convention that the lives of initiates should always be spared. Like small children, they are creatures of God and to kill them would bring incalculable misfortune.

It is as if birth and infancy provide a metaphor, a particular way of viewing a situation, that is adopted for initiation. The repetition of events resembles the practice of leading a bride away when she is first married and then repeating the ceremony years later when her marriage has stabilised by 'leading her with cattle'. In a rather less precise way, the father's Great Ox ceremony repeats his earlier experience of settling down to elderhood. He processes from the bush to the village, symbolising a new life ahead as a 'great' man, dissociated from the wild excesses of his moranhood. Yet this is years after he has been accepted as a committed elder. Putting these together, the sequence of personal ceremonies repeats a pattern:

bride is led away in marriage → husband settles down → children are born → → mother is 'led with cattle' → father kills Great Ox → children are initiated

The most obvious parallel between birth and initiation is a widely felt sense of rejuvenation and promise. Anxieties are real, but the general tone is one of optimism and the anxieties serve to point up the sense of elation when they prove groundless. In the above two sequences, the first is one of promise and the second one of fulfilment. That apprehension is again expressed in the second sequence would seem to reflect an awareness of the exposure of the initiate to the covetous regard – the 'eyes' – of the adult world when he or she emerges from the protection of the family.

Beyond initiation are two further slaughters that complete the process of separation from the village domain for a boy and again are symbolised anachronously but quite consistently by reference to earlier stages of his life. The first is the goat-of-the-shrubs, which he should share with an age mate close to the village where small boys herd goats. And the second is the ox-of-the-wooden-earplugs, which is his inaugural forest feast and for the occasion he wears wooden earplugs like any grown herdboy. Elaborating on Figure 2, one can identify five feasts that mark this transition at increasing distances from his mother's hut and are associated with earlier stages of boyhood.

Successive meat feasts for youths	Stages of growth implied by symbolism
Calf-of-the-threshold and also sheep-of-emergence	Infant leaves his mother's hut
Circumcision just outside the father's village entrance	Toddler leaves the village
Goat-of-the-shrubs near the village (after becoming a moran)	Small boys herd goats near the village
Ox-of-the-wooden-earplugs (formal induction to the forest)	Grown boys herd cattle further afield

In the analysis of Matapato ceremonial behaviour, one is often aware of anachronous features. Fathers avoid any hint of their adult daughters' sexuality and continue to use childhood names or terms of endearment suitable for an infant: 'my child', 'my love', 'my mouth'. Herdboys are cast as emerging from their mother's hut, after years of responsibility for herding away from the safety of the village. These anachronous features are especially intriguing in a society that is organised by age, and hence by definition is very age conscious and also time conscious. It is as if ceremony does not simply reflect stages of social development, but it shapes this development in a powerful way by shaping the perception of ageing.

It is important to bear in mind that nearly all Matapato ceremony is in the hands of the elders, and that this gives them the power to control the rate at which new generations mature. In orchestrating ceremony, they orchestrate time to their own advantage; and by controlling time, they defend their position and control their society. This is not a calculated strategy, but an inherent premise of their culture. Delay and denial of maturity are built into the system. It is the elders who, in sustaining this play on age and time, cultivate the popular awareness of the process of time, and hence the perception of time itself, and of maturity among younger men and women. Meanwhile, younger men – and even women – slowly acquire a stake in this system, which is increasingly to their advantage.

NOTES

1 Cf. Austin (1903:89) who records the reactions of Maasai boys faced with the pain of cauterisation for jiggers: 'Even toddling infants brought to me by their mothers sat down with a grim look on their little faces and uttered no sound, for their mothers kept repeating to them that they were Elmoran, so must be brave and not mind the pain.'

2 Recently, it has become possible for a child to be circumcised even if the mother has not been led with cattle or father celebrated his Great Ox. The degree of relaxation varies between families. Some maintain that it matters less for a mother or for the initiation of a daughter. Typically in such instances, another adult of the family would be asked to deputise in the parent's role at the initiation and to grow their ritual hair afterwards.

3 In a variety of ways the calf-of-the-threshold is an unusual ceremony. Because it is based on the slaughter of a calf, it only provides a token meal and the carcase cannot be divided into the normal pattern of ritual division between categories of feaster (Chapter 14). It has a pattern of its own, balancing certain women's portions with men's and giving the child's mother discretion to allocate ceremonial roles associated with certain cuts. A co-wife with whom she has quarrelled might be offered one role, a shy and overawed bride who has recently been led to the village another, an elder who has recently suffered severe loss of stock another, and so on. The whole village should be involved, and unlike the initiation ceremony that follows, there is a striking intimacy in

this feast. In the evening when the child is given a new name, one of the elders axes a shin bone in two in one stroke, amid general shouting and encouragement. This is a minor feature in Matapato, but it compares closely with the point at which an initiate adopts the food avoidances of moranhood in Samburu (Spencer 1973:90).

The calf-of-the-threshold is the final point in the ritual sequence where the order of birth should be observed regardless of sex. When the late initiation of a son interferes with plans for the early marriage of a younger daughter, some families retain the order of precedence with the son performing his calf-of-the-threshold some years before his initiation. Other families modify the custom, typically by keeping the son away from the village while the feast is held for his younger sister.

CHAPTER 5

INDUCTION INTO THE AGE SYSTEM

Initiation is the principal link between the age system and the series of personal ceremonies outlined in the previous chapter. There is little to add to this outline for girls or for those boys who arrive at an age for initiation when an age-set of junior moran is 'open' to receive them. However, more than half the boys reach this age during a 'closed' period when initiations are suspended. They then encounter the dynamics of the age system that is the principal topic of this work. In order to explain this system as it unfolds to them, it is necessary to revert to an earlier stage in the process leading up to initiation and to follow a parallel set of events in the public domain.

THE 'CLOSED' PERIOD OF SUSPENDED INITIATIONS

The rudiments of age organisation occur in any school, where a group (or age-set) of newcomers are recruited to the lowest form (or age grade), and then are promoted as an age-set to the next grade at the end of each year, climbing an age ladder rung by rung. There are a number of elaborations of this basic pattern in the Maasai system. It is single-sex; a new age-set is formed only about every fifteen years; the system starts during adolescence and spans the remainder of a man's life; and the process of promotion is subject to demographic pressures and to rivalry between adjacent age-sets. There is a certain scuffling on the ladder that is part of the system. In these ways, there is a more complex pattern, although this is still relatively simple as compared with some of the labyrinthian age systems of southern Ethiopia.

Among the Maasai, each tribal section is autonomous in controlling the periods when the most junior age-set is 'open' or 'closed' for initiation. In Case 8, for instance, a critical factor was that the Kisonko were still 'open' at a time when Matapato were 'closed'. It is the elders who control the fifteen year age cycle. More precisely, each age-set is governed at first by the elders of the age-set that is two above themselves, and hence about thirty years their senior. These elders first bring the new age-set to life by kindling a fire; whence the term 'firestick' (*olpiron*) that is applied both to the senior age-set as 'firestick patrons' and to the relationship linking alternate age-sets. Age-set 'A' lights a fire for 'C'; in about thirty years time, 'A' will retire and 'C' will light a fire for 'E'; and in another thirty years time 'E' will light a fire for 'G', and so on. This ritual bond of patronage is seen as uniting alternate age-sets into a political alliance. Over time, age-sets A–C–E–G–etc belong to one firestick alliance although only two age-sets are active at any time. They are the natural rivals of those adjacent to them: the firestick alliance comprising age-sets B–D–F–etc. Thus for the two firestick alliances, successive fires would have been kindled recently as follows, indicating the age-sets and apparent timing:

Dwaati (A)⟶	Terito (C)⟶	Meruturud (E)⟶
(1896)	(1926)	(1955)
Dareto (B)⟶	Nyankusi (D)⟶	Ngorisho (F)
(1911)	(1942)	(1970)

While an age-set of moran (say 'D') is 'open', they will continue to recruit members until their predecessors ('C'), who are by now elders, seize the initiative to suspend further initiations by imposing a curse. Up to this point, boys are eager to become moran and the moran (of 'D') are equally eager to boost their numbers. A threshold is reached when sufficient pressure has built up for a change-over, with a view to forming a new age-set ('E'). Prominent among those petitioning for the suspension of initiations are the older boys. Their ambitions centre on moranhood and increasingly they feel cheated by the prospect of a curtailed period as moran and then an early elderhood. They prefer to wait in order to lead a new age-set to moranhood and serve their full term. The behaviour of the boys is a barometer of the pressure towards change-over. The more convincingly they petition for suspension, by singing, dancing and braving the moran, the nearer they are to a change-over, and ultimately their own moranhood. They need the patronage of their firestick patrons and these elders need the popular credibility generated by the boys at this stage. It is a clear intimation of the future firestick alliance between them. There is no stipulation that the sons of these aspiring firestick patrons should be recruited into this new age-set as their firestick wards, although about 44% of their oldest sons are in fact destined for this age-set, and they in particular have their fathers' encouragement.[1]

The ceremony placing a moratorium on initiations is 'the cutting' (*endungore*), which severs the moran from the boys and places a curse on any boy who is initiated after this point. The ceremony may be attended by relatively few elders and boys, but it resolves the uncertainty and changes the situation significantly. The boundary between the boys and the moran is now clearly defined and a new spirit begins to develop. The oldest youths will definitely remain to become leading moran of the new age-set in due course, and not late-comers to the previous age-set. After it has been performed, groups of boys are sent as delegations to proclaim the event throughout Matapato.

The problem facing the new firestick patrons ('C') at this stage is that they are still relatively young. Certain older men may want their sons circumcised without delay, and may simply disregard this threat of a curse from their juniors. Among the Matapato at the time of field work, this ceremony was not a topical issue. Among their Loitokitok Maasai neighbours, however, it had only recently been performed and this provided a useful insight into the conflicting pressures at this period of the age-set cycle.

Case 9.
In 1976, the Loitokitok elders of Meruturud age-set, now in their forties, assumed the role of prospective firestick patrons of the uninitiated youths and 'cut' (ie. divided) the age-sets. They did this by laying a conditional curse on a firestick, a circumcision razor and a captive bird, which they threatened with blindness and a broken leg before releasing it. It was held that this curse would be transmitted to any boy who was then circumcised and wore the traditional birdskin headdress.[2] At this stage, these elders still lacked experience and were quite unprepared for any evasions. Over the following months, a handful of older men ignored the ban and had their sons initiated. Some lived in remoter areas and claimed afterwards that they had not known of the curse. Others claimed that as they (and now their initiated sons) belonged to the other firestick alliance, the curse could not affect them. It became increasingly clear that the mere performance of the 'cutting' ceremony did not in itself establish the Meruturud elders' claim to have a firestick curse; and each evasion made them less credible. With a mounting sense of frustration, they accompanied delegations of boys to proclaim again their curse. Their aim was to turn local opinion against those who were prepared to flout custom and risk the lives of their own sons so gratuitously. During this period, the circumcision wound of one of the illicit initiates became seriously infected and he was rushed to the local hospital in Loitokitok township. This was seized on by the Meruturud elders as proof of their curse, and pressure mounted in their favour among the elders at large.

A series of incidents of this kind appears typical of the Matapato also, and reveals a jostling between the aspiring firestick patrons and their immediate seniors ('B'). The situation is replicated on the lower echelons of the age ladder, where the moran treat the boys with contempt. For their part, the boys are increasingly aware that each illicit initiation is the loss of a future age mate and a further delay to their own initiations. The boys' mounting concern is perhaps the first significant step in their political education as a group. When the rumour spreads of any further breach,

they should mobilise their numbers. Then as a group, they should rush to
seize the would-be initiate by his left toe, pronouncing their own curse on
him as a future age mate. At least one illicit circumcision took place in the
Meto area at the time of field work.

Case 10.

Kumomati, an irascible member of Terito age-set in his sixties quarrelled with
another elder of his village and migrated to a remote spot during the drought of
1976. His herds became further depleted and he resolved to initiate his son in
order to hasten his elderhood, disregarding the suspension of initiations at that
time. He made surreptitious arrangements, and by the time that news had
spread and a delegation of boys had been mobilised to place their curse, the
operation had been performed. Everyone recognised that Kumomati was a
difficult person who had acted under the duress of a drought. But his action was
widely regarded as a serious breach by elders of all age-sets. Regardless of his
readiness to appease the boys within his very limited means, there was no
guarantee that the curse could be annulled. It was widely felt that Kumomati
had no right to risk his son's life on such an issue.

With mounting support for the suspension of initiations, the ambiguity
concerning the power of the aspiring firestick patrons is resolved. Or
rather, the ambiguity shifts to the foot of the age ladder where the older
boys grow in number and strength and pose an increasing threat to the
moran whom they will replace.

Moran occupy a cherished position, associated with the reputation of
the Maasai as a warrior people. Everyone in different ways is enchanted by
the ideal of moranhood as a climax of male virility. Boys look forward to
this period eagerly; elders hark back to it; girls look to the moran for
lovers; young wives are suspected; mothers of moran dote on their sons'
position; and the moran themselves bask in this limelight. They are held
to excel (*a-isul*) all others physically; and the symbol of their coveted
position is a set of privileges ('excellences' – *enk-isul-ata*) denied to boys.
Boys are not allowed to cross the central corral of any village (*olosinko*), to
dance with girls, to yelp in the bush at night (*a-iseer*), to execute certain
dance movements associated with lion hunting (*a-gilaki*), to carry a haft of
darkwood on their spears or a black ostrich feather pompon on the blade
tip, to put red ochre on their heads or to wear moran hairstyles, to
slaughter an animal in the forest unaccompanied, to shiver in anger, to
hunt lions, or to defend the area against raiders or cattle thieves. These are
pre-eminently the privileges of the moran; and when the current age-set of
ruling moran relinquish these privileges to their successors, they take a
major step towards elderhood.

In practice, the moran overlook minor infringements by the boys when
these are not seen as a direct challenge. They take no notice of smaller
boys who smudge red ochre on their heads at some ceremony or wander
innocently into the central corral to join the outskirts of a moran dance.

There is also special indulgence for younger brothers who herd cattle at the manyata. If on occasion these boys presume a little too freely, then this reflects the extent to which they identify with the moran and is not taken as a direct challenge. Older boys would not take such liberties in innocence, and the moran would lash out at them with their sticks on the slightest provocation. The boys would run away on the instant.

Increasingly as the maturer boys grow in number and confidence, they dare one another to filch the privileges, even hunting a lion on rare occasions. Masiani recalled this period in his own boyhood when they played cat-and-mouse with the moran. 'We would play and sing together rather as moran. This was fine, except that the moran would beat us up if they caught us and we would run away . . . We would go and sleep in the bush . . . Then our spies would creep back to scout around, and when they returned . . . they would say: 'They've gone. They've gone'. And then we would come down from our hide-out and dance again – until one of our lookouts came back to tell us: 'We've seen the moran again.' Then we would run away again. We were frightened of them. It's fine being a boy – but they're cowards. So we waited until we were still bigger, and then when we were circumcised we became really brave moran.'

During the years of waiting, older boys may slip out of control. A minority may desert their herds, and then as truants they may fear their fathers' fury if they return, and become vagrants, pilfering for food. When elders or moran see youths whom they do not recognise lurking in the vicinity, they question them closely – if they can catch them – and disbelieve their answers. It is a time when boys live up to their notoriety as liars, petty thieves, wastrels and fast runners, and pressure mounts for their initiation to bring them again under control.

Truancy apart, the boys are expected to display a spirit of confidence at this time. Those who have remained loyal to their fathers may now be freed from herding so that they can band together. They sing, dance and process from village to village in their area, rousing the spirits of other boys and petitioning their firestick patrons to allow them initiation. As their assertiveness becomes more convincing, they generate a groundswell of feeling that change is taking place. In this way, these youths are pursuing both their own aspirations and also those of their future patrons. When they step onto the lowest rung of the age ladder as moran, their sponsors can also climb an important rung to become firestick patrons with a certain muscle. Meanwhile, the existing moran watch from a distance. If the boys are not escorted and especially if they flout any of the privileges, they may be attacked, beaten and dispersed. News will then spread that they are not yet ready for circumcision and the responsibilities of moranhood.

The next climax in this surge towards moranhood is the boys' dancing festival in which the firestick patrons formally kindle their fire to bring the new age-set to life and lift the ban on circumcisions. Preparing for this festival, the boys dance to muster their numbers, rather as warriors in the past mustered to mount a raid. This dancing is a vivid event in the memories of older men. Referring to earlier alliances throughout Maasai between certain tribal sections, for instance, they recall how Matapato, Loodokilani and Kaputiei danced together as boys, sharing the same festival on this one occasion in their careers. Rarely were other ceremonies shared. Goodwill towards the boys is so widespread at this time that the moran are forced to observe a diplomatic truce. They retain a certain dignity by conceding some privileges for the duration of the dancing. They lend headdresses, short black calfskin capes, and thigh-bells to their younger brothers. The boys may put red ochre on their heads, and reveal some lionskin trophies for headwear that they hunted previously and hid. Had the moran discovered these trophies, they would have cut them to pieces and beaten the boys, but now they stand back and allow them their display.[3]

In contrast to the association with warriorhood in their dancing, the boys must not be armed and they compose a ritual gathering with coercive powers, not unlike ritual dependants. No father would dare refuse them his son when they call at his village. To offend them or to deny any reasonable request would be to risk misfortune. Even Europeans are warned not to drive too fast or too close to such a gathering of boys on the road: if one of them were to hurl his stick in anger after a speeding car, they say, it would crash.

The festival takes place at the village of a father of one of the boys.[4] They converge on this village and continue their incessant dancing, while their patrons supervise the arrangements. The climax of the festival occurs when their sponsors lift their curse on further circumcisions and kindle the fire that brings the new age-set to life. The boys then perform a special dance (a-ipak) after which the festival is named (enk-ipa'ata). There is a notion, once again, of the closeness of God. This is associated with the act of kindling the fire to inaugurate the new age-set as though it is an act of creation. Barren women are encouraged to attend the final blessing, squatting among the boys. There are in fact a number of parallels between this festival and the women's fertility gathering; they share similar ritual procedures conferring new life and hope (Chapter 11). As yet the age-set has no members until the first circumcision. But the elders at least have established themselves as firestick patrons in a formal sense, and the boys have a foretaste of the limelight they will enjoy as moran.

THE CIRCUMCISION ORDEAL

The boys' dancing festival is normally held during the heavy spring rains when a large gathering becomes feasible. The boys then return to their herding duties for the long dry summer season. Those that have truanted have this period in which to face their father's beating and make their peace. The timing of initiation – the lunar month, the day of the lunar month, the time of day – is sometimes determined by family custom, adopted by some ancestor in an attempt to reverse misfortune. The most popular time is during the easier period following the late autumn rains. At this time, each family is better able to adjust to the loss of their most proficient herdboys, who in addition must be fed with special food as initiates. However, as certain families are obliged by their custom to initiate during the summer months, a few circumcisions take place of boys who are the forerunners (*ilngeetiani*) of their age-set. By November when the spate of circumcisions is reached, the sight of initiates is no longer a complete novelty. But this is a point when their numbers steadily accumulate, roaming the countryside in small groups, and gathering together for dances, especially at each new circumcision. There now is a distinct awareness that a new age-set is visibly and audibly emerging.

There is normally only one circumciser covering a wide area, and he can only visit one or perhaps two neighbouring villages on any morning. While the summer demand is relatively light, he can accommodate family preferences simply by staying overnight in one village and then moving on to the next village during the day. The preference for some extended families to come together to initiate their sons in the same village even simplifies his itinerary. However, the spate of demands in the autumn coupled with lineage preferences make it impossible for him to thread his way round his area in a systematic manner, village by village. Because of family custom or because a boy cannot be spared from herding at just this point, some do not take advantage of the circumciser's visit when other initiations are to be carried out in their own village. Families with identical preferences for particular days – say the ninth day of the lunar month – will be competing for his services. The general impression is of a certain confusion that heightens the awareness of change within the age system. As the circumciser zigzags on his itinerary in response to the pressure of demand, he is obliged to modify his plans by the insistence of certain forceful fathers, and in yielding to their pressures, he finds it impossible to keep promises elsewhere. Anxious families are kept in anticipation and eventually may have to bow to expedience and override lineage restrictions adding to their own anxieties. Or they may increase the pitch of their demand, adding to the pressure on the circumciser and to anxiety elsewhere.

This is not the only source of anxiety. It is held that if an initiate has committed adultery with a married women and does not confess, then this will lead to the death of his parents, and the circumciser, and the man who holds him from behind during the operation. On the whole, adultery by boys appears to be quite rare and if the initiate is innocent then this belief does not add to his own apprehensiveness. However, others can never be absolutely certain of his innocence, and Maasai boys are assumed to be unprincipled liars. Disbelieving fathers, adulterous sons and even sons who are quite innocent may find their fears brought to a head at this point by the speculation, boosted by rumours of people in the past who died because boys bluffed their innocence. Some time before the operation, the firestick patrons warn the boys of the circumciser's deadly curse on adulterers so that they can carefully consider their position. When he comes to perform the operation, the circumciser himself explains to each boy that he has placed a curse on his razor that will kill him if he does not confess his adulteries. If the boy confesses, then he is shamed but misfortune is averted. If he asserts his innocence, then a shadow of uncertainty always remains, and this becomes another source of speculation if the operation has any adverse effect.[5]

After being warned by the circumciser regarding any adulteries, the initiate is briefly washed and then signifies his readiness by kicking over a pot of water. One man, usually a mother's brother, holds him firmly from behind while two others hold his legs apart. The operation may last five minutes and during this period, the initiate should not bat an eyelid or even twitch a toe. To do so would be regarded as a sign of wanting to run away. He would be beaten for his cowardice as a flincher (*olkaasiodi*). If he then loses his head and struggles, he would be firmly held down and the operation completed to bring the matter to a speedy end. All festivity would be suspended, his family would be scorned, his mother and their cattle would be beaten. During the coming months he would be avoided by other initiates, at the very time when they are congratulating each other on their courage and forming lasting friendships. Flinching is a disastrous start for a future career as a moran, but it is a disaster from which he can recover. It is recognised that involuntary twitches are possible even among the bravest boys, while cowards may survive the ordeal with unexpected composure. There is even a hint of respect for a flincher in the maxim, 'A man will not run away twice.' In other words, the stigma of having flinched may provide the impetus to assert himself with obsessive courage on all subsequent occasions, just as a moran who loses his nerve in the heat of battle may subsequently show a fierce courage. Others may avoid him for a time, but they are careful not to tease him or humiliate him unnecessarily. Inwardly, he has a burning passion to redeem himself.

The ordeal for the initiate begins from the time that he is made aware of the possibility of flinching as a painful thought. He has years to prime himself for something that can never quite be known until it has been experienced. This is the third source of anxiety and it also bears on the fate of the circumciser who faces a different ordeal. It is believed that if no boy flinches in the course of a season of initiations, then the circumciser will meet an early death. This is one reason why no Maasai would normally accept the task, and it is usually undertaken by a skilled man from elsewhere who is prepared to take the risk. He is despised as a scavenger, a *dorobo*, whose greed for the payment outweighs his prudence. It is therefore in his interest to retain a reputation for skill, while making this a painful operation in the hope that he may snick some hidden nerve and cause an involuntary twitch. Technically, the initiate would have flinched even if someone inadvertently nudges him, and his kinsmen are said to watch the operation very closely: the initiate for signs of a twitch, the circumciser for some dirty trick, and any spectator close by who might nudge him. Sometimes they may even form a close protective ring round the operation to keep possible ill-wishers at bay (cf. Fox 1931:191).

Immediately after a successful operation – with no flinching or admission of adultery – the initiate is offered stock by various close members of his family amounting to perhaps five or more cattle. He then gets up, and in doing so forfeits the right to further cattle on this occasion. He may therefore remain in the circumcision posture until he is satisfied that the gifts he has been promised match the wealth of his kinsmen and his own expectations as a herdboy who has served his family well. He is then carried or led backwards to his mother's hut by the man at his back. Other local elders have a clear idea how many cattle he can reasonably expect and if he stubbornly makes unrealistic demands, they will start to shout at him. In the final resort, he would simply be dragged backwards to his mother's hut, overriding his protests.

Generally, there is a festive atmosphere surrounding a circumcision as described in the previous chapter, and the operation itself is quickly and efficiently dispatched, normally very early in the morning. Even so, it is a tense episode and a degree of confusion and anxiety appears to be an integral part of the ceremony, heightening the sense of occasion. Those close to the initiate and others that have recently been circumcised may deliberately try to provoke his anger, scorning and threatening him, and distancing themselves from him if he does flinch, but also firming his resolve not to do so. In his isolation, he is primed for the ordeal. For want of a Matapato example, it is useful to note an incident that occurred elsewhere.

Case 11.
During a brief visit to the Siria Maasai where the age cycle was several years ahead of Matapato, a male circumcision was performed. At dawn, a band of about ten initiates, who had recently recovered from the operation and wore their full regalia, led the youth from his mother's hut, singing and holding each arm. His movements were wooden and his face seemed drained of all vitality. The circumciser led him outside the village, smeared a line of chalk on either side of his own and the boy's eyes, and reminded him of the procedure (and of

his conditional curse?). The band of initiates then led him by the arm to a nearby spring to wash him and then returned. They paused at certain points, singing and making pointed references to the fact that none of them had flinched. At the father's gateway, he was left standing alone. Following Siria custom, instead of kicking over a pot of water, he was obliged to run from the gateway to his mother's hut where a firestick patron would souse him with water. Then he should snatch a hide and run with it to the circumciser waiting to operate in the middle of his father's corral. On this occasion, he rushed to his mother's hut, was soused and grabbed the hide, and then by mistake he rushed with it back to the gateway. Here, the other initiates grappled with him while he seemed to be fighting his way to leave the village. They dragged him struggling to the right spot, sat him on the hide, and the operation began promptly. Everyone's attention was drawn to the operation itself. No-one seemed to be watching whether he actually batted an eyelid or twitched a toe. An elderly woman (his mother?) with a close view of the operation was shivering throughout, a young elder (a close kinsman) who held his right leg during the operation looked quite shaken, and there was mild shivering among the band of initiates. The initiate himself remained expressionless and motionless. After the operation which lasted perhaps five minutes, he was given milk in a gourd to drink. The two elderly women spectators kissed his cheek, new sandals were placed on his feet, he was briefly offered cattle (the number appeared to have been agreed in detail beforehand) and then led backwards to his mother's hut.

The elders adjourned to a separate part of the hut to drink beer and joke about the operation emphasising gleefully to me how much it hurt: 'like fire!'. No-one suggested that the initiate had tried to run away, or that his shaken kinsman who held his leg felt that family honour had been tarnished. They argued that the initiate was just confused in his 'anger' and had lost his bearings, and that any kinsmen may feel distressed during the operation. Generally, there was satisfaction that the operation had been carried out without a hitch. The elders then called over smaller boys to tease them, playfully dragging them towards the doorway and asking them if they would like to be circumcised. Outside, catching this jocular mood, some women seized several young children. One of them started to prise out their lower incisors as if to emphasise to them the ordeal that awaited them, hooting with laughter while the children howled. (Maasai generally have denied that the ordeal of teeth-prising and circumcision are deliberately linked when I have discussed this episode with them).

Following the operation, the initiate recuperates in his mother's hut, revived by a mixture of sour milk and blood (*saroi*). Prolonging his ordeal with one final gesture, the circumciser may enter the hut and reiterate his curse: if the boy is an unconfessed adulterer, then the drink will 'poison' him.

THE CIRCUMCISION FIRE

After the initiate has been taken to recuperate in his mother's hut, two firestick patrons kindle a fire in his father's corral. Through this act, he is formally incorporated as a firestick ward into the age-set, two below their own. In what is otherwise essentially a family festivity, this is the one feature that is specifically associated with the age system. First, there was the inaugural fire at the boys' dancing ceremony, bringing the age-set to life before it even had any members. Now with each initiation, a new member is recruited with a further fire.

In normal circumstances, kindling this fire is a routine procedure since all boys initiated during an 'open' period belong automatically to the same age-set. However, there are also abnormal situations, and in this respect one encounters the first of a number of recognised loopholes in the age system. It is quite legitimate, though rare, for an initiate to be inducted into a more senior age-set that has been 'closed' for·further circumcisions. This is achieved by asking two older men who are firestick patrons of this 'closed' age-set to light the circumcision fire. It is the father's decision, which would only be made with the blessing of other local elders; and this would only be given when the reason is eminently sensible.

Case 12.
Naru was partially-sighted, and he was constantly scorned and sometimes even intimidated by his younger brother. They were due to be initiated into the same age-set, but their father suggested to the other Matapato elders that Naru should be upgraded on circumcision to the next age-set by asking senior elders of the appropriate age-set to kindle his circumcision fire. In this way, Naru would be poised to become an elder after his period of initiation. His younger brother as a moran would then be forced to show more respect towards him. This proposal for bringing order to the family was generally welcomed, and no-one suggested that the new age-set would be deprived of an active member. With his disability, Naru would hardly have been an active moran – he would even be a liability for them to support – whereas this would be less relevant as an elder.

Case 13.
In another instance, Lemita was the oldest of five brothers. He was a popular boy with great spirit, but lame and delicate. His father recognised that it would be impossible to tie him down to a quiet life as a moran. The temptation for him to join his age mates in the rough and tumble of moranhood would be too great and his health would be at risk. Here also, the local elders agreed with the father that Lemita should be upgraded to the next age-set, although it had been 'closed' for some time. All five brothers were circumcised on the same day. Following Matapato custom, each provided his own firesticks and was incorporated into the age system with his own fire kindled in strict order of birth. First, two elders of age-set B lit a fire to induct Lemita into age-set D and then two elders of age-set C lit four fires to induct each of his brothers into age-set E.

During the period 'closed' to circumcisions, the circumcision fire for each illicit circumcision becomes the key issue. So long as the father can find two suitable firestick patrons willing to collude with him, he can risk circumcision. After a certain point, however, other elders would not want to risk public censure for subverting the system gratuitously. After the illicit initiations in Case 9, the exasperated firestick patrons in Loitokitok insisted that in future *they* would light all circumcision fires. The illicit initiates would then have to remain as ritual dependants, exposed to certain dangers and on an expensive diet. This would only end when the ban on initiations was lifted and the remainder of their age-set would have caught up with them. It was a matter of persuading the elders of more senior age-sets of the effectiveness of their curse, and then any rash fathers would find other elders less willing to light the fire.

CONCLUSION: THE CIRCUMCISION BOND

The circumcision ordeal is a watershed in a young Matapatoi's career. Once he has surmounted the ordeal and proved himself worthy to become a moran, this forms the basis of a pact with his age mates. They have all shared the experience over the same period and in each other's company. Others visit him while he is recuperating in his mother's hut, and then once he has sufficiently recovered, he joins them wearing his regalia as an initiate: a blackened shoulder cloth, scroll brass rings at each temple, and carrying a bow and wax-tipped arrows. With these, they shoot small colourful birds in the bush and arrange their stuffed feathered carcases around a halo-like frame for their headgear. Girls are also threatened with these arrows in exchange for their beaded finger rings, which are then added to the headgear.

The notion of unswerving loyalty to a responsible group of peers who have proved themselves now becomes dominant. It contrasts pointedly with their earlier reputation as cowardly herdboys, ranging from lackeys to wastrels. For six months or more, the initiates band together in increasing numbers, sharing in all things and lending one another moral support. Extending throughout Matapato, there is a sense of becoming a concerted force despite their dispersal, and their age-set acquires an autonomy of its own. They look to one another and not to their firestick patrons for leadership. When one invites another to share some food, it is as representatives of their age-set; and in any request, there is an element of coercion as though coming from the age-set itself. This sharing becomes their dominant ethic throughout moranhood. In their greetings, conversation and demeanour, they are constantly invoking the ideal of their circumcision bond as a coercive force, binding on them all. Potentially, they hold an age-set curse over their future age mates, and as they process together round the countryside, they use this to coerce any reluctant father to relinquish his herdboy son for circumcision. It would be unpropitious for him to refuse.

So long as there are rather few initiates, many of them still striplings, no-one is anxious to promote them to become junior moran. Once they are promoted and no longer protected as ritual dependants, they will again be exposed to the intimidations of the senior moran of the next age-set who still claim the central arena of popular esteem. This is a further source of jealousy directed towards the initiates, although no-one suggested it was related to the threat from 'eyes': moran in general are dissociated from mystical threats. Their scorn remains, and with it the urge to give the initiates a trouncing as though they are still just troublesome boys.

As the autumn circumcisions extend into the spring, the strength of the initiates increases visibly. They band together in growing numbers and with growing confidence. Their singing and dancing acquires a panache and a distinctive style that is their own. Their headgears fill out with bird carcases, and for many this is a period when their voices deepen and they mature physically. Everyone becomes aware of these irreversible signs. There is a widespread anticipation of the impending tussle with the senior moran for the limelight that will send a ripple through the whole age system.

By the summer, all fully grown boys will have been circumcised, and they reach a point where they are eager to brave the senior moran and prove their worth. They proclaim this by discarding the halo-like frame supporting their headgear and the feathered carcases now hang down limply over their shoulders. They then send deputations to some prominent firestick patrons asking for permission to become moran. This can be refused, protecting them until a further season of autumn initiations. Long before this point is reached, however, public opinion is generally in favour of an earlier transition to moranhood, avoiding the expense of feeding them with their special foods during the long dry summer. Senior moran have to accept that their time is slipping away. They are not expected to hand over their privileges at this point. But by accepting the immediate transition with good grace, they take a significant step up the ladder from assertive warriorhood as moran towards the inevitability of their own elderhood.

With the permission of their firestick patrons to become junior moran, the initiates disperse to their fathers' villages. Their period as ritual dependants ends, as it ended in their infancy, with a small ceremony in which the ritual hair that they share with their mothers is shaved. They discard their initiate regalia, shooting their remaining arrows from the doorway of their mothers' huts. Their semi-seclusion as ritual dependants is exchanged for a new set of avoidances associated with their prestige as junior moran. It is as though they have passed through a chrysalid stage and into the most colourful period of their lives as imagos.

NOTES

1 In the Meto sample of 349 males, 99 were the oldest sons of their fathers of whom 44 were also firestick wards, separated from their fathers by two age-sets; 250 were younger sons of whom 62 (25%) were firestick wards. A similar situation is described among the Arusha by Gulliver (1963: 30, 34).

But the Matapato appear to lay less stress than the Arusha on any notion of the patrons as symbolic 'fathers' of their firestick wards; while among the Samburu, the two roles are considered to be wholly incompatible (Spencer 1965: 83).

2   The Loitokitok perform this ceremony independently of the Kisonko of Tanzania. In it, boys and elders faced one another in two lines stretching from north to south, and the bird (*enkumerei*, a white-browed caucal, Mol 1978:31) was released as they shouted and waved their arms to ensure that it flew along the line in this direction as a good omen. The razor and firestick were firmly bound with a strip of sheepskin and given to the custody of an elder chosen to act as the symbolic 'father' of the future age-set for this single context. The Matapato description of this ceremony was very similar, although it was suggested that during the curse, the bird is actually blinded and its leg broken.

3   These concessions are achieved by sending a deputation of boys to the leading spokesman of the moran. He above all other moran is aware of the general desire among elders for a peaceful change-over and of the need for the moran to retain their dignity. He presents the boys with some emblems of his consent: perhaps a dark cape and a pair of colobus monkey-skin anklets, which the boys will hold up high on a stick. When other moran see them sporting these emblems, they should acknowledge the authority of their spokesman and withhold their urge to attack.

4   This is pre-eminently a ceremony that concerns only one firestick alliance, and members of the other alliance, especially moran, should keep away. Even so, the father chosen as host for this ceremony need not belong to the firestick patrons' age-set. It is necessary only that he should be regarded as a highly propitious elder on whom fortune has smiled. The choice of his village for the ceremony is kept secret by the elders as a precaution against any sorcerer who might be tempted to tamper with the site. Lifting the curse is undertaken by unbinding the circumcision razor and firestick and blessing them (see note 2 above). Then after kindling the fire, the elders sacrifice an ox to share with the boys. The blessing concludes the ceremony, and afterwards the barren women who attended it are pelted with cow dung by the boys and are given boys' cloths to wear. The hope is that they will conceive as soon as they return to their husbands' villages.

5   For this curse to take effect, the initiate is made to walk over the circumcision razor. If he confesses his adultery, he averts misfortune by paying a fine from the small herd he has built up: a cow with calf for his father, a heifer for his mother and for the man who supports him during the operation, and an ox for the circumciser. If some persons other than his parents stand in this role, sharing their ritual hair with him, it is they who are endangered and are entitled to the fine.

CHAPTER 6

THE UPSURGE OF RITUAL REBELLION

When an initiate has discarded his ritual hair and becomes a novice moran, he is referred to as a 'shaved male' (*olbarnoti*). It is a term that draws attention to the contrast between his fresh red-ochred baldness and the duller braided hairstyle of seasoned moran whose pigtails reach some way down their backs. Among the Maasai, it is a man's relative age that identifies him in the first instance, and 'shaved male' is a general term associated with inexperience. It is extended figuratively to any man younger than the speaker, alluding to the fact that he can never catch up and relatively speaking will always remain a cub.

Moran novices are at once bound by the two food avoidances of moranhood (*inturuja*). First, they should only drink milk in the presence of other moran, and this forces them into each other's company for their daily needs.[1] Secondly, any meat seen by a married woman or even by an initiate must also be avoided as despised food associated with weakness. This takes them away from the villages, to share any meat somewhere in the bush. When Matapato try to describe the code of conduct of moranhood beyond the outworn claim that they are warriors, it is especially with regard to these two restrictions and the need they place on the moran for one another's company. After their period as ritual dependants, which characterised them up to a point as infants, these new avoidances might be viewed as a form of symbolic weaning, taking them from dependence on their mothers for food as individuals, to dependence on one another. Two of the three most significant steps towards elderhood occur when these restrictions are ceremonially lifted. The first, after about six years, is when they 'drink milk' (alone). Then after perhaps another five years, the second is when they 'eat meat' (in the presence of their own wives).

PREMATURE ELDERHOOD

It is within a father's grasp to deny his son moranhood. In Cases 12 and 13, this was achieved by upgrading the son to a more senior age-set, above his peers. Once the circumcision fire has been kindled, no further promotions of this kind are possible, and the normal course is then for initiates to become moran and to achieve a certain independence from their fathers. There are, however, further devices that a father may exercise to restrict this independence. One of these is to insist that the son becomes a 'premature elder' (*olngusaniki*) by 'drinking milk' alone shortly after his ritual hair has been shaved off, forcing him to discard one of the key avoidances of moranhood almost before he has had a chance to practise it. The son is in a weak position to refuse a determined father at this point. But the father once again must have the compliance of the firestick patrons of his son's age-set, for they play a decisive role in the small ceremony in which he 'drinks milk'. In this way, two minor ceremonies which are both set up by the father for his own son in his own village – when he first becomes a novice moran and when he first becomes a novice elder – are merged into one event. The son does not actually climb to a senior age-set, but remains in an anomalous position until his peers have completed their moranhood about six years later and follow him by 'drinking milk'.

Premature elderhood is only fully justified when a wealthy father cannot manage the herd by himself and has no other son to turn to. He may be too weak or elderly or even dead, and the son is needed to take over active responsibility unhampered by the avoidances of moranhood and the need to seek the company of other moran. Poverty is no good reason, for cattle are not at stake; the son should first serve as a moran, and only then help to build up the family herd. Having a wastrel son is no good reason, for it would only alienate the son further and he would neither learn to devote himself to the herds nor acquire a new sense of respect and responsibility among moran. At most the prospect of premature elderhood for a wastrel would only be an empty threat by an exasperated father. Cattle must be at stake, and with the family herd at risk, some sons grudgingly accept the need to forego their moranhood.

Case 14.
A Meto elder had three sons who were initiated on the same day, leaving him with a larger herd than he could manage alone. Before their initiation, he called them together and told them that one of them would have to become a premature elder to help him cope with the herd while the others were moran. Whether the oldest son volunteered (as I was told) or was persuaded (as seems more likely), he was accepted as the most logical candidate, carrying the responsibility as principal heir.

Not all youths are so compliant; and it is more usual for the father to catch the son unprepared, or he may run away when faced with the prospect of premature elderhood.

Case 15
(a) Lolorion was nearly blind and there was some speculation that his son might become a premature elder and take full responsibility for the family herd. Guessing Lolorion's intentions, the son waited until his ritual hair had been shaved and then in an unguarded moment, he stole away to join the moran in another part of Matapato where Lolorion could not force him to 'drink milk' [continued in Case 19].
(b) In another quite similar instance, a rich father already had forced his oldest son to become a premature elder, and then wished his next son in the next age-set to do the same. Here too, the response of the second son was to run away. On this occasion, he went to a different tribal section (Purko) and associated with one of their manyata villages until others returned to their fathers to 'drink milk', and then he too returned.
(c) In a third instance, a son who had been forced by his father to 'drink milk' prematurely won the respect of his age mates by continuing to act as a moran, sharing their company and still observing the full range of avoidances. For all practical purposes, he was effectively a moran and his father was obliged to reconcile himself to this fact.

Domineering fathers stand to gain if their sons can be bound down meekly to continue as herdboys in the guise of premature elders. However, the resentment of the sons may spread beyond the family. The morale of the novice moran as a group is undermined by each decision to deny one of their age mates his moranhood. Similarly, the firestick patrons feel their authority has been undermined if the initiative in marginal cases is seen to slip from their control because of the determination of a few fathers from other age-sets. For those who have always dominated their sons, it is a strong temptation and inevitably some will risk controversy.

Case 16.
As a youth, Masiani faced the opposition of his guardian uncle to an early circumcision which would entitle him to become the head of his dead father's household (Case 6). There was no question of his becoming a premature elder, as his herd was still small and manageable. In due course, he built up a substantial herd with the help of his oldest son, Kinai, whom he dominated. In an attempt to gain a measure of independence, Kinai pressed his father for an early initiation into the tail-end of one age-set so as to avoid a prolonged wait for the first initiations of the next age-set. Masiani reluctantly agreed with this request. Then after Kinai had shaved his ritual hair, Masiani insisted that he should 'drink milk' and continue to help him with the herd as a premature elder. Before the firestick patrons locally could meet to consider whether they would lend Masiani their support, word spread among the other novice moran. They banded together to insist to Masiani that Kinai should be allowed to remain with them as a moran. His immediate reaction was to ignore them with contempt as mere 'boys'. However, popular feeling was on their side. Masiani was seen as a victim of his own impulsiveness which led him to accept Kinai's early initiation when he could have refused. He was still comparatively young to

be the father of a moran, and his misjudgment was probably also due to his inexperience as an elder. He was in no position to question the general opposition among older men who were the firestick patrons of these moran. He conceded the point, but continued to dominate Kinai as a moran and even later as an elder.

It is widely felt that moranhood is a period in which young men develop a sense of respect as an essential step towards their elderhood, especially in their manyata village. They learn to restrain their desires as individuals in response to the wishes of the group. This ethic of self-denial is a virtue that premature elders are assumed never to acquire. They may be respected by moran for their personal qualities and their closeness to other elders, but they are despised as a category and are unlikely ever to have much influence within their age-set. Any worthy father is expected to promote his son as a worthy moran unless the case for premature elderhood is incontestable, and even then many would want to avoid this course. The short-term benefit of exploiting a son beyond his boyhood is offset by the long-term damage to their relationship and even to the father's reputation. Yet as the above case shows, a father's domination is already an ingrained habit by the time the son is initiated, and the transition to moranhood raises problems of the transfer of power between generations. Masiani himself extolled the manly virtues of a moranhood spent at the manyata in contrast to the meanness and narrowness of a premature elderhood; and he saw his own moranhood as a liberation from the clutches of his guardian uncle. Yet he totally lacked any insight into the corresponding dilemma of his own son, Kinai, who could not be expected to remain as an obedient possession indefinitely. To this extent, Masiani failed to respect his potential as an independent adult.

The two themes – the paternal yoke and the contrary ideals of moranhood – are intertwined in a persisting dilemma. If moran really do cultivate a sense of respect in each other's company while premature elders do not, then this may be as much a reflection of the patterns of development of relations between father and son as of relations among peers. In a variety of ways, the age system relates to the patriarchal family, and has to be interpreted with this in mind.

THE NOVICE MORAN AND THE ADJUSTMENT OF FAMILY TIES

The transition to moranhood entails a range of personal adjustments within the novice's family. The closeness of some brothers may be threatened by their belonging to rival age-sets. This is offset by a series of gifts between them at about this time.

First, the younger full brothers of a novice moran should each give him a gift within their means that confirms their respect for his new seniority.

Giving this gift and invoking it in a reciprocal form of address are expressed by the same verb: *a-imal*. As with the gifts to each other's brides, this respect is reaffirmed whenever they address one another ('pa-heifer', 'pa-kid', etc), avoiding personal names and undue familiarity for the remainder of their lives. In the years that follow when boys dare the moran and are hounded in return, this respect between full brothers is expected to divert tensions from the family itself.

Secondly, when these younger brothers approach their own circumcision and perform their boys' dancing ceremony, it is their *older* brothers who may lend them certain moran adornments to dress up for the occasion. These include ostrich feather and lionskin trophy headdresses and also certain more durable family possessions, such as thigh-bells and black calfskin capes, which will in due course be handed on together with their shields when the boys become fully entitled to them as moran. These are gestures by older brothers who, in handing down tokens of moranhood, take a step towards accepting their own elderhood. The loan of lionskin trophies in particular is a significant gesture. They are treasured possessions among moran that lose their value once they have been displayed by boys who have not earned them, and they are then discarded.

Thirdly, as soon as possible after these boys have actually become moran, each of their seniors of the next age-set should receive just one heifer to relax the food avoidances between them. Ideally, this heifer-of-avoidance (*enturuj*) is given by a younger brother. Until it is given, the senior will order any novice moran out of the hut when he wishes to drink some milk and will spurn any food that they have touched as if they are still just boys. A novice moran could have two older brothers in the next age-set and give this heifer to one of them, say. And yet he and his friends could still be ordered from their mother's hut by the other brother until he too has been given a heifer by some novice. Thus at a time when a novice moran receives gifts of respect from his younger full brothers, he in turn may be giving a heifer-of-avoidance to a senior brother (or possibly a more distant agnate) to overcome the food avoidance between them.

In addition to ending the humiliation of being treated like boys, this third gift has a certain urgency. Each novice whose father can afford it should celebrate his moranhood by providing his first ox feast in the forest for some age mates. To prepare this feast, novices need practical instruction in butchery and roasting, since these skills are treated almost as a privilege in which the moran excel and boys are kept in ignorance. An older brother would only agree to accompany the novices to the forest to instruct them after receiving his heifer-of-avoidance, and then he too can accept a cut from the feast for himself.

For this first forest feast, the novices wear the wooden earplugs used for stretching their lobes as herdboys, and the feast is the ox-of-the-wooden-earplugs (*loonkulaleeti*). It is sited not too far from the village, and the mother and some of her cronies approach to collect certain cuts of meat and fat. As married women they avoid the actual site of the feast so as not to 'spoil' the meat for the novice moran. In Matapato, the novice moran may simply hand over these cuts with some good-humoured banter, for instance threatening to beat their mothers if there is no milk in the village when they return. The women may swear back at them and taunt that they would not dare. In certain other Maasai tribal sections, this teasing verges on horseplay. The women may threaten to come right into the forest mess to peer at the meat as though the moran are still mere boys; and they may taunt them that they seduce the (avoided) mothers of their girls. This reduces the aspirations of moranhood to shreds before they have even been granted the privilege of association with these girls. The moran in turn may tease their mothers of having incestuous relations with their own (highly avoided) fathers. They may raise their sticks and force them to drink their portion of liquid fat to make them feel sick, again with jocular reference to beating them and providing for them.

The spirit of the occasion appears to be a frolic, almost as if with their wooden earplugs, the novices are once again truant herdboys playing at being moran. The various allusions are to the period when they will leave home and take their mothers to live in the manyata (their warrior village); and their fathers, who are conspicuously absent, are the indirect butt of the joke. If mothers have sexual relations with their own fathers and with the moran friends of their daughters and come under the overbearing protection of their own sons and feed them, then their husbands – the fathers of the moran – are superfluous. In this way the joking in this feast draws attention to the prospective shift in the established order within each family when the omnipotence of the family head as husband and father is undermined. For the duration of the manyata, it is the sons who will control (*a-itore*) their mothers and become the possessors (*iloopeny*) of their huts. Building a manyata is still some way off, but the realignment of family relations that it will entail is already anticipated with relish.

THE MOUNTING TENSION OVER PRIVILEGES

It is popularly assumed that their forest feasting builds up the novice moran physically and psychologically, so that they are better able to stand up for themselves. The senior moran by this time have started to settle down, but they still dominate the arena of moranhood. This is symbolised by the possession of their privileges: the right to form raiding parties, hunt lions, assert the marks of bravery on their shields, carry dark hafts on their spears, grunt and yelp as moran, dance in any central corral, and play with girls in every sense of the term. It is their privilege to confer these on the next age-set at a time of their own choosing. Ideally this is the latest possible moment while strength and initiative still lies with them. At this point, they can claim that they will retrieve the privileges again if the juniors abuse them, and no-one would suggest that they have relinquished them under duress. At any time after this point with their failing strength, however, the initiative shifts away from the seniors and any claim of this kind is patent rhetoric. They can no longer stop the juniors assuming the privileges and proclaiming themselves moran in the fullest sense. Once they can do this, they have taken possession of the arena.

In popular accounts, the novices are beaten at every attempt to filch the privileges until one occasion when they beat their seniors. The Kisonko Maasai in particular have a reputation for fierce fighting and even homicide over the possession of privileges. Violence in Matapato appears to be confined to sporadic skirmishes, which serve as a gauge for the strength and determination of the novices. The elders intervene as a moderating force before this builds up to a confrontation. The two age-sets of firestick patrons – for the novices on the one hand and for the senior moran on the other – are both concerned for a peaceful outcome that would demonstrate their authority over their respective wards. To lose this authority would be to lose influence among other elders. Having once been moran themselves, they are sensitive to the feelings of their wards. They seek to steer them away from a confrontation that is bound to damage reputations among moran, among elders, and for Matapato as a whole. The novice moran are persuaded to have patience and demonstrate their mettle in other ways. The senior moran are encouraged to show maturity, gaining in status what they may lose in bravado for the short time left to them. When Matapato fight Matapato over privileges, it is argued, the privileges are reduced to little more than a children's game, and they are not worth a single human life. When they are transferred responsibly, then the status of the privileges and of moranhood itself is enhanced, to the lasting credit of everyone. Under pressure, the senior moran may propose to offer the privileges piecemeal if the juniors ask for them, starting with privileges associated with girls and adornment and withholding those associated with the defence of the land. Their patrons will then point out that the juniors would never supplicate to their seniors. Once they are offered the more trivial privileges, they will accept nothing less than the total range. Under pressure from their patrons and with popular expectation in favour of a smooth transition, neither side normally has the determination to force an open confrontation. The whole issue tends to evaporate in the haze of a shadow contest. A minor incident in one part of Matapato may lead to conceding the privileges, and then other parts may follow without loss of face.

Case 17.
Masiani recalled how his own age-set had wrested the privileges as novice moran

in about 1928, having previously been hounded as boys by the moran of the Dareto age-set (see p. 69). They had been warned not to come near a village where a large number of Dareto moran lived together with their deputy ritual leader, an official with coercive powers to ensure peace (Chapter 9). 'There were fifty-nine of us staying in other villages and we all had shields. They were just driving out the cattle [in the early morning] when we crossed the valley . . . We yelped [a privilege] . . . We went into the [forbidden] village right into the [privileged] central corral as a body [and danced]. The deputy ritual leader led his age mates outside . . . and addressed them. "I have seen that the 'boys' have come after all. Do you want a fight? For now there is nothing [no privileges] that we could take back from them; and there is nothing more that they can take from us. Let me offer them some milk before they return to their villages . . . and do not fight them." They did not try to turn us out of the central corral, for we had shown ourselves to be moran . . . We had brought their [bullying] ways to an end.'

Significantly, in referring to this incident, Masiani recalled how his age-set had 'fought' (e-tarate) for the privileges and had 'routed' (e-tara) their seniors. On this occasion actual fighting had been averted, but a 'victory' had been won. It can never be quite certain that any transition will be peaceful and this gives it a sense of occasion, with the novices claiming a winning edge even when violence is avoided.

Once they have been granted the privileges, the junior moran are no longer novices. They are recognised as an unstoppable force, and deserve the claim that they are now 'the owners of their territory' (iloopeny enkop). Meanwhile, the senior moran come to accept that these privileges are, after all, little more than a children's game, and in discarding them, they prime themselves for a further step to elderhood. They would no longer grunt, for instance, on entering a hut, but would cough instead like an elder to announce their presence. In the past, conceding the privileges was the signal for them to disband their manyat and return to their fathers' villages to 'drink milk' (cf. Case 23 and Merker 1904:81–2). Nowadays, the manyat are disbanded earlier, but the senior moran still cling to the privileges so long as they are able.

THE MANYATA POSSE (EMPIKAS)

Once the novices can claim to be the ruling moran, they are poised to set up their manyata as a warrior village to protect their locality, and this is their crowning privilege. The other privileges pave the way towards establishing this village with a show of force and wearing full regalia to which they are now entitled as they seize the initiative.

This display has to be seen in the context of the uncertainties facing their age-set at this stage. Among the northern Maasai, virtually all moran are expected to live for a period at the manyata. In the south and especially Matapato, there is traditionally a balance between manyata moran who conform with this ideal and non-manyata moran who remain primarily attached to their fathers' villages and herds. Fatherless moran who wish to assert their independence of their older brothers or guardians, as Masiani did, are clearly destined with their widowed mothers for the manyata, and they may wish to take what cattle they have with them. So too are the sons of elders with large polygynous families, though there is a limit to the number of cattle they can take, and only the most senior mother-of-moran goes to the manyata village as the 'mother' of a group of half-brothers (as in Case 4). If an elder has only one wife who cannot be spared, then it is still possible for his moran sons to attach themselves to some other hut at the manyata (as in Case 15b), and they take with them a few cattle to establish their position there. The case for non-manyata moran rests solely with the family's herding needs. They remain with their father's village although they still are identified with the manyata, visiting it from time to time and subject to its discipline. Whatever the solution, brothers should remain together, either as manyata or as non-manyata moran. Only when one of them becomes a premature elder can they be separated (as in Case 14); and even then it is popularly argued that the possibility of remaining as non-manyata moran to tend the herds makes premature elderhood unnecessary. Within these rules there is scope for disagreement between moran who are enthusiastic to join the manyata and fathers who are reluctant to let them go. Each may interpret the balance of the argument quite differently and the conflict of views is brought to a head and manifested in the show of force.

To establish their manyata village, the moran mount a series of recruitment posses. A temporary manyata camp is first set up by a body of leading moran. Armed posses of about half-a-dozen moran each are to be seen leading their mothers and driving cattle to this camp after a dawn raid on a selected village, or heading off for further raids. The camp is the central point from which they plan their strategy for further posses, keeping their intentions a guarded secret. The principal target for each raid is the mother-of-moran who is to be recruited for the manyata. Neither the firestick patrons nor the fathers are consulted; and no-one can predict where the posses will strike or how each father may react to this invasion of his village and property. His moran sons may be in his village unaware that their mother has been selected, or they may be among the posse force, or on a posse elsewhere. Whether they are present or not is immaterial. It is the mother whom the posse have to snatch away in order to establish her hut at their manyata camp, and her moran sons and step-sons will automatically follow her.

Each village raid should be performed with precision. Attacking it as though it were an enemy village, they break in at dawn and tell the mother to pack a donkey with her belongings: hides, mats, milk gourds, and such like. They may help her with this packing while others select one bull and up to twenty female cattle from the father's herd, depending on the wealth of the father and the number of moran attached to her hut. The father may try to reason with them and they may listen, but normally the circumstances have been weighed beforehand and the posse is in no mood to negotiate. If the father tries to prevent them, then two moran will hold him firmly on his stool in his corral, while the others continue with their task and lead the mother away. If she objects, then she too will be held down while they pack and then she will be snatched away.

In this way, the new age-set is establishing its supremacy as a concerted force and dispelling any lingering doubt. It is an episode that strikes at the heart of family paternalism, and fathers respond in very different ways.

Case 18 (follows from Case 16).
When Masiani was forced to abandon his plan to make his son Kinai a premature elder, he remained adamant that he should remain a non-manyata moran as the only able son of his only wife. The point was conceded and no posse was subsequently mounted against him. Masiani's reputation as an uncompromising patriarch hardened further after an incident involving his second son's recruitment to a manyata 15 years later (see Case 22 below). When in due course his third son and foster nephew planned to join their manyata village, they expected trouble. They joined in the posse against Masiani's village, but asked their age mates to take the brunt of Masiani's venom, holding him down if necessary, while they themselves would help their mother pack before snatching her away. They dared not stand up to Masiani themselves. Masiani, however, was keen to improve his reputation, without appearing to submit meekly. When he heard the posse rushing towards his village at dawn ululating with their thigh bells ringing, he went out to meet them. 'I called to them: "Slowly, now, slowly. Don't rush at us like that, for I will give you what you want. Choose your cattle carefully."' From his own account, Masiani instructed them what to do and which cattle to take, as though they might not know. According to his nephew, they knew exactly, but were grateful for his compliance.

Case 19 (follows from Case 15a).
After his son had run away to avoid becoming a premature elder, Lolorion was determined to prevent him going to the manyata, so that he could tend the family herd. The son dare not face Lolorion himself, but asked other moran to form the posse to snatch away his mother for the manyata village. She happened to be Lolorion's favourite wife, and when he saw the posse rushing towards his village, he attacked them with his herding staff. The moran seized him and pinned him down on his stool until they had led the wife away. Lolorion followed them to the manyata camp and cursed both his son and his wife. The local elders were powerless to intercede with the moran; but they managed to persuade Lolorion that he had lost all sense of proportion and forced him to recant the curse.

Case 20.
Kikil was his father's senior and favourite son, with two half-brothers who were expected to join him with his mother at the manyata village. It is said that when

he joined the manyata posse to raid his own village, his father tried to stop them. In the struggle to subdue him, Kikil accidentally speared the corner of his father's cloth. This was a terrible omen. The father immediately submitted, but warned that Kikil would never marry, though he took care not to pronounce a death curse. Soon after this, so the account goes, the father died and Kikil inherited his cattle as senior son. However, the unresolved threat hung over him and no-one would risk giving him a daughter in marriage. He became mad, lost all his cattle and died while still a relatively young elder. His two brothers prospered.

This last instance has a myth-like quality, as if to warn the moran to curb their exuberance, just as the previous case serves as a warning to fathers. Altogether, the period of recruitment is possibly the most vivid collective representation in Matapato. It is a period that buzzes with anecdote and speculation, and the new moran make their imprint on local affairs as the character of the future manyata takes shape. This licence to rebel against their fathers is the bewitching hour of the age-cycle.

THE POSSE AS A BOUNDARY DISPLAY

The division of Matapato into three sub-sections, each with its manyata village, is solely concerned with the territorial organisation of the moran. Maparasha is the largest manyata and dominates the central area, flanked by Silale in the east and Meto (or sometimes Donyo Orok) in the west. The boundaries between these territories are unmistakable features such as wadis, trackways and roads, and the conventions governing them are also clear. Manyata posses can only recruit from villages within their own territory and must not cross any of these boundaries into another part of Matapato. Thus, if a family with moran has associated for many years with the Meto area and happens to have moved temporarily into the Maparasha area at the time of recruitment, then only the Maparasha posses have the right to raid this family. Moran who are no longer under the control of a father or guardian are free to migrate with their mothers to the manyata territory of their choice beforehand. However, those who are still governed by their father or an older brother are not free to migrate at will and have less choice.

It is often claimed that every moran wants his manyata to be the strongest, and this leads to keen rivalry between the three territories. The Maparasha manyata controls the largest slice of Matapato and acts as a magnet for those that are not already committed to Meto or Silali. Manyata posses therefore may place an early priority on recruiting from those families that live close to their boundaries or whose loyalty is in doubt. Moran whose mothers are unlikely to be recruited for the manyata are less easy to trap and they too have to be watched.

Case 21.

As his father had only one wife, Kwemeri did not expect her to be recruited for the local manyata at Meto. But he did expect to be bound to live there himself once a Meto posse had snatched away some of his father's cattle instead. He planned with a friend to abscond to the large manyata camp at Maparasha before this occurred. Then a Meto posse arrived in the area unexpectedly, and Kwemeri guessed that they intended to raid his father's village next morning. He therefore begged an ox for slaughter from his father and went to greet the posse as his guests. Disarmed by this show of friendship, the posse settled down for the evening to prepare themselves meat and soup in the bush nearby. Kwemeri slipped away, collected his friend and a few of his father's cattle and they drove these overnight across the Olpartimero wadi and into Maparasha territory. The Meto posse were powerless. They could not abduct Kwemeri's mother nor take further cattle in a bid for Kwemeri himself, nor cross the wadi to return the fugitives. The cattle were presented to the Maparasha manyata camp for their herd, and Kwemeri and his friend were accepted as Maparasha moran.

Such tactics are recognised as quite legitimate and do not lead to subsequent malice. The Meto posse did not deserve Kwemeri since the manyata exists always to be on its guard, and they were caught napping. When incidentally Kwemeri became an elder, he returned to the Meto area and has lived there ever since. Moran form lifelong friendships within their manyata villages, but as elders they later disperse throughout the Matapato area when their migrations are motivated by hard economic considerations. In this way, they are quite likely to meet up with old manyata friends anywhere in the tribal section. Any tendency for a bandwagon effect in moranhood towards Maparasha is offset by the advantages among elders of dispersing their cattle throughout the whole of Matapato. The role of the two smaller manyata villages in giving effective protection over smaller areas is no less prestigious.

The firestick patrons acknowledge that they have little control over the recruitment posses. But well before these are mounted, they meet throughout Matapato to reaffirm the recognised territorial boundaries and stamp their authority over the moran in this one respect. They can threaten to prevent the moran from forming their manyata villages. Whether they actually have this power is uncertain, but undoubtedly they are a strongly moderating force, and respect for the internal boundaries is a strict condition for condoning the upsurge of moranhood. Within Matapato at least, the patrons confine the moran to their own territories and set face-saving limits to their rivalry at a time when they are dangerously liberated. The moran for their part have a considerable pride in displaying themselves as a disciplined force; and significantly, no informant could recall an instance when the rivalry between Matapato territories had led to a direct clash between posses.

★   ★   ★

The rules and the nature of the rivalry between manyata territories changes radically across the external boundaries that divide Matapato from its non-Matapato neighbours. The boundaries themselves are again well defined, but families are often interspersed, and this gives rise to ambiguity. In these circumstances and by a convention that extends to all Maasai, a recruiting posse may cross into a neighbouring tribal section to snatch back mothers-of-moran whom they claim belong to Matapato; and they must expect similarly incursions into their own territory by their neighbours. The issue is no longer a question of which side of the border a family with moran happen to be living, but which tribal section they belong to. The problem is well illustrated by Case 8 where a Kisonko Maasai was initiated inside Matapato. In this example, it was quite natural that there should be an influx of Kisonko to celebrate the event. The family had only been in the area a few months and were still strangers. In due course the initiate and his mother could conceivably be collected by a Kisonko recruiting posse, crossing with impunity into Matapato territory to snatch away what was legitimately theirs. The Matapato moran at Meto would have no claim and would not seek a confrontation. However, it was also possible that the family would remain in Matapato and that unborn sons would grow up there, making friends with Meto herdboys and regarding themselves as Matapato. When they become moran, these sons would be recruited into the Meto manyata and any Kisonko posse would be met with force, if necessary carrying the battle into Kisonko territory. Recognising the strength of the Matapato claim, on this occasion it is the Kisonko moran who should restrain themselves. Between these two clear-cut instances lies a dangerously uncertain situation when the status of intermediate sons might be finely balanced between two tribal sections, each prepared to assert its rights by force. It was a marginal instance of this kind that provided the critical turning point for Masiani and his family after the initiation of his second son.

Case 22.
In the Rift Valley to the west of Meto live the Loodokilani Maasai who share a tradition of close friendship and common descent with Matapato. Masiani migrated there to build up his herds of small stock in about 1950 and his senior son, Kinai, was initiated there (Case 16). There were many Matapato families interspersed with Loodokilani in this area, and at that time there was no suggestion that any of their moran would be conscripted into a Loodokilani manyata. Matapato posses from Meto came and snatched away what was rightfully theirs without opposition. Fifteen years later, however, Masiani's second son, Kunaiju, was in a very different position. By this time there were only a few Matapato remaining in the area, and he had lived there almost all his life. Masiani on the other hand had no firm commitment to Loodokilani. He had married off one of his daughters there, but had not been offered any wives in return, whereas he was still a popular figure among his friends in Matapato and had recently acquired several wives from there. After his initiation, Kunaiju

joined a Loodokilani posse conscripting recruits for the local manyata, and planned in due course to join in a raid on his father's village to snatch away his own mother, Telelia. Unexpectedly, a strong posse from Meto arrived to snatch Telelia back to Matapato. Realising that there would be bloodshed if the two posses met, Masiani sped the departure of the Meto posse and urged them to rush Telelia to Matapato before there was trouble. The Loodokilani moran heard the news and prepared to attack the Meto posse even carrying their battle into Matapato and the manyata camp if necessary to retrieve Telelia. Before they crossed into the Meto territory, they were intercepted by their own firestick patrons who were as anxious as Masiani to keep the matter within bounds, and bloodshed was averted. Masiani was summoned to account for himself by the Loodokilani elders of his own age-set, who were also the firestick patrons of the moran. Defending himself, he argued that had the Loodokilani posse arrived first, he would have given them the same help and advice for the same reasons. The Loodokilani elders still regarded him as a renegade whose loyalties had always remained with Matapato, and he was expelled from Loodokilani. Kunaiju was still stranded with his friends, and he refused at first to leave them, proposing to stay without his mother at the manyata in Loodokilani. He was eventually persuaded by the firestick patrons that as Telelia had gone to the Meto manyata, it would be ritually dangerous for both of them if he did not join her. He was escorted to the boundary and handed over to the Meto moran.

Had Masiani been allowed to remain in Loodokilani, then Telelia and Kunaiju could have rejoined him years later when the Meto manyata was disbanded. As it was, Masiani returned to Matapato, suspecting that it was his own Matapato age mates as firestick patrons of the moran who had contrived the whole episode in an attempt to force his return. These elders denied any involvement in the affair. During this period of the age cycle, they always see themselves as a restraining influence who would not take such risks, while any posse of moran would not want their advice anyway. Telelia was again recruited as a veteran mother-of-moran for the next Meto manyata by the next age-set (Case 18). She cherished the story of how her husband had averted a war that was nearly fought over her; and how the Meto camp prepared for battle, while she was quaking as their hostage and never expected to see her son again. Kunaiju retained his friends among the Loodokilani and visited them from time to time as an elder. They have told him that he is free to migrate to rejoin whenever he wishes, once he has become fully independent of his father.

Dramas of this kind are comparatively rare, but the possibility remains vivid. The recruitment posses are mounted as mock raids in a spirit that could flare into combat if the conventions are not closely observed. In recruiting within the boundaries of their manyata areas they are establishing the territory that they will defend any time: in a sense they are beating the bounds. In crossing into neighbouring tribal sections, they are again staking a claim, not over territory, but over emigrant families whose marginal status is of as much concern to them as it is to the elders. It is these posses that periodically delineate the boundaries between Maasai.

THE DIVERSE ROUTES TO ELDERHOOD

The manyata posse can be seen as a display of physical power at three levels. It re-establishes territorial boundaries within and beyond Matapato. It proclaims that the new age-set now hold the central arena of moranhood. And it highlights the formal rupture of the paternal yoke. In other words it may be seen as a ritual of rebellion against the father, vividly illustrated in some of the more melodramatic accounts of fathers who have been forcibly put in their place.

Most fathers are keen that their sons should benefit from the manyata experience. They are also well aware that if they try to resist the surge of moranhood, then they are as likely to lose loyal sons as to gain obedient herdsmen. Nevertheless, there are some who succeed in restricting their sons in various ways, either because they have a good reason or because they manage to subvert the system.

It is useful at this point to place the various routes to elderhood in perspective. Figure 3 shows these diagrammatically with a broad estimate of the number within each category for a typical manyata territory.

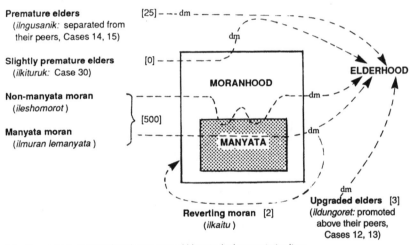

Premature elders [25]
(*ilngusanik:* separated from
their peers, Cases 14, 15)

Slightly premature elders [0]
(*ilkituruk:* Case 30)

Non-manyata moran
(*ileshomorot*)

Manyata moran [500]
(*ilmuran lemanyata*)

MORANHOOD

MANYATA

ELDERHOOD

Reverting moran [2]
(*ilkaitu*)

Upgraded elders [3]
(*ildungoret:* promoted
above their peers,
Cases 12, 13)

[ ]   Suggested number of each category within a typical manyata territory
dm   'Drinking milk' ceremony at father's village

Figure 3.   Career paths towards elderhood

It is evident from this figure that a clear majority of youths serve as moran. Those whom I asked had difficulty in assessing the typical balance between manyata moran and non-manyata moran. Those at the manyata look down on the others and know exactly who they are, but at the manyata and elsewhere both categories intermingle. Non-manyata moran come for extended periods and behave as manyata moran, while manyata moran are often elsewhere. The number actually staying at the manyata fluctuates, and at no time is there a precise tally between them. It is the total that they count.

The Matapato convention that there are these two categories of moran accounts for the small number who arrive at elderhood by some other route. Those that are needed by their fathers for herding can remain as non-manyata moran; and even manyata moran may occasionally be given dispensation from manyata service when the need is pressing. This weakens the case for recruiting a youth to a senior age-set as an upgraded elder, or for forcing him to become a premature elder. If a son cannot be spared for the manyata, then at least he should be allowed his moranhood, and fathers who seek to by-pass the system are vigorously opposed. Some may slip their sons through before the new age-set has properly established itself, but the new moran soon learn to forestall attempts to rob them of active members.

Once their manyata is established there should be no further premature elders. In some other Maasai tribal sections, however, a category of slightly premature elders does exist for certain moran whose circumstances change quite radically, pre-empting an early elderhood. In fact, an unprecedented instance is reported later (Case 30). However, until that point the Matapato moran would not concede any circumstance that could justify this step and effectively opposed it; and the elders had been powerless to force them to change.

Finally, there are reverting moran who follow a delayed rather than a premature route to elderhood. In the past, impoverished moran might fail to build up even the nucleus of a herd, and could revert to moranhood by associating with the next age-set, down-grading themselves in the hope of mending their fortunes through raiding. Today, with no prospect of raiding, the best course for a stockless man is to seek a job at the earliest opportunity. Reverting to moranhood is a course that was always rare and is now only followed by wastrels who have broken loose from all paternal control. They have no thought beyond basking in an unending moranhood, when rightfully they should be elders. The other moran tolerate them because they swell their ranks, but they also despise them as they would any disoriented wastrel; and the girls avoid them because they are old. With their developed age organisation, the Matapato are a highly age conscious people, and a reverting moran today is regarded as an unaccountable oddity, out of place and out of time.

AGE-SETS, AND RIGHT-HAND AND LEFT-HAND AGE-GROUPS

A new age-set is established about once every fifteen years, and it is given a name common to all Maasai at the *olngesher* ceremony, when its members pass the final hurdle to elderhood. Before that point is reached, there are certain conventions concerning the organisation of the moran that vary between tribal sections. Among the Kisonko and related sections in the south, for instance, young men remain active moran for an extended period and there is a major transition from one age-set to the next about every fifteen years $(A \rightarrow B \rightarrow C \rightarrow D \rightarrow)$. In Matapato and most northern Maasai tribal sections there is an elaboration of this basic pattern in which each *age-set* is divided into two successive sub-age-sets. These are the 'right-hand circumcision' and the 'left-hand circumcision', whose names vary between tribal sections. For simplicity here, I propose to refer to these sub-age-sets as *age-groups* and to identify them in relation to their parent age-set: Terito^L for the left-hand age-group of Terito age-set; Nyankusi^R for the right-hand age-group of Nyankusi, and so on. As opposed to the Kisonko pattern, there are *two* successive age cycles during each fifteen year age-set period, and the transfer of privileges among moran is between age-groups $(A^R \rightarrow A^L \rightarrow B^R \rightarrow B^L \rightarrow C^R \rightarrow)$. The same sequence of ceremonies is performed by each age-group until their *olngesher* ceremony, which binds them formally into a unified age-set $(A^R + A^L \rightarrow A)$. Whether one term or the other is more appropriate depends on context. One may refer to an *age-group* of moran when considering their manyata; but to an *age-set* of moran when referring to the firestick relationship for this is shared by moran of both the right-hand and the left-hand age-groups: Nyankusi^R and Nyankusi^L both had Dareto age-set as their firestick patrons. Sometimes, either term is appropriate. For instance, when the privileges were disputed between the Terito^L and the Nyankusi^R who succeeded them, the contest was between age-groups, but the significance of this contest was seen to be in the transition of power between whole age-sets (from Terito to Nyankusi).

It is the right-hand age-group who face the stiffer test of gaining the privileges for their age-set, and carry more prestige in accomplishing this. The rivalry is less fierce within an age-set, and those of the left-hand age-group have an easier task. Boys generally want to belong to the right-hand group because of this prestige, even if this delays their moranhood. And their fathers support them, associating this prestige with manyata discipline and the qualities of respect and wisdom. As a result, in a right-hand age-group, the van tends to be extended by older boys whose initiation has been delayed and the tail-end by younger boys whose initiation has been brought forward. With a larger membership over a wider age span, the right-hand group tends to hold on to the privileges for longer, perhaps even for nine years. Its ceremonial sequence of promotions tends to be more leisurely than the left-hand group, which has a narrower age span and may only retain the privileges for perhaps six years. In this way the right-hand group attracts precisely the qualities that endow

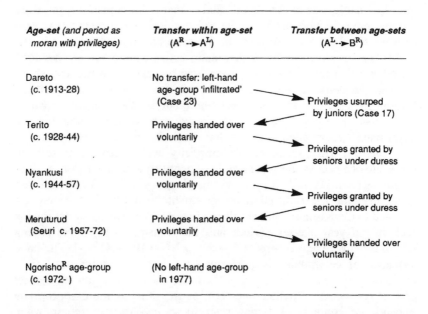

Age-set (and period as moran with privileges)	Transfer within age-set $(A^R \dashrightarrow A^L)$	Transfer between age-sets $(A^L \dashrightarrow B^R)$
Dareto (c. 1913-28)	No transfer: left-hand age-group 'infiltrated' (Case 23)	
		Privileges usurped by juniors (Case 17)
Terito (c. 1928-44)	Privileges handed over voluntarily	
		Privileges granted by seniors under duress
Nyankusi (c. 1944-57)	Privileges handed over voluntarily	
		Privileges granted by seniors under duress
Meruturud (Seuri c. 1957-72)	Privileges handed over voluntarily	
		Privileges handed over voluntarily
Ngorisho^R age-group (c. 1972-)	(No left-hand age-group in 1977)	

Figure 4.   The transfer of privileges within and between age-sets

this prestige and discipline; the left-hand group has a paler complexion and is destined to lose the privileges to the next age-set sooner. The reputation that precedes both of them is self-fulfilling. This difference between right-hand and left-hand is reflected in Figure 4, summarising the manner in which the privileges had been handed over on the eight occasions prior to 1977, with more competition evident between age-sets than within each age-set.[2]

The smoother transition from the right-hand to the left-hand age-group within an age-set is not automatically conceded in a spirit of compromise. The left-hand group have to show themselves worthy of the privileges, and it is by no means certain that these will be granted.

Case 23.
The left-hand age-group of Dareto age-set (Dareto^L) were generally regarded as weak. After some ineffectual attempts to wrest the privileges from Dareto^R in about 1922, they lost heart and this made their seniors even less inclined to concede to them. Without the privileges, the juniors could not build their own manyata villages, and the seniors had no pressing reason to disband their own manyata organisation and settle down to elderhood. The left-hand group lost any sense of collective identity and ceased to exist as a cohesive force. Individual moran tagged onto the tail-end of the right-hand group, joining older brothers already at the right-hand manyata or simply staying as non-manyata moran with their fathers' herds. They were infiltrators (*iloisorokini*) among their seniors,

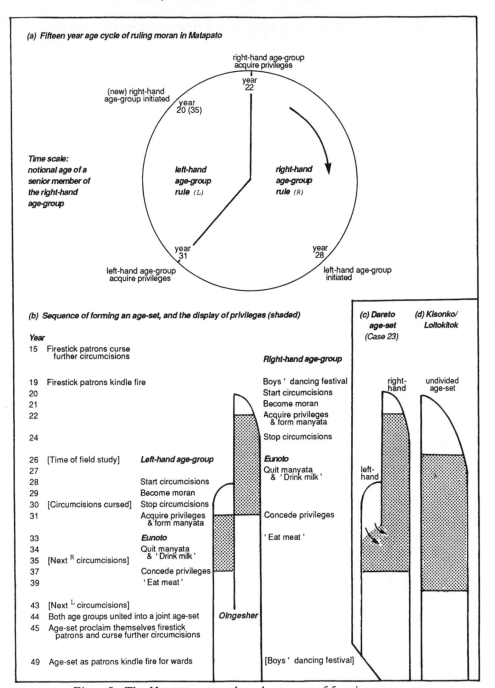

Figure 5   The Matapato age cycle and sequence of forming an age-set

'like smoke'. Once they no longer posed any threat to the seniors, they were allowed to assume the privileges and to join in the ceremonies of the right-hand group; but they were allowed no ceremonies or ritual offices of their own. Thus in Case 17, when the young Terito^R moran usurped the privileges from this age-set, it is said to have been primarily these ex-members of Dareto^L who had been in no mood to hand over the privileges without a struggle after their earlier humiliation. As it was, they were again humiliated, and the instrument was a senior ritual officer whose age-group (Dareto^R) had long since lost interest in these privileges.

No other instance of a left-hand age-group failing to establish itself could be recalled in Matapato and the possibility was even denied in some other tribal sections. However, the fact that in principle it could happen in Matapato and indeed had occurred within living memory was a warning to all left-hand age-groups that they had to earn their recognition. Recognition is no mere formality and the longer the delay, the more an age-group of novices lose in prestige, and the shorter their period as ruling moran.

⋆   ⋆   ⋆

The alternation between right-hand and left-hand age-groups of ruling moran in the fifteen year age cycle and the ceremonial sequence for a whole age-set are represented diagramatically in Figures 5(a) and 5(b). The notional time scale is the age of the oldest recruits into the age-set from about fifteen years old when their firestick patrons curse the circumcision razor until they are about forty-four and perform their *olngesher*.

It may be noted in Figure 5(b) that the preparations for the left-hand group are simplified. Their firestick patrons have already kindled one fire for the whole age-set and have established their authority. They do not therefore curse the circumcision razor a second time or inaugurate a second boys' dancing festival for the left-hand. They simply mobilise small delegations of boys to pronounce a suspension of further circumcisions backed by the threat of a curse (year 24) which is lifted with further delegations four years later. Thus the illicit circumcision in Case 10 occurred in this suspended period and was not an issue between age-sets as Cases 9, 12 and 13 had been. In other respects, the account of this chapter needs no further elaboration, and Cases 14–22 could conceivably have arisen in either right-hand or left-hand age-groups.

Figure 5(c) indicates how this standard pattern is modified when a left-hand group fails to establish itself and merges into the right-hand group. This may be compared with the simpler Kisonko pattern in Figure 5(d) where there are no age-groups and moran retain their privileges for an extended period (shaded). The Kaputiei, incidentally, have a hybrid system, whereby one firestick alliance have adopted the northern pattern with age-groups (Terito^{R+L} – Meruturud^{R+L} –) and the other firestick alliance have adopted the Kisonko pattern without age-groups (Dareto – Nyankusi –). Each firestick alliance regard their pattern as their own affair and in no way an anomaly. The feature that makes Matapato, Kisonko, Kaputiei and others all Maasai is that they all share the same age-sets. The division into age-groups is purely a matter for the organisation of moranhood within each tribal section.

CONCLUSION: REBELLION AND TABOO

In his essay on rituals of rebellion, Max Gluckman (1963) argued that forces of opposition generated by an absolute system may be dissipated through ritual protest. He did not specifically consider systems based on the absolute inequality of age or generation, but the general argument has a clear relevance here. In Matapato, there is a ritualised element in the transfer of the coveted role of full moranhood to a new age-group, marked by displaying the privileges as though they have been usurped. What could have been a true rebellion against their predecessors if this transfer had been opposed takes on the character of a ritualised rebellion when it has been conceded peacefully, as if to emphasise the legitimacy of the transfer to a group entering their prime. The new age-group then sport themselves as the 'rulers of the land' until they in turn are displaced. It is not unlike the Frazer's opening scenario in the *Golden Bough* that gave Gluckman his cue: each vigilant King of the Wood at Nemi was destined in his turn to be deposed by his usurping successor (Frazer 1922:1–3). With regard to the Matapato instance, Gluckman's point would be that by the act of deposing ageing moran, the system of moranhood itself is strengthened.

The episode that follows this presumption of power evokes Freud's elaboration of Frazer in his *Totem and Taboo*: the moran defy the domination of their fathers and snatch away their mothers to live separately at the manyata. The strength of Freud's argument lies in his exposition of the powerful forces generated within each family, and most especially under the tyranny of patriarchy. The crux of his vision was that rebellious sons had a choice. They could either commandeer the father's horde of women and become patriarchs themselves, or they could break out of the impasse by renouncing competition and gratification in order to create a higher form of society. In Gluckman's terms, this would be to convert their rebellion against the father into a revolution against his regime. In the Matapato system, the manyata rebellion represents a reaction against the patriarchal family for a few years only. But they are still critical years that provide a highlight of Matapato culture, and in particular of the age system. As in Freud's scenario, the manyata is modelled on a set of principles that are directly opposed to the self-interest of the patriarchal family. Alternatively, the manyata may be regarded as the Maasai approximation to Plato's *The Republic*, with a pronounced ideal of common property rights taken to considerable lengths to serve the interests of the whole. The prime virtue of sharing within the age-group is geared to the notion of mutual support and fundamental equality. The disposal of women and the concern over incest, which figure prominently in Freud's account, only become critical in the Matapato version at a later stage when the moran are drawn back into the system of patriarchy and are domesticated into elderhood (Chapter 10 below). Among the moran, it is not so much the father's wives that are taboo, as any form of selfishness or self-interest that would be seen as a betrayal of the manyata and of the spirit of moranhood itself. In other words, one has a tension between two opposed structural principles that Gluckman saw as a basis for rituals of rebellion (1963:136), and Freud as a basis for taboo (1950:68). In Matapato, the process of ageing entails a developing interplay between these two principles.

NOTES

1   As a final resort in times of serious hunger, someone else may offer milk to a solitary moran. In Matapato this could be a member of the next senior age-set if there are no other moran at all in the locality. In Purko, it could be a girl who has associated closely with the moran. The essential point is that a moran should never drink by himself.

2   The greater accommodation within an age-set is borne out by the claim that right and left-hand age-groups raided together in the past, putting the issue of privileges to one side. They would not actually fight side by side and their cattle gains would be kept apart, but they would still share in the prestige of a joint victory. Again, the heifer-of-avoidance given to each senior moran is only relevant for relations between age-sets. A moran of a right-hand age-group would not spurn food touched by novices of the left-hand, but he would still expect his heifer in due course, from a novice of the next age-set.

CHAPTER 7

THE MANYATA AS A REPUBLIC

Once the new age-group of moran have the privileges, they are in a mood to show their mettle. Their manyata recruitment posses are mounted in the spirit of a challenge against the world at large and against their fathers in particular. Ultimately, there has to be a limit to their freedom, and it is the firestick patrons who must be prepared to curb them, not as fathers but as patrons showing *their* mettle. In Case 22, the recruitment raid into Loodokilani was widely regarded as the reckless gamble of an age-group of untamed moran. Yet significantly, it was the patrons who averted a major affray. These elders were of Terito age-set and they could not have forgotten that as moran they too had had a major brush with their own firestick patrons in many parts of the Maasai area. It was the age system that was as much to blame as the moran themselves.

Case 24.
During the 1920s, leading Maasai elders accepted the inevitability of change and connived with the British administration's attempts to subdue the moran by abolishing the manyata system. Moran of Terito[R] age-group were forbidden to mount their recruitment posses, forcing them all to remain as non-manyata moran. News then spread to Matapato that the Purko moran had defied this ban and had established their own manyata villages, even though they had been forced to 'drink milk' (qv. Case 15c). A delegation of Matapato moran paid a secret visit to their Prophet, Sendeu. Sendeu's son was an age mate of theirs, and provided them with details of a ceremony in which eight of them should masquerade as their own firestick patrons.[1] This would ritually override the true patrons and enable them to mount their posses. The ceremony was performed and the true patrons had to accept that they had no knowledge that could reverse this ritual anomaly except through the Prophet. However, they could still claim their ultimate power to curse their wards for disrespect. Terito elders recall the histrionic performance of their firestick patrons with awe. The moran were summoned to a harangue, threatened, intimidated, and forced to pay a massive fine of cattle. The patrons then took what was seen as the only realistic and propitious course: they re-established their position by ritually endorsing the manyata arrangements.

This incident is related to each new age-group of moran, emphasising that the Terito[R] were powerless to evade the punishment for their revolt, and the patrons as always, had the last word. However, there was a signal also for the elders, and every age-group of moran since Terito times have been allowed to form manyata villages.

THE ROLE OF THE FIRESTICK PATRONS IN ESTABLISHING THE MANYATA

It is the firestick patrons who select the site for the manyata village within each area and establish it ritually. The ceremony provides them with an opportunity to reimpose their authority after the period of recruitment when the initiative has been seized by the moran. The patrons are in no mood to negotiate. When they are approached by delegations of moran to perform this ceremony, they lay down firm conditions and demand to be honoured as privileged guests with lavish hospitality. Anything less than a show of total respect will be taken as a slight. The patrons will simply threaten to abandon the ceremony – and hence the manyata itself – withholding their blessing and vaguely hinting at a curse. This tactic is repeated at subsequent ceremonies, but on this occasion especially it is critical for them to demonstrate that they can bring a volatile situation firmly under control.

This ceremony is named after the deserted village in which the posses first set up their camp, and also the hatchets used by their mothers to cut stakes for their manyata huts: it is the village-of-the-hatchet. Preparing for the ceremony, the moran buy as much tobacco, sugar and tea as they can afford, and their mothers brew beer. When their scouts report that the patrons are coming, the moran start to slaughter oxen to prepare a lavish feast. When the patrons arrive, they carry long switches and demand a convincing show of contrition before they will touch the feast or enter the camp. The moran and their mothers approach them clutching grass in supplication, and the patrons pretend to take offence and stride away until wooed back by further pleas. Eventually, they agree to start.

Having selected a site for the manyata village, the patrons smear honey on the hut stakes. When the huts have been erected, a young bull is held down in the centre of the manyata, and the patrons kindle the first manyata fire on its back. Each mother then collects a brand to light the fire in her own hut.[2] In this way, the mothers again have a central role in establishing the manyata, earlier as captives of their sons, and now in relation to their own huts. The metaphor of 'cutting' boyhood from moranhood is repeated again. It was first used when the age-sets were divided by suspending further circumcisions, then at circumcision itself, and now at the village-of-the-hatchet, cutting new stakes for new huts. Each cutting is followed by kindling the patrons' fire. Cutting and kindling are decisive acts that structure the age organisation. As women build their huts, so the patrons build up the new age-group.

The patrons impose their commanding role and establish a pattern for future occasions by setting the moran various tasks, including their dancing. The moran for their part, elated by their prospects, are exuberant. A number of patrons hover nearby ready to lash at them with their switches merely because they appear to be idling instead of joining in these other activities, or even without provocation. At any point, the patrons may make an issue out of a triviality, and get up to leave. This will bring the performance to a premature halt unless the show of contrition is repeated. Assiduously the moran order their mothers to prepare more sweet tea for the patrons, and offer them more beef, more beer, more tobacco.

Periodically, the patrons bring the dancing to a halt and harangue the moran, instructing them on the details of the regime they propose. They insist that there must be no further recruiting posses, but a new mood in which the moran serve the wider community. They reserve the right to refuse or delay further ceremonies, or to disband the manyata prematurely. The price they demand for agreeing to the manyata is to bring it within the ambit of their control and to model it on their own ideals of public accountability. The moran must learn to contain their own excesses and to accept an internal discipline. They must first be accountable to themselves through debate at the manyata, and ultimately to the elders through their patrons. It is held that this self-restraint does not detract from the ideal of warriorhood, but enhances their effectiveness. A disciplined group is superior to a horde of individualists both in its fighting qualities and in its ultimate wisdom. The reputation of the manyata hinges on their ability to submit themselves to this discipline and reach for these ideals. These in turn are seen as a shrewd training for elderhood.

THE MANYATA SPOKESMAN

At the ceremony of the village-of-the-hatchet, a central feature is the appointment of a talented and respected member of the manyata as manyata 'spokesman' (olaiguenani). The patrons consult other moran discreetly before they select a candidate, and then direct him to be seized before he suspects and tries to run away from the responsibility. He is installed with the gift of a black club which the patrons bless as a symbol of his office, bearing the authority vested in him at any manyata debate.

On their side, two patrons are chosen to act as 'fathers of the manyata', with an interest in its affairs and a remote overseeing role. Typically, they have sons of their own there, and the manyata spokesman and other leading moran should consult them as necessary, and they in turn should consult other patrons.

The spokesman is responsible for discipline among the moran. When the elders visit the manyata to instruct or harangue them, he must sit among the patrons, and remain silent until they have cajoled the moran into accepting their demands. Then on behalf of the moran, he should repeat in his own way what they have been forced to accept. Similarly, the spokesman is expected to be among the patrons as a peacemaker when they intervene in a local affray between moran, and not among the moran as a warrior. If no patrons are present he can threaten to throw down his black club as a curse on all his followers if they do not obey him.

As with so many other aspects of manyata life, the spokesman's role is popularly explained in the imagery of traditional warfare. In the past when moran planned a raid, he headed the delegation to the Prophet and memorised his instructions and warnings that would ensure success. The notion of a cordial link between the Prophet and the spokesman and the moran generally persists. At the scene of battle, the spokesman was obliged to direct operations from a strategic position in the rear accompanied by a bodyguard and a group of aides. The key to Maasai success was seen as a combination of the courage of their fighters coupled with the spokesman's ability to keep his head in a critical situation. He had to view the battlefield tactically at a distance. He was not allowed to fight, for if he were killed then they would have lost their 'head' (*elukunya*), and they would cease to act as a cohesive fighting force. If the course of the raid went against the Matapato moran, they were expected to group themselves around him, regarding his survival as essential for their own. Even on the battlefield, he was central and yet kept apart. It was not simply that he was not required to develop the quality of bravado that was highly prized among moran: he was forbidden it, for he was expected to excel in other ways that rose above the competition for individual prestige. Only in the confusion of a surprise attack by enemies on the manyata might he be drawn defensively into fighting. Today, he is still prevented by other moran from joining in any lion hunt.

A sensitive issue with which the spokesman had to contend on any raid concerned the rivalry for prestige between families, clans and ultimately between the two moieties (Figure 1). Normally, these agnatic rivalries were contained within the broader display of unity. However, in situations of crisis, agnatic loyalties could become a sensitive issue. In battle especially, oaths invoked honour associated with lineage and clan. Brothers were expected to fight side by side. After the event, the heroic dead were enumerated by clan. This rivalry reached a climax after a successful raid, when minor squabbles over the division of the spoil could precipitate a major affray between the moieties. By dissipating their self-destructive rivalry at this level, so it was argued, there remained a greater spirit of compromise among clans and families over the spoil, and unity at the lower levels would be preserved. In-fighting would not break out a second time. Equally significant, perhaps, if several manyat combined on a raid, fighting between moieties would cut across their rivalry and Matapato unity itself would be preserved. With the advice of his aides, the spokesman had the invidious task of dividing the spoil in the first place to minimise the serious risk of a mêlée. He had to be seen to reward merit where it was due and to balance the competing claims between clans and other groups impartially. Then if fighting erupted, he had to reassert his authority at once to stop it, and then to restore popular confidence in his judgment. Again it was a matter of keeping a cool head, this time when manyata discipline and the unity of the age-group for once could be shattered. Then on arriving at the manyata, the moran divided into two columns according to their moieties, dancing round it in opposite directions. It was the spokesman who gave a tally of those missing to the elders waiting there for the news.

The spokesman's aloof authority is repeated within the manyata. At any debate, he is expected to reaffirm the demands of their firestick patrons. Beyond this he should be reticent until he is in a position to voice the general consensus. Certain moran with strong views may dominate the earlier stages of the debate, but theirs may not be the final wisdom of the meeting after other views have been expressed. The spokesman cannot afford to be seen to adopt a partial view on such occasions. Once again, he is respected for his ability to keep himself slightly apart from the contest in order to see the wider issue. Then towards the end of the debate when a consensus appears to have emerged, he may interpret this clearly and with authority. Speaking for the entire manyata, he will vigorously oppose any moran who do not accept this.

The manyata spokesman is complemented by those moran who are regarded as advocates or 'feathers' (inkopir) and argue on behalf of a particular interest. The imagery is of the 'head' of the manyata – its brain – with the feathers ranged around it, like ostrich feathers in a warrior's headdress. For full effect, every feather (representing every shade of opinion) must be immaculately in place, transforming an ordinary warrior into a composed figure of power. So strong is the notion that their system must ultimately be democratic that the Matapato sometimes say that the power of their society lies with the advocates. When a group of age mates as moran or later as elders nominate an advocate, there is an implicit element of coercion and he 'dare not' refuse. With their backing, the points he expresses in debate carry extra weight. A formally appointed spokesman cannot stand up to a point of view clearly expressed by a decisive body of advocates. He should be at the centre of all views, like the head in the middle of a headdress. He is then well placed to assess how far the more articulate members of his manyata represent shades of opinion that should be taken into account. The debate with different points of view expressed by advocates and converging on the view ultimately expressed by the spokesman is the closest that Matapato come to the notion of a collective mind. It is a process that enables him to voice a more profound wisdom.[3]

To help him in his role, the spokesman appoints any number of personal aides, whom he can replace as he sees fit. Pursuing the metaphor, they are his 'necks' (*imurto*), and without them the 'head' is unsupported and ineffectual. He must constantly keep their company, delegating tasks to them and taking their advice. In his absence, they may act with his authority. The dual accountability of the spokesman (to patrons and moran) is repeated in the role of his aides, who as necks link the head to the body of moran. On the battlefield, it was they who advised him, acted as messengers and also held him down if he showed any desire to join in the fighting. Similarly in the manyata, they are expected to advise him, carry out certain errands, and at the same time ensure that he does not abuse his position. They are manyata moran who should be aware of rumblings of criticism among other moran, and warn him.

A careful tally is kept of the spokesman's shortcomings especially by his aides. Perhaps he has used his authority to settle some issue that should first have been debated; or has failed to convey the feelings of the moran on some matter to the patrons; or has shown weakness in handling a matter of manyata discipline; or is absent from the manyata too often. When the moran can list nine separate issues on which the spokesman has failed them, ignoring repeated warnings, they are entitled to call the firestick patrons to a meeting. The patrons listen to the charges and then invite the spokesman to reply. It is a final measure that is only taken with extreme reluctance. The patrons would not agree to the meeting unless it is quite certain that the spokesman will have to be replaced. It is a possibility that sharpens the popular view of the spokesman's accountability to his peers. They are altogether more likely to contain him, than he is to curse them by throwing down his club.

The spokesman is clearly in a difficult position. Only too easily, he can find that either the patrons or the moran or both feel that he has abused their trust. This is reflected in a number of vivid beliefs associated with the dangers of his position. In order to protect the spokesman and give him strength for his task, he is initially taken by the firestick patrons to the Prophet. There, he presents the Prophet with a heifer-of-respect, as he would an older brother. In return, he is given charms to enhance his powers of persuasion in debate, and to protect him from the harm that success may bring.

The spokesman is the most prominent member of his manyata and this is thought to place him at risk from the envy of others. Other ambitious

Prophets, for instance, may want to discredit the Matapato Prophet by bringing him harm. The moran of his own manyata may resent his authority. Smouldering resentment among the firestick patrons against the moran would be directed towards him. Beyond these are the risks facing a spokesman who has been well chosen for his abilities and embarks on a glittering career of success. If he can dazzle with his oratory and outwit others, then his audience may put their hands to their mouths and gasp at this sheer brilliance. They do not necessarily intend him any harm, but involuntarily their mouths may become bitter and the spokesman is at risk from the effects of this widespread envy. The belief is strikingly reminiscent of the interpretation of people with 'eyes' who bring unintended harm. However, instead of it being the weakest members of the community who are thought to be at risk, here it is the strongest. Because they are so exceptional, they are vulnerable to the concentration of men's envy. As with initiates threatened by 'eyes', this belief lends further glamour to the role of spokesman. Added to his personal charisma, for which he was selected in the first place, there is a dangerous charisma attached to his office.

Among the various accounts that circulate in Matapato concerning the misfortunes of spokesmen who have been exposed to the mystical forces of ill-will, two are remembered as outstanding Maasai moran of Terito[R]. Their position was made more invidious by the attempts of the British administration to destroy the manyata system and ultimately the institution of moranhood itself. Olempaye is remembered as an exceptional spokesman among the Kisonko who was inadequately protected by his Prophet's charms, and went mad because of the envy of others. The early death of Olemutelu as spokesman of the Purko moran has two popular explanations in Matapato. According to the first, he was a powerful rebel who defied the firestick patrons and was cursed by them when he led other moran to establish a manyata illegally (see Case 24). In the other version, he was a pawn in the hands of the patrons at a time when the moran were humiliated and forced to work manually, building roads; he then died from the curse of his own age mates.

The manyata spokesman, however, is not normally seen as a scapegoat, placed in the crossfire between the manyata facing a critical external world and firestick patrons facing high spirited young men. The general attitude towards his installation is that it marks a watershed in the relations between the moran and the remainder of the community. The spokesman's ability to transcend these hazards is seen as a proof of the protection of their Prophet and of the integrity of the manyata.

THE MANYATA VILLAGE AND THE ELDERS' VILLAGE AREAS

The manyata and the elders' villages are opposed precisely as moran are opposed to elders. In contrast to the tight organisation of the manyata, the villages of the elders are dispersed throughout Matapato in loose clusters, and they maintain a more casual network of visiting and communication. This dispersal enables them to graze their herds and flocks over a wide area. The difference is implied in the general term for the elders' village areas: *kerai*, or more literally, 'places where there are sheep and goats'. The products of small stock are pre-eminently the food of elders and their dependants, whereas only cattle are kept at the manyata. Cattle offer the richest prize and it is cattle and not small stock that the moran are obliged to protect. The term *kerai* for the elders' village areas does not contradict the importance of cattle for the elders, but it does express an ideological association

cattle : small stock :: moran as defenders : elders as stock owners :: public : private

This touches on a further polarity between the notion of individual ownership associated with each family head, and joint ownership at the manyata. The manyata moran associated with each hut have immediate charge over their mother and the small herd of cattle that accompanied her, but only as trustees on behalf of the manyata. Telelia who had lived in four manyata villages – as a girl, a young wife (Case 35), an abducted mother (Case 22), and now a veteran mother (Case 18) – was very clear who 'ruled' (*e-itore*). It was the manyata and not her moran sons. The manyata had organised the posse to collect her, and she had more experience in deferring to manyata discipline than any of the moran. To this extent, the authority of the father is not directly challenged by his own moran sons, unless he chooses to make this a personal issue.

Once the period of recruitment is ended with the formal establishment of the manyata, the father's remaining possessions remain securely under his control. He even acquires a certain initiative in deciding which of his uninitiated children may accompany their mother to the manyata, and how many further milch cattle should be sent to feed them. Any very young children would probably go with her, and perhaps an older girl to help her with domestic chores and an older boy to herd the manyata cattle. They all are assumed to benefit from manyata discipline and learn the idiom of manyata speech which emphasises respect and accountability to the manyata. The father is not obliged to send these children; and he can withdraw them at any time if he needs them himself or feels they are not benefiting from the experience or are being maltreated by the moran. If, for instance, the manyata herd dwindles due to negligence then he may recall his uninitiated children and any extra cattle. For the manyata venture has failed and the moran have brought hunger on themselves.

The mothers and the cattle gathered by the manyata posses remain beyond the fathers' control, and none of the huts of the manyata can move from the site. However, the moran cannot reasonably detain the women themselves during a period of intense hunger. Some of them may be allowed to return to their husbands' villages for a time, sleeping in the huts of other women, but they *must* first ask permission of the manyata. In this way, the reputation of the manyata hinges on the extent to which they look after their own herd and dependants, having usurped the paternalistic role and responsibilities from their fathers.

Any father of moran may visit the manyata, but he must first seek their permission, and they would want to receive him with a show of hospitality. He may stay overnight in his wife's hut which effectively becomes his own home again, although outside the hut he is still a guest of the manyata. Generally, an elder keeps his visits as brief as possible. The manyata is regarded as a place for young people that he should respect, and he wishes to avoid any association with their play and the banter of 'children'.

There is one exception to this avoidance. Occasionally, a recruitment posse may abduct the only wife of an elderly man with few cattle. He may then join them at the manyata as their *olodokodonyo*, a kind of elderly mascot. Only benign old men would be chosen, and typically there might be two at a manyata of reasonable size. For such men, the manyata can provide a congenial reminder of their own moranhood now that their interest in elders' affairs is dwindling. They sit around, radiating benevolence, and are greeted cordially by residents and visitors alike. Everyone shows a concern for their comfort, and when there is meat, they are given choice cuts. There is a pride in having them and looking after them. Out of respect for them, there is a limit to the open play between moran and girls, and their presence adds character and a certain dignity to the manyata village. The moran are notorious for their rougher side, but the kindness expected of them towards these old men of the manyata, as towards the manyata herdboys, adds a gentler touch. It makes the manyata a worthier enterprise.

Corresponding to the occasions when a manyata hut in effect reverts to the father during his visit, there are occasions when the huts and even the central corral of an elders' village are transformed into outposts of the manyata. This occurs when some moran pay a visit to share milk together or to dance at night. While they are there, the elders of the village tend to avoid their play as they would avoid the manyata itself.

There are two views of these visits to the elders' village areas, summarised in the terms 'lifting' (*a-dumu*) and 'stealing' (*a-purr*). There is a general notion that the moran bear the brunt of hardship as well as of danger. They may have to sleep rough and go hungry. When there is little food, they are expected to be generous with their age mates to the point of self-denial. Because they above all are expected to protect the community from every type of threat and are dispossessed at their manyata, they are owed a moral debt. This is acknowledged in the right of all moran to have milk when they visit the elders' village areas. They may even take milk from the gourds set aside for the elders, but not from small gourds belonging to young children.

Their first claim is to milk in the huts of mothers of (non-manyata) moran, and they may go from hut to hut until this is all finished. If they want still more, they can then exercise their privilege of forming themselves into a little posse (*enkiti pikas*) and scouring other huts for milk. If the wife of a hut is absent, they may enter as a group and take what they want. If she is in the hut, she is asked for milk and normally complies. If she refuses or pretends there is no milk, then she will be brushed to one side and they will seize her gourds and empty them, pinning her down if necessary. This would never take place in the presence of the husband. When he returns home and his wife tells him that the moran have 'lifted' all the milk, he should accept that this is their privilege in return for defending the herds generally. At any time, his cattle may be stolen or lost, and then he in his turn may call on the moran to retrieve them.

Lifting milk is quite different from stealing. Any boys taking milk in this way would be punished as unprincipled thieves. Again, since moran have to share milk together, if one is seen entering a young wife's hut by himself, then this could not be to 'lift' milk, but only to 'steal' her. The watching elders will converge on the hut to catch him. Few moran would take such risks during the daytime.

The elders face a dilemma. They cannot stop moran exercising their privilege of 'lifting' milk, but this encourages them to assume a privilege to 'steal' wives. The elders wish to avoid the moran but still harbour suspicions when a body of moran enter the hut of the young wife of an absent elder, no matter how brief their visit. They have stories of their own moranhood when perhaps five of them entered a hut together and emerged gratified in every sense in as little time as it would have taken to drink all the milk. The elders can only demand that visiting moran should behave as guests with an outward respect, and the moran are aware that their comings and goings are being carefully watched from a discreet distance.

It is this concern with adultery that places the manyata in a contemporary setting. The decreasing relevance of its defensive role is compensated by the advantages of segregating moran from the younger wives of elders. This is possibly one of the principal reasons why the manyata system has survived attempts to abolish it by successive administrations and the threats and assertions of elders. The dilemma facing the elders is that while all moran should ideally be at the manyata and away from their village areas, they can only fulfil their defensive role by visiting all areas. Even the non-manyata moran play their part in protecting the herds. When an elder suspects that his wives have regular liaisons with lovers and especially with moran living in the area, then this is the time to migrate – but where? A more isolated spot is by definition less guarded by other elders; while a more populated area also attracts more moran.

The elders' attitude towards adultery is at least reinforced in the ideology of the manyata. If a manyata moran stays in the elders' village area for more than the occasional night without manyata permission, he must account for himself on his return. Even if he has permission and a good reason – say to help his father with his herd during a difficult period – he can expect to be teased. His absence is made to imply that he has been malingering with young wives and is already fading into the habits of elderhood. When other manyata moran see him returning, they may call out: 'The donkeys have come.' The manyata women then take up the joke: 'He's just a donkey, for he ran away to the elders' villages . . . Let's grab him and drive him to get some water! Let's put a hide on his back and load him up!' The insinuation is that

manyata : moran wastrels :: disciplined cattle herds : untamable donkeys.

Besides being suspected of 'stealing' women, the moran are also prime suspects in stocktheft. Cattle theft is so sensitive an issue that by convention it should not and apparently does not occur within the tribal section. If a cow is stolen, then the manyata would be roused, for the thief could only come from beyond Matapato and their territory has been violated.

Sheep and goats, on the other hand, are a different matter. Elders regard pilfering small stock during the dry season for the pot as 'stealing' and will try to catch the culprit. However, the moran regard this essentially as 'lifting' and will not join in the search, just as they would not help the elders to trap an adulterer. They share in the hunger at this time and sympathise; and they do not wish to clash with members of their own manyata. This view is also expressed in a custom of not punishing the first moran to call out 'Hind leg!' (*emuro*) when a group of them have been caught by the owner. Moran defend the herds, and they may be given a forelimb of an ox in any legitimate slaughter. They have their due, and in pilfering, just one of them is notionally granted the hindlimb. It is a propitious gesture in a situation that is felt to have vaguely unpropitious overtones, for the herd has been violated.

Small stock like wives are beyond the realm of manyata concern, but not without their attractions for individual moran. In the elders' village areas, therefore, the elders have to help one another guard their possessions. Generally, there is a lingering notion that moran loitering in the elders' village areas are up to no good. If it is not their wives, it is their small stock. The elders keep a watchful eye on moran visiting their area, and with years of experience in bushlore they examine suspiciously any fresh footprints they come across in the vicinity.

UNINITIATED GIRLS AND THEIR PROTECTORS

When the privileges are conceded to a new age-group, the retiring senior moran show no further interest in younger girls that they have not already claimed as their own. Older girls, who remain loyal to the seniors and are soon to be married, also share some of their scorn for the young. Girls between these ages are a possible source of rivalry between the age-groups. At the first hint of trouble, the elders may remove them from the arena by hastening their marriage.

Girls may share in the small talk, the ideals and sometimes even the food avoidances of moranhood as a gesture of closeness, and may occasionally accompany moran to their forest feasts. Those who do not live at the manyata are still treated as manyata girls whenever the moran visit their villages for milk or to dance ('play'). Those at the manyata have a more continuous involvement, until they are returned by their fathers. This is typically for their initiation as a prelude to marriage, but also if it is felt that they are losing rather than gaining a sense of respect at the manyata. On balance, the manyata is held to be a powerful influence for respect among both moran and girls. However, some elders are mistrustful fathers who keep their eligible daughters at home and away from any possible corrupting influence of manyata play. Others are mistrustful husbands who willingly send their daughters to the manyata. In taking their formal avoidance with their daughters to its logical extreme, they provide the moran with less excuse for loitering near their villages.

The new moran claim all younger girls living within their manyata territory, and it is their privilege to overawe, tease, seduce, and playfully molest them. To establish their rights, these moran force each girl to select a protector (olangata). She is still very young and vulnerable, and so long as there is a member of their manyata whose personal honour is associated with protecting her from direct assault or abuse, this ensures a limit to the teasing.

Typically a girl is made to choose her protector when a group of moran first visit her mother's hut by handing to him a gourd of milk to share with the others. Somewhat daunted, the girl is very likely to comply, but she does have the right to name a manyata member who is not present. Certain moran with strong personalities may be chosen as protector by six or even ten girls, while many others are not chosen by any. On a later occasion, such as a dance, she will be made to select a second protector (olkikaji) by planting a spear in front of him. This is almost a casual choice by comparison, and she would not be allowed to nominate anyone who is not present. His honour is less personally concerned with her protection.

From rather different points of view, the girl's protector and her mother share a personal concern that she should develop a sense of decorum beyond the limits of play. The protector is concerned as a matter of personal honour, and the mother for the sake of family reputation. It is the mother who is responsible for her upbringing, beating her if necessary. If she grows up without respect, it is the mother who will be beaten by the father for negligence. The protector is involved if the girl provokes trouble among moran, and he is then entitled to beat her himself or may simply discard her, leaving her unprotected. It matters to the mother, therefore, that her daughter should not choose a protector known to be vicious with girls or of bad character. With considerable influence over her daughter, she may suggest a suitable protector beforehand. If under pressure from the visiting moran, the girl chooses otherwise, the mother may threaten to beat her and insist that the choice is revoked. Whoever makes the choice, a relationship of formal respect should develop between protector and mother. The protector's prestige is further enhanced by being trusted by a discerning mother. He seeks to impress her with his concern for upholding manyata values, and any playfulness merging into sexual relations with the daughter will only take place in other huts. It is this relationship that is taunted by the mothers-of-moran at the first forest feast, when they claim that their sons seduce their 'mothers-in-law'. This is aimed at the very foundation of the respect that the moran have to establish as worthy unadulterating protectors.

As she matures, the girl and her protector may also become lovers. They may compose songs referring with pride to one another. The close relationship that may develop between them still remains within the manyata regime, whether or not they both live at the manyata. They cannot claim any exclusive right over each other, which would contradict the manyata ideal of sharing and dispossession and might almost suggest that they have become like elder and wife. When they sleep together, it should be in company with others. The protector should not be concerned with her casual affairs in his absence; and to prove his selflessness he may offer her on any occasion to some friend. His principal right is that her relations with other moran should be casual in contrast to the constancy he expects. She should be loyal to him, sleep beside him when he visits her village, and normally respond to his sexual advances. If it is quite clear that she is complying with these rules but is becoming increasingly fond of some other member of the manyata, then the protector may be tactfully encouraged by his friends to relinquish his role with dignity, demonstrating again his selflessness. It is when such an affair develops secretly and with an implied slur against the protector that he is likely to react to save his reputation. He is likely then to beat the girl, discarding his title over her, and at some point to attack her lover as a matter of honour.

Girls have no right to sexual fidelity from their protectors except in relation to adultery. A moran who is known to have seduced a married woman is scorned by girls and could no longer be respected as a protector. He has shown himself to be no better than an 'elder', inured to the smell that clings to the clothing of married women, and is contaminated in his turn. His girls would turn to other moran for protection. Over recent decades as girls have been married younger, their influence as custodians of this manyata ideal has diminished, and the attractions of adultery for moran has increased. The aim of moran increasingly has been to keep the girls guessing, neither denying nor admitting their adulteries, and removing this as an issue between them.

In the past when girls were married later, each mother was expected to warn her daughter's protector against the serious possibility of an unwanted pregnancy after her first menstruation. He was then transformed from her lover into the guardian of her chastity, beating her and attacking other moran if she allowed herself to be seduced. If she became pregnant, it was assumed he had been incautious or at least negligent, but either way was to blame. He would lose face among the moran, the mother would be beaten by the father, and the girl would be married quickly to any suitor prepared to take her. If on the other hand she remained uninitiated and seemingly chaste for several years beyond this point, it was a credit shared by both her protector and her mother.

The relationship between protector and girlfriend ends when she is removed for initiation and it rarely leads to marriage which is not theirs to arrange. There are instances where this has been allowed, however, especially where a young wife has run away from an unhappy marriage to her former lover extending his role as protector (Case 41). This raises awkward possibilities when elders learn that their wives' former protectors are in the area. For the most part, however, the relationship ends at marriage. Wives may nostalgically sing the verses composed to their former lovers, just as drunken old men also nostalgically sing theirs. However, if a husband has evidence that there is more to this than a fond memory of a past relationship, then his wife could risk a vicious beating.

Relationships between girls and their protectors vary, and some are closer than others. In the final analysis, the protector fulfils a role on behalf of the manyata, and it is the involvement of a girl with moran in general centering on the manyata that she is expected to cultivate.

Case 25.
Naeku was a widow with no close kinsmen, and her son had difficulty in arranging his own marriage suit. As a girl, she had been very popular with moran of Dareto[R], who were now comparatively senior elders. She therefore approached some of these men and they readily agreed to arrange a marriage for her son. It was not her relationship with her protector that they stressed or her sexual favours towards them as individuals, but the extent to which she shared in their activities. She used to persuade her father to provide an ox for them all to slaughter in the forest; she would lead them to her mother's hut for milk; and she would respond to the high spirit of their manyata. Had she been less sociable or caused trouble through promiscuity among the moran, then she would have been in no position to seek their help now. As it was, with her husband's age-set defunct, they felt obliged to help her as though she were still one of them, and the sense of manyata solidarity lingered with them.

Other women may be less fortunate in later life as a result of their indiscretions when young.

Case 26.
Kesei as a girl allowed herself to be seduced by a relatively senior elder, and she was

ostracised by moran and other girls for her crass disloyalty. Later, she was married to one of these moran, who had to respect his father's wishes on this matter. Her husband absolutely refused to have either sexual or social relations with her, and offered her to his age-set at large. Kesei was obliged to build her hut in another part of his village and to bear children by lovers. She was treated like a widow, while her husband retained the role of guardian and remained a remote and uncompromising figure of authority.

There is no point at which ageing moran are obliged to avoid consenting girls. The closer they are to elderhood, however, the more they would be spurned by the girls and despised by the next age-group. They would then lose respect generally for behaving like reverting moran.

*   *   *

A sharp change in relations between moran and girls occurred when the Nyankusi age-set were moran. This appears to have been a significant stage in a chain of events that stemmed from the general process of adjustment in Matapato to changing conditions (Figure 6).

Traditional feature	Recent modification	Age-set of moran
Large-scale raiding	Raiding effectively curtailed	Dareto[R] (1920's)
Permanent manyata protection for herds	Manyata protection reduced to impermanent presence	Terito (1930's)
Boys uninitiated until physically mature	Lowering in age of initiation by several years	Nyankusi[L] (1950's)
Girls uninitiated and unmarried until mature	(a) Sharp reduction in age of marriage for girls (b) Increase in adultery between moran and wives (c) Marriages become increasingly unstable	Nyankusi[L] (1950's)
Wives 'led with cattle' as a culmination of marriage	'Leading wives with cattle' deferred indefinitely	Nyankusi (1950's)

Figure 6 Perceived changes in Matapato practices over 50 years

The manyata system and the traditional role of the moran diminished in the earlier years of administration; and the Nyankusi[R] were the first age-group of moran with no claim to warriorhood in any traditional sense. It was at this time that the Matapato were faced with an unprecedented number of pregnancies among uninitiated girls. The moran were then roundly blamed for having lost any sense of respect and for abusing the trust that had been placed in them with regard to these girls. From this point daughters were initiated at an earlier age to avoid further pregnancies; and sons were also initiated younger to hasten their development towards elderhood. However, this shifted the problem rather than resolved it. For with more younger wives and fewer older girls, the temptations for adultery among the moran increased and marriage itself became more unstable. The position of girls within the manyata system had not formally changed, but they had less influence over the moran and became less relevant in their affairs.

It was at about this time that decisions to 'lead wives with cattle' were deferred indefinitely, and the custom of culminating marriages in this way has virtually lapsed in Matapato. This is popularly associated with a loss of confidence in marriage as the incidence of divorce has increased. It is not the institution of marriage that has broken down, but the final seal of irrevocable commitment by fathers on the one hand and husbands on the other. By 1976 few women under forty had been 'led with cattle'.

THE LION HUNT AND THE MANYATA BENEFACTOR

Cattle raiding and affrays between tribal sections occur from time to time in the Maasai area, and the Matapato manyata system is still popularly justified in relation to its defensive role. However, such raids are comparatively rare, and it is the lion hunt that symbolises the role of the moran pledged to defend their cattle. The male lion is a highly respected enemy, *olowaru kitok*, 'the great predator' who lurks in the bush to maraud their cattle. A pride of hungry lions may even seek to break into a village, breaching the stockade, and stampeding the herd. When a lion is sighted, a cry goes up and the moran muster themselves in their battle finery, as when recruiting for the manyata, to mount a lion posse (*empikas olowaru, olamayu*). A cornered lion is no easy victim, and claiming his mane as a trophy is an ambition of all moran. If the lion escapes or one of the moran is gored, then the posse return to their villages quietly and without celebration. At other times, they return in triumph and dance their lion dance from village to village. The hero who has won the trophy carries it, and the women dress up and flock to hang beads round his neck and tuck handfuls of grass into his body cloth. The girls later sew the mane into a ceremonial headdress, and it is displayed prominently on a tall post in the manyata when it is not actually being worn.

In most other Maasai sections, the trophy is won by the moran who first spears the lion, and this places them all in competition to be first to draw blood. In Matapato, there is an intriguing variation in which the trophy is awarded to the one who first grabs the lion's tail (cf. Shelford 1910:269). This leads to a number of possible scenarios. The ideal is that one warrior first grabs the tail, placing himself at considerable risk and disconcerting the lion sufficiently to provide an easy prey for other spearsmen. This is no mean feat. When I described the Matapato practice to some Purko, they were quite incredulous. They assured me that the sheer strength and agility of a cornered lion would make it altogether impracticable and foolhardy to grab the tail first. The second scenario is that one warrior spears the lion first and it is a matter of luck who then grabs the tail. This again seems almost calculated to bring the moran into competition. In one version of this scenario, the killer became involved in a brawl with others who were trying to race him to grab the tail. Another version stretches incredulity further.

Case 27.
Merero was in the forefront of an attack on a cornered lion and speared it fatally. Before he could follow through his action, someone else grabbed the tail. Merero insisted that he alone had fought the lion and this entitled him to the mane. His threats led the manyata and then the elders to intervene to avoid bloodshed. With increasing pressure, other Terito[R] moran persuaded him that his role in the hunt and his reputation for courage were widely known, and it was pointless to bring the patrons' curse on himself. He deferred to this pressure, vowing that he would spear the very next lion. That night, so it is claimed, a massive lion sprang into a village nearby and attacked a cow, and it was Merero who killed it on the spot and seized the tail. So it was that while the manyata girls were still sewing the first mane into a trophy headdress, Merero provided them with a second magnificent mane for himself. When the Terito age-set became firestick patrons in due course, they recalled this episode to emphasise the effectiveness of their blessing over moran who deferred to the popular will.

The explanation offered for conferring the honour on the tail-grabber is that it emphasises the importance of group action and devalues the trophy itself. All moran would like to be both killer and tail-grabber, and the lion meanwhile has a more sporting chance in the split second of confusion that this might create. This is the third scenario. Everyone learns of the balance between sheer courage and mere luck or greed in the outcome of a lion hunt. The one who spears the lion and loses the trophy has credit for what he has done. Next time, he is told, he will deserve the trophy, like Merero. Or perhaps, who knows, his renown will soar because he spears a second lion and again loses a mere trophy – so why grieve? The ideal outcome only occurs when the mane is massive enough to be divided into two headdresses and shared by both principals. This practice of sharing out the credit, makes the killing more of an achievement shared by the whole manyata where the trophy is on display. To this extent the tail-grabber is just a trustee.

The ideal of altruistic sharing is personified by the manyata benefactor (*enkaminini*). Anyone who is generous may be loosely referred to as a benefactor, even a girl who always seeks to provide food for moran, or an elderly woman without moran sons, who invites moran to come regularly to her hut for milk. The manyata benefactor, however, is a moran whose outstanding generosity is a by-word. The girls of the manyata are expected to take the initiative in conferring this honour, making him a sleeve armlet from their spare beads that stretches the length of his right forearm. They may even select more than one benefactor.

Because he is known to be quite unselfish, a manyata benefactor's requests are hard to refuse. When the moran debate some delicate issue on which tempers run high and the spokesman himself is compromised in some way, then a popular view expressed by a benefactor carries considerable weight. He has a moral authority that cannot be matched by more assertive moran who might be suspected of self-seeking. The most contentious task that he can perform better than any other because it could risk sorcery is a decision to change the diviner consulted by the manyata. The spokesman should have close dealings with this diviner and is again in a difficult position. However, a benefactor is least likely of all moran to want to cause trouble; and if he is prepared to take an initiative then it indicates the strength of feeling behind him. He least of all should have enemies or excite jealousy, and the diviner is likely to respect him above all other moran. This also emphasises that true generosity requires considerable courage.

Self-denial and courage are linked as the principal altruistic virtues of moranhood, combined in the notion of someone who places himself at risk for others, as in a lion hunt. In the distribution of war gains in the past, the principal shares went to those who had taken the brunt of the fighting and the risks. Generosity also had a special position in this distribution, and manyata benefactors who might not have excelled in the fighting would always receive a generous share (qv. Merker 1904:86). Less distinguished moran might receive good shares, not for themselves but for the sake of their benefactor parents for their lavish generosity with the moran. At the other extreme, really mean moran who had excelled in the fighting could even be denied a share of the spoil. They would still be praised for their courage and would be promised a generous share after the next raid if they showed some true generosity meanwhile. The moral was that if moran were to be truly courageous, risking themselves on behalf of others, they should be truly generous also. Meanness had to be punished, and just as initiates humiliated after flinching would have a burning zeal to redeem themselves with excessive courage; so moran exposed for meanness had a chance to redeem themselves with excessive generosity.

CONCLUSION: THE MANYATA AS A PLATONIC IDEAL

Matapato moran are infatuated with the idea of manyata unity and loyalty. They share in everything and even in their self-government almost to a point of obsession. To do less is to be less than moran. The manyata is a collective representation of an ideal of Maasai integrity that is unattainable at any other time of their lives. In later years as elders, the notion of total selflessness and sharing as a source of community strength is recaptured up to a point in the company of age mates. However, the background to elderhood involves the private interests of the patriarchal family against which the moran have rebelled. Elders have these two sides to their existence, as patriarchs and as age mates. The moran acknowledge only one side, epitomised by their uncompromising loyalty to their manyata and a distant alliance to other manyat.

Parallels between the aspiration of manyata fulfilment and the highest ideals of government in Plato's *The Republic* are considered in greater detail in the conclusion to this volume. Plato himself concluded that his Republic could be no more than an ideal, although a necessary one for any person with integrity, establishing it within himself (Lee 1955:420). The manyata, like other institutions founded on Platonic lines, is only a part of a larger, corrupted whole. The moran are often dispersed throughout their territory, but their sense of belonging to the manyata village at all times remains enveloped in a halo of altruism. It was this exclusive selflessness of the Platonic model that Aristotle criticised, arguing that emotion itself was excluded and thereby the life-blood of community existence at all levels (Warrington 1959:30–38). Certainly, individuality and emotional involvement play a major role in moranhood; and this outline of the manyata system considers the emotional ambivalence that it engenders in the next chapter.

NOTES

1 This ceremony was a sacrifice, in which the patrons normally play a vital role on behalf of their wards (see Chapter 9). Sendeu's son laid stress on the need for a striped ox for this particular occasion, a marking that is particularly propitious for moran, and is used in their body decorations (qv. photograph, Beckwith 1980: 128–135). A similar set of beliefs concerning the danger of overriding ceremonial precedence occurs when circumstance leads to an irregularity that ignores birth order within the family. This occurs, for instance, when sons are married out of order, or when a younger son has to fulfil the role of an absent older son in disposing of their father after death (Chapter 13 and especially Case 52). Such instances are often unavoidable, but the implication is that the junior has acted as though the senior does not exist and in a sense is 'dead'. It is seen as a form of sorcery and the usurper has to pay him a gift, usually a female cow, to remove this threat and to annul any possibility of his curse in response. In Case 24, the action of the moran usurping the role of their seniors *was* avoidable and hence was altogether closer to deliberate sorcery, inspired by the Prophet's son who would be an expert in these matters.

2 For a fuller description of this ceremony in Loitokitok, see Whitehouse 1933:151–3.

3 The Samburu have a similar notion when they suggest that a discussion is like an acacia tree with many branches (ideas), but only one trunk (resolution); Spencer 1965:176.

CHAPTER 8

ANGER, CONSTRAINT AND THE IDEOLOGY OF MORANHOOD

THE EXPRESSION OF ANGER

In Matapato, anger is an emotion normally associated with crying and its significance varies with age. An infant's tantrum is seen as an expression of extreme frustration: it is powerless and angry. If a small boy is bullied by another, then his tears are said to be of anger because he cannot revenge himself. If he goes to his mother crying, then it is with the demand that she should avenge him, and not that he should be pampered. In a fight between two boys, the loser's tears are not seen as a sign of submission, but of anger at the superior strength of his adversary, who should not carry his advantage beyond this point. On the other hand, a boy would be ridiculed if he hurts himself in play and cries. He would be asked if he is just a woman, for there is nothing to be angry about.[1] 'The mustering' (*olkiyioi*) of moran at a time of raiding is a term that may also be translated as a 'tear', implying anger. They 'cry together' (*a-ishiru*) with mounting aggression 'so that they may become many'. The second term is also used when a punitive raid is mounted in anger by women (Chapter 11) or elders (Chapter 12). In times of grief when a child or a parent has died, the mourners cry inwardly; and their sorrow is said to be mixed with a certain anger at their loss. There is even a hint of jealousy, associated by some with the danger from those with 'eyes' (p. 44).

Among moran, anger is associated with the ideals of warriorhood. They are expected to show their fighting spirit in appropriate contexts, and to develop the ability to control it in others. It is then that they experience anger. One of their privileges when angry is to 'shiver' (*a-ikirikira*). Boys in secret may practise this, although never in the presence of moran. At some point, exactly how is not clear, this cultivated expression of anger becomes a habitual response and is no longer merely contrived. If the intensity of a bout of anger increases beyond a certain point, a warrior may shiver more violently and lose consciousness as he starts to 'shake' (*a-poshoo*). At this point, others will hold him to prevent him hurting himself or anyone else. A more general term for shivering or shaking is simply to say that he is 'weeping' (*e-ishirita*). A shaking warrior breathes in audible gasps, as if straining to release some inner pressure, his face wet with tears, mucus, and froth from his mouth. It is also said that his genitals retract and he may pee slightly. Following a fit of shaking, which may last five minutes or more, he regains consciousness, apparently calmed by the experience, and is unlikely to shiver or shake again on that occasion. Other moran draw him back into their company. He has done the manly thing in displaying and at the same time controlling his aggression, and now he has their sympathetic support.

The Maasai term for 'to be angry', *a-goro*, is a reflexive form of 'to suffocate'. There is a notion of breathlessness associated with the heart when they describe a shaking fit. The 'heart is transformed' (*e-ibelekenya*), it becomes 'black', 'anger enters the heart . . . and it rises', and there is a sense of suffocation. In such expressions no clear distinction is made between the function of the lungs and the heart; but it is the heart that is regarded as the most vital organ of the chest and the seat of emotions and of life itself. They see the heart as the direct link between any emotional state and difficulty with breathing.

Elders also may shiver in anger, but in general they should try to suppress this, for it could have the effect of an unvoiced curse. If a father quarrels with his son and starts to shiver, the son should run away whatever his age, as if the father has raised his stick. The incident then becomes a joke at the expense of the younger man. To hold his ground and look his father in the eye or worse still to be seen to shiver also would show gross disrespect and lead inevitably to a curse. In general, a younger man should suppress his anger against his seniors and especially his father. When he backs down from an argument with them, as he always should, others will approve: 'he has been beaten', 'he has run away'.

Thus such English terms as 'crying with anger' or 'shivering with fury' would be meaningful to the Maasai, whereas 'tears of joy' or 'shaking with laughter' would not. One has an institutionalised form of emotional breakdown. Shivering in anger, which begins half in play among boys when there are no moran around, appears to develop into a conditioned response among moran, and then to subside in elderhood. The normal explanation offered by the Matapato for a bout of shaking is that it is triggered off by large quantities of beef and certain roots that moran mix with their soups. These spiced soups are described as the 'beer of young people' that can excite their emotions, sometimes making them happy, and at other times unpredictably irritable. The roots then 'blacken their hearts' so that they become angry and shake, and 'cry with tears like a child'. Analysis of some of these roots, however, has indicated no chemical properties that might induce shivering or shaking.[2] The explanation, therefore, appears to lie in the conditioning of the moran and the beliefs that surround the Maasai concept of anger.

It is the element of frustration that is emphasised when moran shiver or shake. When, for instance, a moran feels he has been provoked by another, he wants to respond with force. Yet he is bound to respect him as an age mate. He must hold back the impulse that would betray the ideals binding all moran of the same age-group. He starts to shiver in his frustration, and then losing consciousness, he will break down and shake. The only action that can avert such a fit is to throw caution aside and attack with his club or even spear. The balance appears to lie decisively in favour of age-group solidarity: fighting is comparatively rare among the Matapato, whereas shaking is common.

Moran in general are expected to shake, and when they display their warrior prowess before a gathering they may respond readily to this expectation. At a dance, for instance, shivering may be seen to spread almost like an epidemic among them, as if triggered off by the sense of occasion and the sight of other shivering and shaking moran. It is the hallmark of a memorable dance. The dancing of moran provokes a culturally defined sense of collective anger, a frustration at nothing in particular. At the same time, these emotions are controlled and contained by the conventions that surround them.

Shaking is a more extreme response to anger than shivering; and in Matapato more extreme still is fainting in anger. As compared with shaking, this type of fainting is rare among moran, and certainly I have seen none. Instead of working up from a shivering into a convulsive fit of shaking, the angry moran suddenly becomes overwhelmed and as he loses consciousness, his whole body becomes totally limp. Any moran is somewhat sedated after shaking, but behaves normally and may even rejoin a dance. After a fainting fit, on the other hand, his whole body is drained of emotion. For several days, he may lie listlessly as if recovering from severe shock.

Beyond fainting, there is the most extreme form of breakdown of all: death. Death from anger is said to have been more common in the past, and I heard of no recent cases. When a moran faints from anger, he feels as though he has neared the brink of death itself, and but for providence might have died. It is as if shivering, shaking, fainting and death in the context of paranoid fury entail crossing successive thresholds of debilitation from which recovery is progressively more difficult. From death, of course, there is no recovery.

There is a story told of a renowned Matapato warrior of Dalala age-set, a diehard, who arrived at the manyata from eating meat in the forest. There he found that his younger moran brother had just been clubbed by another and was being helped back to his feet. The diehard with anger in his heart set off to avenge his brother, but after a few paces, the anger seized him, he stumbled and died. It is a story of the ultimate response, and significantly it is associated with forest feasting.

THE MANYATA AND THE FOREST CAMPS

The moran are not permanently concentrated in their manyata village. They tend to be dispersed throughout their territory and sometimes beyond, engaged in errands, visits to the elders' villages, herding sometimes, and especially feasting on meat in the forest. Dispersed in this way, they are the eyes and ears of the manyata and form a mobile network. They are well informed on all matters relevant to their role, with a shrewd notion of the deployment of villages and cattle throughout their territory and of the possibility of threats from beyond their borders. This role is popularly associated with the sparseness of the manyata fence, which is a matter of pride among the moran, and of concern among the elders because of the risk to the herds (cf. von Höhnel 1894 (I):247–8). The insubstantial fence is intended to proclaim that the manyata never sleeps. The moran may appear to dance or play for much of the night, but they are always on guard for the first sign of trouble: there is no barrier placed between themselves and the territory that they are pledged to defend. News of any raid is promptly relayed to the manyata and to all moran within reach, and they muster to follow the tracks of the stolen cattle. They can follow these quickly, whereas the raiders are hampered by the slower pace of the herd. So long as they are on the trail, the pursuers may cross into neighbouring Maasai areas and they may be joined by moran from other Matapato manyat.

Even at their forest feasts, the moran remain under manyata discipline, and their forest mess is regarded as an extension of the manyata. The moran at the manyata know exactly where they are, and may recall them at any time. When the manyata spokesman himself is at one of these feasts, he is probably accompanied by at least one aide. The focus of manyata affairs then shifts with him, and he remains at the hub of the network of communication.

The forest feast represents the more abundant side of moranhood, offsetting the hardships of other times, although both aspects are regarded as shared experiences uniting the moran as a body. As a result of their feasts, young moran are thought to develop from slender youths into the fullness of manhood with the strength and endurance necessary for their role. They are priming themselves for whatever challenge may be thrust on them.

Typically between four and eight moran share in a forest feast, taking with them a young brother to fetch wood for the fires and water for the soups. When they have finished one ox, they may fetch another. There they remain for days or weeks until there is no more meat. Elders generally approve of these feasts for they occupy the attentions of the moran and keep them away from the elders' villages and their wives. It is the elders who provide the stock for these feasts, for all cattle, even those at the manyata, remain theirs, and the owner's consent is still necessary before the moran can slaughter. Oxen in prime condition may be willingly given, since a father is keen that he should be seen to play a full part in providing for his sons' feasts. This extends to his unmarried daughters who may approach him too for the occasional ox on behalf of their moran friends. Girls may accompany the moran to their forest camps for brief periods as their companions. Unlike married women, whose bodies and cloths are held to smell of putrid fat, the presence of girls is not thought to pollute the meat of the moran. In the forest, the girls are required to do very little apart from eating specially prepared morsels with skewers, keeping their fingers, their bodies and their cloths clean.

There is a sharp contrast in atmosphere between the manyata and forest camp that has a special relevance to the perception of anger. The manyata, apart from its responsibilities, is also noted for its conviviality. The meat and soups of the forest feast generate a more sombre mood in which the thoughts of the feasters turn towards the past ideals of warriorhood. Sexual play with girls is held to be out of place. According to some, a couple making love would be beaten, according to others they would be ridiculed, and the remainder dismiss the possibility because the business at hand is of a quite different kind. Broadly, one might say that the two popular views which portray Maasai moran as endearing playboys on the one hand and as fierce warriors on the other, correspond to the ethoses associated with the manyata and forest camps respectively. The forest camp is more than just an outpost of the manyata, it is also its complement generating a very different perception of the world.

The association between forest feasting and cattle raiding is still vivid, although raids as such are rare. There is a tendency in the forest for thoughts and conversations to turn to warrior ideas. Some moran may go to sleep thinking about warriorhood, dream about it, and then waking with a start they may begin to shake. If one of them has a score to settle, he may brood on this with the thought of fighting his adversary foremost in his mind. If he has no specific score, he may still find himself caught by an edgy mood of aggressiveness, and he is liable to shake at any unexpected event. He becomes enveloped in a fantasy world with anger smouldering in his heart. An emergency recall from the manyata is unlikely, but if it comes, the forest feasters are ideally primed for action.

At any dance at some village, typically celebrating a girl's initiation, the songs of the moran reiterate the themes of raiding, lion hunting, and recruiting for the manyata. These are topics that provoke a display of warrior prowess and shivering. When this leads on to some shaking, onlookers tend to assume that these moran have just come back from feasting in the forest.

When elders recall their moranhood, it is the fights and fracas between tribal sections that are the highlights, and they blame the meat and soups and the intransigent mood that caught them in the forest. Their feasting keeps the moran away from women, but it does not keep them altogether out of trouble.

THE FANTASY OF THE DIEHARDS

Colouring the thoughts of moran at their forest feasts is the fantasy of the 'diehards', *iloontorosi*. This fantasy hovers somewhere between past personalities dimly remembered by older men, and almost mythical beings around whom legends have grown.

The diehards were a small self-selected warrior elite associated with each manyata. They were a crack force. Only fiercely brave moran would be invited to join them, and it is said that they would kill any age mate who refused this invitation or deserted them (cf. Hollis 1905:301n). From the moment that he had been seconded, a diehard was accountable for his behaviour to the others. He was pledged to fight to the death against the enemies of the Maasai and under no circumstances to yield ground.

The diehards would remain almost permanently feasting in a cluster of forest messes, forming a separate community. There, they perpetually primed themselves for warfare, building up their physical strength and training their minds towards the single obsessive thought of fighting without remorse.

A diehard could often be identified by the distinctive emblem he carried instead of a spear. This was a long stick sharpened at both ends and surmounted by knee-bells (bells worn by posses and in battle to rally other moran). When the diehards carried spears, they usually meant business. One of these occasions was when they had exhausted their supply of beef. They could then go as a posse to an elders' village where there was a particularly fine ox. While the cattle were still corralled in the early morning, they would plant their spears in the ground and sing their song, *oloipiri*. This pledged them never to run away in battle: 'I will plant my foot in a termite hole up to my calf, so that it will break if I run away. Our cattle will never be taken by the enemy, nor will they be harmed by drought.' The diehards would then refuse to allow any cattle out to graze until the owner offered them this ox. It was a form of 'lifting'. In return, the owner could expect to be compensated generously from the war-gains of the diehards. Each levy of this kind was an incident that attracted publicity and increased the diehards' obligation to make good their pledges. They were manoeuvring themselves into a do-or-die position, high above the other moran, and priming themselves for action.

The heavy diet of meat and soup was blamed for the dour obsessiveness of the diehards, 'blackening their hearts'. They were morally isolated from other moran and did not want to mix with them. They would hold their own lion hunts for trophy headdresses, and would not join other lion hunts. If a diehard paid an overnight visit to the manyata, perhaps to check the condition of his cattle, his overbearing presence would be felt. Women would only speak in whispers, knowing that as a diehard he could not stand the shrill chatter or smell of wives. Even his own mother would be afraid of him. Other moran would share milk with him as an obligation towards an age mate if no other diehard were present. Otherwise they would avoid and make way for him, and only another diehard would presume to sleep in the same hut. If it was known that he was in one of the huts, then any nearby dance would shift to another part of the manyata. He might decide to join the dance, for after all the idiom of moran dancing was closely associated with the display of warrior prowess. He would at first stand nearby, dour and with an obvious contempt for the element of play between moran and girls. His inside would revolt at the spectacle, he would start to shiver and then leave the dance to find solitude in another part of the manyata village or return to the forest. If he chose to stay at the dance, then his presence would cast a deadening shadow and it would peter out. The dual image of Maasai moran as fierce warriors on the one hand and as playboys on the other is again vividly brought out in such descriptions. The diehards were supremely warriors while the other moran who spent more time in the manyata enjoyed the opportunities of conviviality and play. Like meat and milk among the Maasai, the two did not mix. The one despised the other, and was feared and avoided in return.

Not all especially brave moran became or wanted to become diehards. They had a bleak reputation that repelled many. It was not simply that they were killjoys at any gathering, dour and uncommunicative; but also that they were notorious for showing no quarter, killing mercilessly, and wholly lacking in discretion and moderation. At considerable personal risk, they heightened the probability of military success. But they also increased the vicious hostility, and lowered the chances that enemies of the Maasai would show any mercy when the tables were turned. The diehards associated with the Meto manyata in Matapato, for instance, are remembered as having pursued a party of Kamba raiders from the east who had crossed their territory after seizing cattle in Loodokilani. The story recounts the feat of endurance that led them to recover all the cattle; but instead of being merely satisfied with this clear victory, they pursued the raiders into their homeland determined to kill every one of them.

Major raids were planned by the spokesmen and other leading moran of the manyata after consulting their Prophet and being blessed by the elders. The diehards at their forest feasts would be informed of the outcome of the various deliberations, but they were not involved in the actual planning. They regarded themselves as warriors and not as strategists. They were not interested in the slow build-up to a raid with its tedious negotiations between groups and mustering of forces. They simply wanted to get up and go when the time came. Psychologically, they had been priming themselves for battle, whereas the diplomacy necessary in planning a raid entailed delays, false starts, changes of plan, and so on. Once the forces had been mustered and the diehards had been roused to join with the others, then there was no going back; or at least not for the diehards. Once they had set their course, each diehard had in effect planted his foot and it remained firm. As the time came for setting out, other moran were also expected to prime themselves for war by gorging meat and soups in the forest, with an undeviating concern for the task in hand and no girls. To this extent the gap between diehards and these other moran narrowed. On first sighting the enemy and at no other time, a moran might call out his father's name: 'I am the son of so-and-so'. This was a vow to excel in fighting, or his family honour would be tarnished and he would have to face his father's towering fury. All moran were expected to be ready to throw themselves into the forefront of battle. However, the diehards with their fanatical commitment remained ideologically in the van, and their firm stand in battle would be the rallying point after any setback. They refused to acknowledge the tactical advantages of withdrawal when faced with superior odds and almost certain defeat. Instead, they would hold their ground, remorselessly determined to snatch the remote chance of a surprise victory. In the longer term, this tenacity of the diehards was also held to build up the reputation of the Matapato as fighters, giving them a psychological advantage over their enemies. When a successful raiding party returned to the Maasai area, the diehards had a substantial claim on the captured herds; for besides leading the others to victory, they had a debt to those elders that had supplied them with oxen for their forest feasts.

Other moran might adopt more modest vows. Two close friends, for instance, could swear to fight side by side. If either was killed, the other was pledged to hold his ground at least until he had had a chance to lay out his comrade in the proper manner: on his right-hand side, with his pigtails untied, and his ornaments, weapons and sandals placed beside him. The survivor carried the full account of this to the dead man's family. Attention to such detail in the heat of battle was regarded as a final act of comradeship that deserved praise and gratitude. More generally, he too enhanced the popular reputation of moran for holding their ground.

There is another type of warrior that has an affinity with the diehards
and still exists in Matapato. The term 'bull' (*oloingoni*) may be applied to
any male with outstanding qualities on which the community can rely.
This may be bravery among the moran or generosity and moral courage
among the elders, and it can be extended in mild flattery to almost any
male. In a narrower sense, however, it is applied to a moran who displays a
red device on his shield, rather like a symbolic sun with rays emanating
from it.[3] Moran who sport this device can always be relied on for sheer
courage. It is not sufficient that a 'bull' should have several dare-devil
achievements to his credit, since all moran are expected to be able to excel
themselves on occasion; and it is not necessary that he should have killed a
lion or some enemy since these are recognised as achievements that carry
an element of luck. He must be renowned for his steel nerve that will
never snap in a crisis. He will go into battle displaying his device on his
shield to the enemy as a challenge to their 'bulls'. At home when raiders
suddenly appear, he is the sort of warrior who would instantly take action
and throw himself unprepared into the front line. Courage of this sort is
more spontaneous than that of the diehards who primed themselves as a
group, and to that extent it is rarer and at least as deserving.

Unlike diehards who recruited as a group, and manyata benefactors who
are selected by popular acclaim, a 'bull' is self-appointed. He does not seek
permission to display the red emblem on his shield. To do this might
imply room for doubt, and in any case it is not a decision to be placed in
the hands of less courageous men. He simply displays the device, defying
his own age mates to deny him the right, rather as he defies their enemies
in battle. Other 'bulls' who have already asserted this right are especially
jealous of the honour and will seize his shield and scrub the device off if he
is not someone whom they respect. Other moran who take exception to his
presumption, may refer the issue for manyata debate, and again the matter
is decided one way or the other with a show of force. This is perhaps the
only issue on which a moran is not bound by the decision of his manyata.
If they decide against him and seize his shield to remove the device, he
may replace it, defying them all and prepared to back his claim with force.
He can earn their respect by refusing to bow. This is the way of the moran
and it compares with the time when novices assume the privileges of
moranhood without supplicating for them, and defy their seniors to attack
them. The red emblem is an assumed privilege that 'bulls' are prepared to
fight for, and those who challenge them must take account of this fact.

The diehard and the 'bull' reflect slightly different ideals of Maasai
warriorhood. Some diehards were 'bulls' while others were as yet untes-
ted, although they were committed by their vows. There were also 'bulls'
who preferred not to be diehards, wishing to play a fuller part in manyata
life and perhaps to enjoy the convivial limelight that the diehards

shunned. Yet clearly, these two ideals had much in common, and today only the 'bulls' survive to maintain this tradition. In this respect, a feature of the Matapato *eunoto* ceremony of 1977 was perhaps significant (Case 31). Four or five 'bulls' kept one another's company very closely, touching up the red devices on their shields as a separate group and going to the forest together to share their meat feasting. At a time when the ideal of the diehards was little more than a memory handed down by older men and repeated among the moran, these 'bulls' seemed to have adopted a similar life-style, proclaiming themselves the repositors of a tradition.

WARRIOR PROWESS AND SEXUAL VIRTUE

Compared with other moran, the diehards held stricter views on sexual relations. Some of them might be selected by girls as their protectors, and a friendship could develop between them. However, the diehards regarded sexual intercourse as a diversion from their true commitment to warrior prowess and limited their indulgence. They might lead their girls to their forest camp, but in sleeping side by side, they would place a log between them so as to avoid body contact. Part of their scorn for other moran was that like elders, they indulged in regular sexual activity and, worse still, even with married women. In their pure state, diehards claimed that they could even smell out an adulterer when they came from the unpolluted atmosphere of the forest on a visit to the manyata. They aimed to avoid married women altogether.

It is with this in mind that one can appreciate the incongruity of a popular vignette.

Case 28.
Lesempito was a Meto diehard who obtained permission from his forest messmates to visit his father briefly. During his visit, he seduced the wife of a relatively senior elder in her hut. Her husband arrived outside the hut and realising she had company, he called out to ask who it was. At first the adulterer proudly exclaimed: 'I am Lesempito of the diehards'. Then, as is expected of any moran in such cirmcumstances, his nerve cracked and he implored the elder's mercy.

The joke raises a hilarious laugh. The notion of a diehard who was actually tempted to seduce a married woman, then boasted, and then humbled himself before the husband is triply incongruous. His downfall was complete and he could never be accepted back among the diehards. It was as if he had proudly gone to war, planted his foot firmly on one spot — and had then run away, as any moran faced with a much older men's anger is expected to do. Even ordinary moran and girls would have despised him: he had 'fallen' (*e-sulari*). Adulterous moran in the past who evaded the elders achieved an ambivalent notoriety among their peers; but those that were caught, including the diehard in the story, were handed over by the elders to the manyata for punishment. They would be tied to a post from morning until late afternoon to be pilloried by all; wives, girls and even boys would be told to spit and snot at them. Even a diehard could not retain his respect after such treatment.

The fantasy of the diehards persists as a semi-historical legend, and the role of the elders in perpetuating this legend is important. It is from the elders that the moran learn of the local episodes associated with particular age-groups: the locations of the forest messes of the diehards, the path they used through the hills to cut off a force of enemy raiders, the manyata site where one of them died in a fit of rage, the diehard ancestry of living men, and so on. Such stories evoke the timeless ideals to which they still aspire.

In perpetuating the legend, the elders' hidden message to the younger men seems to be that true warriors avoided wives altogether and even showed a certain respect for girls. They suggest that today there is a lapse in moral standards among moran. There is less shame felt by the adulterers that are caught and rather more open admiration among their peers for those that escape. The legend of the diehards seems to emphasise that a moran adulterer is a mere playboy and less than a warrior in the fullest Maasai sense. He does not show a sense of respect demanded by the elders, and he cannot claim their respect for warrior virtues that he does not have. The elders appear to hold up the legend of the diehards as an apotheosis of one aspect of moran virtue. In freely providing oxen for the moran to slaughter at their forest feasts, they are cultivating the glamour of this aspect. Shivering and shaking as expressions of anger, and even minor skirmishes are shrugged off: moran will be moran. On the other hand, moran who want to parade themselves as Maasai warriors should not be adulterers. The implicit message of the elders seems to be: 'Lay off our wives.'

The response of the moran suggests that the elders have considerable success in cultivating this ideology. Those who cling to warrior virtues are still highly respected among moran. Those who are caught in adultery are verbally pilloried by the elders, despised by the girls, and feel shame in relation to their own parents. The prestige among their peers of those that are not actually caught is tempered by the knowledge that they took a risk that could have brought their age-group into disrepute. Adultery as a self-indulgence remains incompatible with the prudish avoidance of the elders' village areas and the virtue of sharing. In these at least, the diehards excelled. As against the popular image among elders of moran as practised adulterers, one has the alternative image of angry young men. The latter turn against thoughts of sex at their forest camps, their genitals retract when they shiver and shake, and they claim that the very smell of married women makes them want to puke. The antithesis between forest ideals and moran vices persists, but the balance has tipped towards vice in the form of adultery.

In this context, there is an intriguing parallel in the practice of keeping the reigning bull and females of each herd in the owner's corral at night (cf. the elder and his wives), while the younger bulls that might cause trouble are generally confined to the the central corral (cf. the moran as 'bulls' who may dance in this corral as one of their privileges). In being allowed their privileges, the moran are given an arena of their own aimed at confining them beyond the arena of the elders and their wives. Their place is not just in the central corral but more importantly in their manyata and forest camps, which are carefully segregated from the elders' village areas.

CONCLUSION: A DURKHEIMIAN MODEL OF MATAPATO STEREOTYPES

The Matapato view of the emotional crisis that leads a moran to a bout of shaking is that he experiences an overwhelming desire to attack another. At the same time, he feels bound by the rule of age-group solidarity forbidding in-fighting. In restraining himself he experiences a tightening sensation in his chest, suffocating him as anger wells up in his heart. It rises to his throat, and invades his whole being, as he breaks down insensibly in a fit of shaking. It is as if the inhibitions imposed by his age-group and ultimately by Matapato society itself bear down on him like a tightening vice, restricting his impulse and reducing him to an impotent shaking rage. The heavy collective paternalism at all levels of Maasai society leads one almost inevitably towards a Durkheimian analysis. In Durkheim's terms the constraining force is, I suggest no less than a manifestation of the *conscience collective*. One has a form of possession with no corresponding belief in possessing spirits, only of overwhelming anger. A force stronger than the individual, from without and yet from within himself, bears down on him to a point where in losing the struggle to assert himself, he even loses consciousness itself. Far from being a spontaneous response, this phenomenon appears to result from a prolonged process of self-conditioning. From earliest boyhood, the heroic image of moranhood has provided an ambivalent stereotype torn between conformity and competition. On the one hand, there is a subservient ideal of loyalty to peers and on the other the uncompromising ideal of supreme warriorhood portrayed in the legends of the diehards. The diehards resolved the contradiction by their ascetic commitment to self-sacrifice, in effect committing themselves to re-enact the initiation ordeal unflinchingly in the heat of battle, as a supreme display of courageous loyalty. The display of shaking is seen to combine the irresistible aggressiveness of a true warrior and the immovable loyalty of a true age mate. The display of shaking, no less than the legend of the diehards, is a vivid collective representation; and both may be viewed as ways of opting out of a basic contradiction of moranhood. These extreme stereotypes lead one to consider the more general application of Durkheim's analysis of *Suicide* (1897) as a social phenomenon. It is his approach to the problem of opting out that is relevant here, and not suicide as such, which is a more radical form and comparatively rare among the Maasai.

Durkheim's study is not just about suicide, but about abnormal conditions in society that highlight certain critical dilemmas facing the individual in relation to his social milieu. Corresponding to this notion of morbidity is the assumption of normality at other times when society may be viewed loosely as a healthy functioning organism. This led Durkheim to propose four 'morbid' extremes as ideal types to which individuals may be driven, increasing their proneness to suicide. These are the poles of two fundamental dimensions. The first dimension ranges between the extremes of egoism or self-indulgence, and altruism or group-indulgence, with a 'healthy' social milieu maintaining a balance between these two. Altruism is associated with an unswerving loyalty that is exaggerated to a point where individuals may lose any sense of independent identity and willingly give their lives in the wider interest. At the opposite pole, egoism arises when they are so remote from the constraints of society that they lose any sense of involvement or group identity, and life itself loses its meaning. In Maasai society, the emphasis on collective existence and sharing to the point of self-denial, associated especially with the age system, is a leaning towards altruism along this scale. Towards the other extreme, the stereotype of the mean man, who covets his possessions and is isolated and friendless, is a Maasai view of egoism. In Maasai religion, a blessing on those who show respect may be interpreted as a symbolic invocation of the protective goodwill of society, the *conscience collective*, towards the altruistic pole. A curse arising from some act of disrespect isolates the victim from this protection and leaves him dangerously exposed towards the egoistic pole. Case 49 below illustrates the harrowing isolation, verging on madness, of a suspected sorcerer who had been cursed to death and then died.

The second dimension arises from Durkheim's concept of anomie, and he noted the sense of anger and frustration associated with suicides of this type. In his earlier writings, this concept was virtually indistinguishable from egoism (1933:353–73). Then in *Suicide*, a distinction was made and as an after-thought he refined it further to propose anomie and fatalism as the extremes of a further dimension. This concerned the means available to the individual in relation to his aspirations (1951:276n). In the middle range of this scale, there is a moderate balance between means and ends: the individual reaches towards a distant goal and this gives him a sense of progress, even though he may never entirely fulfil his ambitions. If this balance is tilted too far so that means and ends can no longer be related, he loses this sense of purpose and achievement. The two poles may also be viewed in terms of the individual's sense of his own potency. Towards the anomic pole, there is a sense of omnipotence. With no bar on his ambitions, he loses a sense of purpose in relation to the means available, and his ideals range towards the unattainable. This is anomie in its more refined sense. Towards the fatalistic pole there is a sense of utter impotence. He finds himself a victim of ill-fortune, pinned down like a prisoner with no hope of release, robbed of any means of raising himself. Frustration leads to a sense of outrage which may be directed towards those responsible, or it may even amount to a vague paranoia against fate and the world at large.

The first of these two dimensions is a popular analytical theme. The moral involvement of individuals varies from society to society, but it is a basic concept in social science with far-reaching evolutionary significance. The second dimension, on the other hand, has been evasive and its relevance tends to be confined to theories of action with a significance that is more emic and micro-historical than etic and macro-evolutionary. In other words, aspirations and potency tend to be examined with respect to the major premises of the individual culture. They might, for example, refer to a capitalist spirit, a militaristic warrior ethic, some ascribed inequality, or some charismatically based religious movement. Such premises do not readily lend themselves to cross-cultural comparison and hence the deeper relevance is more obscure.

The two dimensions can be represented graphically as in Figure 7. The central area bounded by the circle is the 'non-pathological' norm in Durkheim's sense while beyond the circle tends towards the 'pathological' extremes. Durkheim's discussion of suicide allows for combinations of abnormality in both dimensions, and indeed one rarely finds a pure case that involves one dimension without the other. It could be that an individual who is abnormally placed in both dimensions is doubly at risk, or alternatively that the two dimensions have only a heuristic relevance to reality. The various combinations are represented by the four quadrants of the diagram, numbered here for convenient reference. The 1st quadrant is concerned with instances in which egoism is associated with anomie, and so on. With this model, one may consider various Matapato stereotypes that lie within the circle and towards the extremes, as shown in Figures 8a and 8b. Each stereotype is associated with an emotional state; and taken together in relation to the centre, they express the ethos of Matapato society as a whole.

The emphasis on collective life places the Matapato generally in the 2nd and 4th quadrants. A first approximation of the age system would be to prop the age ladder up this right-hand side of the model, as shown in Figure 8a. Age mates climb together up the gerontocratic scale of increasing potency, while remaining constrained within their age-set. The age system ensures a large measure of stability for men in this respect – except at the extremes. Before they are even allowed onto the foot of the age ladder, boys are pinned down to herding, with little tolerance for their shortcomings. At the top of the ladder, the oldest men are expected to have several wives, large herds, and widespread respect; and yet having fulfilled their role they may lose responsibility and purpose within the age system itself. Among the southern Maasai in particular, this form of anomie poses a crisis in ageing (Chapter 12).

On the left-hand side of the diagram are the misfits of Matapato society. In the 1st quadrant, but still within the circle of normality, are those who are felt to be greedy or jealous, and the term predator (*olowaru*) is loosely used of such persons. Further towards the extreme, with the same faults exaggerated to monstrous proportions is the stereotype of the stranger with greed and jealousy in his 'eyes'. Further out still is the psychopath driven to sorcery. By comparison, the misfits of the 3rd quadrant are pathetic and tend to be objects of ridicule and humour. The butts of

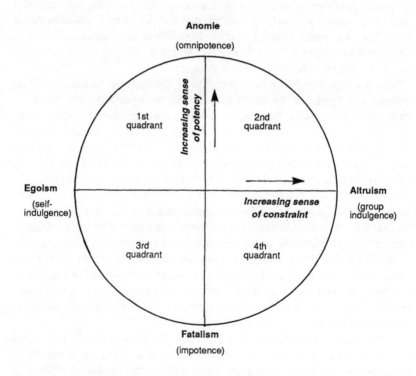

Figure 7 The dimensions of constraint and potency

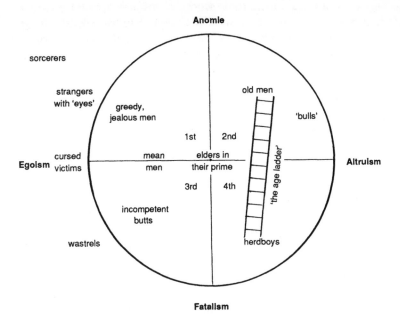

Figure 8(a) Matapato stereotypes associated with elderhood (and boys)

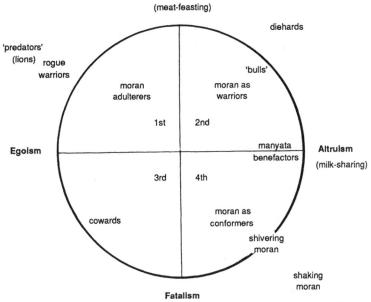

Figure 8(b) Matapato stereotypes associated with moranhood

raiding in earlier times were those whose clumsiness brought bad luck to the raid; and also those who come back empty-handed, silently dragging their spears along the ground, while others twirled theirs in triumph. Today, they are recalled in popular banter: 'Come back empty-handed, you incompetent dupe!' (*Impusu laka ibara*). The response may reverse the terms and throw them back: 'Bungle it yourself, you empty-handed failure!' (*Imbara iyie laka ipusu*). This is also the quadrant of cowards and wastrels. Both are despised and unable to help themselves, but it is the wastrels who are more conspicuous and isolated. The stigma of cowardice matters less among elders, and it can even be overcome in moranhood. The wastrel is undependable and lacks the will to achieve. He is locked into his failure to adapt to the demands of Matapato society, and in their eyes hardly qualifies as a Maasai. As a boy or sometimes even as an elder, he has opted out and these days tends to drift to the towns. On rare occasions, some are even said to resort to suicide.

With regard to the moran, this model has a particular relevance (Figure 8b). First, one may consider their food avoidances. The obligation always to share milk is popularly invoked as a symbol of the perpetual constraint characterising moranhood: they *must* seek out their peers. It is an expression of the age-group ideal of altruistic solidarity centred on the manyata. The obligation to avoid meat seen by married women is closely associated with the notion that the forest rather than the village is the appropriate place for the moran. It is their forest meat feasts that are held to build them up physically and psychologically as warriors.

milk-sharing : meat-feasting :: manyata : forest camp :: age-group loyalty : omnipotent
warriorhood

The anomaly of moranhood can be seen as a tendency towards the extremes of both dimensions.

In their role as warriors, moran belong properly to the 2nd quadrant, where they display their privileges and claim to be the 'owners of their territory'. The diehards represent a more grotesque extreme of this aspect of moranhood. The diehard's pledge to die in battle rather than yield ground is a combination of altruism and anomie verging on suicide. He has placed himself in the impossibly lofty position and no single achievement will satisfy his pledge to live up to his image.

The problem of translating the Maasai term moran (*il-muran*) is that they are more than just warriors. They also rightly belong to the 4th quadrant of the diagram in being forced to submit to the regime imposed on them by the elders and by their own age-group. According to their own code, they are the supreme conformers of Maasai society. The ordeal of circumcision, in which they have no choice other than to submit unflinchingly, binds them for life to their age-group. Ceremony and the obligation to conform is rooted in the 4th quadrant. In being constrained by his involvement with his group the individual can no longer display his potency as a warrior. When moran break down in fits of shaking, losing consciousness and even, it is said, life itself, their state verges towards the extreme of the 4th quadrant.

The linear representation of each dimension in these figures is misleading in that it emphasises the stark contrast of the extremes, ignoring their common features: namely that they are anomalous states with reference to a common axis. Thus while diehards and shaking moran are placed at opposite extremes along the dimension of potency, they share common ideals. The shaking moran wants to assert his warriorhood and yet he is forced to submit. His bout of shaking is regarded by Matapato as evidence of both extremes within him and a sign of his manhood. If he were to attack, however, his aggressive display of pique would betray a lack of age-group discipline and his action would reveal him as a rogue warrior, belonging to the 1st quadrant. The ritual appeal of the lion-hunt is that the 'great predator' in the 1st quadrant is symbolically opposed to moran as a disciplined group defending their society in the 2nd.

Similarly, cowards (in the 3rd quadrant) are sometimes impelled to redeem themselves by a show of obsessive bravery (in the 2nd). Wastrels (in the 3rd quadrant) are disliked because they are more likely than others to resort to sorcery (in the 1st): without the natural ability to achieve their ends they are more easily tempted to adopt unnatural means. In such instances where aspiration lacks a balance with achievement, the flight from one extreme to its opposite reflects the instability of the situation. In breaking the bonds that hold him down, the fatalist is prone to the excesses of freedom of the anomic.

A similar argument links the extremes of the axis of constraint, where individuals can find themselves torn between total involvement and forlorn isolation, reminiscent of a crisis in a love relationship. An experience of this kind is related in Case 36 by a moran forced to 'drink milk' by himself as a step towards elderhood. This precipitated an emotional crisis with his age mates and seemed part of a more general threat to the age-group itself. Similarly, the unity of a successful raid in the past (2nd quadrant) could be shattered by fierce rivalry for sharing the spoil on returning home (1st). Again, the ambivalent reputation of the diehards ranged between supremely altruistic loyalty (2nd) and the roguish vanity of their obsession with personal reputation (1st). Again, the ambivalent reputation of boys is the uncertainty of whether they will submit to the herding regime over the years (4th) or will react as wastrels, throwing away their chances (3rd).

In contrast to this image of violent extremes among younger men, that of elderhood is almost faceless. They have to cope up to a point with wastrels and beliefs in sorcery, and they are bound by loyalty to their age-set. However, as the decisive body of authority in Matapato society, above all they command the central position of the model; and in a sense the stereotypes displaced towards the various extremes are their creation. In thrusting the ideals of moranhood on younger men, they are relegating them to the extremes where they are severely constrained and where the omnipotence of their warriorhood is in the final resort impotent. Their rituals of rebellion against the elders have to be seen in this light.

NOTES

1 It is clear from such remarks that the Matapato also accept that tears may express pain and distress as well as anger, as when a bride approaches her husband's village (p. 31). However, only tears of anger and not anguish are appropriate for men and especially for moran.

2 See Spencer (1965:270): four roots that Samburu claimed have shaking properties were found to be purgatives rather than stimulants. However, note also the contrary view expressed by Fox (1930:454). Of the six roots associated with shaking whose names I collected from Matapato, two were identical to those tested for the Samburu both in name and identification: *olkitalaswa* and *olkinyil* (Merker 1910:363, 365). The other four have not been tested: *oltimigoni, olkiloriti, olkirenyi* (Merker 1910:359, 363, 364), and *encheni enkashe* (unidentified). If a girl shakes, then she is assumed to have shared soup with the moran. If a boy shakes, then he is assumed to have experimented with some of these roots, filching one of the privileges of moranhood. If he even gives a momentary shiver in the presence of a moran, he would betray himself and his desire to attack the moran; he should run away first or risk being beaten. Moran accompany boys who wish to hold their own forest feast as they near initiation and ensure that they do not filch these roots for their soups.

3 One may note the similarity of the various terms: *e-lóngó* (shield), *o-longó* (red sunlike device), *enk-olóng* (sun). However, the possibility of a verbal link between them was not felt to be significant by my informants.

CHAPTER 9

EUNOTO

The Matapato *eunoto* festival is celebrated about five years after the first initiations, and is popularly regarded as the spectacular climax of moran-hood. The term *eunoto* refers to the 'erecting' of the age-group: they are 'planted upright', 'erected' (*e-uno*). The age-group are established, and from that point it is convenient to refer to them as 'senior' moran to distinguish them clearly from their 'junior' successors, whose initiation will follow in another two years or so.

SACRIFICE AND 'PASSING THROUGH THE OX'

All major ceremonies associated with the Maasai age organisation are elaborations of a sacrificial meat feast known as 'passing through the ox' (*empolosata olkiteng*). A sacrifice is strictly a Matapato affair, normally performed by one firestick alliance or the other (ie. by age-set A as patrons and C as wards to the exclusion age-sets B and D and non-Matapato). Typically twenty-nine or forty-nine wards are selected to build a ceremonial village. At *eunoto* as manyata moran, they lead their mothers there; and then in later festivals as elders, they lead their own senior wives instead. They are then joined by all their age mates and by those firestick patrons who choose to attend to supervise the event on behalf of their age-set. In return for this ritual expertise, hospitality is lavished on the patrons as the principal guests of the wards. The festival takes place over a month or more, but the sacrifice itself lasts only one day, starting in the evening when the moon has risen. The ox is first consecrated by anointing it with 'medicines' from head to tail. They sing to it and give it beer to drink, so that it will radiate good will as it stumbles tipsy-footed to its sacrifice. On the following morning, the patrons suffocate it with a woman's apron in the central corral of the village. Its throat is then cut, and the blood is mixed with beer in its dewlap and drunk by those closely associated with the sacrifice. The firestick patrons kindle a fire, and the carcase is cut up and roasted under their direction. All the wards are then summoned and sit in a wide circle, surrounded by a nominal enclosure of green branches. No outsiders or members of the other firestick alliance are allowed into this enclosure, and women are confined to their huts. Some patrons then offer each ward in turn four cuts of meat, notably those closely associated with the chest region. Each cut is smeared from the forehead down the bridge of his nose four times and then held for him to bite off a morsel. Meanwhile, the hide has been cut into slitted strips to be fitted over the right middle finger of each participant by a colleague. It is this act that gives the ceremony its name: 'they pass [their fingers] through the ox [amulets]'. The patrons conclude by anointing their wards with the brisket oil and then give them a collective blessing as they process out of the enclosure. The remainder of the meat is shared among all those at the village to be consumed as soon as possible. The bones and all other remnants are burned on the fire as a precaution against sorcery.

In this way there are two domains: that of the wards as hosts for the festival as a whole, and that of their patrons in supervising the sacrifice. In the more important sacrifices and especially where there is felt to be a serious possibility of sorcery, there is a third domain that concerns the protection given by the Prophet. For Matapato in 1977, their Prophet was Simel, who lived in Loita across the rift valley from Matapato; and before Simel, they had consulted his father Sendeu. Before such sacrifices, the Prophet provides 'medicines' with instructions in their use and advice on matters of detail, and he is paid for these with a herd of forty-nine cattle. He does not attend the ceremony, however, or intervene in any way. It is his clients who send delegations to visit him for his advice, and who manage all other aspects of the festival.

Sorcery is popularly felt to be only a remote possibility provided the Prophet's advice is carefully followed, but the effect of any mishandling (*emodet*) could be catastrophic. If a sacrifice does not have its desired effect, then it is assumed to be the celebrants that have probably misinterpreted the advice rather than the advice itself that is in question. The chosen site is kept secret beforehand, remnants of the feast are burnt afterwards, members of the other firestick alliance are excluded from the sacrificial sharing, and so on. With such precautions, the festivals are conducted in a spirit of extended celebration. They are dominated by the ritual wisdom of the firestick patrons, and not by the Prophet or any marked concern over sorcery. The more festive the atmosphere, the more the possibility of sorcery is felt to recede.

During the period of preparation, those excluded from the sacrifice may allay suspicions of sorcery by sending delegations with gifts to the ceremonial village. They come to 'look toward' (*a-ingoraki*) the event with a display of openness. This gesture of goodwill should be received warmly, and they will be fed and stay overnight with one of the celebrants acting as their host. The visitors may represent the other firestick alliance, or neighbouring friendly tribal sections such as Loodokilani, or even local members of the Loonkidongi dynasty of diviners and Prophets, who above all must avoid other peoples' sacrifices, because of their close associations with sorcery. At *eunoto* very senior members of the other firestick alliance may visit the festival for longer periods. They insist that they are general benefactors and too old to be suspected of sorcery. They have a personal interest in the welfare of their own moran sons who are celebrating there. However, they too should keep away from the sacrificial sharing, for it is held that the presence of even a benign outsider could lessen its effect and weaken the firestick alliance, perhaps fatally.

This is the basic procedure in every Matapato sacrifice, and further elaborations vary with the ritual context. Each of the major rites of transition has its own additional features. The boys' dancing festival, when the firestick patrons first bring a new age-set to life, does not involve the Prophet, and nor does the festival of 'eating meat' (Case 37). The *eunoto* and *olngesher* festivals are the major sacrifices that underpin the Prophet's patronage in Matapato, and it would be inconceivable and highly dangerous to hold either without consulting him. From time to time, the Prophet may recommend other ad hoc sacrifices with ad hoc variations to reverse misfortune. On occasion, for instance, he might propose any of the following variations: (a) instead of building a ceremonial village, the sacrifice should be performed in the existing village of some propitious elder, or (b) even at some location in the bush; (c) several ceremonial villages should be built in order to extend the same ceremony over various parts of Matapato simultaneously; (d) both firestick alliances should simultaneously perform sacrifices in separate linked villages; (e) the sacrifice should be of a sheep rather than an ox, or (f) of a pregnant heifer to cure women's infertility, as in Case 49. The Prophet may also divine where a propitious animal can be found for the sacrifice. He may simply describe the markings it should have, as in Case 24 when it was even suggested that the role of the firestick patrons should be usurped. With this wide scope for elaboration in their communal festivals, it is useful to emphasise again that the formal procedure for 'passing through an ox' is the basic recurring motif.

Referring to the meat feasts as 'sacrifices' is to emphasise their sacred and ritualised nature. The close bond between the celebrants and the ox is a religious expression of the symbiosis between people and cattle and their relationship with God. They live off their cattle, which feed on grass, which is nurtured by rain, which is a gift from God. In myth, this food chain is condensed in the notion that cattle themselves were once a direct gift from God to Maasai, and there is a similar condensation in sacrifice. There is no suggestion of sacrifice as a piacular gift *to* God that reverses this process. The act of suffocation, for instance, is explained in terms of containing God's gift within the ox for men to consume: it must not vomit its cud, for this would be to return the grass to the ground. In this way, the link with God is intensified, as if it is the gift of life itself that is 'passed through the ox', directly from God to the celebrants.

The death of the ox is complemented by associations with birth as a metaphor for regeneration noted in the context of initiation. There appears to be a symbolic link with birth when a manyata-mother sprinkles milk at the moran as they pass out of her gateway on their way to *eunoto*. There is a similar link when the firestick patrons kindle the fire for the sacrifice as they did when they first brought the age-set to life. Again there is the notion of a threat of jealous sorcerers, which may be compared with the threat of strangers with 'eyes' following birth. At the *eunoto* sacrifice, there is also the rather more tenuous link when the manyata-mothers are confined to their huts during the act of sharing the sacrifice. The festive atmosphere at *eunoto* and other sacrifices is an expression of the general sense of communal rejuvenation fully consistent with symbolic expressions of rebirth.

In Matapato, feeding on the herd is a natural life-sustaining aspect of the symbiotic relationship between people and cattle. Killing an ox in sacrifice does not in itself constitute a contradiction: but it does sharpen the mystery of life itself. The symbolic overtones of the whole performance of sacrifice are matched by a keen attention to detail and a lively sense of communal identity that extends beyond the immediate participants to all Maasai.

PRELUDE TO THE MATAPATO *EUNOTO* OF 1977

This chapter provides an extended account of the *eunoto* of the Ngorisho[R] age-group in 1977, as it unfolded over a period of months. The setting for this whole performance was the predicament of the moran and especially those in the Meto area that had built up over several years.

Case 29.
In about 1972 it was decided to restrict the size of the next manyata at Meto in order to avoid unnecessary stock movement during the local epidemic of East Coast Fever. This was quite consistent with the Matapato tradition of maintaining a pragmatic balance between manyata and non-manyata moran, placing prudence before prestige, especially in changing times. The effect of this decision on the morale of the moran could perhaps explain an incident shortly after the inauguration of their manyata. The period is remembered as one of disappointment among the Meto moran because of the stunted size of their manyata after their high hopes earlier on. Their local diviner, Olairumpe, prescribed a minor manyata ceremony to cure their malaise. During its performance, several of the moran started to faint, not from anger it was said,

but quite inexplicably, rather like women. Sorcery was suspected and they returned to their diviner for further advice.

Four years later in 1976, the situation had deteriorated further, especially in the Meto area (Case 1). The drought and murrain coincided with the moranhood of Ngorisho[R]. By chance, a similar episode had occurred nearly thirty years earlier when their firestick patrons of Nyankusi[R] had been moran. There was a widespread notion that this revealed some cosmic pattern and that the sequence of disaster would only be broken with the initiation of the next age-group. Increasingly, with their depleted herds, the Meto moran had good reason to seek work in Nairobi or elsewhere, but they were caught in a vicious circle. They could only 'drink milk' alone to end the restrictions of moranhood after their *eunoto*. However, this in turn could only be mounted when the drought had broken and food was again relatively plentiful. Some tribal sections had compromised their traditions previously to make this possible. In Loitokitok, for instance, junior (pre-*eunoto*) moran who badly needed work could obtain permission to perform the ceremony of 'drinking milk' prematurely, before *eunoto* instead of after. This freed them from the obligation to constantly seek one another's company. Tradition in Matapato in this respect remained intact. Once a youth had been launched into moranhood he ran the full course until *eunoto*, and there had never been any 'slightly premature elders' (Figure 3). By autumn 1976, however, the untenability of this tradition came to a head.

Case 30.
Sarengei was a member of Terito age-set with a dignity and charm that made him generally popular, both among elders and as the father of two non-manyata moran. By 1976, he had lost nearly all his cattle, his older moran son was weakened by illness, and his younger son was anxious to find work in order to remit wages to his family. Sarengei therefore argued to the elders locally that Matapato restrictions on junior moran seeking work was outmoded. He proposed that three moran of his village should be allowed to 'drink milk' immediately: his younger son in order to find work, his older son who had to precede him ceremonially, and the son of a stockless widow who also badly needed to find work. Anticipating trouble from the Meto manyata, Sarengei consulted the local elders surreptitiously. These included especially those of Nyankusi age-set as firestick patrons of the moran and his own age mates of Terito, most of whom had moran sons. His calm manner in the face of hardship readily convinced them; and they only informed the three moran shortly before mounting the ceremony for 'drinking milk'. The privilege of remaining moran in the fullest sense held no further glamour for them, but they still had their commitment to their age-group. They were torn between this loyalty and respect for Sarengei and the force of his argument. They therefore told their age mates and shifted responsibility from themselves. A deputation of moran from the Meto manyata was promptly dispatched to Sarengei's village to challenge the elders' right to override traditions upheld by the manyata. The deputation appeared at dusk just before the ceremony was to take place, and delayed it for four hours while they pursued their case with the elders. The firestick patrons played the principal part in dismissing

their arguments, while Sarengei himself remained subdued. The patrons maintained that it was they who knew best how to interpret tradition, especially in hard times. They pointed out that the moran should not threaten their age-group curse. This would harm their own reputation and the prospects of three innocent moran, who had no stock to pay the fee for annulling the curse. Having at first been aggressive in their demands, the delegation were forced into a more defensive position. They then insisted that there should be no further attempts to force other moran into 'drinking milk' prematurely before *eunoto*. Even this promise was withheld, since the elders could not bind themselves or other elders when no-one knew when the drought would end. The outcome was precisely as Sarengei had predicted. The moran had mobilised themselves to defend the manyata domain in debate, but the elders doggedly maintained that realism has always been a foremost consideration in Maasai society, and it was they who pinned the moran down. The 'milk-drinking' ceremony followed at once. For the first time ever, it was claimed, Matapato now had three 'slightly premature elders', two of whom went off at once to find work.

A factor that may have influenced the timing of this incident was that the manyata spokesman was absent and the manyata delegation had to act quickly without their normal leader. Generally, there was a sense of disarray among the moran. The manyata was unusually small. The age-group were popularly associated with the persisting hunger and misfortune. Many of them badly needed work. Then at the height of the drought, communication among moran had broken down as many dispersed with their surviving family herds. Some had even reached the foothills of Kilimanjaro, well beyond the border with the Loitokitok Maasai, and no-one knew quite where. There could be no mobilisation for *eunoto* until their return. However, the normal period of dry season was now behind them. It was November and the drought could reasonably be expected to break at any time. The absent spokesman and some other leading Meto moran had in fact gone to Loita with the formal delegation to consult their Prophet Simel about the drought and the forthcoming *eunoto*. Even if Sarengei could not wait, there was a general feeling that with some rain and a few months for the herds to fatten, the *eunoto* would not be far off.

EUNOTO: PHASE I. THE DEPUTATION TO THE PROPHET

Eunoto is the only occasion that actually brings the whole age-group together before the three manyat are disbanded. When they act together, one of the three manyata spokesmen becomes senior spokesman for the whole age-group. Usually he is appointed from Maparasha as the largest manyata, while the spokesmen from Meto and Silale serve as his principal aides. When they are first presented to the Prophet after their installation and on subsequent occasions, it is as a joint delegation with a single 'head' and two 'necks' (p. 106).

The *eunoto* festival is based on the standard procedure for any sacrifice, except that the importance of the occasion is marked by two sacrifices: the first in the *eunoto* village and the second in the forest nearby. The Prophet, therefore, has to advise on *two* sites and on the choice of *two* oxen, and he provides a wider range of instructions and 'medicines' than at a more routine consultation. In payment, he is given a larger herd of cattle than normal, collected from each of the three manyata areas.

Among his instructions, the most closely guarded secret that overshadows this particular consultation is the choice of moran to fill two highly respected but unpopular roles: the man-who-is-planted-upright (*olotuno*) as their ritual leader, and the man-of-the-cut-thong (*oloboruen-keene*) as his deputy. There is a belief that the destiny of the ritual leader is inversely linked to that of his age-group. They are expected to prosper while he will be dogged by misfortune – it could be poverty, childlessness or even an early death. This belief is more strongly developed among the southern Maasai than in the north; and in Matapato, which is regarded as closer to the south, opinion is divided. Some point sceptically to the success and long life of certain ritual leaders recently. Others suggest that this is simply because the misfortune has bedevilled the whole age-group instead. Others insist that the deputy ritual leaders are also at risk. One young elder of Meruturud[R] enthusiastically described signs of premature senility in his own ritual leader, regarding this as an omen that his age-group would remain mentally agile as old men. Even sceptics admitted that the 1977 *eunoto* was overshadowed by the knowledge that the ritual leader of Nyankusi[R] had died prematurely at their *olngesher* festival, which is a sequel to *eunoto*. Misfortune in Matapato eyes has the habit of history repeating itself. The period when the Nyankusi[R] had been moran had been disastrous for their herds, and now this had again occurred while their firestick wards of the Ngorisho[R] were moran. It therefore seemed plausible to expect that the Ngorisho[R] ritual leader would die early, like his predecessor. In health, wealth, offspring, and life itself, both ritual leader and his deputy are thought to be at risk, and differences of opinion concern the level of that risk rather than the general premise.

Before asking the Prophet to determine the choice of ritual leader and his deputy, a shortlist is prepared by the patrons and moran spokesmen. The ideal candidate should be unflappable, unblemished and with a pure Maasai ancestry. The Prophet is expected to question them closely on these aspects before secretly consulting his oracle. His choice is only divulged to the senior spokesman and one or two other members of the delegation, who maintain a discreet silence. This is not just to hoodwink sorcerers, but more specifically to prevent the news from spreading to the victims who could run away to some other part of East Africa if they learned beforehand. The secret is only shared with other leading moran and patrons closer to the time when the two will be seized and installed by force.

The delegation, which was absent on this business during the previous example (Case 30), returned to Matapato with 'medicines' to distribute and instructions for coping with the immediate drought. At the same time, the knowledge spread that they had brought back the secret of a choice that was a disquieting possibility for all pure-bred moran and their families.

PHASE II. THE CONVERGENCE OF THE MANYAT FOR *EUNOTO*

Manyata villages in Matapato must not move from the sites on which they were first established until they migrate together for their *eunoto*. This festival is always held somewhere on the western side of the Doinyo Orok, the 'Dark Mountain' whose sombre hulk is visible from almost every part of Matapato. However, the chosen spot varies, and this is kept secret by the deputation after their return from the Prophet. Each manyata first moves to its own temporary site close to the mountain before processing together to the secret joint site for the festival itself.

Up to this point the three manyata villages have maintained their separate identities. Moran will have visited neighbouring manyata territories typically to attend dances, or even to pay prearranged courtesy visits to the manyata itself. Beyond this, the relationship has been one of careful avoidance. For instance, they will not have taken the same liberties with girls, milk, small stock and married women in neighbouring territories as in their own.[1] So long as this respect is carefully maintained, their rivalry remains indirect and damaging confrontations are avoided. In the event of a breach, the manyata spokesmen accompanied by some aides quickly meet to negotiate peace. It is precisely such matters that are their particular concern.

When the manyat converge for their *eunoto*, however, this avoidance is ended, and the possibility that their rivalry may erupt into open competition becomes less remote. In all tribal sections, this is recognised as a tense period that can lead to fighting. The evidence suggests that manyat come together for *eunoto* in a spirit of friendship, but it is always possible that their incipient rivalry will be provoked to a flash-point. Only a year before my fieldwork, a serious fracas erupted among the neighbouring Loodokilani between those manyat that supported the decision to hold their *eunoto* at once and those that wanted to delay. In 1967 an almost identical incident had occurred among the Purko for similar reasons. The fiercest battle remembered by my informants also concerned the Purko in about 1945, when the manyat moved from their temporary villages to their joint village. As they arrived, there was a spontaneous outburst of fighting over which manyata should occupy the prestigious eastern end of the village. Women and elders were hurt when they tried to intercede. The moran were then ordered to disperse to their original manyata villages, postponing the festival for several months.[2]

As compared with such incidents, the Matapato *eunoto* of 1977 was by comparison a low key affair. It took place after the drought had broken with a widespread sense of relief that the moran could be released to find work and help rebuild their families' herds. The majority of participants simply came to attend the two climaxes (as indeed we did) and then dispersed after each. Local resources simply could not feed large numbers for more than one brief burst at a time. Even so, in these unpromising circumstances, there was a genuine sense of occasion, and the rivalry between manyat was self-evident.

Case 31. The Matapato eunoto *of 1977*
Episode 1. The rivalry between manyat over trophies. The 1976 drought in Matapato broke in December, and by February conditions had improved sufficiently to allow the manyat to move to Doinyo Orok for their *eunoto*. Normally, the three manyat are expected first to build temporary villages before migrating to the site chosen for their joint village. On this occasion, the manyat from Maparasha and Silale arrived in the area at about the same time and chose to share the same temporary village at once, each with their own sector. The firestick patrons approved of this show of solidarity and confidence. The Meto manyata, however, delayed their arrival, arguing that Meto had borne the brunt of the drought and their cattle were not yet able to cope with the migration. This excuse concealed their disappointment at being the only manyata without even a single lionskin trophy. In a desperate bid to retain some prestige, the Meto moran scoured the countryside for a lion. When eventually they mobilised to join the others, they still had no trophy, and cynics from the other manyat claimed that the ceremony had been delayed a further month for nothing. Worse still, the Pleiades constellation would soon become invisible in the evening sky. From this point, no major ceremonies could take place until the Pleiades reappeared at dawn, for it is assumed that the elders' prayers cannot be heard during this hiatus (between about 28 April and 10 June). It was now increasingly unlikely that the *eunoto* could be completed in time. Normally, such delays would merely extend the period of festivity. However, on this occasion no extended festivity was possible and the delays caused by hurt pride at Meto delayed those other moran who badly needed to search for employment. When the crestfallen Meto moran arrived, they built their village containing nineteen huts. This was about 100 yards from the other village, which had sixty huts and displayed five lionskin trophies on tall flag poles in the Maparasha sector and two more in the Silale sector. It was the Maparasha-Silale village that was the natural centre of this complex with dancing each day and night, and the Meto village that was late, overshadowed, and right out of centre. (Later when we arrived, having previously associated ourselves with the Meto area, the insistence of the Meto moran that we should camp close to their village seemed to suggest that they were claiming us as surrogate trophies.)

Two dances recur in *eunoto* and express complementary aspects of moranhood. In the 'lion dance', the lion-skin trophy headdresses are worn by their owners or on less formal occasions by some other moran. This dance is a motif that encapsulates the exuberant spirit of moranhood. The other dance, *emosiroi*, is the exact converse: subdued and lacking the element of exuberant spontaneity. It is performed by visiting delegations and by moran when their patrons wish to impose their authority. The elders themselves may join in and married women may faintly follow it as onlookers. This dance seems to express unity and submissiveness to ritual obligations. It bears the imprint of peace and conformity as opposed to the competitive associations of the lion dance: the 4th quadrant of Figure 8b as opposed to the 2nd. In Maasai idiom, dancing tends to be synonymous with 'play', but *emosiroi* is a dance when this would be an inappropriate term.

Episode 2.   Ruffling the firestick patrons and the ritual of counter-rebellion. The Meto manyata arrived too late to allow the first stage of the *eunoto* proper to be performed at the new moon towards the end of March. It was therefore necessary to delay this stage a further month. During this period, an incident in the Meto village provoked the firestick patrons and dealt a further blow to the prestige of the Meto moran. One of the firestick patrons at the festival was Mebugu, the ritual leader of Nyankusi[L]. His wife was a manyata-mother at Meto and it was highly appropriate that he should attend the festival. However, it was important that he above all other firestick patrons should be respected and maintain his dignity, and also his wife, who by custom had been chosen for him by his age-group. One evening, a Meto moran entered her hut and started to make love with her daughter, ignoring the mother's presence and protests. She was furious and complained to the patrons. They regarded the incident as an outrage against Mebugu himself, and a symptom of the prevailing disrespect among all moran. When Mebugu heard next morning, he could not conceal his anger. As ritual leader, he had a powerful curse, but he was also obliged to respect the collective will of his age mates. Their first task was to coerce him to restrain himself while they took on themselves the responsibility for castigating the moran.

The Meto moran were assembled to the west of their village and moran from the larger village were called over to join them. The response of the patrons throughout the morning was similar to that described for all such occasions when they assemble to harangue the moran. They emphasised their power to curse and simply abandon the festival, while signalling at the same time that the harangue was an end in itself that stopped short of fulfilling these threats. This is, in other words, an established procedure when elders seek to establish their authority over the moran: an authoritarian ritual of counter-rebellion. About 40 elders ordered about 100 moran, 30 wives and 10 girls to sit in separate groups. The three moran spokesmen sat with their spears among the patrons. The general description by elders of such occasions emphasises the fear it generates among the moran and their mothers. Certainly everyone seemed to take the harangue itself seriously enough. Three times in the course of the morning, firestick patrons worked up a display of exasperation, ordering the moran to leave the meeting. This then prompted a number of elders looking seriously shaken to leave the meeting and by implication abandon the festival also. A cry would then be raised and moran and wives rushed to them clutching fistfuls of grass in both hands, invoking its life-giving powers and in effect appealing to a higher authority. The elders could not ignore this, and were forced to turn back. In some instances, this was more than just moral coercion that would in any case have obliged the elders to return to their places. There was even a hint of physical coercion. One slight elder who neatly dodged fistfuls of grass waved at him found his way barred by two strapping moran thrusting grass within inches of his face until he turned back, their broad grins contrasting with his trembling anger. This note of hilarity among the younger people at the more histrionic moments, countered the counter-rebellion. It set a limit to the freedom of the elders to abandon the moran to their fate. Following the third outburst of anger, the harangue wās adjourned until the afternoon. Meanwhile, the moran were told to brew tea for all the elders and to perform the subdued *emosiroi* dance in each of the villages.

When they met for the second session, some of the patrons had cut fresh whips up to ten feet in length. This was to become a feature at certain points throughout the festival. The patrons agreed not to threaten to abandon the festival. At the same time, they warned the moran not to attempt again to coerce them with grass that God had placed on the ground. The moran were again ordered to leave the meeting several times when the elders' anger mounted, as if to exercise their right to obedience, but no elders stomped from the meeting. During the breaks in moments of pique, certain patrons occasionally cracked their long whips at unsubdued groups of moran as though they were frisky cattle. The moran would dutifully retire to a safer distance, 'running away' from the elders' anger, although still sometimes giggling. In the course of the afternoon, the elders appeared to have established control over the moran and over their own anger. The offending moran was ordered to pay Mebugu a heavier fine than he could readily afford. Mebugu by now was quite mollified, and led the blessing of all the moran. As the elders dispersed, he remained with a small group of age mates, entertaining them with a display of joking and good humour. They encouraged him, rather as moran closely support an age mate after a bout of shaking.

That evening, the Meto moran and six elders processed dancing *emosiroi* to the larger village. They were received by a line of moran, wives and girls, greeting one another in turn with touching palms. Later that night, the largest dance I had seen up to that point built up in the Meto village with many visitors from the larger village. Prominent in the dancing was the exuberant 'lion' dance, displaying the less submissive aspect of moranhood. It also suggested a new spirit of solidarity between the two villages that had been absent earlier, when the larger village was the focus of all dance and play, and the smaller, newer, gaucher Meto village had a deserted air.

Descriptions of other occasions suggests that the threat to abandon the ceremony and the coercion with grass is an aspect of Maasai rhetoric. When some of these elders (of Nyankusi[R]) had previously performed their own *eunoto* as moran, their firestick patrons of Dareto age-set had complained that they were not being properly fed. Repeatedly, they staged walk-outs and were repeatedly forced back by grass-clutching moran – and then were offered more beer and meat. The patrons can only threaten to postpone ceremonies up to a point. In a society based on the periodic upgrading of men with age, they can bully, cajole, stomp and threaten, but they cannot bring the process of ageing to a halt. Time, if not always the broad grins, is on the side of the young. It is as if the patrons have to display their anger histrionically to have credibility just as moran have to shake. Then rather like shaking moran – and indeed Mebugu that very morning – they have to be held figuratively from hurting themselves (by fistfuls of grass). For like the moran they are impotent in their anger.

Episode 3. The absconding ritual leaders. By now, the move to the secret *eunoto* site and the seizing of the unsuspecting ritual leader and his deputy was imminent. A precedent for this event was that Mebugu as a moran twenty years earlier had learned from a sympathetic kinsman that he was to be seized as ritual leader. He had then run away to hide in Loodokilani, and the *eunoto* was postponed while a manhunt was mounted, since no-one else could be installed in his stead. Largely by luck, they found him after only three weeks, but he could have run much further afield and kept hidden for months. Possibly because of Mebugu's prominence in the previous episode, and certainly because the two secret victims would be seized shortly, there was general apprehension. This was shared among those moran who feared they might be seized, and also among the spokesmen who were responsible for keeping a wary eye on the unwary victims. However, forestalling any escape meant sharing the secret more widely, increasing the possibility of the victims' being forewarned, and risking a leak. This would lead to further immeasurable delays that their age-group simply could not afford. On the day after the crisis over Mebugu's daughter, the two victims were reported to have set off separately for Namanka on the other side of the Doinyo Orok. This coincidence raised the unnerving possibility that someone had broken the secret to them and they were actually running away. A discreet search was mounted and the spokesmen in some agitation asked me to drive some aides to Namanka. (Having had no experience of either my discreetness or my bush driving, this amounted almost to panic). Later that day, the victims and their companions returned innocently to the villages totally unaware of the sensation they had caused among the few who knew the secret. It was a trivial event that highlighted the principal concern among the moran at this time.

PHASE III. MIGRATION TO THE *EUNOTO* SITE

As the time for moving from their temporary villages to the *eunoto* site draws near, the manyat are joined by non-manyata moran and they migrate as a whole age-group. The apprehensiveness of sorcery surrounding this move helps to build up a sense of occasion. The *eunoto* site itself is kept secret so that it cannot be tampered with beforehand. A protective line of chalky 'medicine' provided by the Prophet is traced on every forehead from ear to ear for the move. There is also a false start to divert misfortune from the migration proper that follows. This is a theme that is repeated later that day with the installation of the ritual leader, for he too is thought to divert misfortune from his age mates who follow him to elderhood. This concern with threats from sinister forces coincides with the transformation that the age-group of moran undergo through *eunoto*. It marks an implicit shift in the distribution of power with age more generally. The juxtaposition of large numbers of older men and younger men sharply differentiated by age highlights their differences. The maturation of the moran is a fact of life that arouses ambivalence, clearly expressed in Episode 2 and other incidents of the kind. Even the firestick patrons, whose future is ritually linked with that of their moran wards, have a vested interest in delaying the reality of the present. This is to suggest that the kind of insight offered by some informants, that the danger from 'eyes' emanates from society at large, could logically be extended to interpreting the dangers that are felt to surround *eunoto*.

Episode 4. Seizing the ritual leaders. The migration to the *eunoto* site had to take place on the fifth day of a Maasai lunar month, reckoned from the morning when the old moon was no longer visible (24th April 1977). When the time came, moran feasting in the forest nearby were summoned and the number in the villages increased overnight from about 100 moran to perhaps 450. This was the first time that the whole age-group had ever been assembled in one spot. Forty-nine of the moran were selected to lead the procession. Singing *emosiroi*, they were followed by a herd of forty-eight white heifers and a young black bull, and then by all the other moran. They were blessed by a manyata-mother, who dipped a handful of grass into a milk gourd and flicked milk at them as they passed through her gateway and out of the larger village. This was the false start, and when all the moran had passed out, the patrons ordered them to disband. (Coining the metaphor, the ritual rebirth had been aborted.)

The procession proper had to wait until the manyata-mothers packed their donkeys and had left to be at the *eunoto* site before the moran. During this lull, the patrons directed the moran to process between the villages performing their lion dance. Some patrons, who were trying to slow down the tempo, were visibly moved, two with tears down their cheeks. It was the lion dance, I was told, that stirred their memories – and it was being performed too fast. In other respects, the patrons clearly showed that they had total control and were determined to dominate this occasion. Throughout the day they marshalled the moran for instruction, for dancing, and for the chores of moving, and one or two lashed out with their long whips on impulse. The moran seemed drained of their earlier confidence, for the migration was a prelude to the evening climax when the identities of the ritual leader and his deputy would be revealed. Later, several moran described to me their feelings of apprehension on this day: a dread of the approach of evening and of the awful possibility that they themselves or perhaps one of their close friends might be seized as a ritual leader. One moran whose ancestry made him ineligible expressed his own vicarious fears. Whoever they were, two of his age mates were to be plucked away, violating the manyata bond of sharing in everything including a common destiny. The ritual leaders were to be condemned to an uncertain future, even an early death, and he felt as though a part of his own self was condemned.

Eventually all was packed for the migration. The procession was led by a few firestick patrons who knew the secret location, a spot about four miles further south. Then came the manyata-mothers with their laden donkeys, some straggled from time to time, and others stopped to readjust their loads, halting the procession that followed. Then came the remaining patrons, and at their rear a few with whips to control the pace of the moran, so that they did not overtake the straggling women. Then came the moran in four files, two for Maparasha and one each for Meto and Silale, wearing such lionskin trophies and ostrich feather headdresses as they had. They carried their shields, held high their manyata flags, and raised their spears to the rhythm of their lion dance. Each time the procession was halted by the patrons, the dancing would intensify and minor epidemics of shaking broke out: a yelp, some shaking, and then more yelps and more shaking. Possibly thirty of the moran shook, while many more were shivering. Finally at the tailend of the procession, came a file of about thirty girls, escorted by four moran.

By the time that the body of the procession arrived at the *eunoto* site, the women had already been directed by the leading firestick patrons to build their huts in a large circle. This was the point, incidentally at which the violent *eunoto* affray had erupted in Purko in 1945 when rival manyat competed for the prime position in the village. In Matapato, there was no prime position to be fought over; and here in any event, manyata rivalries appeared to have dissipated before the migration. When the moran arrived, they were directed to fetch logs for the fire and to cut thorn branches for the village fence. In a matter of hours an unremarkable stretch of open bushland overshadowed by the mountain was transformed into a joint manyata village. Meanwhile, the patrons blessed the forty-nine young cattle in the centre of the village; and then holding down the young black bull, they kindled the manyata fire on his back. The manner of lighting this fire is popularly related to the misfortune that dogs the ritual leader. According to one version, it is the unpropitiousness of lighting it on a living bull that has the effect of a firestick patrons' curse. According to another it is 'medicine' provided by the Prophet which they put in the flames that has the effect of sorcery.[3] Various moran looked on, aware that their patrons were performing an essential preliminary to installing the two incumbents in a matter of hours.

As the shadows lengthened and the new moon was just visible, all the huts had been erected and the moran were called to the village. Most of them were quickly rounded up, but some were found lurking in the bush nearby, apparently hoping that their absence would not be noticed. There were rumours that several had already run away. Once assembled, the moran were mustered round the patrons' fire, singing *emosiroi* and facing inwards in a double circle, about thirty yards in diameter with a pathway between the outer and inner rings. Then further delays prolonged the suspense when it was discovered that some of the manyata-mothers had not yet taken a flame from the patrons' fire to kindle their own hearths. This prompted a routine check on all huts. Eventually the patrons were satisfied that the procedure for seizing the two ritual leaders could continue. A posse wearing capes and consisting of the three moran spokesmen and four strong aides ambled round the pathway between the two rings. They glanced over the moran as they passed, and were poised at any moment to seize the ritual leader. In the gathering twilight, they continued to circumambulate for perhaps twenty minutes while the other moran continued the slow measured tones of *emosiroi* with tense shivery expressions. One or two yelped and started to shake from time to time. As darkness closed in, it only became clear that the posse had seized the ritual leader when there was a cry and a scuffle. Other moran near the spot joined in to hold him, while a woman's apron was forced over his shoulders. Shivering, screaming, and throwing his limbs violently in all directions, he was half dragged and half carried to his mother's hut and forced to sit beside her fire opposite three firestick patrons. For a time he continued to scream and seemed almost delirious, while his mother and his young brother, who was a manyata herdboy, were also overcome with grief. About fifteen of his closer moran friends gathered, singing to comfort him, and a cow with male calf was tethered in front of the hut as a gift from his age-group.

The commotion eventually subsided and the moran were again assembled into their rings to sing *emosiroi*; and the same procedure was followed to seize and instal the deputy ritual leader. Once this too had been completed, the circle was finally broken. With a sense of general relief there was dancing and high spirits in various parts of the village, by groups of moran with their girls, and also by manyata-mothers in their own groups. For the first time that day, the festive atmosphere returned and continued into the night.

The Pleiades star cluster was by now barely visible in the evening sky, and the *eunoto* sacrifice, which formed the next climax, could not be performed until the cluster had reappeared in the early morning in two months time. The sheer size of the gathering in these hard times could not be sustained for more than a day. Next morning, there was a general exodus by both elders and moran, seeking food elsewhere. Some moran made their way back to their forest camps. The parting gift for elders was one mug of tea to be shared among every four men, and it was accepted that there was no point in remonstrating for more. There was no more. Those that remained in the vicinity were primarily the manyata moran and their mothers.

PHASE IV. SETTING UP THE RITUAL LEADER'S VILLAGE

On the morning following the installation of the ritual leaders, the braided hair of forty-nine leading moran is shaved. This act establishes an order of precedence that is followed throughout the festival: first the senior spokesman, and then in order, the ritual leader, his deputy, the two other manyata spokesmen, the four moran who seized the ritual leaders, and finally all other moran. Three days later, selected manyata-mothers move their huts to set up a smaller village. This is the 'village of the ritual leader', sited to the north or south of the larger village, which remains as the joint manyata, displaying the flags and trophies of the three original manyat (qv. Map 4, where 'south' appears as a south-easterly alignment).

For the duration of the festival the ritual leader and his deputy wear women's aprons and brass earrings and are confined as 'ritual dependants' to the vicinity of the two villages. Each carries a thin bamboo staff crowned with an ostrich feather as insignia of office. During this period the four moran who seized them become their aides and close companions. Because the ritual leaders are ritually confined, they cannot join other moran at their forest feasts during this period. Instead, they have their own mess close to the village, and are presented with specified cuts of all the oxen slaughtered in the forest to share with their entourage.

In the 1977 *eunoto*, the installation of the ritual leaders resolved the uncertainty regarding their identities. General concern for their position now shifted from apprehension at their prospect as ritual victims to deep respect for their seniority as ritual leaders. Shortly after the installation a firestick patron took me to one side to emphasise in tones of awe how much everyone – and not just the moran – respected these two men because they were truly 'great'. Meanwhile, they could be seen in the two villages with their distinctive insignia. They walked together, visited various huts, exchanged quiet greetings, but did not join the dancing that attracted other moran so readily. In their presence, the other moran had to restrain their high spirits. The notion of the 'greatness' of these two was

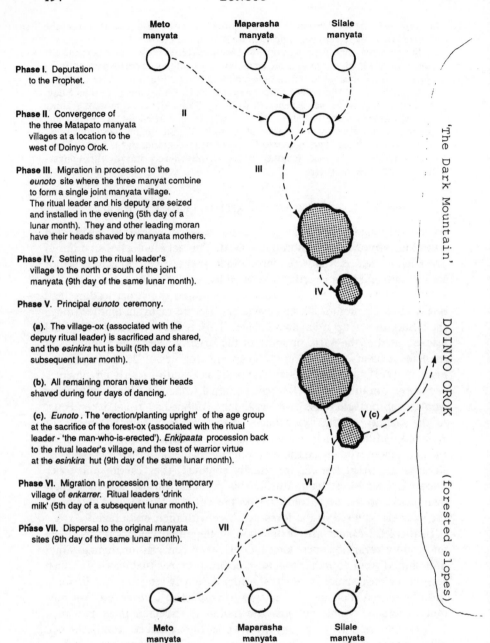

Phase I. Deputation
to the Prophet.

Phase II. Convergence of
the three Matapato manyata
villages at a location to the
west of Doinyo Orok.

Phase III. Migration in procession to the
eunoto site where the three manyat combine
to form a single joint manyata village.
The ritual leader and his deputy are seized
and installed in the evening (5th day of a
lunar month). They and other leading moran
have their heads shaved by manyata mothers.

Phase IV. Setting up the ritual leader's
village to the north or south of the joint
manyata (9th day of the same lunar month).

Phase V. Principal *eunoto* ceremony.

(a). The village-ox (associated with the
deputy ritual leader) is sacrificed and shared,
and the *esinkira* hut is built (5th day of a
subsequent lunar month).

(b). All remaining moran have their heads
shaved during four days of dancing.

(c). *Eunoto* . The 'erection/planting upright' of the age group
at the sacrifice of the forest-ox (associated with the ritual
leader - 'the man-who-is-erected'). *Enkipaata* procession back
to the ritual leader's village, and the test of warrior virtue
at the *esinkira* hut (9th day of the same lunar month).

Phase VI. Migration in procession to the temporary
village of *enkarrer*. Ritual leaders 'drink
milk' (5th day of a subsequent lunar month).

Phase VII. Dispersal to the original manyata
sites (9th day of the same lunar month).

Figure 9 Principal phases and movements of the Matapato *eunoto* festival

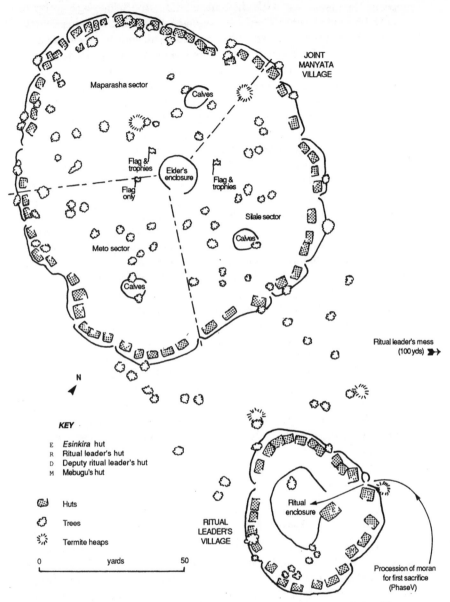

Map 4 Matapato *eunoto* 1977: the joint manyata and ritual leader's villages.

echoed in the claim that with their installation, the whole age-group of moran had become 'great'. They were one age-group. In future there would be a more marked sense of respect between them all and the world at large.

The regard for the ritual leaders as individuals is very similar to the normal deference expected in the presence of any gathering of age mates, for they carry the authority of the whole age-group. The moral authority of the ritual leaders is expressed in the form of a powerful curse. If the ritual leader plucks out one of his hairs or throws away a bead from his blue necklace as he utters the name of an age mate, then the victim's 'heart has been plucked out and thrown away for predators, and he will not live two days.' In practice, it is the positive aspects of the role of ritual leaders that are emphasised, but their power to curse looms over this role. Two months after the installation in 1977, the ritual leader was still an isolated figure. While others chatted, he had an aloof manner and was indecisive in his actions, as if uncertain of his role and preoccupied with his inner thoughts. The deputy ritual leader, on the other hand, now appeared relatively relaxed and able to enjoy the company of other moran, taking events in his stride.

After the installation, there is always a lull in the proceedings for at least one month until another new moon. It is during this period that delegations may come with gifts as in any other festival of sacrifice. At *eunoto* it is felt especially fitting that among these should be boys who will shortly press to displace the moran as the next age-group. Goodwill at this stage is valued, and boys are primed by their fathers to mobilise themselves as a delegation.

The fire that was first kindled by the firestick patrons in the centre of the joint manyata is kept alight throughout this period. An enclosure is built beside it for the elders, where they may sleep at night if the huts are full; and there should always be plenty of meat and beer, and pots of tea. Increasingly as the time for celebrating *eunoto* approaches, close kin of the moran – fathers, brothers, married sisters – converge on the two villages and in good years they can expect lavish hospitality. As an *eunoto* year, 1977 had a bad start.

PHASE V. THE *EUNOTO* SACRIFICE

The sacrifice at *eunoto* is the second occasion when all Matapato moran of the age-group are mustered together. By mid-June in the 1977 *eunoto*, the condition of the cattle had improved considerably, and the festival built up briefly to a reasonable tribal gathering. In addition to Matapato, the event attracted an assortment of tourists, including a professional film crew, a freelance journalist and his photographer, and at one point a party of school-children. Our presence did not appear to have a pronounced effect for two reasons. First, the visitors were only interested in the high-points of action, and these were precisely the times when the celebrants were too busy to notice and patrons briskly removed any prying visitor that got in their way. Secondly, this was traditionally a festival featuring display before an appreciative audience, and the fact that the Matapato were augmented by a few outsiders heightened the occasion without detracting from it. Over the years, the routine of *eunoto* had been extended to fit in such tourists. The Prophet (no doubt with an eye on his fee) had reassured Matapato that tourists are innocent of sorcery and could· even be a commercial asset. The patrons saw no reason for excluding them, but insisted that the visitors would have to negotiate a fee directly with the moran spokesmen. The spectacle of *eunoto*, and hence the bounty offered by voyeurs, belonged to the moran.

It is an indication of the importance of *eunoto*, that they sacrifice two oxen and not just one as in other festivals. The first is the village-ox in the central corral of the ritual leader's village, and this is associated with the deputy ritual leader. Then four days later, the forest-ox is sacrificed beside a wild-fig tree in the forest; and this is associated with the ritual leader himself.

In the past, on the evening before the village-ox was sacrificed, the animal was separated from the herd and there was a contest between manyat to be first to grab its horn. As the herd was being driven home, moran from rival manyat would hide at strategic points. The first hint of a move to anticipate the ox by members of one manyata would be a signal to others to race them to grab its horn. No-one could predict precisely which path home the ox would follow; and the first to start racing could not always be certain that they were closest. Having been a game at one time, this built up to a vicious competition for prestige between manyat.

Case 32.
When Maasai herds were severely depleted by a series of disasters in the 1890's, Matapato, Loodokilani and Kaputiei merged and held joint *eunoto* festivals. As their herds recovered, rivalry developed between the Kaputiei and the other two and this came to a head over the issue of grabbing the ox's horn. According to popular Matapato accounts, they did not mind if it was Loodokilani who won the contest, but they did mind if it was Kaputiei. As the time for this contest approached at the Dareto[R] *eunoto* festival, some Kaputiei moran attacked a smaller group of Matapato feasting in the forest. The Matapato moran responded in force, driving the Kaputiei from the area just before the contest, and then grabbed the ox's horn without them. When the Kaputiei returned, fighting broke out at a dance in the joint *eunoto* manyata, and one Kaputiei moran was killed. This was taken by the elders as a signal that the three tribal sections should separate, each once again with its own *eunoto*.

At the next *eunoto* festival, intense rivalry over the race to grab the ox's horn again built up, this time between Matapato manyat, and fighting was narrowly averted. The Matapato elders then decided to ban the contest in future, although it is still held among the Loodokilani. Kaputiei is now regarded as a distant ally that no longer shares the close friendship of the other two tribal sections.

*   *   *

Sacrificing the village-ox closely follows the procedure outlined at the beginning of this chapter. The most significant addition is the erection of a large hut, *esinkira*, as the central feature of the ritual leader's village. The exact siting of this hut is first outlined by a thick thong cut from the hide of the village-ox after its sacrifice in the early morning, and the hut must be completed before the moran can share the meat of the sacrifice later in the day. The manyata-mothers work continuously at this task, pegging the wall stakes along the line of the thong in mid-morning and binding cross-pieces while patrons place a central post with a single cross-beam to bear the weight of the roof. Finally, the women plaster the walls and roof with cow dung by early afternoon.

Two roles are associated with the start and the completion of the *esinkira* hut. The deputy ritual leader's formal title, the man-of-the-cut-thong, refers to his role as future custodian of the thong used to outline the hut initially. It is then knotted forty-nine times, greased, and bundled safely away in his hut. He also keeps one of the ox's horn shells as a container for fat to grease the thong regularly so that it remains supple. If it were to become dry and crack, then this could threaten his whole age-group. At any time, therefore, he can ask an age mate for fat to maintain his supply. Figuratively, the deputy has 'tied the hearts of the moran so that they will not die'. His power to curse would be to untie one of the knots and utter the name of an age mate as his victim. At the festival of 'eating meat' about six years later, the knots are finally untied and the thong ceases to have further significance.

The other role is performed by a small girl who climbs onto the roof of the *esinkira* hut as it nears completion to plaster it with dung. Just as the ritual leaders and their wives are sexually avoided as titular 'parents' of the age-group, so this girl is adopted as the age-group's titular 'daughter'. She must be too young to have had any sexual relations with the moran; and she is given a sheep as a gift of respect emphasising her avoidance with the moran in future as their 'daughter'.

Case 31 (ctd.)
Episode 5. 'Passing through' the village-ox. The routine procedure for building the *esinkira* hut was followed closely at the *eunoto* in 1977. With the hut completed, a temporary ritual enclosure of green branches was laid out in the centre of the village and the whole age-group of moran were summoned to share in the sacrifice. They were led by the senior spokesman, and then the ritual leader, and so on. Carrying long stripped staves, they processed from the joint manyata in a sweeping circle to enter the ritual leader's village (see Map 4). This was the part of the ceremony that all members of the other firestick alliance especially had to avoid absolutely. The wives of this village were now confined to their huts so as not to see the moran taking their bites of meat. Among the tourists, the women were told to leave the village, and the men were kept outside the ritual enclosure. In order to fit into this enclosure, about 450 moran were seated in three

concentric circles, supervised by about seventy-five firestick patrons.[4] Starting with the senior spokesman, a patron smeared him with a cut of meat four times down his forehead and then told him to bite a piece off (no simple task). He then passed on to the ritual leader, and so on and on. Other patrons followed with the other three cuts of meat. During this lengthy procedure, the women could be seen peering curiously through their doorways, and this was ignored by the patrons.[5] A knot of about thirty-five girls in turn ignored the hisses of some of the seated moran, who tried to frighten them away, and looked on in curiosity. Then the moran filed out to be blessed individually with a smear of brisket oil down their bodies, and the remainder of the hide was distributed as finger amulets. The ceremony ended with the moran dancing through the ritual leader's gateway. They squatted between whiles to be blessed by eight firestick patrons spraying mouthfuls of beer, twice within the village and twice outside, and then the moran would stand up waving their staves to continue their dancing between blessings. Some moran started to shiver at this point, and for the first time that afternoon a few even shook.

*   *   *

Up to this point, only forty-nine moran have had their scalps shaved following the installation of the ritual leaders. After the sacrifice of the village-ox those that remain unshaved loosen their pigtails, and dance in and around the villages and further afield with their hair flowing freely.[6] On each of the following mornings a quarter of these moran have their hair shaved off, ideally by their own mothers. Each should have his own stool with him, which becomes one of his principal possessions as an elder. Some non-manyata moran by family custom have to return to their own homes to be shaved by their own mothers during this period. Others whose mothers are absent may arrange to be shaved by any manyata-mother at the festival. By the time the second ox is sacrificed four days after the village-ox, all the moran will have been shaved.

[*Episode 6.* In the 1977 *eunoto*, confusion over the procedure for shaving the moran led to a heated argument between elders. This introduced a new theme that is more relevant to a later chapter (Case 48).]

The act of sacrificing the ritual leader's ox in the forest is held to be the crucial event of the whole festival, and once again all the moran are assembled. The ritual leader is the 'man-who-is-erected' (*olotuno*), and through him the whole age-group is 'erected' (*eunoto*). For the sacrifice of the forest-ox, the Prophet selects a site beside a wild-fig tree, a species popularly associated with prayers to God that often towers above the forest. After the hide has been removed from the carcase, it is held spread out. Beer mixed with 'medicines' is then poured into it, and tossed several times up to ten feet high so that it falls in small showers, accompanied by a prayer. In the final blessing, the age-group is given a new name that is closely linked to the ritual leader. In other respects, the sacrifice again follows the routine procedure.

The return of the moran to the ritual leader's village is marked by performing their *enkipaata*, the ritual war dance previously performed as boys at their dancing festival.[7] Their arrival at the village introduces a new and more secular theme. It is a moment when those moran that have had sexual relations with married women will be exposed before the onlookers, rather as boy adulterers are exposed at their circumcisions (p. 72). The whole episode is contrived by the firestick patrons who have dug a hole inside the *esinkira* hut and have placed a conditional curse on it. On their arrival from the forest, all moran are invited to enter the hut and to pee into this hole. It is maintained that the curse will not affect 'moran-of-the-girls' – those that have had no sexual relations with married women and can now prove their warrior virtue. However, it will kill any adulterers who pee. Everyone is said to be fascinated by this revelation, looking on to see which moran enter the hut and which try to sneak away unnoticed. Some moran urge their fathers to come to *eunoto* as their guests, and especially to see the proof of their virtue, for they expect promises of a number of cattle at this time. Adulterers may be less pressing, for their lapses have provided their fathers with an excuse for only token gifts. Others have been constantly taunted by their mistresses concerning their adulteries, and may lead these girls to the entrance of the hut to see for themselves the final proof that will shut them up. Some moran, it is said, get to this point, and then at the crucial moment, apprehensive and shivering, they find themselves unable to muster even a trickle and are mortified at their impotence. Among the less virtuous moran, some are goaded to the brink – by mothers and sisters as well as mistresses – and bluff their way through until the final moment when they evade the occasion. They later claim that they forgot, or got lost, or were violently sick elsewhere. The spokesmen and ritual leaders may claim that they are already virtually elders and are exempt from such tests of virtue. Others take advantage of the incongruity of the whole episode, and drift away from the scene after the *enkipaata* dance, muttering that it is a stupid idea and they would not pee into any hole for anyone. No-one, however, seems to question the seriousness of the elders who contrive the occasion or the efficacy of their conditional curse; and it is firmly maintained that no moran would risk his life for the mere sake of reputation or a few cattle.

Increasingly over the years, fewer and fewer moran have entered the hut, and the loss of face that adulterers once experienced has become almost a matter of tacit prestige among moran. However, there is still a sense of shame before all other persons, and especially their own fathers. With the lowering of the age of marriage for women, girls are smaller and have less influence over the moran and young wives provide a more attractive temptation. The critical question at the 1977 *eunoto* therefore was: how many or how few moran would dare to enter the *esinkira* hut to pee.

Episode 7.   The moment of truth at the esinkira *hut.* At the 1977 *eunoto*, a small advance party of patrons and moran led the forest ox to the wild-fig tree selected beforehand by the Prophet. The patrons suffocated the ox, kindled the fire, extracted brisket oil for the blessing, prepared the hide, and invoked God as they tossed beer high into the air. Meanwhile, the moran were given the more routine tasks of fetching firewood, cutting up and cooking the meat, and building a more substantial ritual enclosure than before. The routine was virtually identical to that for the village-ox except that the patrons were if anything more domineering. As if anticipating trouble, a number were armed with long whips. When the remainder of the moran processed to the spot to share in the sacrifice, they were closely marshalled by whip-cracking patrons. The meat giving routine was speeded up and at the final blessing the new name *Ilbarisho* was given to the age-group. This was followed by an address by patrons who in high spirits warned the moran of the conditional curse placed on the hole in the *esinkira* hut. The patrons then went on ahead to the village. The moran prepared themselves for their *enkipaata* dance, decorating their bodies with chalk in a variety of patterns, and stripping themselves to a modest loin covering (and without even this in the days before photographers and official feedback had made them self-conscious of their manhood). Then they surged, yelping, half dancing and half running down the hillside to reassemble close to the ritual leader's village while patrons ahead of them cracked their whips to check the rush.

With the high level of adultery, no-one expected many moran to enter the hut; and reports from recent *eunoto* ceremonies in neighbouring tribal sections bore this out. However, an appreciative audience for those moran-of-the-girls that could and would enter the hut was expected. As the moran danced into the village, however, there was no sign of the knot of girls who had looked on curiously at the village-ox ceremony, nor of the mothers-of-moran who traditionally are especially keen to see the proof of their sons' virtue. As the moran processed in a wide circle several times inside the village, they were watched by some elders and just one solitary girl – Mebugu's daughter who had been ordered to attend following the earlier episode. At the critical moment as the leading moran approached the entrance to the hut, one elder broke down shaking and was dragged by other elders into the hut. There was some laughter at this incongruous diversion and the dancing came to an abrupt halt. The moran then simply dispersed to various huts and to the joint manyata to dance. None of them entered the hut. The inference was not that every moran was a self-confessed adulterer. With so little virtue left, the age-group had apparently decided that it was a silly idea and had told the women beforehand not to attend their return from the forest. The elder who had shaken had in his time been a moran-of-the-girls, it was said, and his seizure had been brought on when he realised just how far the ideals of moranhood had been reversed. It is now very unlikely that the Matapato elders will ever again try to impose this test of virtue, which in the event only tested the ambivalence of their own authority over the moran.

Generally in the course of this century the autonomy of the moran has been eroded with the curbing of the manyata system. However, in rejecting a divisive test that was associated with a dubious prestige, the moran in the above instance appear to have reasserted a degree of solidarity against the elders. It is as if the right to 'steal' wives without being caught was closer to becoming a tacit privilege of moranhood. In reducing the age at which girls were married, the elders had, perhaps, pushed the moran too far.

★   ★   ★

On the morning after the forest-ox, the moran are blessed by their firestick patrons in the joint manyata. Non-manyata moran are no longer obliged to remain in the vicinity. However, there is no quick dispersal of the *eunoto* villages, and in normal years the festive atmosphere continues. At any time, a proportion of the moran will be at their forest feasts nearby, reserving cuts of meat for the elders who remain at the manyata, and for the ritual leaders' mess nearby.

The moran want their *eunoto* to be remembered for its lavishness, and elders are encouraged to stay as their guests, while the moran cultivate their friendship. Individually, they invite certain elders to small beer parties in their mothers' huts: especially their fathers, and also other elders who may have grievances against them or daughters they are seeking to marry. Generally it should be a sociable time between elders and moran.

The *esinkira* hut is a club-house for the firestick patrons, and it should be guarded at all times against the possibility of sorcery: other elders should avoid it. Inside, the patrons are supplied with meat, tea, beer and anything else they might want. A row of milk gourds round the wall should be replenished constantly. One of the few customs associated with the moiety division between clans relates to this display of milk gourds, which are placed on opposite sides of the *esinkira* hut. As on other occasions that involved moieties, this led in the past to competition.

Case 33 (follows shortly after Case 32).
At the *eunoto* of Dareto[R], moran of the Loodomongi moiety tried to place their milk along one side of the *esinkira* hut to the right of the doorway. Moran of the other moiety at once objected, claiming this superior side for themselves as both the ritual leader and his deputy had just been selected from their moiety. Fighting flared up between them, and was quickly quelled by the firestick patrons flaying with their sticks at every moran within reach. Since this time, patrons have taken care to forestall any repetition by instructing the moran which side of the hut each moiety should place their milk.

As compared with the affrays considered previously, this fighting would have cut across rivalries between manyat, and again suggests a shift in the focus of competition. In this respect, it is not strictly comparable with the Purko fight between manyat over possession of the most prized sector of the *eunoto* manyata.

Corresponding to the row of milk gourds inside the hut, the moran place the skulls of oxen slaughtered at their forest feasts in a row round the outside of this wall displaying the lavishness of their feasting. One has, in other words, a neat representation that is repeated in *eunoto*, linking the inside of the hut with the elders and the milk product of the village and the outside of the hut with the moran and product of the forest feast. The ritual leaders, spokesmen and other more mature moran are encouraged to join the elders inside the hut and taste the beer. The majority of moran, however, prefer simply to glance inside from time to time in curiosity and then to join the company of other moran elsewhere. They avoid both the elders and any suggestion that they might be partial to beer. They do not want to be seen to be elders just yet.

During this period, the moran have to collect together forty-nine oxen as a gratuity for their patrons, and there is a notion of redistributing wealth. The donors should be sons of comparatively wealthy men. The recipients should be poorer firestick patrons or at least those who have undertaken a heavy share of responsibility during *eunoto*. Worthy patrons show considerable reluctance before accepting one of these oxen. It is for this reason that the *eunoto* attracts one or two stockless patrons who have drifted away from Matapato society, and are less reluctant to accept these gifts. They can be seen hovering close to the other patrons when the moran are harangued, and enthusiastically undertaking some of the more routine chores that might otherwise have been left to the moran. Their odd manner and appearance gives the assembly of firestick patrons an uncharacteristic motleyness; but at least those present are a representative cross-section of the total age-set. This ensures that the very kind of men who might in other circumstances be suspected of sorcery are drawn in, and the transition that the moran have undergone has the unreserved blessing of their patrons at large. The *eunoto* can only move to its final phase when these forty-nine oxen are corralled together in the joint manyata village. If just one of the donor moran has difficulty in persuading his father to part with a beast, proceedings may be further delayed.

PHASE VI. THE MIGRATION TO THE VILLAGE OF *ENKARRER*

The two villages remain at the *eunoto* site for at least another month, and the festival ends as it began with a migration to a new joint village, the 'village of *enkarrer*'. The procession there is danced with full regalia – spears, shields, lionskin or feather headdresses – and again it is to a secret location on the fifth day of a Maasai lunar month. During the next four days, the ritual leader and deputy are headshaved and cease to be 'ritual dependants'. They can now return to as normal an existence as their new roles permit. They and the three spokesmen 'drink milk' alone, and the forty-nine oxen are handed over to the firestick patrons. On the ninth day of the month, the festival ends. The three manyat migrate to their original sites at Maparasha, Silale and Meto (Phase VII). There, they may remain a while longer, but from this point any moran is entitled to return to his father's village to 'drink milk'. Then those who wish to leave the district to find work may do so.

By the time the 1977 *eunoto* in Matapato had reached its concluding stage, the long summer dry season had again begun and dispersal was an overdue relief, even for the moran. At the previous *eunoto* about seven years earlier, however, conditions had been quite different, and the attitude of the moran towards dispersal was more spirited.

Case 34.

The *eunoto* festival for the Meruturud[L] had taken place in a period of good times with a large gathering, and they remained *in situ* for several months. After the migration to the village of *enkarrer*, the moran refused to disperse. They maintained that as the privileged defenders of the land and sole owners of their manyata, they had a right to remain together for as long as they chose, regrowing and rebraiding their hair as in the past. Their firestick patrons of Terito age-set systematically coerced them from this defiant stand. They first pointed out that in the past, a prompt dispersal from the village of *enkarrer* had always been observed and was a necessary part of *eunoto*. Then they threatened simply to abandon the rebellious moran to their own ways. They would refuse the moran further ceremonies so that they would remain and die as moran with no prospect of elderhood. Then, striding away from the meeting, the patrons left the moran with little option other than to rush up with fistfuls of grass, forcing the patrons to recant, but at the same time submitting to the inevitable. They dispersed to their separate manyata areas almost at once.

*   *   *

Through *eunoto*, the whole age-group are mustered as never before in their existence, and the principal dance that expresses the triumph of this mustering, as in war, is their *enkipaata*. In precolonial times, a successful *eunoto* is said to have culminated with a flamboyant raid against some established enemy of the Maasai. This flamboyance is evoked by the term used elsewhere in Maasai for this raid, coupled with a vow to excel in fighting. It is the term that in Matapato refers to their diehards, *iloontorosi*. The raid is seen essentially as a display of supremacy at a supreme moment for the age-group, and not as a desperate bid by cattle-hungry marauders; although this may have been true of some of the younger or less successful moran. According to informants, the majority of moran by this stage in their careers would have established themselves sufficiently to have lost their aggressive edge. Memory of this tradition is vaguer in Matapato than among the Purko, for instance. Nevertheless, Case 34 suggests that even in modern times, the Matapato *eunoto* can still unite and enthuse an age-group of moran and goad them to assert themselves in a crowning display.

DISBANDING THE MANYATA VILLAGES

Nowadays, each manyata village is formally disbanded quite soon after the return from *eunoto*. The disbanding ceremony (*enoonkureeta*) repeats the earlier scene at the inauguration of the manyata when the patrons marked their arrival with a display of authority. The patrons are expected to come with long whips and an assortment of warrior headgear in the spirit of a burlesque on moranhood. Again they play on the apprehensions of their hosts in a mood of mock aggression. Yelping, singing their past moran songs, they crack their whips as they approach the manyata, and hurl mock curses and accusations of incest. Their aim is to frighten the manyata-mothers who are less certain that these mock curses are harmless play. The mothers urge the moran to join them with fistfuls of grass, imploring the patrons to eat the meat and drink the beer that has been prepared for them. As in the inauguration ceremony, the elders show some reluctance and turn their backs contemptuously on the moran. Their strategy is to prolong this show of irritation until the show of contrition by the moran is at least equally convincing. Once this is achieved and the patrons allow themselves to be persuaded to accept the hospitality, their curses earlier in the day can have no effect. However, by this point, they have achieved their purpose. The abusive idiom of the patrons recalls the first forest feast when joking abuse between moran and their mothers was indirectly at the expense of their absent fathers, whom they were about to desert for the manyata. At the disbanding ceremony, the moran are on the point of leading their mothers back to their fathers' villages. The joke is now turned against them with the patrons (many of them their fathers) hurling sexual abuse at their expense.

With the disbanding ceremony, the ritual of rebellion symbolised by the whole manyata episode is over. Indeed, it seems likely that it must be a spent force before there can be sufficient accommodation between moran and elders even to mount *eunoto*, let alone disband the manyat. Both moran and patrons would undermine premature attempts before this point. Richard Waller (personal communication) has suggested that this disbanding ceremony may well go beyond a 'merely ritualistic attack'. The Terito[R] age-group in Loita told him that when they were moran, they were terrorised by one of the patrons who sat outside their rebel manyata with a firestick over his knee and asked repeatedly: 'Do I break it? Do I break it?' Magical elements in the patrons' threats were held to have led to monkeys invading the manyata and to lions lying down on the beds of moran. This incidentally was the age-group that defied their patrons by building their manyat in the first place, and they appear to have been threatened with the withdrawal of the patrons' mystical protection, leaving them exposed to the untamed forces of the bush (qv. Case 24).[8]

After moran have dispersed to their fathers' villages to 'drink milk', the manyata site is gradually eroded by the natural encroachment of the bush. The lionskin trophies too lose their glamour after *eunoto*. They can no longer be displayed and are discarded as mere toys. They may be handed on to younger brothers to give them a final display at their *enkipaata* dance, when the new age-set is inaugurated. Then after initiation they too will refuse to wear trophies that they have not themselves earned as moran in their own lion hunts. They are again discarded and either thrown away or with luck sold to tourists seeking their own Maasai trophies according to their own notions of prestige.

CONCLUSION: INTERPRETING EUNOTO

Eunoto is the climax of moranhood that extends to an expression of unity throughout Matapato. This unity builds up with each successive phase as the boundaries of tension and rivalry shift outwards. First rival manyat are brought together and the possibility of some fracas between them is very real. Then as these are surmounted, there is an implicit tension between the patrons asserting their authority and the moran resisting it. Then with the easing of this tension during the period of sacrifice, concern switches to the threat of sorcery from the other firestick alliance or non-Matapato. This is followed in good times by a period of general festivity when the moran make their peace with Matapato elders at large. Finally, there was in the past a flamboyant raid against some enemy of the Maasai peoples, and an expression of unity consummating the festive spirit.

As the next chapter will show, the period following *eunoto* is a time when the younger moran especially may resent the enforced step towards elderhood. Elders too may show ambivalence towards a transition that places moran in more direct competition for wives and the favours of other men's wives. The manyata system is a short-term expedient to a problem that is never quite resolved, and the return of the moran to their fathers revives it.

Apart from a few premature elders who are shadowy anomalies and in no sense moran, the ritual leader should be the first of his age-group to settle down. At a time when the moran are promoted to become 'great', he is installed as the figurehead and becomes greater still. He is obliged to adopt a lifestyle that is a caricature of docile elderhood. By becoming an elder, he makes the elderhood of all other moran more credible and imminent. Given the mystery that surrounds him (and his deputy to a lesser extent) one is led towards surmise and a suspension of anthropological disbelief in psychological arguments. Because he should be wholly uncontroversial as an individual, there can be no resentment at who he is, but only at what he stands for. On the one hand, he is 'great' and has a powerful curse, but on the other he is threatened by an uncertain misfortune. This ambivalent notion suggests that he is the focus of powerful forces converging on the whole age-group at this point of their career. Some Matapato suggested that his misfortune lies in the manner of his installation which is devised to divert the smouldering resentment of the firestick patrons away from other moran. An informant in Loita suggested that it stems from the resentment of his age mates because of his coercive powers (as in Case 17).[9] However, most informants refused to be drawn into speculation: no-one really knows, not even the Prophet.

This misfortune threatening the ritual leader is quite separate from the notions of sorcery that threaten the *eunoto*. The threat to the ritual leader is diffuse, whereas the threat posed by sorcerers is altogether more specific. If anyone, it is the senior spokesman who is the most obvious target for jealous sorcerers, for he has power and his death would throw the whole age-group into disarray. It is for this reason that the Prophet gives the spokesman 'medicines' and charms to protect him, just as his age mates surround him in battle. It is the senior spokesman who is first to perform each act required of the moran at *eunoto* precisely because he has the protection of the Prophet and the ability to cope with his instructions. Provided he can follow these exactly, the wiles of sorcerers cannot get past him to the ritual leader who performs these acts next, or to others who follow. However, the ritual leader is in no way protected from his own prospect of misfortune, and it is popularly held that this is beyond the Prophet's powers. The Prophet is expert in coping with man-made sorcery, but he cannot intervene against providence itself. At most he can help select an ideal candidate as ritual leader, in order to protect the age-group at his expense. The threat of misfortune persists at least until the ritual leader is mature enough and prosperous enough to confound popular belief. Even then the belief may persist in the rumour that the patrons or someone else fudged *eunoto*, and that misfortune after all has bedevilled the remainder of the age-group instead.

A variety of symbolic clues seem related to the beliefs surrounding the role of ritual leader. Both he and the spokesman are liable to run away from their installation, given a chance. The complementary positions of these two can be related to the metaphor of the feather headdress: the neatly arranged circle of ostrich feathers that enhanced the stature of a moran in battle. The spokesman is described as the 'head', and those who surround and advise him are the 'feathers', enhancing his effectiveness (p. 105). The insignia of a ritual leader is a feather plucked from one of these headdresses and erected on a cane staff, rather as he was plucked quite literally from the circle formed by his chanting age-group at his installation – to be erected outside the circle and by himself. From this point, a veil of cultivated respect is drawn around him, cutting him off from the intimate camaraderie of his fellows. This respect is not unlike that for an age-mate from another part of Maasai. He should lead a quiet life and remain insulated from controversy and even gossip that might irritate him. The spokesman on the other hand is thrust to the centre of age-group affairs and plays a key role in resolving any controversy. The intriguing feature of the incident that involved the ritual leader Mebugu was that he was precipitated into a controversy. His age mates then had to exercise their coercive powers over him as a group to restrain him from venting his natural feelings and the damage this might cause (Case 31 Episode 2).

Another peripheral figure, but in a quite different way, is the diehard whose insignia was a battle knee-bell mounted on a staff. The depersonalised role imposed on the ritual leader contrasts strikingly with the highly personalised stance chosen by the diehards. In terms of the model of Matapato stereotypes (Figure 8b), the diehards thrust themselves towards the extremity of the second quadrant as assertive warriors. The ritual leader, on the other hand, is thrust towards the submissive extremity of the fourth quadrant. In these two representations, one has a contrast between a commitment to warrior values as against an imposed and peaceful elderhood: anger as against equanimity, resort to physical force as against powers of moral coercion, the avoidance of married women as against an arranged early marriage, and the possibility of great fortune as against the threat of poverty and misfortune. Both representations are placed in the forefront of the dangers to which their age-group is exposed. The diehard is a warrior who plants himself as mainstay in the battle-line. The ritual leader is the man-who-is-erected (or planted upright) as the mainstay in the transition towards elderhood. *Eunoto* is associated on the one hand with the ritual leader and on the other with the flamboyant raid that follows, a raid known in some parts of Maasai by the term used for diehard in Matapato.

This leads to a further possible metaphor associated with the role of ritual leader. The most critical event of *eunoto* is held to be the sacrifice of the forest-ox, when the ritual leader is 'erected' and through him, his entire age-group. The site recommended by the Prophet must be close to a wild-fig tree, *oreteti*. These are impressive trees by any standard, towering above the forest. One used by Matapato is even said to have reached a girth of some 30 feet and a height of 150 feet (Dallas 1931:40). An immediate relevance of this tree is that it provides the firesticks invariably used by the patrons (cf. Huntingford 1931:143). Other writers have commented on this species. Jacobs (1965:139) notes the distinctiveness of its numerous aerial roots which give it the appearance of standing on top of the earth rather than arising out of it. The Hindes (1901:102–3), in writing of its significance for the Maasai, note that: 'It originates in an ivy-like growth, which climbs up a well grown tree of another species, the shoot sending out stalks and roots until its support is completely surrounded. The various stalks then all coalesce, and the bark unites into one piece, the irregularities of which disappear after a few years, leaving a perfectly smooth surface. No sign of the supporting tree is visible with the exception of its crest, which rises from the middle of the [wild-fig tree]. About fifty or sixty feet from the ground, the [wild-fig tree] throws out large branches, which support both their own weight and that of the heavy foliage and fruit they bear. Eventually the original tree is completely swallowed up, and its usurper represents the only indication that it has ever existed.' There is a neat parallel between the notion of a vulnerable creeper with no substantial roots that smothers its host as it acquires strength and longevity, and the heavy dependence of the age-group of moran on their unfortunate ritual leader. My informants emphasised that it is the act of sharing in the sacrifice of the forest-ox that raises the moran to a higher status and not the presence of the wild-fig tree nearby. Nevertheless, at a metaphorical level, it is as if the act of 'erecting' the age-group in the forest is a sombre re-enactment of the transfer of life and strength. It seems to simulate the transfer from the host-tree to the parasite, with the ritual leader – the man-who-is-erected/planted-upright – as the principal stake.

This brings the argument back to the principal features of sacrifice noted earlier in the chapter, and the transfer of life and renewal from the ox to those who share in 'passing through' it. The parallels with the transformation of the ritual leader at *eunoto* are striking. A sacrificial ox is selected by the Prophet from anywhere in Matapato for its propitious markings: the ritual leader is selected by the Prophet from anywhere in Matapato for his propitious and unblemished credentials. The patrons kindle the fire for roasting the sacrifice and imparting life to their wards: they also kindle a fire for installing the ritual leader and this imparts life to their wards. The sacrificial ox is suffocated with a woman's apron: the ritual leader is installed by seizing him, forcing a woman's apron over his shoulders, condemning him to a constricted future and possibly an early death. The sacrificial ox is made happy beforehand with singing and beer: a belated attempt is made to bring happiness to the ritual leader with singing and the gift of a cow with calf, and later a wife. Finally, the sacrifice of the forest-ox is the act of erecting the age-group through their ritual leader: it is 'the ritual leader's ox'. The parallels and associations are so close that one is led to view the imposition placed on the ritual leader as a form of sacrifice. If there is a certain analogy with birth and renewal in the sacrifices of *eunoto*, then equally one can point to an analogy with death in the transformation of the ritual leader. This goes beyond the sense of suffocation experienced by a shaking moran when he feels his basic urge to fight constricted by the conscience of his age-group ideals. In the case of the ritual leader, he is singled out and the vitality of his being is consumed by his age-group. His misfortune is their fortune and his early death is their long life. He is close to Frazer's concept of a divine king, with all that this implies for the transference of evil onto the sacred object, or as Freud might have put it, the projection of the guilt of their rebellion. However, in Maasai terms he is more than a scape-goat that is driven out. He leads his age-group upwards, bearing the brunt of the dimly perceived resentment against their passage towards elderhood. This is not expressed in terms of 'eyes' or of sorcery, but of destiny itself; and it is this that marks him out as great.

NOTES

1 It is probably significant, for instance, that I did not collect any examples of fracas between manyat that stemmed from competition over girls, whereas this had been a recurrent problem among the Samburu where rival clans were interspersed. (Spencer 1965:113–7).

2 The fracas concerned respectively the Ngorisho[R] among the Loodokilani, the Meruturud[L] and the Nyankusi[R] among the Purko. The Annual Report for 1945 (AR/Kaj-Nar/1945:3) presumably refers obliquely to this last incident.

3 Regarding a comparable practice among the Rendille where the fire is actually kindled over the lap of the ritual victim, see Spencer 1973:49.

4 This gathering at *eunoto* provided an independent check for my assessment from official district censuses of 13,600 people in Matapato. The distribution of population by age among the Samburu for whom I have fuller data (Spencer 1965:320, settlement census) coupled with the figure of 13,600 would imply some 700 moran spanning 7 or 8 years in the Ngorisho[R] age-group, nearly all of whom should have attended this ceremony. This compares with 600 claimed by some Matapato and 450 according to my own count on two separate occasions (Episodes 4 and 5 above). My informants denied that any moran were away at work and only a handful would have been premature elders or at school and not required to attend the ceremony. If these informants, and my count, and the extrapolation from Samburu data are all correct, then this would imply a truer figure of about 9,000 people in Matapato.

5 The prescribed cuts of meat offered the wards at a sacrifice are the chest (heart, lungs and diaphragm: *enabooshoke*), inner forelimb (*enashe keju*), brisket (*emputuei*) and flank (*enkalemian*). See Chapter 14. All the moran were intended to take each of these bites, but due to the toughness of the cuts there was only time to complete the first ring of moran before evening and the remainder were in fact offered no meat. Because this is a ritual occasion, the Matapato maintain that the moran have special dispensation to eat the meat that the women have seen, and the ritual enclosure is a purely nominal fence of branches. In some other Maasai areas, there is a substantial screen of matting intended to blot out the gaze of inquisitive women (photograph: Beckwith 1980:100–3). For other photographs relevant to *eunoto*, see Jacobs 1971 (kindling the patrons' fire, shaving the moran, the *esinkira* hut) and also Hamilton 1963.

6 When a moran has loosened his hair, it becomes known as *ol-masi* (s. and *il-masin* pl. for the hair of several moran), a term that otherwise refers to the ritual hair grown by 'ritual dependants'. Among the Samburu, this is the term used for the free-flowing hair of their moran.

7 According to some, the term *enkipaata* can be applied to the dancing performed during the festival on four occasions: on the move to *eunoto* wearing full warrior regalia; during the four days following the sacrifice of the village-ox (without weapons or chalk decoration), and again most importantly after the sacrifice of the forest-ox (with chalk decoration and little else); and then on the move from *eunoto* again carrying full regalia. Others suggested that the dancing on these occasions was *oloipiri*, the dance associated formerly with the diehards. More cautious informants, however, emphasised that the procession from the forest back to the ritual leader's village was the most important of these occasions and the only true *enkipaata* in Matapato. It was a term that should not be applied loosely to the lion dance, for example.

8 The most graphic description offered of the disbanding ceremony was among the Loitokitok Maasai where it is still deferred until the next age-set have been

initiated years after *eunoto*. Forty-nine firestick patrons cowl their heads with sheepskin caps, *inkureeta*, whence the name of the ceremony, *enoonkureeta*. Their abuses against the moran incorporate such phrases as: 'become bitter; be finished off; become lost for ever; you have fucked your mothers when they denied us [this right]; I have come and hear and see that your mother has nothing left to fuck'. As with the joking between moran and their mothers at the first forest ox (of-the-earplugs), the Matapato acknowledged but did not stress the element of joking abuse. The disbanding ceremony appears to have lapsed among the Purko, and its future is uncertain in Matapato.

9   In Loita, the ritual leader's hut is regarded as a place of sanctuary for homicides and for boys who are being hounded by moran after filching privileges. Much of the resentment of moran was said to result from this protection given to fugitives. The Matapato denied this practice among themselves. However, they accepted that it would be a legitimate use by any ritual leader of his powers of coercion to bring his age mates closer to the ideals of elderhood.

In relation to these beliefs regarding the source of the ritual leader's misfortune, one may compare similar notions concerning the early death of the Purko senior spokesman of Terito, Olemutelu (p. 107). In Purko also, Terere of Talala age-set was unique in combining the roles of both senior spokesman and ritual leader on the advice of their Prophet. However, even in Purko as in Matapato, there is an emphasis on the separateness of these two roles normally.

CHAPTER 10

THE TRANSITION TO ELDERHOOD AND RELATIONS THROUGH WOMEN

It is useful to look beyond *eunoto* as a rite of transition, and to regard it as a significant stage in a more inclusive rite of this kind that encompasses the whole period of moranhood.[1] The ritual of rebellion after initiation separates moran from the paternal yoke and the domain of elderhood generally. The manyata episode is a ritualised form of segregation from this domain. *Eunoto* is the first of a series of steps that incorporates them into elderhood, culminating in their *olngesher* festival more than a decade later. As the surge of moranhood loses its momentum, the initiative reverts to the elders, both as firestick patrons and as fathers. The period of moranhood, which asserts the primacy of youth, ultimately defers to the moral supremacy of ageing. This process entails a transformation from the food avoidances that define moranhood to a new set of avoidances associated with the dignity of elderhood. It is a process that concerns men's changing relations with women, and through women with one another as they marry and settle down.

MORAN AND MARRIAGE

Moran may marry at any time after their initiation although they are not normally expected to do so before *eunoto*. An early marriage is often a logical solution for a wealthy moran whose father is dead. It may simply be the whim of a wealthy father who sees some advantage in establishing the next generation of his family while he is still relatively young. Such marriages are regarded as the father's concern, and they should not interfere with the obligations of moranhood. In the past, for instance, a married moran played a full part in raiding. Today, his bride is normally expected to start rearing a family in his father's village and under his protection as a 'father'. Meanwhile, the moran husband continues to live at the manyata and shuns any suggestion that he is in any sense an 'elder'.

He avoids meat seen by her because she is a married women, and he will not even drink milk in her presence. He will be even more circumspect than his age mates on his occasional visits at night. He will seduce her furtively, and then creep away under cover of darkness to avoid any reputation of domesticity. She also should avoid him. In Loitokitok, a highly extroverted and popular moran pointed to a retreating group of women and whispered to me: 'Did you see my wife?' This would have been impossible for she had hidden on the far side of the group, covering her head with a cloth. In fact I had not even noticed her.

A married moran with no close kinsmen may find it necessary to take his bride to the manyata. This will place her in a particularly vulnerable position. Unlike girls whose lovers are also their protectors, she has only a husband who will avoid any action that might be construed as jealousy, associated with the possessiveness of elderhood. She is exposed to the moran rather than protected, and a manyata marriage is an expedient only as a final resort.

Case 35.
As a fatherless moran with good prospects, Masiani married early and was obliged to take his bride, Telelia, to his manyata at Maparasha. She recalled life there with some three hundred moran of Terito[R] and only seven young wives. 'The young wives at the manyata . . . were frightened of the moran, for the Terito were vicious. They did not want to see any of their young wives passing by them inside the village; if they saw one, they would throw a club at her. We dared not even go round the outside of the manyata to visit other huts, for the moran would beat us; they were that bad. Then at night when we just had to go out to milk our cattle and put the calves back in their pens, the moran would stay right away over there so that they would not accidentally stumble across their own wives [in the darkness]. They avoided us and hated to see a young wife in the village . . . You would only go to the hut of your mother-in-law to sleep. When it got light, there was just the gap between the hut and the outside fence where you could go [qv. Map 4]. Once the cattle had gone grazing, your mother-in-law would lead you outside to rest in the shade of a tree beside the other young wives of moran and cover you [with a cloth].'

Under no circumstances can the young wives of moran attend the *eunoto*, and for the period of the festival, they return with their children to their own fathers' villages. The most pragmatic reason for this is the fear that they would be treated even more roughly at *eunoto*. They would be too terrified to refuse moran from rival manyat claiming their sexual rights as age mates, and they could be maltreated with impunity; whereas the same moran would have to be very circumspect in approaching each other's girls. The wives of moran also pose an anomaly in relation to the *esinkira* hut: no-one is quite certain whether moran who have had intercourse with them should be excluded as adulterers or be permitted to enter for having merely exercised their full rights as age mates of the husband. The problem is regarded as relatively new as it is only recently that moran have begun to marry before *eunoto* in any number (about 16% by the 1977 *eunoto* according to Table 1).

Eunoto does mark a turning point, however. Once performed, it is no longer an anomaly for moran to marry nor to have sexual relations with their own wives. This takes them a step further towards domesticity and elderhood and away from their girls.

The ritual leader should marry soon after *eunoto*, ideally before any other moran, and his wife too will be respected as though she belongs to a senior generation. She is a gift from his age-group. If he dies young, then at least they have tried to ensure that he has had a chance to found a family of his own. Like the ritual leader, she is chosen secretly from a propitious family and is co-opted through a form of coercion. In place of a conventional gift of 'anointment', moran from another manyata area slip into the village of the unsuspecting girl and place round her neck a chain that has been doctored with the Prophet's 'medicines'. She too is expected to scream and rage, and then her mother, realising what has occurred, tries to prevent her throwing away the chain – and her own life. The mother may then slip it round her own neck for safety. This form of betrothal overrides any other arrangements the father may have made for the girl.

AGE FELLOWSHIP AND RELAXING MILK AVOIDANCES

Following *eunoto* and the disbanding of the manyat, moran return to their fathers' villages. Each father decides when to organise the 'milk-drinking' ceremony for his sons, releasing them from the obligation to share milk with other moran, as occurred in Case 30. Normally, when moran share milk, one of their number – ideally the host – picks up the milk gourd, shakes it, removes the cap, hands it to his age mates to drink, and then replaces the cap. In the 'milk-drinking' ceremony, the performer is seen to drink alone and to replace the cap for himself, and the obligation is ended.

There is a belief that if a moran has at any time 'stolen' milk by himself, he will splutter during the 'milk-drinking' ceremony, rather as if he has inadvertently swallowed a drowning fly. This test of integrity once again introduces a minor element of ordeal, even for those that have never violated the prohibition. It is never certain that an innocent moran can avoid choking involuntarily at the critical point. Moran and firestick patrons witness his performance inside his mother's hut. First another moran takes a flame from the household fire to inspect the milk inside the gourd and make quite certain that there *is* no drowning fly. He then shakes the gourd and hands it to a firestick patron, who holds it to the mouth of the solo performer to drink. If he splutters, then he will have to provide an ox feast for his age-group, regardless of his protests of innocence or submerged flies. This is a standard punishment for violating the obligations of moranhood. If he emerges honourably, he can expect gifts of cattle from his father and close kinsmen, and a small feast is prepared for the guests.

The real ordeal for each moran at this time, however, is to adjust his drinking habits after the ceremony. For perhaps six years, he has shared the close company of age mates, popularly expressed in terms of the daily need to find one another in order to share milk together. Once he has 'drunk milk' alone, he cannot pretend that he is still bound by this restriction. To do so and neglect more urgent tasks would be widely regarded as the response of a wastrel.

Case 36.
Kunaiju expressed his disorientation somewhere between moranhood and elderhood after the 'milk-drinking' ceremony. 'On that day, I became an elder [sic]. My whole body hated it. I was alone, yet did not know how to stay that way. I would set off to find some age mates. I would fetch Lekwemeri and together we would search for other moran [sic]. At Embukani where we lived, we were looking for one another all the time. Yet we had "drunk milk", and in time I came round to drinking it by myself. My body did not want it – it detested it and I was apprehensive; and that was how we stayed for some time. You would go out with the cattle and herd them until nightfall – by yourself. You would say: "Whuh! I just can't go on. I'll lie down now". You would drink just a little milk, for your body did not really want it. You would put just a little in a cup, enough to taste, and then you would step up [to the sleeping hide] to sleep. You would hate to be seen [drinking alone]. Next morning when it was light you might go to meet another moran of your age-group. You would drink together, but now neither of you would open up the gourd for the other [and it was no longer quite the same]. So we all disbanded to look after our cattle, and we broke up our earlier fellowship (*oloosiat*) to become accustomed to drinking milk [alone]. If you immediately turned to herding cattle, you would be very busy; and those who had cattle to tend got on with it and went off in different directions . . . It was the men who had no cattle who would keep together and share milk together, though without opening up the gourd for one another. In the end, it was those who turned to herding their cattle alone who soon got used to milk alone.'

The nausea expressed here accompanies a sharp change in diet. It is at this period in their lives that the daily intake of milk for men is said to drop very considerably from the large quantities they claim to have drunk as moran. In this way, at about the time that an incipient age-group of adolescent boys increase their appetite and capacity for milk, an age-group of incipient elders are adjusting physiologically as well as psychologically to a more moderate intake. Correspondingly, this is a time when the senior moran take over more responsibility for herding as some of the most experienced herdboys are poised to become moran. It is a step towards a more general change-over, and the seniors adjust themselves to the inevitability of handing on the privileges of moranhood in due course.

Having 'drunk milk', those moran who are married may take up residence with their wives. For others, marriage is the next logical step, although some may still have to wait many years.[2] Widespread marriage raises a further threat to the close fellowship of the age-group. Ideally at least, the sexual services of their wives, like food, can be shared as an aspect of offering hospitality. However, beyond usufructuary rights of this sort, each husband has sole right to the growth of his herd and family and this is potentially divisive. No-one questions this right, and there is no attempt to delay marriage further in the spirit of age-group solidarity; but in this spirit, food avoidances are maintained in relation to their own wives, and this extends to drinking milk in their presence. A young wife is expected to keep her husband's milk-gourds full for him and his guests as a matter of pride, but she is first ordered to leave her hut whenever he or any of his age mates come to drink. She is not just despised as a threat to the bond between age mates, but they actually express a sense of embarrassment (*esora*). She has no business to be there while they are drinking.

An elder is only prepared to drink in his wife's presence after she has returned a heifer to him from her herd. She may quickly volunteer this *heifer-of-avoidance* (*enturuj*) to overcome the constant humiliation of being ordered from her own hut. However, a ready submission can also imply fickleness in not really valuing the small herd allotted to her on marriage, and she may hold out for a long period, while this herd builds up. Meanwhile she is not mistress of her hut in this respect, and ultimately her exasperation at the high-handedness of her husband is expected to overcome her pride. If it does not, the husband can end this avoidance at any time and on his own terms. He may claim to have found a fly in the milk gourd, and teasing her for her negligence, he may demand that she pays him the heifer, which in this instance is referred to as the heifer-of-the-flies. If the issue develops into a battle of stubbornness with neither prepared to budge, one of the husband's visiting age mates may help the couple through this impasse by introducing a fly surreptitiously into the gourd and then complaining as he is about to drink. Either way, she pays a heifer and the avoidance is formally ended. The husband may continue for a period to order her out of her hut until a time of his own choosing, emphasising his prerogative to modify the rules as well as to win the game. Even after he consents to drink milk in her presence, he continues to conceal from her for some time that he goes to his mother's hut to eat porridge. This is not a food for young men, and he still wishes to retain his dignity and avoid embarrassment in front of his own wife. Progressively, these avoidances are relaxed, but taking food in the presence of his wife remains a gauge of domestic relations. If these become strained, his first impulse will be to avoid food in her hut.

There is another *enturuj* avoidance between husband and wife that has to be resolved as their marriage consolidates. Neither should touch the other's head, and until this avoidance is relaxed, senior moran have to solicit each other's wives often in other villages to shave their scalps. At first, this may be an acceptable aspect of sharing their wives' services or displaying their hair as moran. However, the ideal for an aspiring elder is to display self-sufficiency by being shaved regularly in his own village; and this can only be done after his senior wife has paid him a further heifer to relax the avoidance. She may then delegate the task of shaving to a more skilled co-wife or even to the wife of an age mate. He should not then be shaved in any other village, and his hair should be allowed to grow when he is on an extended visit elsewhere. Increasingly among age mates, a man who continues to let his hair grow or to be shaved elsewhere is felt to be a wastrel. It implies either that he has no wife, or that his wife has no cattle to relax this avoidance, or simply that he neglects his domestic responsibilities through his aimless wanderings. He is behaving like a moran. As he settles down to elderhood, it is a matter of decorum for the husband that he should be close shaved. For the sake of her own reputation, his senior wife has little option other than to give him this heifer.

ADULTERY AND RELAXING MEAT AVOIDANCES

The avoidance of meat seen by married women during moranhood is more rigorously observed than the demand by elders that they should avoid these women sexually also. The transition to elderhood entails a complex transformation of these avoidances corresponding to an elaboration of the relations between the sexes.

There are various degrees of adultery. It is quite legitimate to have discreet relations with the wife of an age mate. Adultery with the wives of other age-sets provokes a variety of responses. If the cuckold is two or more age-sets senior, then would-be adulterers have to be especially careful, for these are the age-sets of men they must respect as their firestick patrons and often their fathers. There is less respect for the age-set of their immediate predecessors who have no direct curse over them. The risks of adultery with their wives are lower and the temptation is greater, especially for unmarried senior moran whose *eunoto* has removed any lingering ideals of chastity. The underdeveloped girls with whom they used to consort are now frequently the fully grown wives of this next age-set of junior elders (as I shall call them). These moran previously tried to filch the privileges of moranhood from this age-set, and now with less justification they may seek to filch the favours of their wives in a game of cat-and-mouse. At first, these adulteries may appear sporadic and individual husbands may nurture their grievances, determined to prevent those they suspect from marrying any daughter of an age mate or of their clan, by using their marriage veto (p. 29). Meanwhile, they can only wait patiently for opportunities that may never arise: the adulterers may be looking elsewhere for wives. As suspicions mount, these junior elders watch the comings and goings of moran and of their own wives more carefully. They often move to live together in one village to share their vigilance. At some point, the mounting sense of grievance is brought to a head at a meeting of their age-set; and they agree to obstruct the marriages of all moran – guilty or innocent – to their daughters. All existing betrothals are suspended and any daughters of their age-set already married to the senior moran are recalled with the threat of a paternal curse. The senior moran are in no position to negotiate, and can only plead for a settlement on any terms. Once this position has been reached, the problem resolves itself. The junior elders have no wish to withhold their daughters indefinitely, since the only alternative suitors would be men older than themselves or non-Matapato. The ideal of relatively local and younger sons-in-law would be lost for a time, in addition to the disruption of existing marriage arrangements that have been carefully fostered. Typically, the senior moran would be required to pay forty-nine heifers, forty-nine blankets, forty-nine cloths and forty-nine gourds of beer to be distributed among those junior elders with outstanding grudges. The gaming on the one side and the grudging on the other should then be at an end.

A more structured relationship now crystalises between the two adjacent age-sets with the notion that the junior elders are highly eligible fathers-in-law for the senior moran and there should be mutual respect. They refer to each other loosely as 'affines' (*ilaputak*). The senior moran have now taken a significant step towards elderhood, and the junior elders a further step still. As table 2 suggests, perhaps one-quarter of all marriages link these two age-sets in this way, although the evidence is somewhat indirect.

Age Difference	Proportion of marriages	Comments
father-in-law older by:	%	
+5 age-sets	1	father-in-law probably dead when daughter is married
+4 age-sets	6	father-in-law probably dead when daughter is married
+3 age-sets	21	
+2 age-sets	44	father-in-law also a firestick patron of son-in-law
+1 age-set	25	'affines' (loose Matapato usage)
0 age-set	0	age mates: marriage with daughters prohibited
-1 age-set	3	'affines' (loose Matapato usage and unusual)
father-in-law younger		

Source: interpolated from Samburu data and extrapolated to Matapato[3]

Table 2 Age differences between fathers-in-law and sons-in-law

A major step in adjusting to elderhood occurs when a new age-group of junior moran is established. The senior moran grudgingly concede the privileges and obtain wives in increasing numbers. As the juniors emerge into the limelight and develop a roving interest in these wives, suspicions of adultery shift in their direction. Beyond this is the remoter possibility that some senior moran have consorted with the neglected wives of those junior moran that have married very early. What may be regarded as a sport by the junior age-set (and even possibly by their wives) is treated as a serious lapse on the part of their more mature partners in adultery. It entails a loss of dignity. Such lapses by either the senior moran or their wives – hypo-adultery so to speak – are on a par with the infringements of the food avoidances of moranhood. The same term, *enturuj* is used of both, but not of their hyper-adulteries with the wives (or husbands) of more senior age-sets.

About two years after handing over the privileges, the senior moran 'eat meat' in a ceremony that relaxes the avoidance of meat seen by married women. Unlike the private ceremony of 'drinking-milk' alone, 'eating-meat' is a festival shared by the age-group in four or five specially constructed villages in different parts of Matapato. Participants attend the most convenient venue to where they live. Many, perhaps even most, of the senior moran are married by this time and their wives take the place that their mothers occupied at the *eunoto* festival. Typically forty-nine moran are selected as hosts to found a village on each of the selected sites. The ritual leader and his deputy join the same village, and this is the occasion when the deputy unties the forty-nine knots in his *eunoto* thong which then loses further significance. On this occasion, there is no concern with sorcery and the patrons conduct a sacrifice in each of the 'villages-of-meat' without consulting the Prophet or using his 'medicines'.

For some time before the festival, the firestick patrons warn the senior moran and their wives that they have placed a curse on the meat that is to be tasted by each senior moran at the festival. The wives must confess their hypo-adulteries with junior moran of the next age-group and the senior moran must confess both their hypo-adulteries and any lapses in avoiding meat. They are all warned that anyone who does not confess could die on the next occasion when the wife shaves her husband's hair; or their children could die. This is a concern that builds up again to an ordeal at the ceremony itself when the moran have to taste meat in front of their own wives.

The critical point of the ceremony occurs after selected cuts of meat have been cooked in the central enclosure and cut into morsels. Some young wives then collect these in their outstretched aprons and take them to one of the huts. Meanwhile throughout the village, patrons heighten the drama by warning both moran and wives to admit their guilt, and they

chant 'Confess! Confess!' (*Tilimu!*). The moran then process into the hut
to be offered a morsel each from the hand of a wife or a firestick patron,
while other wives and patrons look on. If a wife has infringed, she should
take care not to witness any moran tasting meat. If a moran has infringed,
he should refuse the meat offered by hand and indicate that he wishes to
pick it up himself. She by staying away and he by refusing have confessed.
If he refuses, he should make it clear to his wife whether his lapse concerns
forbidden meat or adultery. However, neither moran nor their wives are
expected to reveal the identity of their lovers or recriminations would be
endless, and perhaps no-one would be safe. A man who tries to force the
whole truth from his wife would be restrained by his fellows.

It is not only the guilty who may find this an ordeal. Men with nothing
to confess may find themselves nauseated by the experience of tasting meat
in front of women, and leave the hut to vomit. They may remain
embarrassed at eating in the presence of wives for a while. Some even
continue to old age, steadfastly refusing to eat meat inside a village, and
clinging to the virtues of moranhood, rather as some diehards are said to
have done in old age.

Those that have confessed have a debt to settle with their spouses. The
innocent marriage partner is entitled to eight female cattle and a bull,
although popular pressure normally reduces this to one female or perhaps
two in the spirit of reconciliation.

Case 37.
The Meruturud[R] age-group succeeded the Nyankusi[L] and had early evidence of
the effectiveness of the patrons' curse on 'eating meat'. One of them as a young
moran had seduced the wife of a Nyankusi[L], and this woman had concealed the
fact when she and her husband went to 'eat meat'. Subsequently, she lost her
son and bore no more children. The husband was never told the truth, but the
Meruturud[R] at least drew their own conclusions. In about 1968, it was their turn
to perform the festival. For some time beforehand their firestick patrons (of
Terito age-set) had warned them of their curse, and this raised some awkward
questions. Koileken took the initiative and ordered his wife to tell him if she had
had any dealings with junior moran, pointing out that she could not conceal the
fact much longer. She coolly retorted that she had 'gone to the moran'. and that
she knew that he had 'gone' to one of their wives, and she named the woman.
Neither owed the other cattle. In another incident, Resia's wife ran away one
month before the festival. He guessed that she had concealed from him an
adultery and had run to her father's village, confessing there and soliciting cattle
from close kinsmen to appease him: this is the expected procedure. She
returned, escorted by one of Resia's age mates to dissuade him from any violence
and told him from which villages he could collect the cattle she now owed him.
Then the age mate begged Resia to settle for just two heifers. Some other wives
kept a cooler nerve until the time of the festival itself. Most of the husbands who
were not already at the 'village of meat' as hosts collected there beforehand and
expected their wives to follow. On the day of 'eating meat' they looked keenly at
the approaching groups of dancing women for a glimpse of their own wives. As
the day advanced and still some women were absent, the keenness of some men

turned to anxiety and then, with full realisation, to bitterness. They resented the lies and reassurances that had been fed to them, and vowed that they would demand the full payment of nine cattle without remission.

At the height of the ceremony, the ordeal switched to the husbands. Those women that had arrived for the celebration were confidently proud of their fidelity. Singing and dancing jubilantly, they were aware that a moment of truth had now arrived for many outwardly confident men. None of these husbands, it was said, felt easy as the women gathered to peer closely at each in turn; and some had good reason to feel nervous. Moiyoi's wife was prominent among the women spectators and clearly expected him to accept his morsel of meat from the hands of the woman selected for this task. He gave no hint of any breach until it was his turn, and then averted his head as the morsel was offered him. Following this signal, the woman laid the morsel on a stone and he picked it up himself. Other women started to titter, and outside the hut his wife lost her temper, and started to hit him while he tried to reason with her. She made the most of one of the few occasions when women may mount a histrionic display against their husbands with impunity. His age mates intervened to restrain her, promising at first that she would be given her nine cattle. They then tried to persuade her to accept a smaller number when she had calmed down. Other husbands found themselves similarly trapped. It made no difference to the offended wives whether their husbands had tasted forbidden sex or meat. It was not simply a question of infidelity to their wives but also of hypocrisy and infidelity to the obligations of their age-group which infused their marriages. Now the wives were entitled to cattle for the slight. Melita refused the meat in his wife's presence with greater ease. It had been she who had persuaded him to share some of her meat during a period of drought when he was ill with hunger; and she did not demand any cattle. As the day advanced, the tally mounted of husbands who had refused meat and had been attacked by their wives, and of wives whose absences had infuriated their unsuspecting husbands, and even of husbands whose unexpected absences had infuriated their wives. Rumour and counter-rumour spread. As long as the young elders still waited in a queue leading to the hut, their wives hovered nearby, and the firestick patrons continued to chant: 'Confess! Confess!' The occasion polarised into those who were dancing, singing and joking, and those who skulked elsewhere, feeling their shame and humiliation.

The ordeal did not end on that day. Some of the wives had arranged not to attend the ceremony, perhaps to look after their children or because they were still confined after giving birth; and these women still had to face their husbands with the truth on both sides. Jubilant after the ceremony, the husbands processed home from village to village, singing and dancing. At each village, those wives that had stayed behind were expected to put on their finery before coming out to greet their husbands with their own dance. As any husband who had not yet confronted his wife approached his own village, his unease would increase until he saw his wife among the other women. If there was no sign of her, it was clear that she was either hiding or had run away, since the firestick patrons had extended their curse to this occasion also. The husband would detach himself from the group and storm into his village demanding to know where his wife was. As the procession approached Leken's village, on the other hand, he behaved differently, lurking inconspicuously on the far side of his dancing age mates and hoping that his wife would not notice him. In fact, rumour had already reached his village that he had refused the meat offered him at the ceremony, and this wife had had time to prepare his reception. She came out dancing with the other women and carrying a stick. Then, she detached herself from the dancing and went up to beat him, demanding to know why he had not told her previously and why he was trying to hide from her now. She was restrained by the other men, and then returning to her hut she produced Leken's stool – the symbol of his mastery within his own home. She left it in the corral, announcing that Leken could sleep there since he was not going to enter *her* hut. Leken was persuaded to offer her nine cattle to make his peace, and she resisted all attempts at coercing her to concede a single animal. She had now completely upturned the situation of a few years previously when Leken had ordered her out of the hut so that he and his age mates could share milk together. And she had added substantially to her allotted herd.

This series of episodes suggests a remarkable increase in the confidence of the young wives when there were enough of them and with enough experience of married life to muster as a group. The principal hazard faces the wives, who are all exposed to the lures of adventurous young moran of the next age-group. Fewer junior elders are expected to have tripped over the avoidance of either forbidden meat or forbidden wives who hardly as yet exist: they are expected to have more foresight in controlling their appetites. Any man who could not resist the temptation has 'fallen' (*e-sulari*) to a degree that cannot be matched by the fallen wives. His age mates will loyally rescue him from the assaults of his wife, but they will not shelter him from his humiliation. Quite gratuitously, he has infringed their integrity as an age-group. In celebrating their own achievement through a display of dancing and making him the butt of their joking, they isolate him, and indirectly conspire with the women in exposing him. In addition to his payment to his wife, he will have to provide an ox feast for his age-group as a fine for his lapse.

OLNGESHER: THE FESTIVAL UNITING THE AGE-SET

By the time a right-hand age-group have 'eaten meat', they are effectively junior elders and their left-hand successors are close to their *eunoto* and senior moranhood. Over the next ten years or so, those of the left-hand 'drink milk', 'eat meat', marry and settle down until they are ready to proceed with those of the right-hand to the *olngesher* festival. This unites the two age-groups into a single undifferentiated age-set.

The process of union between the two sides has in fact been taking place for a number of years prior to the festival. The intense solidarity within each age-group cracks as they disband and 'drink milk'. When the left-hand too have reached this stage, then the basis for rivalry shifts from the division between right and left to the new challenge that unites them against the next age-set of boys who are now becoming troublesome moran. Meanwhile, the right-hand seniors have adopted a tolerant view of any minor excesses by their left-hand juniors. They themselves had enjoyed the kudos of wresting the privileges from the previous age-set, of being stronger, and of leading a more leisurely way to elderhood. When it is the turn of the left-hand to follow the same path for a briefer period, those of the right can afford to concede to them their lesser share of glory. Personal resentments over adulteries do not build up to a major issue between them as age-groups. As the left-hand also mature, there is a growing awareness that their strength lies in uniting as an age-set, and they accept the respect and sharing due to each other as age mates.[4]

There is an intriguing parallel between this union of an age-set and preparation for a meat feast. At any sacrifice, a barbecue is constructed for roasting the meat, and the term for this structure and particularly for the bridging struts, *olngesher*, is also the name of the final festival in the series of promotions. Figure 10 illustrates how the sequence of ceremonies appears to be modelled on the principle of a barbecue framework. The firestick patrons kindle the fire that first brings the age-set to life. The senior age-group is metaphorically a right-hand stake which is cut by their mothers at the village-of-the-hatchet and then 'planted upright' at their *eunoto*. The junior age-group as the left-hand stake follows the same course. Finally, the two sides are united into a composite age-set at *olngesher*, the strut bridging the stakes on either side. There is a further symbolic parallel in the principal term for an age-set, *ol-aji* (m) and a hut *enk-aji* (f). A barbecue and a hut have a similar structure, with a fire at the centre, and stakes at either side supporting the cross-struts. At each stage,

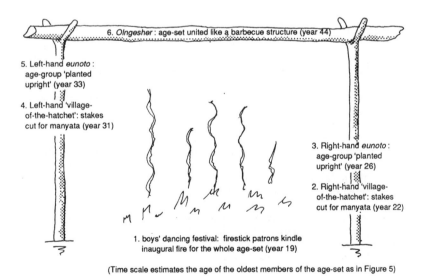

6. *Olngesher* : age-set united like a barbecue structure (year 44)

5. Left-hand *eunoto* :
age-group 'planted
upright' (year 33)

4. Left-hand 'village-
of-the-hatchet': stakes
cut for manyata (year 31)

3. Right-hand *eunoto* :
age-group 'planted
upright' (year 26)

2. Right-hand 'village-
of-the-hatchet': stakes
cut for manyata (year 22)

1. boys' dancing festival: firestick patrons kindle
inaugural fire for the whole age-set (year 19)

(Time scale estimates the age of the oldest members of the age-set as in Figure 5)

Figure 10:   The barbecue (*olngesher*) and the construction of an age-set

it is the firestick patrons who build up the structure, rather as wives build huts, pegging the stakes and building the cross-pieces, and the *olngesher* is the final touch, completing the process. The barbecue analogy would be even neater if 'eating meat' followed *olngesher* instead of preceding it. And in fact among the Kisonko, who are the leading performers of *olngesher* for all Maasai, 'eating meat' is indeed an immediate sequel of *olngesher*, and the metaphor is even more apt.[5]

In Matapato, the 'eating meat' festival is essentially a reduced and premature version of the more elaborate and important *olngesher*. Instead of a number of smaller villages for each age-group, *olngesher* has just one village for the whole age-set, ideally with 149 huts. All members of the right- and left-hand sides are expected to come to 'pass through the ox'; and for the first time since their circumcisions, they are now joined by the premature elders.[6] Each participant should have his own wooden stool, a thick bamboo tube for tobacco, and a switch from an *esinoni* tree (lippia sp.) tipped with sprouting green leaves. The firestick patrons bless the stools in the evening. Then next day when the ox is sacrificed in the centre of the village, the celebrants eat meat in front of their wives and again this becomes the focus of an ordeal for both sexes. If either have stooped below their age-set in adultery since their last confessions when 'eating meat', then again this should now be confessed. This normally occurs at about the time when fury at the adulteries of the moran of the next age-set reaches its climax, and there is no spirit of tolerance.

Case 38.
When the Nyankusi age-set were preparing for their *olngesher* ceremony in about 1966, they were infuriated by the scale of their wives' adulteries with moran. They flatly refused the customary visit of good-will by any deputation of moran of the Meruturud age-groups, and their venom turned on their own wives. Their firestick patrons of Dareto age-set gave warnings of their curse and helped to precipitate an early panic. Wives began to run away to their parental homes. At this stage it appears to have been the husbands who effectively held the initiative, pestering those wives who had stayed with awkward questions and looking for signs of anxiety. By the time of the festival, it was assumed that most of the wives' indiscretions were already known. This left those wives that had not run away in a stronger position at the ceremony itself, since this would now reveal the hypocritical indiscretions of the husbands. Ntoipo had concealed his own adultery with the wife of a moran. When the firestick patrons gathered their wards together to taste meat before their wives with final warnings on everyone to confess, Ntoipo's wife realised that he had slipped away. She raised a hue and cry that became the most memorable event of the entire ceremony. Eventually, some of his age mates found him hiding in an empty hut and persuaded him to offer her nine cattle at once. She railed at him, shouting, shivering and struggling to beat him until the firestick patrons themselves intervened to quieten her, and ordered Ntoipo to keep his promise. While this scene was enacted, another couple, Kisali and his wife, were sitting quietly in their own hut. They had been selected to migrate to the *olngesher* village as hosts, and she

at once had confessed her adultery with a moran to Kisali. He then responded by confessing to her a hypo-adultery of his own. Both had stooped, but neither had fallen because of the dignity with which they had confessed. They agreed to sit the ceremony out, neither to eat meat nor to watch; and neither owed the other cattle. A third husband, Parsoi, who confessed by refusing the meat proffered in front of the women was later the butt of a joke among his own age mates. It transpired that he had infringed the avoidances before the ceremony of 'eating meat', and then as a bachelor at that time, he had sneaked away unnoticed, evading the chance to confess. Now at *olngesher* the firestick patrons maintained a tighter security, emphasising that their curse extended to earlier unconfessed infringements. Parsoi was trapped. If he had had the courage to confess when they 'ate meat', he would only have paid the minimum penalty to his age-group. Now as a married man, he was obliged to face his wife and the humiliation of paying cattle to placate her as well.

The culminating blessing uniting the age-set is pronounced by the firestick patrons after this test. Their wards crouch down, wearing their tobacco tubes as elders, clutching their *esinoni* switches so that the greenery splays above them 'like a forest'. Thus while the ritual climax of *eunoto* entails the moran going out to the forest for their blessing, at *olngesher* at the corresponding point, the forest has come to the ceremonial village, as it were. The moran of the forest have been transformed into established elders of the village. They are then told that they should all reach their homes before the leaves of their switches have dried up and on no account to have sexual relations with any women on the way. The triumphant dancing and home-coming follows a similar pattern to the earlier ceremony of 'eating meat' with a similar delayed ordeal for some. Once home, they should collect their wives and children together and whip them gently with the 'living' switches which still retain the life-giving powers of the patrons' blessing.

From this point, they may display certain privileged symbols of elderhood: they may herd cattle with switches of *esinoni*, they may wear long ceremonial capes on ritual occasions instead of just short ones, and above all they may wear tobacco containers round their necks. This is a privilege associated with their greatly enhanced power to bless and to curse. When tobacco is chewed and mixed with spittle, it provides a bitter taste on the one hand, and yet a feeling of well-being on the other. This expresses the ambivalence of the power of creativity and destruction which elders have to learn to control.

In bestowing this power to curse on their wards, the firestick patrons urge them to use it responsibly, reminding them of the misfortunes of the Dareto age-set.

Case 39.
The Dareto are said to have been appalled at the sheer magnitude of the confessions from their wives at their *olngesher*. Very few it seemed had resisted the temptation of 'going to the Terito moran'. The husbands are said to have refused placatory cattle, and the strength of their grievance had the effect of a

curse on their own wives. This is the reason put forward for the early deaths of so many of their children. They had been endowed with the full power to curse as elders, but had responded in pique as moran. They had not yet learned to control the destructive power of their emotions, and then they paid the price.

With *olngesher*, the firestick patrons are said to 'lie down' (*a-irrag*), having transferred responsibility to their wards who are now elders in a full sense.

THE IMPLICATION OF DAUGHTERS FOR THE DOMESTICATION OF THE MORAN

Among moran, the term *enturuj* applies specifically to their food avoidances. As these are relaxed in stages, the term acquires a new connotation and refers to the avoidance of wives of younger men of the next age-set who are already beginning to marry. In 1977, members of the Meruturud age-set were mostly in their thirties and claimed that as moran they had weighed up the seducibility of every young woman. The prospect of being exposed by their patrons at *eunoto* had been no disincentive for adultery. However, as junior elders anticipating their *olngesher*, they now had to take greater care. They found themselves embarrassed in the presence of the wives of younger men and would avert their gaze. Any men who were caught out during the meat test at *olngesher* deserved their discomfort, and any wives who emerged with credit deserved respect.

Underlying the shame of hypo-adultery for junior elders is the notion that indirectly their own daughters are involved, and this is the crowning avoidance for all Maasai. The growing concern for sexual dignity in the transition from moranhood to elderhood is linked to the fact that increasingly their own daughters number among the unmarried girls. In time, these girls will be among the wives of the next age-set, nominally their 'sons-in-law'. It is 'daughters' of their age-set whom they must avoid above all. Symbolically, the young girl who plastered the roof of their *esinkira* hut at *eunoto* was the first girl they avoided as their 'daughter'. She represented a new generation of avoidances that elevated them. Being senior moran implied becoming fathers who should acquire a new respect. Increasingly as they marry, they avoid familiarity with any young female whom they do not actually recognise, for she could be the daughter of an age mate. Ignorance of this fact is no excuse for presumption. As they become elders, even familiarity with younger men's wives that are not their daughters could be seen as a step towards familiarity with those that are: it is transgressing into a forbidden domain.

This avoidance should be especially pronounced between a man and his own daughter. She is brought up from infancy to leave the hut whenever he or his age mates enter and above all to avoid them when they have food. For the young elder, having a daughter introduces a new constraint on his freedom within his own hut. Their relationship also conceals a deep affection, and its development is a significant aspect of the domestication of young men. At the time that the husband is still uncertain of his relationship with his wife and is not yet reconciled to the inevitability of his own elderhood, they may well have a small daughter with whom bonds of affection and avoidance are being nurtured. The mismatch between husband and wife in the early stages of their marriage is resolved through redefining their roles as parents. They refer to one another and become generally known by their teknonyms as father/mother-of-so-and-so. While the father has a direct responsibility for aspects of his sons' upbringing, responsibility for daughters lies wholly with the mother and the father maintains a discreet distance. The conflict of emotions facing the father is well expressed by his urge to beat his wife on one occasion because she has not instilled their daughter with enough respect, and on another occasion because he feels she is being too strict. When Matapato claim that girls can learn respect at the manyata, it is not just from the moran, but also from their mothers and in the absence of interfering fathers.

As the daughter grows, the father and his age mates avoid any reference to her sexuality. Throughout her adulthood, she will continue to greet them with a bowed head for their palmed blessing like any child. Even when she is a mature woman, they will not call her mother-of-so-and-so, as this would allude indirectly to her capacity to bear children; instead they continue to address her by terms of endearment suitable for small children. She remains their 'child', dependent and sexless.

The avoidance between father and daughter is associated with his power to arrange her marriage with prime concern for what he regards as her best interests and no consideration for her personal wishes. Above all she must be taught not to bring her grievances to him or she might constantly run back to him after her marriage. If he can obtain a good match for her, and she has acquired an unquestioning trust in his judgment and the wisdom of his choice, the credit devolves on his household. His reputation and the marriageability of his family is enhanced by her eligibility.

After the oldest daughter has married, there may be a partial relaxation of her avoidance with her father and his age mates, enabling them to drink milk in her hut. She must first offer her father a heifer from her allotted herd, a gift which he frequently bestows on an age mate.[7] Underlying this gift is her eagerness to encourage him to visit her and see the success she has made of the marriage he arranged and to accept her hospitality and relax in her hut. He should avoid sleeping there, but if he has drunk so much of her beer that he falls asleep, then in his drunken insensibility, he 'sleeps with respect'. She would be thrilled and would leave a full gourd of beer beside him before finding some other hut to sleep in herself. It is the fulfilment of their relationship.

This relaxation of the milk avoidance of a young woman with her father and his age-set is in striking contrast to the relaxation of milk avoidances with her husband and his age-set, which is also settled by the gift of a heifer from her allotted herd at about this time. On the one hand there is the awkward interplay and sullen reluctance to give her husband the heifer-of-avoidance (*enturuj*) that is virtually forced from her. On the other hand there is the sense of loyal affection with which she seeks to repay her debt to her father with the heifer-of-milk. It is a measure of her upbringing that she feels she owes this debt. It is also a measure of the domestication of young elders that they should be transformed from awkward husbands in their own huts early in their marriages into dignified fathers in the huts of their daughters a short generation later.

*   *   *

The crux of the avoidance of daughters is the right of fathers to determine their futures. Increasingly as they accumulate daughters, junior elders become aware of their power to select suitors, to veto marriages, and ultimately even to insist on the temporary return of a daughter that has already been given away. As individuals, they have direct authority over their wives and offspring; but through their daughters, they have a taste of the power of their age-set over younger age-sets. In their relationship with various categories of female, it is the avoidance of daughters that is in a class of its own and associated with the integrity of their age-set as a whole. Even their wives may run away and be remarried to some other age-set, but daughters remain uniquely their own, and they regard this right as fundamental.

Case 40.
Sirere was a wild and impulsive boy (*osarkioni*) who became the butt of his Terito age mates after initiation. On one occasion they seized and slaughtered a large striped ox and at other times they beat him, but each attempt to teach him respect simply increased his alienation. Eventually, when he was close to elderhood, he brewed beer for a meeting with local members of the preceding age-set, Dareto. He renounced his own age-set and asked them to accept him as a member of theirs. They were unenthusiastic, but saw no obvious reason to refuse him. However, their spokesman made one clear stipulation: Sirere would have no power to curse their children and above all no right to veto the marriage of any of their daughters if he had a grievance. He was therefore accepted into their company without the fundamental right that membership of an age-set normally confers. Sirere adjusted himself to elderhood as well as he could, and eventually succeeded in marrying a woman who was considered as uncontrollable as he was, and not sought by other men.

THE AMBIVALENCE OF HOSPITALITY AND WIFE-SHARING WITHIN AN AGE-SET

Two Maasai terms, *olporror* and *olaji*, express the expectations towards an age mate. Very broadly, the transition to elderhood entails a shift from the first to the second. This corresponds to the extension of affiliation from the age-group associated with the manyata period inside Matapato to the age-set which extends to all Maasai. The two terms do not so much refer precisely to age-groups and age-sets as to ambivalent aspects of the bond uniting age mates. They are coined to emphasise one aspect or the other, according to context.

This ambivalence is well illustrated with reference to the rights that age mates can claim in each other's wives. A husband can regard his children as possessions. However, the fact that his age mates have sexual access to his wives means that in a sense the begetting and the children themselves also belong to the whole age-set. In this context, he is a trustee rather than a sole possessor. For the husband to be jealous in this respect (*a-lom*) is dangerous, for it can provoke the resentment of his age mates and their implicit curse on the children. The idiom of age fellowship is sharing, and junior elders are self-conscious as they emerge from the intense sharing of moranhood to a personal concern for the growth of their households. They feel vulnerable to any resentment among their age mates, especially while their children are still very young. When a man allows a persistent age mate to browbeat him into parting with some minor possession, he will argue that the lives of his children are altogether more precious.

It is in this vein that each husband is expected to fulfil his obligations as host scrupulously. When an age mate visits him overnight, the husband should sleep elsewhere. Whatever his wife may consent to in his absence is none of his business; he has no right to probe. This obligation to vacate his hut may be relaxed among those who shared a close companionship at the same manyata and have remained intimate friends. When they visit one another, the guest may press the host to remain in his hut, so that they can continue to chat as they settle down for the night side by side. In such company, there can be no suggestion of jealousy between them, and their willingness to put this obligation to one side for the night is an expression of their trust. It is this warm aspect of age fellowship that is expressed in the term *olporror*. It evokes the spirit of sharing among moran of one manyata and may be readily extended to any other context when there is an unreserved bond of trust between age mates.

When a less well known age mate visits the village, the husband should be punctilious in his hospitality for the sake of his children, born and unborn. In this context, the opposite term, *olaji*, evokes the overriding constraints of age bondage. It may be significant that the masculine form *ol-aji* is the counterpart of the feminine *enk-aji* (hut) for in describing the obligations between age mates in elderhood, it is their rights to hospitality in each other's huts that they stress: they are all one 'hut'. The most extreme obligation is towards a visiting age mate from beyond Matapato. His popular image is a stark caricature of the uncompromising demands of the age-set itself in its sternest guise. When Matapato describe their obligations towards age mates, it is such a visitor that they portray: he is of *olaji*. This reflects a general mistrust of strangers expressed also by the beliefs in 'eyes' and in sorcery; but visiting age mates are still age mates and cannot be shunned.

When Masiani first settled as a stranger in Loodokilani and when he was formally expelled years later, it was as a member of *olaji* (Case 22). Whereas during the intervening years, he cultivated new friendships in the spirit of *olporror*; as indeed Lepunian did when he first settled in Matapato (Case 8). When age mates sit together at a meat feast, the spirit of *olporror* is generated, but a prized flank of beef should be reserved for a highly respected age mate, typically a visitor from elsewhere. This cut is for *olaji* as the widest expression of age affiliation. One has a contrast between the intimacy of the particular relationship and the principle of its universal application.

The rule of hospitality is always a sensitive issue, and the age-set locally act as the guardian of *olaji* against abuse. If a husband seems to covet his wives too closely, his age mates will seize one of his finest oxen for a meat feast and sleep in his huts with his wives to annul any lurking curse. However, the husband can forbid his wives consorting with a man who has a bad reputation; and he can complain to his age-set if a particular age mate is having a regular affair with one of his wives. The age-set would first warn the lover and then if necessary punish him; for persistent philandering can provoke husbands and this too would be dangerous for the children. Moderation should be shown on all sides, and the telling criterion would be whether visiting age mates clearly have a good reason for their visit and limit themselves to casual liaisons.

Coveting a wife – either ones own or another man's – is seen as a disloyalty, a threat to the age-set itself in the emotions it can rouse. One elder in the Meto area was criticised because his possessiveness over his four wives had led him to move to a smaller village. It was felt that he spent too much of his time guarding them instead of seeking the company of other men. It was felt to be only a matter of time before his age-set would mobilise to punish him. Another man who was very hospitable in relation to his senior wives was still felt to be too possessive over a more recent favourite wife. His age mates were watching to see whether he would moderate in time. Masiani's generosity and loyalty to his age mates was widely acknowledged; and yet he too was held to betray a streak of jealousy by scorning his senior son, Kinai, whose natural father had been an age mate whom he despised.

THE TRANSFORMATION OF AVOIDANCES IN ELDERHOOD

As a man reaches elderhood, the range of avoidances in relation to different categories of women becomes increasingly complex. When he pays a visit to a village he does not know, he should enquire regarding the huts of his own age mates and clan 'sisters', and also those of 'daughters' and 'mothers-in-law'. This helps him to map out the village in his own mind as an array of expectations and avoidances. The total pattern is summarised in Figure 11, plotting food avoidances against sexual avoidances, and grouping the array into four logical zones, I to IV.

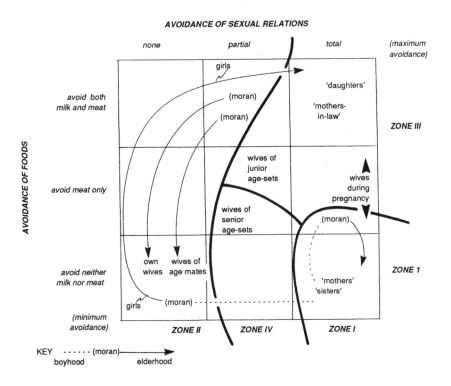

Figure 11   The development of men's food and sex avoidances

Zone I in the lower right-hand corner concerns the close family links with 'mothers' and married 'sisters'. Boys belong to this zone without either sexual involvements or food avoidances. During their period as moran, they avoid meat seen by these women, but after moranhood the relationship is again associated with the close family bonds built up in childhood. When they become elders, they can relax in the huts of these women in relation to food especially, and concern with sexuality is unselfconsciously absent. It would be unnatural, for instance, for an elder to avoid his sister's hospitality since this might imply resentment and his curse as a mother's-brother on her children. He should eat her food and even stay the night with a blessing.

Zone II on the left-hand side of the diagram is the area of legitimate sexual relations, at first between moran and girls and then with their wives. The modification of food avoidances is an especially sensitive issue in this zone, and an admission of approaching elderhood. Moran do not want girls to see them relax their food avoidances (eg. p. 159). As they settle down they increasingly avoid these girls with respect to food and their company. At the same time, they progressively relax their food avoidances with their own wives, and one category of partner is replaced by the other.

At the foot of the diagram, an elder's food avoidances correspond to those on hair shaving. The only women allowed to shave his hair in his village are those whose meat he would be prepared to eat: his own wives, the wives of his age mates, and also at a pinch his mother or a very close sister.

Zone III towards the upper right-hand portion of the diagram has a crucial significance, with the most strongly expressed avoidances extending to the whole age-set. It is primarily associated with the paramount avoidance between fathers and daughters. Other categories of women in this zone can be indirectly related to this relationship. The avoidance, for instance, between a girl and her mother on sexual matters, and between a man and his mother-in-law are extensions to the spouses of father and daughter, maintaining separate spheres of sexual activity. Just as the food avoidance with a 'daughter' may be partially ended with the gift of a heifer, so a woman may make a similar gift to her son-in-law. This will make it easier for her to visit her daughter, especially at times of child-birth. The strict avoidance of intercourse with a pregnant woman could be explained as an attempt to avoid contact between the semen of the father and what might be an embryonic daughter. The punishment for infringing either avoidance is the same (Chapter 11).[8]

Zone IV, ranging over the centre of the diagram, concerns the wives of other age-sets with whom there is partial avoidance. The wives of junior age-sets tend to be more avoided because they are the co-wives and close associates of 'daughters'. This argument is not extended to the wives or widows of senior age-sets, and these are the target for discreet adulterous pursuits. Sexual indiscretions apart, there is a general feeling of unease in relation to food prepared by the wives of other age-sets. Generally elders maintain that wives simply do not have the skill to prepare and cook meat properly. Within their own age-set as they mature, they may concede that their own wives' cooking is not quite as awful as the cooking of wives of other age-sets, and meat prepared by their wives is not altogether avoided except by the most fastidious elders. However, as guests in the huts of other age-sets, even when offered beer and good company to soften their inhibitions, elders express a sense of unease. These huts and these wives do not belong to them, and this is expressed in a feeling that their meat is not quite fit to eat. To this extent, the meat avoidances of moranhood linger as an expression of age-set solidarity.

Each of these zones can be regarded as a sphere of interaction with distinctive characteristics. Boys are first confined to the domestic sphere in Zone 1, and then after initiation, they encounter each of the other zones. The system of relations with and through women takes shape in an array of avoidances that modifies during their transition to elderhood.

CONCLUSION: THE AVOIDANCE OF DAUGHTERS AND THE SYSTEM OF ALLIANCE

The array of relationships between men and various categories of women is riddled with double standards. Men exploit their own wives beyond the limits set by custom. Adultery with the wives of other age-sets is held to be as common among elders who should have developed respect as it is among moran who maintain that they are nauseated by their smell. The sexual avoidance of mothers and close sisters is accepted without question, but the principle is not extended to any marked degree. It is not heinous to seduce the wife of a 'father', but it is still foolish for he has a potent curse. It is not heinous to seduce a distant 'sister', but it is a matter of ridicule which grows stronger with degrees of closeness.

Against this broad leeway for interpretation, the age-set avoidance of 'daughters' on the one hand and 'mothers-in-law' on the other stands out as a monument of precise structuring. These are sensitive restrictions to a degree that simply does not occur in relation to 'mothers' or 'sisters'.

This selective concern over incest leads one to look for some underlying structural pattern. Among the Trobriands, for instance, it is the avoidance of brother-sister incest that Malinowski stressed (1929:448), and this had to be examined in the broader context of Trobriand society. In Matapato and among the Maasai generally, the fundamental avoidance is between father and daughter, and it is linked quite explicitly to the regulation of marriage. Daughters must avoid fathers to be marriageable, and sons-in-law must avoid mothers-in-law as an extension of this.

This leads one to reconsider Lévi-Strauss's analysis of the link between exogamy and the horror of incest. Tylor (1889:267) originally suggested that exogamy is the 'simple practical alternative between marrying-out and being killed out': through intermarriage, society is transformed from the level of fragmented families to a higher level of coexistence with a greater chance of survival. Elaborating on this, Lévi-Strauss (1969:478–85) argued that the system of alliance through wife exchange could be threatened by in-marriage. This led him to suggest that the horror of incest extends beyond the biological family to the culturally defined wife-giving group precisely because it stems from a social rather than a biological incongruity. It is of major concern to public morality because it poses a threat to the foundation of society itself. The immediate point to note is that Maasai clans do not have a strongly corporate nature, nor is there a pronounced concern for avoiding marriage with distant clan 'sisters'; but then nor is incest with 'sisters' a matter of special concern. Lévi-Strauss's model has to be modified to adapt it to the Maasai context where hypersensitivity over incest concerns daughters and the relevant corporate group in this avoidance is the age-set. It is the strict avoidance of each 'daughter' by the age-set of wife-givers and of her mother by the age-set of wife-receivers that structures the system of marriage.

The significant point here is that a daughter is uniquely linked to her father's age-set. She can have only one father, whereas mothers can have sons and sisters can have brothers in two or even three different age-sets. Whence an age-set of 'fathers' can assert exclusive possession over a category of marriageable women – their 'daughters' – in a way that brothers cannot over their 'sisters' or sons over their 'mothers'. This correlates neatly with the absence of a widespread concern over the possibility of incest with either 'mothers' or 'sisters'.

This leads one to coin the term 'age-set exogamy' in relation to marrying 'daughters' out. Clearly, however, age-set 'exogamy' is not a system of exchange between self-perpetuating groups. The age system is self-perpetuating, but the age-sets themselves by definition dissolve into old age and oblivion as new age-sets are generated. The flow of daughters tends inevitably to be towards more junior age-sets (Table 2). This provides a basis from which the more senior age-sets can exercise power over their juniors, demanding respect as potential fathers-in-law with the power to withhold their 'daughters'.

With their strong bonds of friendship and competition for wives, what if age mates were not prohibited from marrying each other's daughters? A system of exchange of daughters *within* the age-set would then be possible. In the spirit of age-set loyalty and sharing, a father could be under irresistible pressure from age mates to give them priority over suitors from other age-sets. To prefer some other suitor could be construed as an act of disloyalty to his own age-set. 'Daughters' would then accrue as wives of the most senior age-sets instead of being handed downwards. Younger men could be starved of wives and of the opportunity to generate daughters of their own. This could even drive them to rebellion against the senior generation for wives, reminiscent of Freud's scenario in *Totem and Taboo*. In fact in northern Uganda, a rebellion of this sort appears to have been characteristic of the periodic change-over of the generational age systems of the Karimojong and related tribes (Spencer 1978b:142–3).

Paraphrasing Tylor, the Maasai are faced with the simple practical alternative between age-sets marrying daughters out (and down) and families dying out. In denying each other 'daughters' as age mates, men are ensuring the succession of their families as fathers. This is consistent with a popular preference for offering daughters to the sons of age mates in the spirit of age-set loyalty: it is the next best thing. Out of the ten marriages that Masiani had arranged for his dependants, for example, eight were with the sons or daughters of age mates. This was perhaps an unusually high proportion, but it was not regarded as excessive. Through being in cohoots with his age-set, he was well placed to maintain a prudent concern for these marriages. As Matapato express it, the girl has a 'father' in her new home to look after her, in the person of her father-in-law.

What at first sight might seem a negative example that throws further doubt on Lévi-Strauss's argument concerning the link between notions of incest and clan exogamy, turns out to be an impressive vindication of it in another respect. This is not to confuse incest avoidance with exogamy or sex with marriage; and the Maasai are least likely to be confused. The way in which the horror of incest is expressed is consistent with the social solidarity of the connubium of age-sets. This entails a type of hypogamy, with the avoided daughters married downwards to younger men, who in order to qualify as eligible suitors are obliged to show respect for their seniors. The double avoidance of 'daughters' and 'mothers-in-law' is the bedrock of social morality in a society where other categories of women tend to be only partially avoided. Or to express this slightly differently, the pride and affection that fathers and daughters have in their exemplary avoidance is also their pride and affection for the age system itself.

So fundamental is this system of exchange in Matapato and so far-reaching the influence of the Maasai in the past, that one is led to note clear evidence of the system elsewhere in the region. A prohibition on marrying age-set 'daughters' is extremely common. It has been reported for the Nandi (Snell 1954:32), Kikuyu (Lambert 1956:66), Kipsigis (Orchardson 1961:76), Arusha (Gulliver 1963:34), Samburu (Spencer 1965:82), Embu (Saberwal 1970:33), Rendille (Spencer 1973:34), Sebei (Goldschmidt 1976:99), Meru (Fadiman 1982:126) and Marakwet (Moore 1986:58). Indeed, one is tempted to suggest that institutionalised handing downwards of daughters is as central to age organisation in this area as generational constraints are to the age systems of their distant northern neighbours, with a shift from a concern for 'alliance' in the south to 'descent' in the north.

NOTES

1 Cf. Spencer 1965:259–60.
2 The sample in Table 1 suggests that in 1977 at their *eunoto*, 16% (14/86)

of the Ngorisho[R] moran had married, and that in Meruturud, about fifteen years after the right-hand and seven years after the left-hand had performed their *eunoto*, this proportion had increased to 79% (84/106). Between these two estimates, Fosbrooke's survey of Kisonko in 1939 suggested that ten years after performing their *eunoto*, only 32% (145/460) of the Terito[R] had married, assuming that the 145 do not include any Terito[L]/Merisho (Fosbrooke 1948:32,45).

3 Unfortunately, it did not occur to me to collect the relevant data for this table when I was in Matapato. Table 2 is based on data collected among the Samburu who have a similar system, though with later first marriages and slightly lower polygyny rates among the most successful men and altogether fewer bachelors among the least successful. It is possible that highly polygynous Maasai Prophets in particular have a larger proportion of fathers-in-law who are actually younger than themselves. The table was concocted by assuming (a) that the Samburu are sufficiently close to the Maasai in all relevant respects, allowing for the slightly longer span of Maasai age-sets on average; (b) that the profile of age differences between fathers and daughters is identical to that between fathers and their sons (for whom I had reasonable data; Spencer 1978b:137); and (c) that women of each age cohort are distributed among husbands of the various age-sets in direct proportion to the distribution of age differences recorded between husbands and wives, excluding marriage with the daughter of an age mate (Spencer 1965:322 aggregating age differences).

4 A mass veto on marriage described previously (p. 178) can only develop *between* age-sets and not between the right- and left-hand sides *within* an age-set, since they cannot marry each other's daughters, and there has to be a realistic accommodation of adultery. Among the three age-sets prior to 1976, the Meruturud were forced jointly to make reparation as an age-set to their predecessors of Nyankusi; and Nyankusi were similarly forced to do this in relation to the Terito age-set. However, Terito[R] had to settle with Dareto alone, since Terito never ran seriously foul of Dareto.

5 At non-ceremonial meat feasts, it is more usual to place the meat on skewers planted in the ground around the fire. This is a quicker, but less thorough method than a barbecue which is always constructed at sacrifices. In addition to the barbecue (*olngesher*), a Maasai elder's stool is another structure supported at each corner, and the *olngesher* village and ceremony are also known as the village-of-the-stools in the northern Maasai tribal sections, such as Purko, because each young elder's stool is blessed by his firestick patrons. A symbolic association between festivals for the moran and the preparation of a meat feast occurs also among the Samburu in their *ilmugit*-of-the-roasting-sticks (*lowatanda* qv. *olngesher*) when the right- and left-hand sides of an age-set are *divided*, and in the *ilmugit*-of-the-smell-of-roasting-meat when morale is at a low ebb (Spencer 1973:90, 93).

6 Premature elders, who were made to 'drink milk' as soon as they became moran, are required again to 'eat meat' shortly before their age mates, and this is performed as a simple family ceremony, similar to 'drinking milk'. Their reunion with their peers at *olngesher* is total and the age-set as a whole is united.

7 The milk avoidance between married sisters and their father's age-set may be relaxed once the oldest sister/daughter has given the heifer-of-milk, and there is no need for further gifts from younger daughters when they too marry. This gift is also known as the heifer-of-the-girls or heifer-of-avoidance (*enturuj*), and may be dispensed with if the father has already died. A woman may relax her avoidance of milk or tea in the presence of her son-in-law by giving him a

heifer, but he is unlikely to want to drink also until she is well beyond child-bearing. This is a matter of embarrassment (*esora*) between them and not of formal avoidance (*enturuj*).

8   This is an inference that was not suggested by Matapato informants, but it does closely parallel their explicit argument that any pregnant woman should avoid the 'sheep of the emergence', because she could be bearing an embryonic male, and all males are at risk from this meat (p. 59). With regard to the extension of this avoidance towards intercourse with all males, it was pointed out to me that for women who had extramarital affairs, any lover could conceivably be the father of the infant. Moreover, the infant's life might be at risk from the husband's anger if he discovers she has been having intercourse with other men. Cf. incidentally, Llewelyn-Davies (1978:226) who stops just short of drawing this inference from similar material gathered among the Loita Maasai.

CHAPTER 11

THE WOMEN'S COLLECTIVE RESPONSE

SUBMISSION TO VIOLENCE

The undisputed right of men to own women as 'possessions' is emphasised by both sexes in Matapato. A girl is brought up to accept that women have a restricted role, and there is no contradiction when in later life she is expected to accept the arbitrary authority of her husband in domestic affairs. For younger wives especially, and ultimately all women, married life is bounded by the threat of violence. From the outset of their marriage, it is the husband who holds the whip-handle, bullying any negligent or defiant wife into submission, rather as he should control a troublesome cow. She is his possession and he would lose respect if he overlooks serious lapses. When the occasion arises he should lash out with a stick before she can run to the sanctuary of another hut and before anyone, even a small child, can intervene on her behalf. If he hesitates he may lose the initiative on this occasion.

The worst outcome for the husband is that his wife might slip out of his control. Once this happens, he should chose his moment for a sound beating carefully. One elder described with graphic frankness how a man should tame a disobedient wife, especially one who appears to continue affairs with moran after being warned. He should lead her to the bush away from the interference of villagers, take off her clothes and ornaments, and tie together her hands and her feet. Then as she lies helpless on the ground, he should whip her with a long switch as thick as his finger, perhaps ten times, or twenty, or thirty, or forty or more. He might have several switches in reserve. He would take care to avoid her breasts, her head and especially her eyes: a blind wife, after all, would be a liability. The point he wished to emphasise was not the sadistic appeal of such a punishment, but that it was intended as a final lesson to her, for all time. Subsequently, a single lash delivered in a moment of anger should be enough to remind her of her place and, he claimed, she would never go to the moran again. On another occasion, a Matapatoi was incredulous when I mentioned that I had been told by the Loitokitok Maasai that they have no traditional bloodwealth payment for women because no woman would ever be killed. He pointed out that any man might accidentally kill his wife when beating her: he had heard of such instances, although he could not recall an actual case.[1]

If a wife has a grievance, she may brew beer for a meeting in her hut and put her case to local elders, especially those her husband should respect. This is a measured response that requires a considerable maturity and confidence. It hardly applies to issues that erupt unexpectedly during the earlier unsettled years of a marriage. A younger wife is more likely to run away on impulse. She may go to one of her husband's age mates or senior kinsmen locally to ask him to intercede, or to a former lover, taking her destiny into her own hands. Or she may run away to her parental home as a natural retreat, especially if she has a deep grievance. At her parents' home, she can only expect their full support if she has been generally maltreated by her husband. If it is felt to be a trivial issue by a recently married daughter, she will be led back with a request that her husband should overlook the matter. He cannot easily refuse this intervention. Occasionally, the unsettled marriage of a high spirited wife is punctuated by episodes of this kind. Both her husband and her father or brothers come to accept ruefully that these outbursts tend to resolve themselves and should subside once she has children that need her constant attention. Where the lapse is more serious or running away becomes an unrestrained habit, then the wife is threatening her own marriage. She is also bringing into question the marriageability of her father's agnatic group. If she then runs back to her own kin, they may seize the opportunity for maintaining their own reputation. Her father is in no position to beat her: he should avoid her and any act that might derange her clothing. He may therefore direct his sons to deliver a beating out in the bush, which is intended to be no less severe or final than a husband's beating.

The following case is illuminating in contrasting the violence that surrounds the relationship between the sexes with a touch of sentimentality and realism for the happiness of the daughter (and sister).

Case 41.
When Talengu ran away from her elderly husband, her father ordered his sons to beat her and escort her back. On the next occasion, she ran to her former moran lover, Kwemeri. Her father ordered her brothers to fetch her, beat her and return her again to her husband. They refused partly because they were Kwemeri's age mates, and also because as children they had been very fond of Talengu and did not relish beating her a second time. The father is then said to have taken the unusual step of beating his own daughter and returning her to her husband himself. He argued that this was a more humane measure than cursing

her and risking her life. She then ran away to live among the Keekonyukie Maasai, and the father again went to fetch her back and almost strangled her in the effort. At her parents' home, she vowed to him that she would never go back to her husband; she would continue to run away, or be killed by the beatings. Her brothers and mother then connived with Kwemeri to subvert her marriage ritually, while she was still less than a wife in the fullest sense, and before she was returned to her husband. Kwemeri secretly drove the formal bridewealth into her father's corral at night, precipitating the final marriage ceremony by fait accompli (p. 30). At this point, the father let the matter rest. He could not be accused of disregarding the reputation of his agnatic group, and he too was fond of Talengu, who had been a loyal and dutiful daughter before her marriage. Kwemeri was ordered to settle the marriage debt of the first marriage in full and to pay a heavy additional payment to discourage other young men that might be tempted to interfere with the marriage plans of elders. Talengu had already paid her own heavy price.

THE WOMEN'S FERTILITY GATHERING

The importance of fertility to women has to be viewed against the backcloth of this regime to which they are subjected by older men. Children give them hope for a less restricted future. Moreover, because their fertility is seen as a vital force that links women uniquely to God, it provides them with an inviolate arena when they act collectively. It is a means to defend their position, hedged with its own ritualised form of violence.

Women's songs on most festive occasions include prayers for children, coupled with sexual obscenities and taunts against men in general: as husbands who maltreat their wives, fathers who abuse their daughters, and lechers who bring trouble. Their prayers, dances and mockery complement the more comprehensive and calculated involvement of the elders in ritual. These women's activities are proper to the occasion; it always has been this way, they say. It could be a bad omen if there were no women's dancing at an initiation or other popular ceremony. The abuse of women individually is accepted as a fact of every day existence, and their collective counter-abuse has a sanctity of its own. It is unanswerable.

During any good wet season, when there is plenty of milk and less work to be done, a women's gathering may develop into a festivity in its own right. They may band together in small groups praying for children, dancing, processing from village to village, recruiting further wives, and building up their number into a substantial gathering. The general term for such a gathering employs a very apt metaphor 'that which is heavy' (*oloiroishi*), as when a woman is pregnant, and with a similar coercive gravity (p. 40). Through their prayers they bear the promise of future life for the community as a whole and must be respected. In large homesteads, some wives may join the gathering while others remain at home. Those that are less free may remain away or join the gathering for only a few days; and those that are still ritually confined after giving birth must return to their own villages each evening. As a body they are self-governing and plan their tour round the countryside for themselves.

Drawing on the weight of their coercion, small delegations of dancing women are sent to the villages of rich or popular elders. These elders should offer them food and (today) money in return for the women's blessing – or they put their own wives and children at risk if they refuse. The money is shared to buy new cloths and ornaments, and poorer women especially are given generous portions, to emphasise the gathering's universal ideal. Normally, this is treated as a festive occasion and it was in this spirit that Masiani described how he had welcomed a visit of this kind. 'They came to all our villages and elders would only give them ten shillings. When they came to my village, I gave them thirty shillings and told them that rich men should give them more: "Make them all give you thirty shillings – and thirty and thirty. Go to my own age mates and tell them that Lechieni [Masiani] has given thirty shillings and that they should not bring ruin on themselves." Aha, the women liked me for that. They liked me and blessed me and danced in my village. I collected all the milk there was and gave it to them to drink together with the thirty shillings. And they went away.'

Those husbands who beat their wives at this particular time or prevent any of them from joining the gathering, are harried. If the women hear of such an elder, they will storm his village dealing tit for tat. If he has beaten his wife, they will want to beat him and seize some of his best cattle. If he has tried to detain any wife, they will snatch away all his wives, and leave him to feed the children, milk the cows, and fetch wood and water. No other woman – and certainly no man – would help him. This is a severe degradation, and it is held to be dangerously unpropititious for elders to undertake such tasks.

Elders that have bullied their wives at other times are not normally singled out for punishment in this way. However, the notoriety of women's gatherings is that for once the initiative slips from the elders, and no-one can be quite certain how the women will interpret their rights or how far they will take their licence. This casts a different slant on Masiani's enthusiasm for the women's cause. His cavalier treatment of his own wives was such that he had as much reason as any other elder to be apprehensive of the women's gathering. (Qv. Case 18 where he moderated his behaviour towards moran when confronted by a posse.)

Descriptions of these gatherings give a striking impression of mounting hysteria over their fertility. The gathering of women and their shared anxiety feed on one another and the rumour spreads that they are somehow threatened. Barren women especially are said to be agitated, breaking down in tears, shivering, shaking and even fainting; and their apprehensiveness spreads to other women. It is believed that any encounter in the bush with a man provides them with a better than normal chance of pregnancy, and men keep a very respectful distance at these times. To be caught by a gathering of rampaging women is to risk manhandling, stripping and rape. 'Daughters' of the victim, pregnant women and confined mothers would avoid such a scene. All other women are held to be desperate for their next baby.

The women's fertility gathering is in some ways dangerously out of control, and yet it is sanctified like fertility itself, bringing women closer to God. From a safe distance, elders accept it philosophically as an outburst that should be allowed to run its course. The notion that it brings the blessing of fertility from which they all gain may be seen as a symbolic and face-saving expression of this insight. For a brief period during favourable conditions, the normal social order is upturned and women take over a domain that lies outside the normal bounds of village existence.

Once the gathering loses momentum, the initiative returns to the elders who alone are held to understand how to settle the powerful ritual forces that the women have stirred up. The whole episode should be brought to an end with an elders' blessing. In the course of their gathering, women choose some particularly propitious man to provide the feast for this blessing which is shared by other elders. He provides the ox-that-smears-the-women for the feast, and its rib-fat mixed with red ochre is smeared on the women's necks and shoulders. There is a rather obvious sexual symbolism in this blessing. The initiative returns to the elders, whose 'hot' spittle in the blessing is thought to bring fertility to the women (cf. p. 49). Those that are pregnant should stay away, just as they should avoid intercourse or they risk miscarriage.

The women then disperse to their homes immediately after the blessing. Their return is not quite unconditional, and the tit for tat spirit lingers. If one of their number returns home and is beaten by her husband for deserting him to join the gathering, the wives may reconvene to mob him. They slaughter his favourite ox and even snatch away his wives, leaving him to fend for himself and his children, while they again start to dance.

RITUALS OF REBELLION AND OF PROTEST AMONG WOMEN

It is useful to compare two explanations put forward by other anthropologists for gatherings of this kind. Max Gluckman coined the term 'rituals of rebellion' in his analysis of women's seasonal reversals of behaviour among the Zulu and commonly reported elsewhere in Africa. The Zulu were a society in which women were normally subservient to men, he argued, and in the easier period following months of hunger and drought, there was a natural outburst of pent-up energy. Suppressed rivalries had to be given free rein to reinvigorate society and sustain the sexual *status quo* (Gluckman 1963:112–8). Rituals of rebellion are thus presented as seasonal spasms that maintain stability, reflected in the popular belief that they bring good fortune to society generally and not just to the women. In his analysis of similar women's dances among the Gogo, just to the south of the Maasai, Peter Rigby shifts the focus from sexual inequality to the notion of ritual contamination affecting women's fertility that can be 'danced away' (Rigby 1969:159).

At first sight, the Matapato women's gathering is closer to the Gogo, where the women also sense a threat to their fertility, and where the element of violence and obscenity appears to have been more pronounced than among the Zulu. On the other hand, whereas Rigby insisted that the status of Gogo women is equivalent to that of men, among the Matapato they are clearly subordinate, and in this respect the Matapato are similar to the Zulu. The question therefore arises: can the Matapato women's gathering be more aptly regarded as a 'ritual of rebellion' (following Gluckman) in which the frustrations of male domination are danced off? Or should it be regarded as a 'ritual of purification' (following Rigby) in which their reversal of behaviour is an attempt to reverse misfortune, to dance it away?

Here I would question Rigby's argument that the two explanations are incompatible, and suggest that among the Matapato at least they have a close bearing on one another. The intriguing feature is the conditions under which a rumour of misfortune spreads, threatening the one affliction that all Maasai women dread, typically at the height of the wet season when food is abundant. This is a season that brings a whole range of disturbances after months of drought and hunger (cf. Gluckman 1963:131–2). The expected reaction is one of relief; but there is also a restlessness, a surplus of nervous energy that even affects the cattle: a month at the height of the wet season around March or April is known as the time when 'the bulls are tied up' – to prevent them fighting and frisking the herd (*oenioingok* cf. Hollis 1905:334). It is as if life is disoriented by the sudden change of circumstance, instead of adjusting smoothly. Unlike the dry season, which builds up slowly and relentlessly and gives Matapato time to adjust themselves mentally and physically, the onset of the wet season has an immediate impact. The herds require less intensive management, water is readily available, the food supplies are assured, and options open out for migration. As elders turn their attention from the rigours of economic survival to broader issues, they are freer to make journeys they have planned for months. They visit close friends, call in cattle debts, broke marriages, and so on. The moran too are expected to display themselves and fulfil their traditional role as defenders of the herds. For stock raids can be expected in this season if at all, when cattle are in their prime and rain can obliterate the tracks of the raiders. With this change in tempo, however, no new options open out for the women, and they remain subservient. They may become more aware of their vulnerable position, and more sensitive to the matter of the elders' cavalier schemings elsewhere at this time. These concern redeployments of the household, daughters to be married away, brides to be brought in, and give and take in cattle, all without consulting any wives. The gulf of inequality that divides husbands and wives seems to widen. During the dry season with the survival of the family and herd at stake, at least there is a spirit of cooperation; but this spirit does not appear to carry over to the easier times of the wet season. It is at this time especially, I suggest, that the women have good reason to experience a sense of isolation and resentment and to become unusually aware that their fertility is their most precious asset. Any rumour of a threat to their reproductive powers may well be fed by their anxieties at this time. It is even seen to threaten the future of those with children, who need to reassure themselves of their condition by bearing yet more children.

If this is to be explained at a symbolic level, the credibility of the rumour seems to indicate a loss of confidence among women in their domestic status. Within each household this loss of confidence may appear at first as an idiosyncratic domestic issue. Repeated over a whole area at this time, and a sense of crisis gathers momentum. It seems to reflect the breakdown of normal communication between the sexes and a widening of the gulf that separates them generally. The rumour appears as an apt expression of this crisis, raising the whole issue to a metaphysical plane. The loss of role among women is offset by their growing awareness that they share a common condition. As they begin to unite, their unity gives them the potential to recover from their inertia and to assert their rightful role as the reproducers of Matapato society. The process of revival among women appears to be linked to reviving their confidence in their own fertility. From their situation of semi-isolation and domestic discord, the gathering brings large numbers of women together where in militant mood they act in concord. Their awakened consciousness at a super-domestic level, their notion of a direct contact with God, and the widespread respect they acquire from the elders, seem to revive their flagging spirits. It gives them a renewed confidence for re-establishing themselves with greater self-respect within their own households. Ritual reversal and a notion of impending ill-fortune (Rigby) may thus be linked to ritual rebellion in a system of oppression (Gluckman). Through a ritualised expostulation, a slump in morale among women is reversed. It is not just the women who are purified, as Rigby suggests, but the whole atmosphere in this reassertion of the importance of womanhood. Their gathering has a brief reality of its own, which readjusts the balance of power between the sexes, and is seen to bring with it a diffuse blessing that ensures the birth of future generations.

THE WOMEN'S MOBBING AND THE ABUSE OF THEIR FERTILITY

When a women's fertility gathering erupts in violence because of the opposition of some elder, there is an underlying fury. There are two other occasions that may go a step further and lead to a mass mobbing. The first may follow a miscarriage or stillbirth, which are assumed to have been caused by wanton intercourse during the tabooed pregnancy period. A single early miscarriage would normally pass without serious comment. Gossip and resentment mount if a woman has a series of miscarriages, especially during the later months of pregnancy, or if she is known to have maintained sexual relations during this period. It is this sort of flagrant abuse of her reproductive powers amounting to infanticide that provokes other women to act as a mob. She has flouted a gift of God, and other women must bring her to her senses in a punitive act of atonement. This also dissipates their anger and is held to remove the possible threat to their fertility.

When there has been a serious miscarriage, word passes from village to village among women. They cry to one another (*a-ishiru*) and as their anger wells up, so does the urge for a mobbing (*ol-kishiroto*). It is more than just a Matapato issue: it is a threat against all women and even non-Matapato women living in the area may join the others. Each woman cuts for herself a stick and at dawn while the cattle are still corralled, the mob descend on the victim's village. They seize her, beat her with their sticks, and wreck her hut. She is stripped to the waist, and a chunk of flesh is sliced from her brow. The mob will also seize one of her husband's finest oxen, and beat it with their maternity belts. This ox is then slaughtered by some elder to provide a feast. Its intestines are draped around the victim's neck, and she is driven from the village with her own blood and the animal's chyme spilling down her body. If the husband has not run away or at least persuaded the mob that he is wholly innocent, they will seize him also and beat him. If he escapes, they may turn round his thorn barricade so that the inside faces the bush; and he has to contend with the possibility of sorcery associated with this act. Finally, with their anger abated after the feast, the women should leave their sticks under a non-thorny ('cold') tree and disperse in peace. The episode and the anger are at an end, but the damage to the victim's reputation lingers and she carries the white scar on her brow for life. Women in Masiani's village pointed out a former victim who had suffered a series of miscarriages during a prolonged affair with a lover. When the mob raided her village, her husband persuaded them of his own innocence and they had let him volunteer and slaughter an ox of his own choosing. Several other victims in the Meto area could also be readily identified by their scars.

Less common and altogether more notorious is the mobbing of an elder who has abused a 'daughter'. He can have no excuse and any intercourse between them would be construed as rape. Again, there are shades of abuse.

Case 42

(a) In Meto, a habitual drunkard had started to show unbecoming familiarity with a 'daughter' of his age-set, pawing at her arm or her body on several occasions. At first this had led to uncertain speculation. Then all his 'daughters' began to regard him with contempt and no longer greeted him with bowed heads, but avoided him altogether. His age mates of Nyankusi warned him, but took no further action for this was a matter for Meto women. It was felt to be only a question of time before they would collect together for a mobbing, intent on slaughtering his cattle and beating the culprit himself if they could.

(b) In another instance, an elder of Terito age-set was assumed by the women to have seduced his own daughter. This was construed as rape, although he was widely believed among elders to be the victim of malicious gossip and entirely innocent. When he heard that the women were gathering to mob him, he was not tempted to argue his innocence, but fled to another locality. He later returned discreetly to lead his family in migration to Loodokilani before the women had time to remobilise

(c) Legena was less prudent. He was accused of raping a 'daughter' of his age-set in the central corral of a village. Everyone in the locality was outraged, but his age mates argued that this was a matter to be settled by the women and took no action. The women gathered together in a mounting fury. When they appeared at Legena's village, other men fled, but Legena himself was determined to stop them killing his favourite ox and tried to hold them at bay. They seized him, hit his head, tore off his earrings severing his lobes, pounded his back, pulled his legs apart and stamped on his genitals. They then seized, slaughtered and cooked the ox themselves since no elder would venture near to undertake the task. Legena lived for another 30 years, but he was maimed for life.

This last example has become a local tale of horror in which the initial outrage almost palls beside the fate of the victim. In Matapato terms it was not just the attack on his genitals that made other elders wince, but also the attack on his head and earlobes and by women, since these parts are inviolable among elders. The story testifies that when women are mobilised for a purpose, nothing is inviolable. The women's mobbing more generally rattles the elders' sense of decorum, reinforcing their view that as possessions wives are sometimes dangerously out of control, and as a species women are incomprehensible.

It is revealing that a women's mobbing normally relies on a local elder to slaughter and cook their ox. The popular explanation is that women do not have the strength or knowledge to do this for themselves. Yet it is clear that they are quite capable. One woman conveyed the spirit of piquish independence when she claimed that the women in their fury may slaughter several animals themselves, taking what cuts they want and leaving the remainder of the carcases to rot. An elder also reflected this when he claimed that women's mobs abandon all respect, taking for themselves the most revered elders' cuts, and he would take no part in such a feast. Even so, a prescribed part of the normal women's mobbing is that an elder should act as butcher and cook after the women have selected their ox. Other elders have their prescribed cuts which they eat away from the village. This sharing in the feast – at a distance – lends it a legitimacy in its final phase. Like a women's fertility gathering, it culminates with a feast provided by the elders in which both sexes share.

CONCLUSION: WOMEN AS CUSTODIANS OF THE MORAL ORDER

As in women's rituals of rebellion elsewhere in Africa, those in Matapato have features associated with warriorhood. The women's fertility gathering has some clear parallels with boys gathering together for their dancing festival before circumcision. Both gatherings dance from village to village recruiting members from ambivalent husbands or fathers. Both gatherings lead up to a feast prepared by the elders, who then pronounce their blessing. The link is further established by encouraging barren women to crouch among the boys in the final blessing by the firestick patrons (p. 70). Similarly in the past, the moran are said to have recruited for a raid by coercion as they danced from village to village. This culminated in a feast and blessing by the elders in which they smeared their bodies with the rib-fat, as the women do at the end of their gathering.

When they are gathering together, however, the women do not identify themselves with boys or ordinary moran. In their songs as viragos, they assert their independence by comparing themselves with diehards. They scorn the opposite sex, warning men to keep away, and naming their potential victims who are thought to have cohabited with pregnant women. Arming themselves with sticks, they make sorties to selected villages with demands for food and gifts as the diehards did.[2] Beyond the notoriety of the women's gathering is their mobbing. When they muster together as a punitive force, then like the diehards they are unstoppable and no sensible man would attempt to stand in their path.

There is an intriguing complementarity between virago wives and diehards. The diehards' supreme aim was to ensure that Matapato were supplied with cattle, while the women's gatherings are oriented towards the supply of children. The symbiotic relationship between humans and stock is reflected symbolically in linking the ideal of virile manhood with the ideal of fertile womanhood. The analogy also brings out very clearly the obsession that women have with their fertility that matches the obsession of the diehards in popular belief. Women proclaim themselves prepared to face the dangers of childbirth with a similar fortitude. Thus virago wives : diehards :: children : cattle

The parallel between the conditions of women and those of moranhood can be explored by comparing Figure 8b with Figure 12.

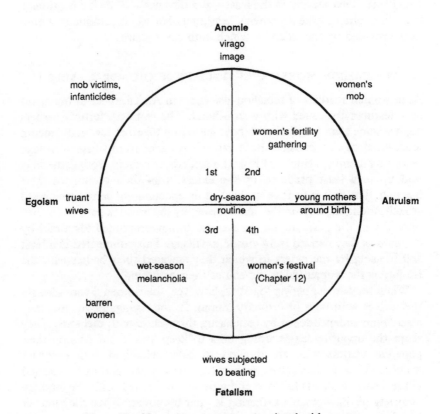

Figure 12   Matapato stereotypes associated with women

The women's mobbing is more than simply an outlet for pent-up feelings. At a deeper level of analysis, it plays a strategic role in the age system with reference to the handing down of 'daughters'. It was suggested in Chapter 10 that the close bonds between age mates are dangerously exclusive and their avoidance of their 'daughters' is critical for the age system. Marrying these 'daughters' to younger men underseals the respect that develops between age-sets and the domestication of the moran. In this way, the avoidance of 'daughters' provides a bedrock of social morality on which the age system as the principal edifice of Maasai society is founded. This extends to the other avoidances associated with Zone III of Figure 11: pregnant wives who may well be carrying embryonic daughters, and 'mothers-in-law' who as wives of the wife-givers are the converse of 'daughters'.

In this model, women are pawns in a system of exchange controlled by the older men. In the context of their mobbing, however, the women have the final word. They assert themselves primarily as the custodians of these sexual avoidances associated with 'daughters' on the one hand and pregnant women on the other, and above all with their own fertility. Women are not concerned in this way with other male abuses and they do not, for instance, mob all rapists, but only men who have abused their 'daughters'. Other rapings are the concern of the husband supported by his age-set or of the moran protector. Similarly, women do not punish all husbands who maltreat their wives, but only those who do so at the time of their fertility gathering. The women collectively have their own domain that the elders must respect. When some abuse is clearly the concern of a women's mob, as in Case 42, the elders stand to one side.

The women's mobbing, then, is more than just a wild and unstructured outburst. It provides a cornerstone to the moral foundation of the Maasai age system, which depends on the sanctity of 'daughters'. In the first instance, the women are mere pawns of the system, and certainly as 'daughters' or young wives, they are hardly more than this. However, as mature viragos with an increasing stake in the system, they defend it collectively and provide a formidable force for maintaining the status quo. Overtly, this expresses a concern for fertility and for the perpetuation of the Maasai as a people. In its effect, however, it helps perpetuate the Maasai as an age system. Women's gatherings and mobbings may be regarded as rituals of rebellion. Yet paradoxically in the final analysis, it can be claimed that it is women as an angry mob rather than elders in their harangues who are the ultimate custodians of the morality underpinning the system.

NOTES

1 The Matapato tradition is that the bulk of a murdered woman's bloodwealth (twenty-nine cattle as against forty-nine for a man) should be paid to her possessor: to her father when she is young and then to her husband after she has been led with cattle. If the husband happens to kill her himself after this point, then he bears full moral responsibility as a homicide for what he has done, and there is no bloodwealth payment, for it could only be to himself.
2 The Matapato term for diehards (*iloontorosi*) is incidentally the Samburu term for the women's gathering (*ntorosi*) (Spencer 1965:228, 1984:158–9).

CHAPTER 12

AGE BONDS AND RITUAL POWER IN ELDERHOOD

When elders are involved in a blessing for women or in some other community issue, it is as a body without regard for age-set affiliation. Yet significantly in the traditional system, the only control that a local community has over any individual elder is through his age-set, represented by those living in the area. If one age-set locally does not concur on some issue, there can be no consensus within the community. It is an elder's local age mates, for instance, who can summon him to attend a discussion or to account for himself in some way. Only they can censure him if he has disobeyed their wishes without good reason. On any occasion when a simple request is made by an age mate, it cannot easily be refused, and when an elder is formally approached on behalf of a group of age mates, he would not be expected to dare to refuse. This sense of respect for age mates is cultivated during their time at the manyata, and submission to the will of the age-set among elders is axiomatic. A firmly held view among certain men may switch radically as a result of consensus reached at a local discussion. It is loyalty to the principle of unity that is unswerving, and there is no loss of face if this overrides a personal view on some lesser principle. When they say they 'dare not' refuse or disobey on some issue, it is a pledge of this loyalty to the age-set. They accept unquestioningly the age-set's view of the good of the community at large.

THE AGE-SET POSSE IN ELDERHOOD

With the performance of the *olngesher* ceremony, the transition to elderhood is ceremonially complete. However, a certain spirit of youthfulness may linger, and faced with any situation that demands joint action or even individual courage, elders still pride themselves in responding positively. This is well illustrated in the continued use of the posse as a mode of age-set coercion in preference to their curse. Used as a punishment this is comparable to the women's mobbing and sometimes it is given the same name (*olkishiroto*), although it is more usually known as *esoogo*. Among moran, the standard response against those that have infringed their food restrictions or manyata discipline, is to mount a posse to seize a fine ox for a feast. This is regarded as a particularly apt form of punishment. The victim learns a harsh lesson, and is then reincorporated fully into his age-group as the provider of a feast. Only if this fails to cultivate respect will they resort to a beating, as in Case 40.

Among elders, *esoogo* has some ritual elaboration and is a preferred form of punishment against an age mate who has placed self-interest above his age-set obligations. Once the decision has been taken to inflict this punishment, the victim's age mates muster to raid his herd at dawn, yelping as they rush his village, prepared to overcome any resistance. They formally claim one fat ox for immediate slaughter and eight heifers to be dispersed among the age-set. At this point, others living locally may come to plead on his behalf. One heifer may be returned to him out of respect for the women, and one for each of the age-sets of elders who plead. Typically five or six animals may be returned altogether, depending on the seriousness of the offence and on the grace with which he accepts his punishment. The victim is then blessed after the meat feast by smearing him with the brisket-fat, and a slitted strip of the brisket hide is placed around his neck. The confiscated cattle may be given to prominent members of the age-set, such as the ritual leaders or spokesmen, or they may be set aside for the Prophet's next consultation payment.

Sometimes, an elder knows that a posse of his age-set are coming to punish him. When he hears their yelps in the distance, he may drive a fine ox outside the village to forestall them and slaughter it himself. This is a gesture to the raiding party to accept the meat feast as a gift in the hope that they will not then confiscate further cattle. For a lesser offence this might be acceptable. However, if he has been mean in sharing food, then they will be generous in disposing of his stock and may even slaughter a second fine ox. If he has been covetous with his wives, then they will again be generous both with his stock, and on this occasion with his wives also, asserting their sexual rights as his age mates. *Esoogo* is also the age-set response to members who fight and draw blood once they have 'drunk milk'. Both antagonists must submit to this punishment separately, even if the fight was unprovoked or the blood letting was quite accidental. It is argued that even an innocent party is too closely involved with this breach of age-set unity, and the automatic effect of the incident is to place an age-set curse on both men. The meat feast and blessing of the *esoogo* dissipates their anger and removes any curse. An elder who has been dogged by misfortune may even be advised by his age-set to provide an ox feast similar to *esoogo*. This clinches their blessing and removes even the remote possibility of some lingering curse.

The colourfulness of Masiani's account of his own life is that he never quite mastered the impetuous spirit of moranhood that led him into trouble with his age-set. He was forced to pay *esoogo* on two separate occasions, which even he regarded as excessive.

Case 43
(a) After Masiani's age-group (Terito[R]) had handed on the privileges of moranhood to their successors, a considerable number of them migrated towards the lowland regions of Loodokilani to build up their flocks of small stock. Those that remained sensed that their age-group was fragmenting. After meeting to discuss the problem, they sent a messenger to order the migrants to go no further. Four or five of them, including Masiani, took no notice. Posses were then sent out to inflict *esoogo* punishments and to confiscate more cattle than they could readily afford. It was made clear to Masiani that in ignoring the messenger, he had defied his whole age-group, and that his past loyalty to them did not mitigate this offence.
(b) About 25 years later, when Masiani was in his fifties, he was involved in a drunken brawl with an age mate. He claimed to be the innocent victim of an attack, but it was he himself who had drawn blood in self-defence. His description of his own feelings as he heard the yelps of the posse coming to seize his cattle indicated how keenly he felt this punishment. He had always been loyal to his age-set, but still his initial impulse was to go out to shoot at them with his bow as they came for his cattle. The restraining hand of a friend by his side prevailed, and he put down his bow.

A posse, which is used in the first instance to recruit for the manyata, may be used subsequently whenever an age-set prepares to build a festival village – also known as a 'manyata'. The victims on these occasions are not reluctant fathers or mothers, but any of their own age mates who show reluctance to be involved and their senior wives.

Case 44
(a) Masiani's son, Kinai, had been denied a manyata moranhood so that he could continue herding in Loodokilani with only infrequent visits to his manyata at Meto (Case 16). After the family had been evicted from Loodokilani (Case 22), Kinai devoted his attention to herding in a remote border area, and remained aloof from the affairs of his age-group, Nyan-kusi[L]. He was absent when they met together to select those who should migrate first as hosts to set up their *olngesher* village. Having just married his second wife, he felt he was too busy to become involved in the minutiae of planning for a ceremony that did not even interest him. Kinai was censured in his absence, and to draw him more closely into their affairs, he was nominated as one of the hosts. He was not informed of the decision. Instead, a party of his age-group were mustered as a posse, rather as moran recruiting for the manyata, and they raided his village at dawn. They seized some of his cattle and forced his senior wife to pack her domestic belongings on a donkey and led her to build her hut at the *olngesher* camp. Kinai had been absent at the time. When he returned and learned of the incident, he followed meekly to join in the preparations for the ceremony (Case 38 follows).
(b) About 10 years later, Kinai's fortunes had altered (Case 1). The family herds

had been depleted by drought, his first wife had died in childbirth leaving him with a large number of small sons, and he started to drink heavily, which he could not afford in any case. In a matter of months his whole outlook changed and even his devotion to his herds and ultimately to his own family faltered.

Misfortune had been widespread and Nyankusi age-set were advised by their Prophet to try to reverse this through a festival of sacrifice. Also their patrons of Dareto age-set were dwindling rapidly, and this was perhaps their last chance to host them in this way and solicit their blessing at the sacrifice. Again Kinai was selected to act as host, leading his surviving wife. On this occasion, it was with sympathy rather than irritation and there was no need for a posse. A delegation of his age mates visited him to inform him of the arrangements to be made, and he complied with considerable enthusiasm, emphasising his loyalty to his age-set and minimising the inconvenience. Co-opting him was a gesture that emphasised their need for unity and compassion within the age-set in a revival of confidence.

THE RITUAL DELEGATION AND THE POSSE

The ritual delegation (*olamal*) provides a more conventional method of age-set coercion, stressing the bond that unites an age-set. Its members are unarmed and similar in some ways to ritual dependants. They must be given hospitality, they must not be involved in controversy of any kind, and they are confined to villages overnight while the cattle are at home. A ritual delegation is selected for a purpose. On one occasion this might be to prepare for a festival, perhaps soliciting cattle for the Prophet. On another occasion it might be to persuade an embittered age mate to withdraw his veto on the marriage of a 'daughter' and accept compensation. Either way, the request to give or to accept the cattle should not be refused. As with the women's fertility gathering, the delegation are 'heavy', or better 'pregnant' (*e-iroishi*), with all that this implies for bearing something close to God. There is a gravity, a hidden power that must be respected. They speak for the age-set.

The powers of moral coercion of an unarmed ritual delegation contrast with the physical powers of the armed posse, rather as the concept of elderhood contrasts with moranhood, as women's fertility gatherings contrast with their mobbings, and as the *emosiroi* dance contrasts with the lion dance. They represent two types of coercion associated with contrasting moods. The sheer muscle and angry determination of a posse have the appearance of being the more draconic measure, but Matapato stress that there is no malice or aftermath. The posse get their own way, and that is that. The ritual delegation go beyond mere requisition and the possibility of their curse is invidious if their anger is aroused.

Moran also are obliged to mount ritual delegations in their routine preparations for *eunoto*, and this is a distinct step towards elderhood. However, they still prefer to resort to physical force when they are crossed rather than invoke an age-set curse, which is quite alien to moranhood.

Case 45.

A ritual delegation of Meruturud[R] moran was formed to collect cattle for the Prophet's fee for their *eunoto*. Wearing short ceremonial capes and carrying only staves, they were obliged to avoid all controversial situations and to proceed in peace. One of their number, Sayianka, was generally disgruntled and argued persistently with his companions. The more they tried to restrain themselves, the more provocative he became. Eventually they decided to give vent to their welling anger physically. The more outraged members wanted to flog him without further discussion, but others urged a more disciplined punishment. They set aside their ritual regalia and four moran seized Sayianka and beat his back, buttocks and thighs with sticks, avoiding his head and front. As they let him go, he stumbled into four more moran who repeated this treatment, until he ran off. The delegation then recomposed themselves and continued without him in peace.

The moran on this occasion had no brief on the way to cope with such a situation. They balked at any resort to their curse, which as young men they did not understand and could not control. The elders thoroughly approved of their response: intuitively, they had made the right decision. Having resorted to physical punishment there could be no possibility of bitterness or a lingering threat of misfortune.

Even when elders find their path crossed on a ritual delegation, they may be reluctant to curse, preferring the more wholesome resort to naked force.

Case 46.

A ritual delegation of elders of Nyankusi age-set visited selected age mates to collect together a herd of cattle for the Prophet in return for advice before a sacrifice. They were frustrated by the repeated appeals for dispensation by these age mates, who pleaded hardship. Having shown compassion to a few, the delegation lost credibility as a coercive force, and others turned their coercion against them with similar appeals. They were now faced with a threat to the authority of the age-set, but had no wish to inflict a damaging curse. They therefore decided to lay aside their ritual regalia and to reconvene as an armed posse. They then confiscated the cattle they needed from age mates by force rather than by threat, in a series of raids and without consultation.

In these cases, as in the women's fertility gathering, the interplay between physical and moral coercion is seen to respond to the context. Within an age-set, the armed posse, like the *esoogo* punishment, evokes the incisive spirit of moranhood while the ritual delegation invokes a higher domain of authority that elders alone know how to control. It is this higher domain that elders must invoke in their dealings with other age-sets and ultimately in any bid for power within Matapato as a whole.

THE FIRESTICK PATRONS AND THE CLAIM TO 'RULE'

Once the manyat are disbanded after *eunoto*, the three spokesmen are no longer under the same intensive constraint to lead their age-group. When two age-groups in turn are amalgamated into an age-set after their *olngesher*, the six spokesmen have no unique authority. Their role is maintained, however, until the *olngesher* of their firestick wards about thirty years later. During this period, these spokesmen may be replaced by new men who emerge as more adept in sensing which way the local breezes of opinion are blowing. The most influential elders are those who brief themselves before any local discussion and win the confidence of their age mates. The metaphor of moranhood persists, and in addition to spokesmen, those who hold sway are known as the 'feathers' or advocates. Advocates are not formally appointed; they have a mandate that is retained for as long as they are seen to fulfil the role. When any perceptive elder is approached by a group of age mates, asking him to be their advocate on some issue, he may be reassured by their trust in him. At the same time, he 'dare not refuse', and he confirms his position through his performance in debate. It is not just a matter of trust to be asked, but also a matter of obligation to respond. The claim among elders that it is the advocates who 'rule' the country, draws attention to the extent to which age mates rally behind such men. Together, they unceremoniously by-pass any traditional spokesmen or government appointees who do not have this popular trust. The future of a spokesman or advocate who is appointed to any official position depends on his ability to cultivate trust as an advocate among advocates.

Very broadly, the period when the elders of an age-set are in their political prime corresponds to the span of about fifteen years when the privileges of moranhood are claimed by their firestick wards in their physical prime (as right and left age-groups). During this period, their firestick alliance is pre-eminent at both levels. They eclipse the other firestick alliance: the older men who have been superseded and the younger men who still aspire. Nowadays with local government positions to be filled, firestick patrons of this age are the most suitable candidates for appointment. More than this, they claim a right to these appointments as the age-set who 'rule the country', coining the phrase used by the moran who 'rule' among younger men in a physical sense (p. 86). In Matapato, there is an element of rhetoric in this claim since each firestick alliance is wholly autonomous. It appears to be a recent innovation, but certainly the willingness of the administration to accept that there is one 'ruling' age-set in principle for new appointments lends considerable prestige. To this extent, the claim 'to rule' has acquired a new meaning and has become a self-fulfilling reality.

The topic of formal administration in the area is beyond the scope of this work. However, it is worth noting that the claim over government appointments as a privilege of the 'ruling' age-set serves to bridge the gulf between the government sector and the traditional system. It reduces the ambivalence of these appointments, for in the face of criticism from other age-sets on controversial issues, the 'ruling' age-set are more likely to share some of the dilemma of those representing them. As they rally behind these men, they are well placed to perceive the external realities. To this extent, if no more, the position of such men bears a certain resemblance to the strength and accountability of the spokesmen in the traditional Maasai system. This may be regarded as one of the strengths of what is often a much criticised system in the modern era.

During the period of fieldwork, it was Nyankusi age-set who organised the ceremonial advancement of the moran as their firestick patrons. They dominated community affairs, and held virtually all administrative appointments. About eight years previously, Terito age-set had monopolised this position, but Nyankusi were poised to challenge them for control.

Case 47.
In about 1969, the elders of Terito enjoyed considerable prestige in Matapato. They could claim to have excelled as moran to a fuller extent than their successors. Now as elders, one of their former moran spokesmen, Koileken, had become a particularly effective government chief, and they maintained a firm control over their wards, the high-spirited Meruturud ^{L} (Cases 22 and 34). Then a series of cattle thefts by the Dalalekutuk Maasai to their north provoked these moran. Against the wishes of both administration and their patrons, they retaliated in a concerted raid to restore their prestige as the traditional defenders of Matapato herds. Their Terito patrons had now lost temporary control over them, and this provided a pretext for a campaign mounted by a clique of younger elders of the next age-set (from Nyankusi^L) against the Terito. They argued to both the administration at Kajiado and to the Matapato elders at large that it was time for the Terito to 'lie down'. Younger literate men who were more active and closer to modern trends should take over responsibility. In other circumstances, the Terito elders might have stood up to this challenge to their authority. However, having lost the initiative locally and the sympathy of the administration, they lost the will to fight. Their time was running short and they regarded the impropriety of this campaign as distasteful. In relation to administrative appointments, they agreed that Nyankusi elders should fill new posts (or perhaps they were given no option). Chief Koileken agreed to retire, but only on condition that none of the clique responsible for this vitriolic campaign should be eligible for appointment to office: only older men should be chosen (from Nyankusi^R). The Terito argued that so far as their traditional domain was concerned, nothing had changed and they retained their role as firestick patrons of Meruturud. It was more generally agreed, however, that they had effectively been forced into formal retirement three or four years prematurely. The right to administrative appointments had now become a privilege that could be claimed by each age-set as their turn came, rather as retiring moran are forced to pass on the privileges to their successors. To this extent, Nyankusi could claim to 'rule' Matapato several years before the circumcisions that would make them firestick patrons of a new age-set. However, there remained considerable bitterness that they had achieved this by mobilising government support for an unprecedented innovation. They now found themselves in an

exposed position, with the ear of the administration, but with little experience or widespread confidence in their advocates or their ability to 'rule'.

This episode provides the back-cloth to relations between the two age-sets subsequently. The Nyankusi were an easy butt for popular gossip. The vignette of the adulterous diehard (Case 28), for instance, whose arrogant career ended abruptly with his total humiliation, was enjoyed all the more by Terito elders because they claimed he was the grandfather of a leading member of the Nyankusi clique who bore the family name. The vignette was in fact an allegory, for just as the fallen diehard got himself into trouble and was pilloried, so the grandson too was tempted by illicit opportunities and later was sent to prison for fraud. It was as if he too had paraded his ambitions with excessive duplicity, was caught out and fell.

About eight years after they had been forced to 'lie down', the Terito elders, and ex-chief Koileken in particular, were still far from a spent force.

Case 48 (Episode 6 of Case 31).
The *eunoto* of Ngorisho[R] was the first major festival that the Nyankusi elders had ever organised, and for most of them only the second *eunoto* they had even attended (previously as moran). This placed them in a vulnerable position in relation to leading members of Terito age-set who were present at the festival. As members of the other firestick alliance, these Terito kept discreetly away from the sacrificial sharing. However, as respected elders and fathers of moran, they had a right to share in the festivity and to take part in discussions held at other times. Having been patrons at the previous two *eunoto* festivals for Meruturud[R&L], they could speak with authority on matters of ceremonial propriety that were obscure to the Nyankusi. Koileken, the ex-government chief who had retired early, still had a lively interest and an unrivalled experience. He appeared to have a clearer grasp of the total procedure for *eunoto* than any other elder present, and the Nyankusi majority were obliged to listen to his views with a certain respect. Discussion was interspersed with one or two heated exchanges on points of detail between Terito who claimed relevant experience and Nyankusi who claimed sole responsibility for the festival. Then on the evening before the first sacrifice when patrons and moran congregated to bless the ox, Koileken appeared and led the singing of traditional warrior songs that the Nyankusi had never properly learned.

The irritation of the Nyankusi patrons finally erupted several days later over the arrangements for shaving the hair of the moran during the four days between the two sacrifices (p. 159). Prompted by Koileken, the Nyankusi had tried to ensure that an equal number of moran from each manyata and also from each sub-clan would be shaved on each of the four days. In the event, no clear directive had emerged from the elders' discussion. Manyata mothers shaved every moran who presented himself so that virtually all had been shaved by the second morning. A meeting was then convened by the Nyankusi, and the Terito elders were roundly blamed as muddle-headed busybodies whose interference had led to the confusion.[1] The Nyankusi patrons' anger flared up. Discarding all courtesy, they shouted at the few Terito who were present to leave the meeting and stay away. For the remainder of their stay at the festival, the Terito elders drank and sang and kept to themselves in the joint manyata.

No-one seriously questioned that the Nyankusi at this time were wholly in control of the moran and their ceremonial activities, or that this would continue for some time. On the day after the above episode, at the height of the *eunoto* gathering, there was a prolonged meeting of the elders. They considered a variety of intractable issues that could only be resolved on an occasion such as this when so many were gathered together. It was clearly the Nyankusi who dominated in number and vigour, while the few Terito who attended were hardly sober. The rest were still drinking.

On the evening of the second sacrifice, Koileken again appeared and sang the traditional warrior songs, again stealing the limelight. He at least was determined to show himself a 'bull' who would not 'lie down', and no-one could stop him.

The political importance of major festivals has to be stressed. The heated exchanges between the ageing Terito and their Nyankusi success-ors barely concealed the competition between them over power itself. It again raised the question of the credibility of Nyankusi as firestick patrons and ultimately their control over their wards. The topic of disagreement was a trivial matter that in private discussion might have led to a lively but friendly exchange of views between elders of any age-set, with the more senior men claiming more experience. In the context of the festival, however, the Terito were felt to be challenging the authority and status of the Nyankusi in the wider community. There was no clear dividing line between sharing their knowledge and parading it to dominate a meeting. Having placed themselves in the forefront, the Nyankusi were now exposed to those Terito who were still active enough to exploit their inexperience.

The precise transfer of power from one age-set of elders to the next is not as clear-cut as the transfer of privileges from one age-group of moran to the next. One age-set may claim formal acknowledgement by the administration. Their seniors can always cite the Maasai proverb that 'the neck [of a cow] cannot overtake the head': that is, an age-set cannot overtake its predecessor in ritual status within the community at large.

Generally, the Nyankusi were obliged to show respect towards Terito, and they must have been aware of a new threat to their rule. They had now set a precedent for their successors of Meruturud, and already these junior elders were claiming that when they performed their own *olngesher* in perhaps three years' time, Nyankusi should retire and give way for younger and more vigorous men. This too was rhetorical, since a complete age-set cycle of fifteen years would have to elapse before they would have been expected to 'lie down' in the traditional system. Meanwhile, it was judicious for Nyankusi to show respect for their Terito seniors, so that they could claim it from their juniors.

As they neared the top of the age ladder, the Terito could claim an august dignity. At the same time, they were aware that they were a dwindling force and they would soon be as sparse and inactive as their predecessors of Dareto age-set. The gradual demise of an age-set with creeping age lies beyond my own field experience. However, Richard Waller witnessed this process between 1972 and 1982 in his own study of Maasai oral history, which necessarily relied on elderly men (personal communication). During this period, the survivors of Dwaati age-set completely died out, and Dareto age-set, which had earlier been a group with sufficient corporateness to form their own small circle at any meat feast, ceased to exist as an age-set. As they dwindled in number, some elders of Dwaati and Dareto expressed their feelings that they were no longer really part of society, and had no one to talk to. Waller gathered that once an age-set no longer has sufficient active members for any sort of corporate existence, its surviving members will lose heart and get tired of living and wish to follow their age mates. In terms of Figure 8a, this suggests that as ageing sets it, inactive elders find that the top rung of the age ladder slowly disintegrates under their feet and they drift towards the left-hand side of the diagram. They have outlived the ageing model.

SORCERY AND THE CURSE

In Case 48, the Terito elders were blamed for interfering at *eunoto*, but no-one suggested that they had intended sorcery – for this would have harmed their own sons. Like sorcerers, however, they were seen as intruders who managed to create confusion, increasing the risk that the *eunoto* would not promote well-being. They drew upon themselves the hostility that might otherwise have been directed towards younger members of their firestick alliance – the Meruturud – as the more likely sorcerers. The possibility of sorcery between firestick alliances complements the belief in the curse within each firestick alliance: by the firestick patrons over their wards and by each age-set over its members.

The belief in the power of the blessing and the curse is associated with legitimate authority, underpinning social order in Matapato. The belief in sorcery, on the other hand, expresses forces of chaos and evil that undermine this social order, and it is quite distinct from the curse. A curse is compared with arrow poison placed on the skin, which has no effect unless there is a cut; in other words, unless a wrong has been done. Sorcery, on the other hand, is like poison in the hands of a malicious person. It requires only technique and no moral justification to be effective. A curse can be revoked by a blessing when amity has been restored. Sorcery can be countered up to a point with the help of a diviner, but it remains incomprehensible and can never be properly revoked.

Between these two clear-cut beliefs lies an anomalous area of overlap, for the curse is insidious in its effect and an elder who curses too readily is himself acting with malice and spreading discord. The acts that accompany a curse (*oldeket*) are sometimes loosely referred to as 'sorcery' (*esakutore*), hinting at an amoral element of irrevocability that sharpens its potency. A ritual leader has the power to throw away one of the blue beads of his necklace, his deputy can untie one of the knots in his thong, a mother's-brother can pluck a hair from his fly-whisk, and any disgruntled elder can throw away a lump of chewed tobacco. Such deliberate acts would bring misfortune even if unprovoked, and it is never quite certain if a curse that has gone that far is truly revocable. Predictably, a blessing would follow in due course, but if the victim then suffers misfortune, the curse would be seen to have prevailed. If the curser dies before giving his blessing, then the victim and his future descendants live with the threat of misfortune hanging irrevocably over them. They have *engooki* and would be avoided for as long as the stigma attaches to them. Worst of all would be a decision by the firestick patrons to break a firestick as a curse over their wards, severing the chain of their alliance. The wards would be unprotected and could never become patrons in their turn. Even when the Terito^R age-group resorted to rebellion to found their manyata, their patrons did not go this far (Case 24).

Elders disclaim any detailed knowledge of the techniques of sorcery, since this could raise awkward questions as to how they know. Everyone is expected to adopt a lifestyle that would neither attract the jealousies of sorcerers nor the suspicions of others that he might himself be a sorcerer. Yet the notion of sorcery is as much a dimension of elderhood as the staging of major ceremonies that elaborate these beliefs. The sorcerer is a shadowy threat at any festival, and to this extent a part of it. He is perceived as an ill-wisher who has tampered with the site of the festival village beforehand. He creeps surreptitiously through the bush to pilfer one of the cuts of meat 'like a dog' and contaminates it with some evil charm (*esetan*). He may tamper with personal possessions that have ritual associations: a stool, a sleeping hide, ash from a fire, a snick from a cow's ear, a blood-letting bow or arrow. The concern over sorcery at a festival is that a would-be sorcerer has a superior knowledge that he can use to disrupt the proceedings. The organisers keep the secrets of the Prophet's advice until it is time to use them, but the sorcerer is even more secretive. He understands their game, but they do not understand his. As a symbolic figure in the cosmos, he plays as full a role as the stranger with 'eyes' whose hidden jealousy can harm weak people: the young and ritual dependants during transitional periods of their lives. The sorcerer, however, is an altogether more sinister figure. He does not just gaze with involuntary malcontent, but deliberately seeks to harm his victims. He poses a threat to strong people as well as weak, and even to age-sets or whole communities through their major festivals.

Sorcery is a topic that tends to be avoided until a combination of circumstances leads to a flurry of speculation. Elders claim that their ability to curse is superior to the power of any known sorcerer. However, they are powerless to direct this curse against a phantom suspect. They feel that they are visible targets for an unseen enemy who comprehends their moves and forestalls them. It is the vicious idiosyncracy of some psychopath acting in a wholly inexplicable fashion that is feared. His identity is unknown and his nefarious ends are incomprehensible: in these lies his power.

The possibility of sorcery from the rival firestick alliance is a belief that prevails among the southern Maasai; whereas in the north sorcerers are generally assumed to be from other tribal sections. Both possibilities are accepted in Matapato and above all the belief shared everywhere that the principal sorcerers are the Prophet's jealous rivals seeking to discredit him. Always, whatever their motives, sorcerers are envisaged as wastrels that have developed into malevolent freaks.

The Prophet plays a key role in this, for his expertise lies in being himself a sorcerer and a member of the Loonkidongi dynasty from which all sorcery is assumed ultimately to derive. The strength of his patronage over Matapato lies in the unquestioning trust they have in his ability to 'see' from a distance the traps that sorcerers are laying. He cannot normally help them identify the sorcerers, but in providing them with effective counter-sorcery he gives them a winning edge. At the same time, in offering this esoteric advice, he is nurturing their concern for sorcery and their dependence on him. As one firm believer put it: 'If we did not have Loonkidongi, we would not need Loonkidongi.'

In addition to age promotion ceremonies the Prophet's advice is sought for other ad hoc festivals of sacrifice. These especially concern times when there is a sense of persistent misfortune and a suspicion that sorcery could perhaps be implicated in some way. If the elders can stage the festival successfully, then there is a euphoric sense of achievement. Heightened morale is translated into belief. Implicitly they have triumphed over adverse forces and reversed their misfortune. After the undercurrent of anxiety, the community has emerged in good shape. The sacrificial festival planned by Nyankusi in 1977 after years of drought and misfortune was of this sort (Case 44b). The other firestick alliance were in no way involved and they were careful to disclaim any interest in it or detailed knowledge.

When the sense of misfortune is more widespread, the Prophet may advise both firestick alliances to hold a twin festival. Each have their own 'manyata' and there may be regular visiting between them until the time of sacrifice. Then simultaneously they segregate themselves in their separate 'manyat' and they each sacrifice an ox. More inclusive still is a 'women's festival' (*emasho oonkituak*) when a pregnant heifer is sacrificed and elders attend without regard for their age-set differences. The most vivid example illustrating the popular reaction to sorcery at Meto derived from a festival of this kind, and this reintroduces the concern among women for their fertility which was considered in the previous chapter.

THE WOMEN'S FESTIVAL AND THE POWER OF THE ELDERS' CURSE

The range of women's fertility rituals may be viewed along a scale from the extreme of a mob fury from which all men flee to an increasing involvement of elders in restoring normal relations. Elders share in the feast after a normal mobbing; and they provide the blessing that concludes any fertility gathering. Towards the other end of the scale, they organise a 'women's festival'. This may be mounted whenever women's anxiety over fertility reaches serious proportions. It can follow a fertility gathering that has still left a residue of uncertainty or it can occur at any other time. In this festival, the elders are cast in a role comparable to patrons at *eunoto*, the women have a client role comparable to the moran, and the animal sacrificed is a pregnant heifer rather than an ox. As in *eunoto*, the sacrifice is assumed to bestow life on those sharing in it through the death of an animal. However, on this occasion it violates the belief that to kill any pregnant female is a heinous act. In other words, the same logic as in *eunoto* is extended across the threshold of what is normally permissible. In effect the normal protection of all pregnant beings is reversed in an attempt to reverse widespread unpregnancy. There is a shift in emphasis in this festival from the women's ritual of rebellion against the elders to a ritual reversal shared by both sexes and the notion of purification in a matter that poses a threat to the whole community. It would only be contemplated when forces destroying reproductivity are already felt to be rampant. These have to be met with a sorcerous act of similar magnitude, after close consultation with the Prophet as an expert in sorcery. It is comparable with the heinous act of installing the ritual leader at *eunoto* from which others that have a close sympathy with the victim stand to benefit. As in Case 31, the widespread apprehensiveness that such an act provokes may be judged from an example.

Case 49.
By 1976, those adult cattle at Meto that had survived the East Coast Fever epidemic seemed to have a certain immunity to it. However, their calves were still vulnerable, and the years of drought left the stock in very poor condition, with few calves, little milk and the local population generally demoralised. It was in this situation that a rumour spread among women that their own fertility was also affected. It was generally assumed that fewer babies had been born recently, and this prompted a women's festival. Following the instructions of the Matapato Prophet, the festival centred on the sacrifice and feast of a pregnant heifer. As in *eunoto*, the elders offered each woman prescribed cuts of

meat to taste. They then blessed each woman in turn, smearing the heifer's brisket-fat and foetal fluid across her forehead and down her stomach. As the wives queued for this blessing, some started to faint. Then, according to one elder, the fainting spread: 'They fainted inside the village. They fainted outside. Some cried, some shook, they all shivered like moran. Even a few men fainted. The elders said: "Get up, for there is sorcery in the village". Yet they continued to faint even [when they had returned] to their homes, and there were a few who continued to faint for three – six – seven months afterwards.' According to one of the women: 'There were some of us who had been blessed so that we would bear children and some who had not. We circled round and round dancing. Then someone [accidentally] kicked up the skull of a partly buried bush-pig. Then we trembled and trembled-trembled-trembled-trembled-trembled and cried. When you cried, you would fall on your back in a dead faint. The whole lot of us fainted *pii*! Milk spurted from the breasts of young mothers, and babies struggled in the wombs of pregnant women. Many people were [as good as] dead, and then when they woke up they would cry and go crazy. We all cried – everyone in the Meto area. So the elders picked us up. Your husband would pick you up and lead you home, or some other elder. And the elders said: "Let's clear out for there is sorcery in this village."'

Such accounts are prone to exaggeration. No woman known to be pregnant, for instance, would have been allowed to attend this ceremony, for the attempt to reverse the misfortune of barren women by deliberately killing a pregnant heifer would have been highly unpropitious for other pregnant beings. Yet there remains a vivid sense of a collective hysteria as the fainting and then panic spread. It is revealing that the serious loss of stock and the deaths of many calves should have been associated with a mounting concern for the women's own fertility. In their close symbiotic relationship with the herd, women have an intimate responsibility for tending calves. The incident suggests that the widespread loss of calves culminating in a deliberate killing of a foetal calf roused a sympathetic response in relation to their own reproductive powers that built up towards an emotional climax.

It is perhaps also significant that drought and hunger in the Meto area had prevented women from mounting their fertility gatherings for some years. In addition to their general misfortune, they had been denied the normal outlet for their anxieties. It is as if the sacrifice centering on a ritual outrage was in a sense a ritualised rebellion against the cosmic order itself in the hope that this would reverse their misfortune. In the event this play with cosmic forces appears to have heightened rather than calmed their anxieties. It left the elders with a still more serious problem before confidence could be restored. The remarkable sequel to this episode has the flavour of a witch-hunt.

Case 49 (ctd).
After leading their wives back to their villages, the Meto elders sensed a certain urgency to root out the sorcerer. They therefore referred the incident

to a well respected local diviner, Olairumpe, since their Prophet was too far away. As the incident is remembered, the divination confirmed sorcery and implicated two suspects, Lepusi and Malaso, both of whom had non-Maasai connections. Lepusi was a diviner with a bad reputation and a relative stranger to the district. It was he who had previously been suspected (by Olairumpe) following the episode of fainting at the Meto manyata (Case 29). Malaso was a controversial Matapatoi who was living in Lepusi's village, close to the border with Kisonko. His mother had been a Kikuyu and he had a reputation as a wastrel. Previously, he had been suspected of killing his half-brother and also his wife's lover by sorcery. Now it was assumed that he had developed into a more sinister kind of sorcerer, bent on undermining Meto life by attacking their unborn children for some quite unfathomable reason. It was held that Malaso had obtained some harmful charm from Lepusi, which he had either planted in the festival village or thrown over the outer fence to land among the cattle.

Elders of all age-sets gathered to summon the two suspects from their village. Lepusi heard in advance of their approach and fled to Kisonko in Tanzania. No-one at Meto expected ever to see him again. Malaso, however, responded to their call, and invited the elders to place a conditional curse on him to prove his innocence. Two left-handed and two one-eyed elders were chosen to voice this curse, and kneeling on their left knees they each threw some chewed tobacco towards the setting sun. Three of them were of Malaso's age-set, Terito.

Malaso had been ill for some time. After the curse, he made his way to Namanka township to buy some European medicines from a local non-Maasai practitioner. For eight days, he travelled along the Matapato-Kisonko border towards Namanka, only twenty miles away. People would give him milk to drink when he visited their village, but threw away the cup afterwards. Even his own age mates would not allow him to sleep in their huts. It is said, a madness (olailiruwa) settled on him. On the ninth day he was found dead in the bush, stenching, his stomach distended. His spear was planted in the ground beside him and his pouch was full of money to pay for the medicines. No-one would touch the money or bury him.

When collecting accounts from informants within only a year of this incident, it was not possible to separate the facts from the elaborations of legend. So far as the Meto community were concerned, and particularly the women, the episode vindicated their beliefs in the ultimate power of the elders to protect them from sorcery. Olairumpe was a local elder as well as diviner; he had identified the sorcerers, and then it had been the elders at large who had finally vanquished them. The legend provides a vivid image of a controversial man who had sealed his own fate by living in the village of the sort of person that normal elders should avoid. The story is steeped in symbolic imagery. The good diviner and the bad diviner, the triumph of the curse over sorcery, the nine day ramble (a ritual number) by a madman along the border of Matapato and on the border between life and death, leading to a desolate end, rejected even by his own age-set. In general, sorcery is seen as a major source of disorder in Matapato society, whereas the elders' power to curse, to bless and to organise ceremony is the very foundation of order. The problem of sorcery is that it is insidious with no obvious pattern or predictability. The sorcerer creeping through the bush is always one pace ahead of the elders, but once he has been exposed, they hold the initiative.

CONCLUSION: SORCERY AND THE TWO DOMAINS OF ELDERHOOD

In Matapato there is a fundamental contradiction between the ideal of close community living and the need to disperse their herds for grazing. Large gatherings and large villages simply cannot be sustained. Even the manyata which is the symbol of close fellowship among moran tends to seem depleted when its members are dispersed at their forest feasts and elsewhere. This strong sense of fellowship shifts perceptibly when the manyata is disbanded. The effect of this transition was well described by Kunaiju after he had 'drunk milk' (Case 36). His whole being and outlook had to adjust to a new isolation, and he coped with his nostalgia by devoting himself to his father's cattle in which he had an interest in the longer-term. This illustrates the shift from age-group to family loyalties with more independence and self-sufficiency. It accompanies a radical change in the age-group itself, first with the disbanding of the manyat after *eunoto*, and then with its incorporation into the more inclusive age-set at *olngesher*. As moran, their unquestioning loyalty to their manyata was demanded and they were held to have no possessions of their own. On becoming elders, they acquire possessions and they have more to lose: cattle, wives and then children. The fear of an age-set curse develops as they feel themselves more vulnerable and as the scope for a conflict between personal and age-set interests increases. This conflict is clearly brought out in a number of earlier examples (eg. Cases 9, 10, 27, 28, 30, 36, 40, 44a, 45a, 47).

It is this development of self-interest in elderhood that appears to be projected in the belief in sorcery. The sorcerer is the exact reverse of the ideal age mate and good neighbour. He is jealous and mean in all matters, an odd man going his odd way who keeps his knowledge and his designs to himself. The life-style of the moran, which emphasises their gregarious interdependence, makes it difficult to pin this image on them. However, the transition to elderhood lures them in this direction with an element of enforced remoteness.

Any elder may prefer a measure of remoteness for a time, giving him more personal control over his family and more room to graze his stock. However, if he adopts too remote a life-style, cutting himself off from his age mates, and does not share the risks, then he is himself at risk. If good fortune does not come his way, this may make him a prime suspect for sorcery when circumstances seem to point accusingly in his direction.

Among elders, the tendency towards dispersal is offset by the rich collective life of all ceremonial activities and especially their festivals. Self-interest is put to one side, and they rebuild their 'manyat' and briefly recapture the spirit of age fellowship. It is at such events that the sorcerer (or rather his image) has a special role. He is the antithesis of this collective spirit. In contrast to the nostalgic whiff of moranhood recreated by their gatherings, the sorcerer is a caricature of the other side of elderhood taken to its grotesque extreme. This is to suggest that the spectre of the sorcerer is a projection of the part of themselves that they disown on such an occasion. It is somewhere out there, creeping through the bush, a malcontent or perhaps a visitor from some other Maasai tribal section. Most suspect are the Loonkidongi dynasty of diviners and Prophets who are notoriously competitive and jealous. So long as the participants at the festival can recapture their ideal of selfless unity, the spectre is banished and loses its potency. However, if confidence in the occasion fails to develop or is lost, then the belief in sorcery expresses the apprehensiveness of some malignant force, bent on mischief. In women's fertility gatherings and festivals there is a similar pattern, illustrated strikingly in Case 49.

Elders are surely sincere when they claim that they do not understand the techniques of the sorcerer: he exists primarily in the collective imagination. However, their ability to vividly portray the motives of the jealous sorcerer going about his business is a virtual admission that jealousy is a familiar streak in Matapato experience, just as every man up to a point is thought to have 'eyes', to covet his own wives, and to be envious of those who are remarkably successful. All men are initiated as equals and carry this ideal though to their moranhood, but with elderhood the unequal distribution of wealth and influence can no longer be concealed, and their society is seen to be unfair (qv. Table 1). In losing their youth, the elders also lose the selfless purity of the manyata ideal. The idiom of worthiness and sharing among elders as matters of principle is interspersed with fretful gossip at the selfish success of some men and suspicions of malpractice, frequently verging on sorcery. To fully appreciate the strength of this concern with personal success, it is necessary to return to the topic of family development. This is now considered from the point of view of a young elder who has put his moranhood behind him and is approaching his first marriage under his father's heavy hand.

NOTES

1   It is quite possible that each firestick alliance has developed its own diverging traditions in relation to the major festivals, and that the confusion was caused by the Terito elders inadvertently introducing variants that were peculiar to their own alliance. Informants denied that this could occur in Matapato where some of the most enthusiastic conversations between elders of different age-sets

concern ritual protocol with no secrets or suggestion of diverging traditions. Evidence collected among the Purko Maasai, however, did suggest a distinct divergence in the order of events in *eunoto* between firestick alliances, although again the possibility was regarded as incongruous and denied by my informants (*Models* Chapter 5).

CHAPTER 13

ELDERHOOD AND THE PATERNAL YOKE

In the analysis of patrilineal societies, the term complementary filiation normally refers to a man's links with his maternal kin. Among the Maasai where the age system is strong and maternal kinship is of little relevance, this term can more usefully be applied to his links with his age-set. The privilege rights shared with his age mates in their wives and the produce of their livestock belong to a domain that complements the patrilineal family. The family domain is more concerned with a long term interest in the well-being and growth of these as breeding possessions. In the context of the family, the son's moranhood is just an episode. It is critical in the development of the relationship with his father, especially for those that go to the manyata. When the son leaves for the manyata, his father may regard him as little more than a herdboy. When he returns after about five years, he is poised to settle down to elderhood, but once again he remains under the father's authority. The earlier account of an elder as an independent stock owner (Chapter 1) and marriage negotiator (Chapter 2) applies to any mature man with no living father. For other elders, whatever their age, the existence of a living father is an overriding factor.

THE FATHER'S CONTROL OVER HIS SON'S MARRIAGE

Marriage broking is pre-eminently a speciality of older men. This is popularly justified in terms of their greater wisdom, with a wider social network and an ability to discern the more marriageable families. This claim barely conceals the power that it gives them in a society where polygyny increases the competition for wives and delays the first marriages of younger men. Moreover, the notion of marriageable families implies a network of marriage that excludes unworthy families, whereas with high polygyny, virtually all girls are highly sought after and hence all families are marriageable. The network to a considerable extent may be regarded as a diffuse cabal of older men including those who may no longer have influence in community affairs. Beyond the father of each compound family, who is in a key position, are other senior kinsmen of the *agnatic group*. They comprise a dispersed patrilineal family, typically descended from a common grandfather beyond whom precise details of ancestry are uncertain. At a time when their dwindling age-set has formally retired, these older men may be at the height of their influence within their individual agnatic groups, until they lose interest in such matters. They have a right to be consulted on matters of marriage. They can even have a decisive role after the father's death when his younger sons are in no position to pursue their suits unaided (eg. Case 25). Their involvement may work in two directions. When the older men are negotiating for brides on behalf of younger kinsmen, they use their personal network, especially within their age-set, and increase the moral indebtedness of the younger men. This in turn reinforces the right of these senior men to influence the choice regarding the marriages of girls of the agnatic group, including the sisters and daughters of the younger men. In other words, as wife-receiving marriage brokers, the older men add to their fund of influence within the agnatic group by drawing on the good will of their friends. And then as wife-giving brokers, they draw on this fund of close agnatic influence to cultivate the good will of their friends.

For as long as he lives, the father remains the key figure. He is at first subject to the influence of senior kinsmen when his older daughters are married while he is still perhaps in his forties. As these die off and his sons reach an age for marriage, he is in a more commanding position. He has a genuine interest in seeing these sons married to establish a further generation of his family. At the time of fieldwork, Masiani had arranged five marriages for his two senior sons. The earlier marriages were quite atypical because of his flamboyant disregard for convention, but they well illustrate his sons' dependence on him and the nature of the system he had to contend with. Significantly, of the four marriages arranged with 'daughters' of his own age-set, three stemmed from friendships and episodes of his moranhood. He displayed his own role as broker prominently and pared down each son's role as groom to a minimum, even springing marriage on them without warning.

Case 50

(a) Masiani arranged two marriages for his senior son, Kinai. The first marriage was with a divorcee, who had returned to live with her parents after her husband had lost all his stock and then abandoned her. There was still no settlement of the earlier marriage debt, and this gave the first husband the right to claim any of the children she bore. Also he was a member of Kinai's age-set and this made the match especially sensitive. Masiani was an age mate of her father and argued that he himself would bear full responsibility for this marriage. He negotiated it, offered a token gift, and led the wife back to his own village as a 'father'. As she was a divorcee, it had only been necessary to agree in principle on her remarriage without any form of wedding or celebration. Kinai was about thirty years old at this time and knew nothing of his father's plans. When he came home from herding one evening, he was greeted with the news that Masiani had returned with a 'bride' for him. He was overwhelmed with delight at this unexpected present. In due course, the outstanding marriage debt was settled and only then did she become Kinai's wife in a fuller sense.

(b) Negotiations for Kinai's second wife stemmed from an earlier broken marriage of Masiani's with the sister of a close age mate living in Loita. He now asked for a daughter from his friend – a niece of the previous wife – to settle the earlier marriage debt. On this occasion, Masiani himself presented the opening marriage gifts (the 'anointment' and the 'favourite'). He only informed Kinai of his arrangements and of the reasons for his recent visits to Loita when it was time to remove the bride after her initiation. Kinai was then obliged to fulfil his ceremonial role as groom in a properly conducted marriage. However, Masiani accompanied him to Loita and directed him at each stage of her removal to Matapato. Kinai's role appears to have been almost as passive as his bride's.

Case 51

(a) Masiani had an altogether warmer regard for his second son, Kunaiju, but he still played a dominant role in arranging his three marriages. The first marriage was again with a divorcee and even more bizarre. This was with the daughter of Merero, a lion killer whom he had supported when he was denied the trophy (Case 27). Merero had later migrated to Loitokitok and this daughter had run away from two successive husbands, leaving him with an outstanding marriage debt. Masiani visited Merero and agreed to settle the debt, in return for the girl. Once again, he had given no hint to his family of the reasons for his absence in Loitokitok. As in Kinai's first marriage, he led the bride back himself. Then to tantalise his family, he sent a message ahead to tell them that he was returning with a bride, implying that they were to prepare to receive his own fifth wife. As he neared his village, he sent a further message to the astonished Kunaiju, summoning him to lead his own bride for the last few miles. This marriage also failed (Case 5c), and after the woman had left Kunaiju, it became obvious that no other man would want to marry her and settle the debt. Her father was still impoverished and Masiani was forced to accept a nominal repayment without much hope of a fuller settlement.

In the relationship between agnatic groups, the success of one marriage may be invoked to arrange further marriages. There is no suggestion of direct exchange, but it is intended that wives given in both directions will broadly balance over time, and they claim a certain prestige in sharing a marriageability (*enkaputi* qv. p. 29).

Case 51

(b) As a moran, Masiani had saved the life of a close friend with the deft use of his shield; and Kunaiju's second marriage with this friend's daughter was seen as the fulfilment of a moral debt. Kunaiju's third marriage was with another girl from the same agnatic group. Both marriages were local affairs and Kunaiju was well known to the brides' agnatic group. Masiani himself remained a key figure in the negotiations, but he allowed Kunaiju to present the formal gifts and perform his ceremonial role as groom without interfering.

Shortly after this marriage, Masiani was approached by an age mate from this other agnatic group, asking for Kinai's daughter (Masiani's granddaughter) as a bride for his son. It was the marriageability between the two agnatic groups that was emphasised, but having given two of their own girls to Masiani for Kunaiju, they undoubtedly wanted a return in kind. Masiani agreed at once without even consulting the girl's father, his son Kinai. Kinai acquiesced, arguing that Masiani had more experience in such matters.

The role of senior men in arranging marriages emphasises that the affinity is between agnatic groups. This is made quite explicit when one broken marriage leads to arranging another (Case 50b), or when circumstances lead one of the parties to switch either the groom or the bride so that the suit itself survives changes in casting.

Case 52.
Leminto's eldest son was widely regarded as an unsettled wastrel. In arranging a marriage for him with an agnatic group who had recently been given a 'daughter' of theirs, Leminto emphasised that he would personally ensure the marriage's success. At first, the son fulfilled his ceremonial role adequately. Then after the girl's initiation, instead of coming to lead her away as his bride, he left Matapato abruptly on an indefinite visit to Kisonko in Tanzania. His younger brother was sent to fetch him back, but was unable to trace him and returned alone. The two fathers agreed that the marriage should continue and the younger brother was substituted as groom. By proving himself a wastrel after all, the oldest son forfeited his bride and the right to marry first.

Fathers do not always persevere with their wastrel sons. Many are simply left to fend for themselves without stock or wives until they are seen to have mended their ways. Or they may drift away to places like Nairobi as vagrants in search of work and never return. Wastrels disgust their fathers, but they do not necessarily bring them discredit or affect the marriageability of their brothers. They tend to be regarded as inexplicable and random casualties that occur too often in any family. They are irrelevant. However, any younger man who marries before his older brother, as in the above example, should pay him a heifer. For in breaking the rule of precedence by birth (Figure 2), it is as if the older son does not even exist or is dead, and this is akin to sorcery. It could kill him or at least provoke his curse. The heifer formally acknowledges the senior's existence in return for his blessing.

In another instance, it was the bride that was switched, while the suit linked to a marriage debt was maintained.

Case 53.
Kwemeri had arranged the marriage of his second son to the daughter of an age mate. The girl's father died shortly before her initiation and custody over her passed to his senior brother. This brother had previously supported another suitor and was now in a position to rearrange the marriage. Out of respect for Kwemeri, he was reluctant to do this, but he also found the obligation to

maintain his earlier promise of support to the rival suitor irresistible. He handled the issue with considerable tact, inviting Kwemeri as a special guest at the girl's initiation and discussing the matter over beer. He suggested that the marriage debt and friendship between the two families should be maintained, and that Kwemeri should accept some other girl of the family in due course. Kwemeri at the time was involved in three bids for wives for himself and three others for his sons. He could not afford to press his claim unduly or he would have damaged his marriageability and his chances of success in these other suits. He concealed his disappointment and accepted this offer in the spirit of friendship. To the other elders he acknowledged that good faith had been maintained and judged beside that, the substitution was a mere trifle.

In Chapter 10, within the domain of the age system, marriage was examined as a structured exchange that bridged the gulf between age-sets by handing girls down to younger men. In the domain of patrilineal families, marriage is part of a system of patronage, debt and self-interest that invokes the loyalties of age affiliation to its own ends. This domain is altogether more individualistic than the collective ideals of the age system, and as they age, elders are less bound by the influence of senior kinsmen.

THE FATHER'S CONTROL OVER HIS SON THROUGH STOCK

Each Matapatoi builds up his stock from the herd originally allotted to his mother on marriage. Full brothers grow up with a shared interest in the development of this herd. Some of their cattle are formal gifts at birth, initiation, and 'drinking milk' and others are added as occasional encouragements, especially when they have excelled in herding. The principal initiative in these gifts comes from the father, but any unmarried son can press his mother for further cattle. In a rather loose sense, a woman is constantly bargaining with her sons over her allotted cattle. She has to use discretion in making these gifts and to avoid allowing herself to be browbeaten into parting with her cattle too readily. Even in this matter, she is subject to the control of her husband. He can direct her to give one of her cattle to a deserving son, or forbid her giving further cattle to a son he considers undeserving, or even confiscate the odd cow. Favouritism apart, the principle of seniority within each hut means that each successive son is in a weaker position than his older brothers to solicit cattle. He is also less immediately in need of a herd than they are. By the time a son marries, he should have acquired sufficient cattle to be independent of his mother. As she ages, these demands dwindle together with her herd. Eventually she hands over the few remaining cattle to her youngest son when he too marries, and she then becomes dependent on him. It is he who inherits this rump if she dies before this point.

Moranhood does not increase a son's rights in cattle, and those taken to the manyata still belong to his father so long as he lives. Only when an *esoogo* punishment is levied by other moran can an ox be slaughtered without the father's permission, and then the son has to face the added shame of accounting to him for its loss. In the past, even the war gains of moran belonged to their fathers. When moran returned from a raid, suspicious fathers are said to have rushed out to greet their sons, hoping to claim these cattle before the moran could lodge them elsewhere or give them away to form stock friendships as a personal investment.

On the whole, however, especially with senior agnates lurking in the background, younger men feel their dependence on their fathers more keenly than their need for independence. Kunaiju lacked neither spirit nor friends and his father's impulsiveness had lost him nearly all his stock and had forced him into a disastrous first marriage (Cases 1, 22, 51a). Yet at the age of about thirty, he was still doggedly loyal and denied any wish for independence: 'I want to be where papa is, for a "child" who does not accompany his father is pestered. If there is some elder who wants to trouble you, he will wait until he sees that your father has gone away, and then he will come and harass you. Whereas at other times, he dare not argue with you because your father is nearby.' Such expressions are general among junior elders, fostered no doubt by their fathers, but suggesting even so that they are not straining for independence.

Following his first marriage, the development of a young elder's rights in his cattle is the development of his relationship with his father. There are three steps in this process: the segregation of his cattle at night, the right to dispose of these cattle, and the right to herd his own cattle and migrate independently. The first step is taken when he builds a separate corral in another part of his father' village with its own gateway. This step is ostensibly to segregate the two parts of the herd at night where they can more easily be checked by their owners (father and son) and milked and tended by the wives. A quarrel between wives over cattle returning in the evening is a frequent pretext for segregating the stock in this way. The separation of Kunaiju's sector of the village from Masiani's in Map 2, for instance, was precipitated by Kunaiju's neurotic first wife who had to be separated from the other wives before she eventually ran away. In another instance at Meto, an elder had even insisted that the hut of a particularly disruptive wife should be fenced off from the remainder of the village so that it could only be approached from the outside. He forbad any of his other wives from visiting her sector and forbad her from visiting theirs. The elders maintain that men have to segregate their cattle to keep control over their wives. Nevertheless, this segregation also reduces the chances of the father quarrelling with his married sons, which would be regarded as a more serious matter. The segregation of wives is therefore also an indirect step towards the autonomy of each son, and it follows a line of segmentation within the family.

A fuller step towards independence is to grant the son the right to 'control' (*a-itore*) his cattle. With this, he can dispose of stock without first seeking his father's permission on each occasion. He can slaughter at will and build up his own network of stock friendships with gifts of cattle and respond directly to any requests from his wife's kin. With this freedom and with the father's consent, it is now easier for the son to migrate elsewhere adding flexibility to the management of the total herd. The father expects to be informed of all his sons' cattle transactions, and he must always be given the brisket-fat of any slaughtered ox or a portion of the money from the sale of any animal. A Matapato image of filial piety is of an elder carrying some brisket-fat. This implies that his father is still alive and that he is making a special journey, perhaps of some distance, to fulfil this obligation. The father has the right to withhold this concession indefinitely rather than put his cattle at risk, and it would be formally granted only in the presence of other elders. They admonish the son not to abuse this privilege and remind him of instances where the concession has been reversed after men have returned to their fathers' with depleted herds and hungry families.

In most other parts of Maasai and for the majority of families, the concessions to any son go no further than this. Very occasionally in Matapato, however, the son can take a further step towards full independence over his cattle. This is normally an indication of friction with his father, which is to be avoided at all cost, for the father's anger could have the effect of a curse. If he becomes exasperated, as in Cases 54 and 56 below, he should confiscate perhaps two cattle (and no more than nine) and then he cannot grudge his blessing. However, he may also be persuaded by other elders that it would be in his own interests to 'divide' (*a-or*) his herd. This would separate his son and grant him total autonomy with his cattle, so that he can migrate where he pleases and shake loose the paternal yoke.

Case 54.
Masiani habitually dominated his senior son Kinai during the years of his moranhood and subsequently as a young elder (Cases 16, 44, 50). He claimed credit for Kinai's skill with cattle, and because he could always rely on him, he maintained an extroverted social life. He often visited friends elsewhere, even beyond Matapato, while Kinai remained with the herds, loyal, aloof, and relatively friendless. A hint of future trouble occurred when Kinai was refused permission to 'control' (dispose of) his own cattle. He then appealed to other elders; and members of Masiani's age-set, including Kwemeri whom Masiani respected, persuaded him that Kinai deserved this concession. Even then, he was still tied to his father's herds and was slow to use his new freedom to build up stock friendships of his own.

A highlight of Kinai's uneventful life occurred when some Arusha Maasai of his age-set were passing through the area and were attacked by a drunken group of younger elders of the next age-set (Meruturud). Kinai and another elder happened to be close by and rushed to defend the visitors. One of them had been badly clubbed and Kinai led him to his home and nursed him for two days.

Some years later, when Kinai had migrated with the small stock to a remote area, the Arushai returned with a stool and tobacco as gifts. Masiani, who remained with the cattle, hosted Kinai's friend and accepted the gifts for himself. Then, after a further lapse of several years, a messenger from Arusha came to inform them that their friend was celebrating his son's initiation. Both Masiani and Kinai were invited to attend. Masiani decided that he would accept the invitation, leaving Kinai to tend the herds as usual. Probably for the first time in his life, Kinai dared to argue with his father, pointing out that the Arushai was his own friend and age mate. Masiani was unyielding. Next morning before dawn, Kinai slipped away from their village, rather like a truanting herdboy, and accompanied the messenger back to Arusha. There he was treated as a special guest, and given another stool and promised further gifts.

Masiani stayed at home and later claimed that he had tied a knot in the strap of his tobacco tube to avert the effects of his anger. Yet, he continued the argument when Kinai returned, and with such vehemence that Kinai ran away to Kwemeri. Kwemeri led him back with two other elders of Masiani's age-set to intercede on Kinai's behalf. They persuaded Masiani that in his present mood, he and Kinai should separate and the herd should be 'divided'. Kinai was now quite responsible enough to manage on his own and had earned the right to manage his family independently. The formal ceremony of separation was supervised by Masiani's age mates and marked with blessings at each stage. The father's and son's herds were first confined in separate parts of the village, and a bull from Masiani's herd was exchanged for a heifer from Kinai's. Then Kinai migrated with his stock through a separate gateway to a village nearby. With this separation, the relationship between them improved and Kinai eventually came back to live with Masiani. He still retained the right to migrate independently, and refused to move away with his father to another area during the 1976 drought. He only rejoined him at a time of his own choosing (Case 1).

Kinai's outburst against his father may be seen as a mild rebellion by a son who had been denied a manyata moranhood or any clear break with his past as a herdboy. Just as young moran are not granted the privileges until they are prepared to claim them for themselves, so no-one interceded on Kinai's behalf until he asserted himself. While some aspects of this case are atypical, all the ingredients were familiar to Matapato. Masiani was a Maasai through and through, in some ways still a moran at heart, and this was an episode that could be understood by everyone, except perhaps Masiani himself.

The role of Masiani's age mates here is intriguing, since relations between father and son are logically a matter for senior agnates or other close clansmen. A generation earlier when Masiani had rebelled against his guardian uncle, for instance, it had been his senior agnates who had been a moderating influence (Case 6). Confronted with his father's anger, Kinai knew that Masiani was too senior and intractable to listen to arguments from his kinsmen, none of whom he altogether respected. Yet even in his most intractable mood, he would defer to his age mates. This had always been his saving grace; and Kinai knew those he respected most in the area.

Personal concern among close age mates extends quite reasonably to domestic affairs that affect 'their' wives and 'their' sons. Once they had been appealed to, they intervened quite legitimately – on Masiani's behalf as much as Kinai's.

'Dividing' the herd and granting a son this right to manage independently has a note of finality. Yet in practice it is as reversible as the concession to dispose of his own cattle. In the final analysis it is an act of expedience rather than of irrevocable commitment, and it can be expediently reversed.

Case 55.
Lodorkiook had formally 'divided' his herd, and his son subsequently migrated with his two wives to another part of Matapato. The son then started drinking heavily, selling off his cattle and neglecting his family. A visitor passing through the area carried back the wives' complaint to Lodorkiook. He walked to his son's village to investigate for himself: he had negotiated both marriages and accepted personal responsibility for the well-being of his son's family. When he arrived, the son was away and the plight of his family was immediately apparent. Lodorkiook told the wives to pack their donkeys, called in his grandsons who were herding the cattle, and led them all back to his own village. The son returned to a deserted homestead. So far as Lodorkiook was concerned, his son was free to continue as a wastrel or to return under his authority. The herd was no longer 'divided', and he himself would now take care of his own personal 'possessions', including his daughters-in-law and grandchildren.

Quarrelling between wives may also determine an elder's decision to 'divide' his cattle just as it may lead him to segregate them within the village. These are aspects of the same process of segmentation as the family grows.

Case 56.
As she grew old, Taraiye's senior wife started to quarrel incessantly with his five younger wives. He recognised that the family had grown too large to remain viable. He therefore decided to 'divide' his herd, separating this senior wife and her three married sons, and placing them under the direction of the eldest son whom he trusted absolutely. During the drought of 1976, both parts of the herd suffered heavy losses, and Taraiye recalled his wife and her sons. He wanted to supervise matters personally during this critical period to ensure that everyone and all the cattle were adequately cared for.[1]

LOSS OF RESPONSIBILITY AND THE INCONGRUITY OF OLD AGE

Success in pastoralism is only possible for those prepared to nurture their herd as the capital on which they depend. The possibility that some may lose the will to persist is serious when they are themselves the heads of their own families with no living father to take the matter in hand. They are not in the same category as those that have been wastrels since boyhood. These are simply left to themselves, without stock or wives until they are seen to have changed, if they ever do change. An established elder who unexpectedly becomes a wastrel is quite different. He has dependants who suffer and his closest agnates are held indirectly responsible if they allow this to go too far. His disregard for his own marriage reflects on their own marriageability. In the final resort, they should be prepared to take collective responsibility, or who else will entrust them with their daughters as wives? They find themselves forced to display this concern. The key problem is: who should grasp the initiative? For once grasped, as in Kinai's appeal above his father's head in Case 54, matters tend to take their own course.

Case 57.

Moikan had a good reputation as an elder, and then unaccountably his whole lifestyle changed. He started to have affairs with unattached women, selling off his cattle to give them money, and he neglected the increasing hunger of his wife and children as the herd dwindled. He ignored the advice of his age mates. His closest kin in the area were members of his clan, Makesen, who were only sparsely represented. At first they were in no position to interfere with the way a distant kinsman treated his own possessions. When eventually his oldest son, a moran, approached these clansmen to complain, their indignation erupted, aware that their reputation was now at stake. They mustered themselves as a punitive force, seized Moikan, tied his feet together and whipped him as he lay on the ground. Then they called for a whetstone to file down his front teeth, as the traditional punishment for men who behave like predators. At this point, onlookers from other clans intervened, arguing that the punishment had already gone far enough: he would never risk another beating.

In this case, there seems little more that Moikan's age-set could have done, having failed to intervene by persuasion. For his clansmen in default of closer kin, however, there appears here to have been a deliberate display of zeal to chastise the prodigal father, as custodians of their marriageability. It was ultimately a clan matter. The way they handled it resembles the age-set punishment when the demand for nine cattle is moderated as a concession to an appeal from outsiders. Here too, they swooped on their victim in anger, and then could afford to make concessions once the extent to which they were prepared to go could not be doubted. The victim, apart from being humiliated, was indebted on all sides for clemency.

This problem of a loss of will may develop in any family when a father reaches old age. Ideally, effective responsibility will have devolved on his senior son before this point. However, if this son himself is inadequate for the task, then his brothers may be forced to take the initiative. Even senior wives can become involved in order to save the herd and ultimately the family itself. As they say of a crisis with the herd, 'Cattle have their own law!' (p. 9).

Case 58.

When his father became old and weak, Enkashi as senior son was entrusted with responsibility for managing the whole family. Then Enkashi started to drink heavily, and left the day to day management of the herd to his younger brothers. He sold many of his own stock to buy spirits, and then, assuming the full privileges of his father, he started to sell off other family cattle. At this point his mother, Kiranda, took the initiative and called together all Enkashi's brothers. In the morning, when the cattle had just left the village, they seized Enkashi, bound his legs and arms, and led by Kiranda they started to beat him. The father had been totally unaware of the developing crisis, and when he heard the commotion and saw the beating, he ordered his sons to stop. Kiranda, thoroughly worked up, swore at him and told the sons to carry on. Other village elders by this time had arrived on the scene and persuaded the old man to let the punishment take its course. Enkashi did not filch further cattle and later admitted that it had been his passion for spirits that had led him to abuse his privilege.

In another instance, the source of the problem was the obstinacy of the father himself as his senility advanced. His family had to be more circumspect to save the situation.

Case 59.
In the course of a serious drought, Marasiwa migrated from Matapato to Kisonko and then settled there. He allowed his senior wife and her two senior sons formal separation, and then found himself in a similar position to Lodorkiook (Case 55). His senior wife complained that the sons were squandering their cattle, and he returned both the cattle and the remainder of his family to his own village. He then told his sons that they were free to do as they pleased – elsewhere. In due course, the sons returned to him and settled down more responsibly.

Meanwhile, a serious problem had developed: Marasiwa's family was large, and he had been unable to arrange marriages for his other sons. Matapato elders were not prepared to offer him their daughters while he remained in Kisonko, and Kisonko elders would not do so because it was uncertain that he would stay. By this time, he was quite senile and because of the earlier incident, he refused to allow any of his sons to return alone to Matapato and obstinately refused to return himself. His age mates and clansmen in Kisonko sympathised when they were approached by his sons, but felt unable to intervene. Taking matters into their own hands, therefore, his eight adult sons led other members of his family back to Matapato a few at a time. Eventually, the old man remained with only two of his five wives and a few cattle. It was these wives who were left to explain the situation to him and to persuade him to return. Marasiwa agreed, and the whole family were reunited in a single village on the Matapato side of the border shortly before his death.

★   ★   ★

Concern for a loss of responsibility is expressed in a variety of ways. One of the threats hanging over a ritual leader is that he may age prematurely. Certain ritual infringements are thought to impair reason: when for instance a girl tastes the gift of her 'anointment' or when any male tastes meat of the (women's) sheep-of-emergence before an initiation (p. 59). In Meto, the premature senility of four elders is said to have been the result of helping themselves to some of this meat stewing in one of their huts. They only realised their mistake when the wife returned and shrieked at them in horror. The episode is not related as a warning to elders to keep their fingers out of their wives' pots, but as proof that there are aspects of the women's domain that are dangerously debilitating for men. In a society where the adept are highly regarded and popular slanging makes fun of the incompetent (Figure 8), there is an apprehensiveness of losing control and reason, and ultimately of ageing itself.

The butts of Matapato jokes tend to be mimicked in the high piping staccato of an exasperated old person who panics at having lost control over a situation. Stories of a woman harassed by her grown sons or of a father, spluttering with indignation as moran hold him down on his stool and snatch away one of his wives for the manyata, are typical of this kind of joke and are told with relish. If the butt happens to be a younger man who has lost his head or is running from the anger of an older man, then the imitation is similar, even though he is actually being humiliated by someone older. Like the adulterous diehard, he has tripped up, and his dilemma is epitomised by the frailty of old age.

There is an incongruity in ageing that contradicts the respect for age on which social order is built. There is in this humour also a certain gentleness and absolutely no suggestion that the frustrations of the elderly are in any way linked with sorcery or with the unrestrained use of their curse. The father in old age may on occasion be foolish or selfish. He may even be feared for his curse. However, he remains the family figurehead, and he retains his integrity and the loyalty of his sons.

DEATH AND THE 'FATHER'S CHEST'

As he ages, an elder is less concerned with manipulating his herds for his own personal ends. He may reduce his residual herd of unallocated cattle, giving his sons a better chance to build up herds of their own. After his death, these sons will have an inalienable right to their cattle, whether or not they already 'control' them, and the father can do much to smooth the transition beforehand. However, he should retain at least some cattle in his residual herd. They are the cattle-of-his-corral (*eboo*), the source of all his marriages and a symbol of his authority. On his death, these cattle are inherited by his oldest surviving son together with his stool, his outstanding debts, and the right to dispose of his unmarried daughters. They are all 'of his corral'. This rule of residual inheritance matches the rule that the residual part of each wife's allotted herd must be inherited by her youngest son. Both rules are geared to the survival of the parents to old age, when they can expect to be dependent on their oldest and youngest sons respectively; and both rules are invariable. It makes no difference if the oldest son is of a very junior hut; he is still senior to the other sons. Similarly, if a wife dies young then it is still her youngest son who inherits the entire herd of unapportioned stock, even if he is a newborn infant with several older brothers, as in Case 1. Any anomaly that this gives rise to will be offset by the manipulations of the father or guardian over time to redress the balance (p. 34).

A father cannot disinherit his senior son, for whatever reason. At most he can call in his debts, promise all his daughters in marriage and allocate the cattle-of-his-corral among his other sons as he sees fit. He knows that when he dies, the senior son will not be able to revoke these decisions. For this would flout his final wishes with the same effect as some unresolved curse that can never be put right once he has died. The son would have *engooki*, the sin of an unresolved curse, hanging over him and his family until his line dies out (cf. Case 20). An elderly man who mistrusts his senior son may even make a point of publicly pronouncing a conditional curse against any future attempt to tamper with his final wishes.

When the father's life is clearly ebbing away, any sons living elsewhere are expected to migrate to be together with him. To allow a parent to die in neglect would again impose an irrevocable *engooki* on them. Ideally, the father should die in his senior wife's hut after his hair has been shaved, and before his personal ornaments are removed. The shaving severs his link with the living, otherwise others would follow him to death. An ox-to-smear-the-corpse is slaughtered a short distance from the village and the feast there is shared by all males, including moran, with no grouping by age-set. The brisket-fat – the father's portion in life – is extracted and his senior son smears it over the father's body and personal trinkets. Then the sons, with the senior at the head and the youngest at the feet, carry the body to this spot. It is laid on a hide, on its right side with the head facing north or south. The disposal of a dead mother is similar, but a sheep is slaughtered instead of an ox.

Traditionally, the dead were simply laid to rest in the shade of a 'cold' (non-thorn) tree away from the village. A hyena or other predator was expected to devour the body during the night. If it did not, then this was seen as a sign that the dead person might have *engooki* from some earlier incident in life that could still bring misfortune to the successors. Sheep fat would then be left beside the body to attract predators on the second night. The longer the corpse remained undevoured, the more serious the omen. This did not apply to men or women who died with no sons. Such a death was (and is) unpropitious, but any *engooki* they carried died with them; if possible the dying person would be taken outside the village to lessen the risk of pollution for the living, and the corpse would not be smeared with fat.

In the past, important elders, if they so wished, could be buried under a cairn of stones or in the centre of their village with a sprig of wild olive planted above them. There was no regular practice of burial, but just occasional final wishes that had to be honoured. Today, discreet burial is the principal concession to the influence of Christian missions in the area.

Some suggest that it is because with less game there are fewer hyenas around. Others argue that it reflects a new acceptance that this is a more sensitive way of showing respect for the dead than leaving their bones exposed, where they can be kicked around by any animal and even by unknowing children in play. No-one suggests that burial is associated with a new belief in afterlife. The closest that the Maasai have to any belief in immortality is the establishment of a family and ultimately an agnatic group that survives the father (or mother) and prospers. In other words, it is the total absence of any suggestion of the destructiveness of *engooki*. A peaceful death in old age, surrounded propitiously by the family with sons is felt to be the best guarantee of this.

The final settlement of a dead man's estate is supervised by a group of his surviving age mates. Each of his sons should be given some trinket, while other elders can beg for individual items. Then symbolically, his senior widow sweeps the hearth area and his age mates bless her hut to make it 'smell sweet' after his death, and they sleep there for the night.

Although the father's dying wishes cannot be ignored, it is still felt dangerous if there are too few cattle-of-his-corral left for the senior son to inherit. He is principal heir, and any sense of grievance at his brothers' better luck could bring them misfortune. In such circumstances, the younger brothers should present him with some cattle known as the 'father's chest'. Ideally, they should collect together nine cattle, but fewer are normally given except in the most unpropitious circumstances. This gift resolves any ambiguity, and they would be immune to the mystical effects of any smouldering curse the senior brother might harbour. There the matter must rest. The payment of the 'father's chest' acknowledges the father's residual authority within his senior son at a time when the family has been weakened by his death and fragmentation is imminent. Like the payment of cattle by an adulterous wife to her husband or by a rebellious son to his father, it automatically annuls the effects of anger. This is especially important in the slightly unpropitious aura surrounding the death of an established personality.

The term 'father's chest' was linked by one informant to a proverb alluding to the son's trust in his father's disinterested advice: 'You like the chest that joins together the two arms.' The father, he pointed out, is the chest, the owner of his corral and village entrance. He is the central figure of authority in his homestead, and can override any wrangling between his wives and children. They are the two arms, with their huts allocated to the right and left of his entrance. When an ox is slaughtered, the brisket-fat, underlying the chest belongs to the father and ceremonially meat from the chest region has a special significance (Chapter 14). In referring to the father as the 'chest' there is also reference to the legitimacy of his authority. The chest especially is regarded as the source of towering anger and the spittle of a blessing comes from somewhere in the chest region. The chest is generally associated with emotional strength (Chapter 8). In these ways, the term 'father's chest' evokes the paternalist bent of Maasai society, with the father controlling segments of his family, backed up by the awful possibility of his death curse.

The length of time that brothers remain together after the father's death depends on the manner in which the corpse is discarded. In the past when the body was exposed in the bush, they might stay for two months to give the bones sufficient time to separate. Today with burial, it is felt that this may take several years, and they should remain together for as long as they can without strain. Behind this is the hint that the father's uniting personality lingers while his bones still remain articulated; one might say that the chest still 'joins together the two arms'. When eventually the brothers part, it should be with good will and the senior brother retains a moral authority associated with inheriting the 'father's chest'.

Each brother's rights over his own possessions are now quite unambiguous. However, there is a lingering notion that the brothers still share a residual concern in the marriage broking of their girls. This continues for as long as there is trust, and it is a sign of strength that this should persist. Where it does so, they take care to consult one another over the marriage of any daughter and may be offered a token animal as part of the marriage debt. Any brother asking for such a gift may even refer to it loosely as 'the father's chest', invoking the lingering authority of the father which it would be unpropitious to refuse.

THE AGNATIC GROUP AND THE RULES OF INHERITANCE

The balance of concern between the day to day influence of a man's age mates in his domestic affairs and the longer term interests of his agnatic group is displayed again after his death. His age mates dispel the odour of death in his homestead and oversee the disposal of his trinkets among his sons as their 'fathers'. However, it is the agnatic group who are especially involved if there is any problem over the inheritance of stock, typically when there is no adult son to take authority. This is an agnatic matter that cuts across the divisions between age-sets. The order of precedence for transferring and inheriting stock is very explicit and is summarised in Figure 13. The elaborateness of these rules in the absence of a close heir is an indication of the intense concern to avoid squabbling, both for the sake of reputation and at the slightly unpropitious time of death. It is the elders of the agnatic group who determine the interpretation of these rules and who nominate a guardian if one is needed. If there are no close kinsmen locally, perhaps because he is an immigrant from some other tribal section, then elders of the sub-clan or even clan fill this role by default, as in Case 57. They are concerned to uphold their reputation for scruple in a situation that may tempt opportunism.

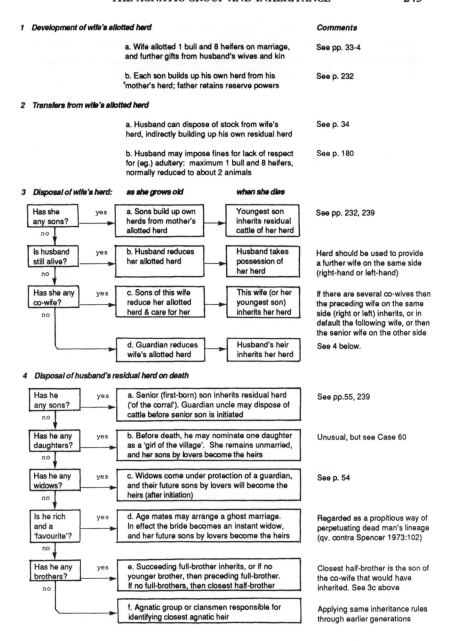

1 Development of wife's allotted herd · ***Comments***

a. Wife allotted 1 bull and 8 heifers on marriage, and further gifts from husband's wives and kin — See pp. 33-4

b. Each son builds up his own herd from his 'mother's herd; father retains reserve powers — See p. 232

2 Transfers from wife's allotted herd

a. Husband can dispose of stock from wife's herd, indirectly building up his own residual herd — See p. 34

b. Husband may impose fines for lack of respect for (eg.) adultery: maximum 1 bull and 8 heifers, normally reduced to about 2 animals — See p. 180

3 Disposal of wife's herd: **as she grows old** **when she dies**

Has she any sons?	yes →	a. Sons build up own herds from mother's allotted herd	Youngest son inherits residual cattle of her herd	See pp. 232, 239
Is husband still alive?	yes →	b. Husband reduces her allotted herd	Husband takes possession of her herd	Herd should be used to provide a further wife on the same side (right-hand or left-hand)
Has she any co-wife?	yes →	c. Sons of this wife reduce her allotted herd & care for her	This wife (or her youngest son) inherits her herd	If there are several co-wives then the preceding wife on the same side (right or left) inherits, or in default the following wife, or then the senior wife on the other side
		d. Guardian reduces wife's allotted herd	Husband's heir inherits her herd	See 4 below.

4 Disposal of husband's residual herd on death

Has he any sons?	yes →	a. Senior (first-born) son inherits residual herd ('of the corral'). Guardian uncle may dispose of cattle before senior son is initiated	See pp.55, 239
Has he any daughters?	yes →	b. Before death, he may nominate one daughter as a 'girl of the village'. She remains unmarried, and her sons by lovers become the heirs	Unusual, but see Case 60
Has he any widows?	yes →	c. Widows come under protection of a guardian, and their future sons by lovers will become the heirs (after initiation)	See p. 54
Is he rich and a 'favourite'?	yes →	d. Age mates may arrange a ghost marriage. In effect the bride becomes an instant widow, and her future sons by lovers become the heirs	Regarded as a propitious way of perpetuating dead man's lineage (qv. contra Spencer 1973:102)
Has he any brothers?	yes →	e. Succeeding full-brother inherits, or if no younger brother, then preceding full-brother. If no full-brothers, then closest half-brother	Closest half-brother is the son of the co-wife that would have inherited. See 3c above
		f. Agnatic group or clansmen responsible for identifying closest agnatic heir	Applying same inheritance rules through earlier generations

Figure 13 Rules for the transfer and inheritance of stock

A loophole in this system is when the agnatic group of a dead man is represented by just one surviving brother or cousin. This leaves his wishes open to abuse in the first instance. Once again more distant clansmen will only intervene after a direct appeal has been made to them.

Case 60.
Silaloi had three daughters but no sons. He therefore informed other elders that his youngest daughter, Siekwa, would remain unmarried as a 'girl of the village' to bear him a male heir (Figure 13:4b). After his death, his agnatic cousin, Naporda, became guardian of the household, and assumed control of his herds. He then arranged a marriage for Siekwa, and there were no other close agnates to object.
  Siekwa's husband died soon ('days') after the birth of her first child, a daughter. She ran away with the infant to a sub-clansman who was also a spokesman of her father's age-set. There, she claimed that the death had occurred because her father's wishes had been ignored: his death curse was hanging over them. The spokesman had no hesitation in leading a deputation of sub-clan elders to Naporda. It took time and a lot of pressure to persuade him to restore Siekwa to her legitimate position before there was further misfortune. Siekwa only bore one more child, a son who became Silaloi's heir. By 1977, she was a formidable lady living with this son at Meto, and he had four wives and ten sons of his own. This was taken as a sign that the elders had been right to respect Silaloi's wishes.

The remarriage of widows is another somewhat anomalous area where expedience may overrule the norm that such women should remain under the protection of a guardian to bear children and an heir for the dead husband. If a widow is to be remarried, the consent of her father is vital, and this is then confirmed by placing an iron ring round her ankle.

Case 61.
Soibe's husband died soon ('days') after he led her to his village as his first wife. Masiani as the closest half-brother was ideally placed to become guardian and consort on behalf of her husband. Instead of following this course, however, he proposed that he should take over the dead man's role *in toto*, as she was still only a girl and her marriage was barely established. She would become his own fourth wife and would retain the cattle of her allotted herd, while he would manage the rest. There were no closer brothers of the dead man to object; and Soibe's father readily agreed: he had no wish to see his daughter a widow so soon.

An intriguing feature of this case is that it was open to two interpretations. The first was the widely accepted view that Masiani had become Soibe's husband in the fullest sense, in effect inheriting both wife and stock. The second was that the only propitious outcome would be for Masiani to remain as her guardian. Her sons would then be recognised at initiation as sons of the dead man. Yet neither interpretation made any difference to the practicalities of day to day existence while they were still children. As there had been no misfortune and Masiani had placed an iron ring round her ankle at her father's home, the issue seemed unlikely to be raised in future.

Where a dead man already has sons, there can be no denying their right to inherit his stock, and with full independence once the oldest has been initiated. However, they may still be faced with a request for cattle from the senior uncle, who again may invoke the 'father's chest', implying that the bond uniting brothers in the previous generation still lingers. In the context of recent death, it would again be unpropitious to refuse this. If he was particularly close to the father and well respected, then each of the sons might offer him a cow. Otherwise, he might be given just one animal by the senior son, and only if he asks for it. Again there is a notion of finality, and further requests of this sort cannot be made by more distant kin.

This gift of the 'father's chest' is only intended to be final in relation to stock. It does not lessen the dependence of the younger generation on their senior agnates for powerful support in arranging their marriages. Then, not surprisingly, when it comes to the marriages of their own sisters and daughters, they may find themselves exposed to these same uncles asserting their patronage.

At some point, the brothers, may feel they have acquired sufficient seniority to dispose of their own sisters and daughters, without the interference of the senior generation. The correct way of retaining their good will is to offer their most respected uncle the right to dispose of just one further girl. While the agnatic group remains strong, the older men may still seek to use their influence. From this point, however, the nephews can persuade them to accept instead the occasional animal from the marriage debt of subsequent girls.

Case 62.
Mebugu's father had already promised two of his daughters to other men before he died. His surviving brother then proposed to rearrange their marriages. Mebugu was obliged to respect this uncle, especially as he had been very close to his father and was of the same age-set. However, he was himself a well established elder and was also determined to respect his father's wishes with regard to these two girls. As a ritual leader he already faced the prospect of misfortune without compounding it further. He offered his uncle the right to choose a suitor for a younger girl of the family on the definite understanding that he would not again try to influence further suits.

Comparing this with Case 53, it may be noted that no-one on that occasion was prepared to stand up for the wishes of the dead man, and his daughter's marriage was expediently rearranged.

THE DISPERSAL OF BROTHERS

Concern for reputation is a characteristic feature of the agnatic bond at every level, ranging from control over unruly members to negotiations over contentious divorce suits. Oaths frequently invoke the clan or sub-clan or agnatic group, by name or by some allusion to their cattle, expressing pride and loyalty. Brothers on a raid were expected to fight side by side. When first engaging the enemy they could invoke their father's name as an oath that implicated the honour of the family. The diehard who died in anger had wanted to avenge his brother. And so on. After the death of the father, brothers continue to share this sense of deep loyalty, and they should disperse before any strains appear between them. They can come together again at any time, but only in strict amity.

This closeness of brothers is partly explained by the rigid rules of inheritance that preclude rivalries between half-brothers, whose mothers have separate allotted herds. Even the ambiguity of the division of the mother's allotted herd among full brothers is offset by the random fluctuations in fortune in the pastoral economy. As a result, no regular pattern of friction between brothers appears to emerge from the available data.

Given this background of loyalty, it is also characteristic that the Matapato should idealise instances where particular friendships between brothers coincide with the bonds of age-set loyalty. These may date from the time when they were together in the same hut as manyata moran, as full or half-brothers. There is no suggestion that age-set bonds and family loyalties belong to separate domains, but only that the one is expected to reinforce the other.

Case 63.
Adoli and his four brothers remained very close friends after the death of their father, and continued to share the same village regularly. Adoli as senior son had the right to dispose of their unmarried sisters, but to maintain their unity, he always first consulted his brothers (B to E in the diagram). This practice of consultation was continued when they started to marry off their daughters, and they boasted that they had never disagreed in giving away any girl. However, no-one expected this idyllic unity to be maintained indefinitely and the inevitable strains appeared over four successive marriages (a to d in the diagram).

(*a*) During the period of close harmony, the two youngest brothers (D and E) supported the suit of an age mate (Y) for one of Adoli's daughters. Adoli had no firm plans for her, and agreed to this proposal.

(*b*) The first sign of strain emerged over the marriage plans for another of Adoli's daughters. D and E supported the suit of another age mate (Z) whom Adoli mistrusted. D and E then called a meeting of all the brothers, and asked Y to attend to lend his support as another age mate of Z. Rather than argue with his brothers in front of his son-in-law, Adoli again deferred, though with reservations.

(*c*) It was this episode that apparently led Adoli shortly afterwards to support a suitor of his own choice for D's daughter. He called on his son-in-law Y to persuade D as an age mate to agree to this, although D had favoured another man. D agreed, also reluctantly; and Y for the second time had been put in a compromising position to resolve the differences between Adoli and his brothers.

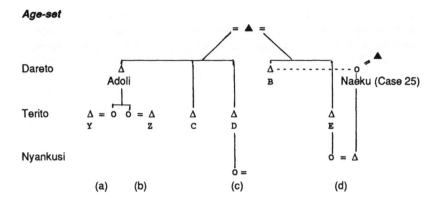

(a) (b) (c) (d)

(d) The second brother B was of the same age-set as Adoli and was approached by a widow, Naeku, to arrange the marriage of her son (Case 25). He suggested that E should offer his daughter, and this was supported by Adoli, who again called on Y to use his influence as an age mate to persuade E. E deferred to this pressure.

Unity was maintained, but the brothers now agreed that family loyalty had been stretched to its limit. The older brothers felt that D and E had been too ready to exploit Adoli's good will (a and especially b). The younger brothers felt that Adoli had overreacted (c and d). Y as their son-in-law and age mate wanted nothing more than to be allowed to mind his own domestic affairs. A point had been reached whereby the marriages of two daughters of Dareto age-set had been arranged by brothers of Terito age-set, and then their roles were exactly reversed in the next two marriages. The symmetry suggested that this was a suitable point to moderate their overbearing unity. By 1977, the brothers no longer made a point of consulting one another regarding the marriage of every daughter. However, each suitor selected for their daughters was told to present a cow and some beer to Adoli as their senior brother. They still retained a reputation for close loyalty towards one another.

The brothers in this case took pride in the fact that the strain that inevitably developed had not been between the two sides of their father's polygynous household (Adoli/C/D v. B/E), but between age-sets (Adoli/B v. C/D/E), and to this extent no lasting rift in the family had occurred. A less glossy view would be that the relationship between half-brothers is easier than between full brothers. Full brothers grow up in tacit competition over the allotted herd of the same mother, and tend to be spaced apart by age. There are stricter rules of respect and precedence between them, typified by the gifts of respect to older brothers and to each other's wives. Half-brothers do not make these gifts and are ideal consorts for each other's widows.

As against the ideal of close fellowship between brothers, there is a recognition that they also have some of the bitterest quarrels. These are felt to be altogether more intense than between unrelated elders. Beliefs in sorcery are frequently associated with jealousy and mistrust between brothers. This is regarded as primarily a family affair that does not concern other people; and it is not thought to operate on the same catastrophic scale as the sorcery that may threaten a major festival. However, it does have a wider relevance in that the worst kind of indiscriminate sorcerers are also thought to be fratricidal. In Case 49, the accused sorcerer Malaso was also thought to have killed his half-brother. Again, the most notorious sorcerers are held to be among the Loonkidongi diviners, inspired by jealousy of their more successful brothers and other agnatic kin: as they say, 'The Loonkidongi have no brothers.' Another popular image of sorcery is when a wife who has just lost her baby blames a jealous co-wife who is barren (qv. Case 4). Accusations between women do not appear to excite the same degree of concern, however, and no-one suggests that the sorcerers who threaten whole communities by interfering in festivals are women. Like the Loonkidongi diviners, they are all assumed to be men. Allegations of sorcery against brothers are rare, but they are still altogether more common than specific accusations of sorcery beyond the family. In these respects, Matapato beliefs in sorcery are very much to do with brothers.

Three examples that reverberated round the Meto area suggest no clear pattern other than that brothers are at risk from one another after their father's death. In the first, the fact that the suspect was the senior brother gave him no immunity. Through his sorcery he lost his moral authority over his younger brothers (qv. Case 57). In the second, there was a suspect without misfortune, and in the third there was misfortune without a suspect. All three allegations were resolved by moving apart.

Case 64

(a) Saigol was the senior son of a large family who had been forced to become a premature elder by his father and was despised by his younger brothers who had all been manyata moran. After his father's death, four of his brothers died and a fifth became mad. Saigol was then found to possess some bright red powder and his surviving brothers accused him of sorcery. They beat him and sent him away, warning him that they would beat him again if he ever returned.

(b) Olaitei was the second of seven brothers who had remained together after their father's death. They suffered no misfortunes, but Olaitei was irascible and a vicious circle of bad faith developed with his brothers for which they roundly blamed him. Eventually, they accused him of sorcery and told him to move away, while they themselves stayed together.

(c) Mitikini had three wives and a large family, and then suffered a spate of bereavements. None of his brothers had been so successful and he suspected sorcery although he did not know which brother to blame. His misfortune preyed on him, and he migrated from Matapato to settle down in Kisonko, leaving his brothers with the problem of coping with the sorcerer in their midst.

Better by far, they say, that brothers should move apart before their rivalries reach this pitch. No-one likes to see elders quarrel, and when they happen to be brothers then there could be an even darker side.

CONCLUSION: THE HYPOTHESIS OF THE WASTREL AND THE COMPLEX OF FAMILY RELATIONS

The possibility of sorcery between brothers after their father's death should be seen as an aspect of the complex of family relations. This extends to the related concern over wastrels and also to the popular fantasy of the guardian as an unscrupulous ogrelike brother of the father. Incidentally, Masiani suggested that his father too had been killed by the sorcery of a brother who then became his guardian (Case 6).

It is intriguing to consider the possibility that the root of this complex could be embedded in the experiences of boyhood coupled with the ethos of Matapato society. Brothers are drawn together from an early age in defence of their family reputation and herd. The father plays an important role in fostering this and encouraging them to respond readily to the challenge of herding. However, fathers also have a quite arbitrary power. In selecting those sons who are favourites and identifying those who are wastrels at a relatively tender age, it seems quite feasible that some fathers overreact. They may even drive their less adept sons towards defeatism. Alternatively, the negativeness of the wastrel, like the truanting herdboy, might be regarded as a passive form of rebellion by those who are driven too hard by their fathers. Whatever the precise cause, there is disgust at the number of boys who become wastrels, giving a distinct impression of a vicious circle between some fathers and their sons (Chapter 4).

The father's arbitrary power leaves scope for unequal opportunity and rivalry between brothers. It is the father who is free to encourage favourites, possibly discourage others, and decide which should be circumcised early or late, or be denied the kudos and discipline of a manyata moranhood. Those that become premature elders and especially those that are wastrels are despised. For such men are felt more likely to resort to sorcery in sheer jealousy and spite. Generally among brothers, their concern for family reputation prevails over their rivalries, especially if they are of the same age-set and while the father is still alive. They share a deep trust in his protection, expressed by the young elder who claimed that he wanted to be with his father so that he would not be pestered by older men. When the father grants his sons some independence or dies, his heavy dominance over them is lifted. Instances of discord between brothers after the father's death are unusual, but they conform to a recognised pattern, and this is why brothers should move apart. The two strands of the paternal yoke – the father's partiality to certain sons and his unremitting protection – leave the sons exposed after his death. They are not just exposed to the demands of some senior agnates, but also to one another, and to their own weaknesses. A recurrent theme in some examples cited in this chapter is of worthy elders who lose the will to persist and become wastrels once they are free of the father's influence. This is to suggest that the phenomenon of wastrels among the Maasai is the product of the competitive pressures generated within the family.

A strong argument in favour of this interpretation lies in the quite different configuration of wastrels, clans and family relations among the Samburu, which supports some kind of correlation (Spencer 1965). It was noted in Chapter 2 that unlike the Maasai, the Samburu have exceptionally strong clans. Ties of clanship and clan reputation do not merely become significant by default. They are of the essence, and clansmen are very ready to constrain the arbitrary excesses of any individual member. When a stock owner overreacts, his local clansmen do not wait for an appeal from wives or brothers or sons before they can intervene. The more ramshackle appearance of Samburu architecture also means less effective sound-proofing, and a domestic dispute can very quickly become a local clan matter. Unlike the Matapato, Samburu are more constrained to conform to clan ideals and the principal arena of competition is between clans. There is fierce rivalry between clans among moran, and in family life those who are feared for the trouble they might bring are not brothers or father's-brothers, but affines and mothers'-brothers from other clans. In Matapato, a firestick elder who is also a mother's-brother is an ideal ritual sponsor in any personal ceremony, such as circumcision or 'drinking milk'. In Samburu he would be avoided.

The age system cuts across Samburu clans as it does in Matapato, but age-sets are organised on a clan rather than a territorial basis. Through their clan-based age system, the first marriages of moran are delayed. The age gap between generations is therefore high, and few fathers are below sixty-five when their oldest sons marry. Many do not live that long. With this delay, there is less scope for conflict between fathers and sons. The clan is *in loco parentis* in a very real sense, and continues in this role throughout the remainder of a man's life. In contrast to the Matapato system in which a proportion of sons marry early while others who are wastrels may never marry, Samburu moran have to wait longer for their first marriages. However, it is relatively certain that they will all marry when their time comes: the clan will see to it.[2] Correspondingly, there is little concern about wastrels, who in the more conformist milieu of Samburu appear to be altogether more rare (or at least more containable).

And there is no serious concern over sorcery and little truck with Prophets, whom they associate with the more thrusting nature of Maasai society. The domestic problems of Samburu society relate to the gerontocratic delay in first marriage, which brings the moran into more direct conflict with their firestick patrons; and these by convention cannot be their own fathers. This contrasts with Matapato society, where the father is thrust into a more prominent role, and there is a radical shift in popular concern towards the contradictions of patriarchy and its aftermath after the father is dead

NOTES

1 It may be noted that the formal division of wives into right-hand and left-hand sides had no bearing on Taraiye's decision to divide his family. Similarly, it does not relate to any elder's pragmatic decision to separate wives to different portions of the village with independent entrances. Apart from loosely structuring the general pattern of friendships among wives, other things being equal, the division between sides is most relevant to inheritance when a wife leaves no son.

2. In a clan sample among the Samburu, virtually no moran under thirty were married as compared with perhaps one quarter in Matapato. Correspondingly, only 3% of Samburu elders above that age were unmarried (mostly widowers) corresponding to perhaps 14% in Matapato (mostly regarded as wastrels).

CHAPTER 14

THE MEAT FEAST

A study of Matapato society is necessarily a study of the ritual process associated with ageing, for this provides the major dimension of their system. Within this process, their collective ceremonies are the nodes in what is otherwise a largely dispersed existence. At these ceremonies the meat feast is the one event that is guaranteed to draw a crowd and promote an awareness of the occasion. It is a topic that is complex to handle and too important to ignore. It bears on many points of this study and provides an opportunity to supplement earlier chapters, ending on a festive note.

THE FEAST OF THE GREAT OX (*LOOLBAA*)

As an introduction to the topic, one may consider a personal festival that is regarded as a high point in an elder's career, corresponding to the high point for each wife when she is 'led with cattle'. The Great Ox is the last of a sequence of feasts that should have been celebrated by each elder before any of his children are initiated (Figure 2). It finally settles his transition to elderhood with a symbolic return from the bush to the village domain. At *eunoto*, when moran process back to the village after the feast of the 'forest ox', the ritual leader is symbolically first to settle down to elderhood. In a sense this is *his* Great Ox; he is given a name and becomes great for his age-group. Years later, when his age mates hold their own Great Ox feasts as individuals, they too renounce traces of moranhood, and they are endowed with new names and the attributes of greatness. It is a ceremony that is nurtured by older men, demanding respect and overawing younger men with the responsibilities of full elderhood, and endowing old age itself with a charisma.

For the Great Ox feast, a really fine ox is suffocated in a ritual enclosure in the bush. The left-hand column of Figure 14 indicates the order of

Details of the Great Ox feast (loolbaa)	*Comparable details elsewhere*
1. The ceremony is normally delayed until just before the initiation of the first child (but could take place earlier depending on family tradition).	*Calf-of-the-threshold.* Performed for the celebrant's first child at about this time (ie. shortly before initiation), but it could be performed sooner by certain families (p. 58).
2. The ceremony enacts an elder's symbolic return to the village domain with the solemn procession from the feast in the bush to his village (see 10 below). It is associated with three earlier feasts representing his removal from the village domain as a boy (opposite), also performed by brothers in order of birth.	Three feasts precede the Great Ox (p. 62). *Calf-of-the-threshold* entails his ritual emergence from his mother's hut before initiation (p. 58). *Goat-of-the-shrubs* is a diminutive version of the Great Ox performed near the village (p. 62). *Ox-of-the-wooden-earplugs* marks his induction into the forest as a feasting moran (p. 84).
3. The feast is sited inside a ritual enclosure under some non-thorny ('cold') trees away from the village. The celebrant has a wholly passive role. Elders do not sit grouped in their age-sets.	*Death ox.* Consumed under 'cold' trees where the (passive) corpse will be laid away from the village. Allocation of cuts of meat are similar to the Great Ox feast, and this is the only other feast where elders are not grouped in their age-sets (p. 240).
4. Celebrant and age partner wear ceremonial gear (black calfskin capes, scroll brass ear-rings, red ochre) and remain placid as ritual dependants while the meat feasting progresses.	*Initiations.* Father and an age partner wear ceremonial gear and sit in vigil throughout the heat of the day while the festivities progress, and they must remain placid throughout. (But this takes place in the village and not in the bush; p. 59).
5. Celebrant also carries an unstrung bow, a quiver, an unpointed arrow, and in some other Maasai sections he wears a head feather.	*Male initiates* after circumcision carry bows and blunted arrows to shoot birds for their headdresses (p. 76).
6. Two firestick patrons kindle the fire for the feast - even if they are by now so old that they have to be carried and helped with the kindling.	*Male Initiations.* Two firestick patrons kindle the circumcision fire to induct the initiate into his age-set. This is the only other occasion when they kindle a fire for individual males (pp. 74-5).
7. This is the last act that the firestick patrons perform for their wards individually.	*Olngesher.* This is the last collective act of the firestick patrons inducting their wards as an age-set into elderhood (p. 186).
8. The entrance of the ritual enclosure faces north or south. Possible sorcerers are not allowed inside, and remnants of the feast are burnt afterwards as a further precaution against sorcery.	*Sacrificial festivals.* A ritual enclosure is constructed with an entrance facing towards north or south, and there are similar precautions against sorcery (p. 140).
9. In late afternoon, the celebrant's senior wife joins him and they give each other a token whipping providing neither have 'stooped' in hypo-adulterty since *olngesher*. Otherwise they must confess beforehand, or risk death.	*Olngesher and 'eating meat' festivals.* Wives watch their husbands accept meat offered by a woman unless either has 'stooped' in hypo-adultery, when they would risk death. They should confess beforehand. On returning home, *olngesher* celebrants give their dependants a token whipping (pp. 179-85).
10. The celebrant and his age partner lead the senior wife in procession back to the village, leading to a teasing display of mock aggression between the sexes (see 11 below).	*Marriage.* Groom and best man in ritual gear lead the bride to his village where she is teased (p. 31). *Eunoto.* Procession back from the forest to the ritual village leads to a semi-mocking test of sexual virtue for moran (p. 160).
11. On returning to the village, there is a boisterous whipping contest between the sexes for possession of the rib-fat. The women should be allowed to win. The celebrant and his wife remain aloof, but his age mates and their wives are prominent. Note that this is a burlesque of the token whipping in 9 above.	*Women's mobbing.* May lead to attacks on elders, countering beatings inflicted on women (p. 201). *Ox-of-the-wooden-earplugs.* Entails verbal teasing between moran and their mothers over allocated fats – in some other Maasai sections especially (p. 84). *Calf-of-the-threshold.* Wives of the two moieties playfully vie for the rib-fat (p. 58).
12. In the celebrant's hut in the evening, the firestick patrons offer him and his ritual partner the brisket-fat (normally the father's cut). He is blessed and is given a new name.	*Calf-of-the-threshold.* The initiate is offered the brisket-fat by the elders, given a new name, and blessed (p. 58). *Eunoto.* Age-group of moran are blessed with brisket-fat in the forest and given a new name (p. 159).
13. The celebrant and his age partner must each treat the other and his wives with great respect and should never refuse any request.	*Eunoto.* The reciprocal relationship between each age-group as a body and their ritual leader is similar and extends to their wives (pp. 156, 174). Distant age mates are also feared (pp. 189-90).

Figure 14   The Great Ox feast compared with other rites of transition

events of this feast; and the right-hand column identifies parallels with other feasts or festivals. Many of these parallels are features that are central to these other occasions, and this colours their meaning at the Great Ox feast. And indeed vice versa: in some other parallels, it is the Great Ox feast that is the more significant, and this colours the other occasions. Thus, the celebrant's placid vigil at his Great Ox while the elders prepare and eat their share of the feast is very similar to his vigil at the initiation of each of his children (4). However, it is the Great Ox vigil that is of prime significance. There is a more pronounced concern to avoid sorcery (8) or any discordant note; and the gravity of his future relationship with his age partner does not apply to his partner at an initiation. Confessing hypo-adultery before the Great Ox, on the other hand, is less significant than at *olngesher*: there is no build-up to a confrontation between the celebrant and his wife over their sexual indiscretions (9). On this occasion, any confession is a mere detail rather than a major issue; but still, it must be settled with the gift of a heifer well in advance. Any bitterness is then resolved and the feast will not be marred by revelations that would shatter the serenity of the celebrant. The firestick patrons warn the couple beforehand to confess to one another and make their peace with dignity.

After the elders have finished their feast, the celebrant's senior wife comes to the enclosure late in the afternoon. Standing on the unslashed reticulum (second stomach) of the ox, the couple gently whip each other with four token strokes. Then they sit side by side on the ox's head facing the direction of the village, before returning there. The procession back to the village symbolises the celebrant's final reincorporation into the village domain as a mature man who must be highly respected by all.

As in some other feasts, the ox's fat has a special role. On their arrival at the village there is an abrupt change in mood. Age mates of the celebrant armed with switches impale the rib-fat of the ox on a stick and plant it firmly just inside the village. They then defend this against their wives (also armed with switches) who try to seize this fat (11). Other women may join in, provided that they are not 'daughters' or 'mothers-in-law' of these elders. By convention, the women should be allowed to run away with the fat on their fourth attempt. This is the one ritual of reversal in which both sexes confront one another on equal terms. The four sorties with whips are a burlesque of the four token switches between the celebrant and his wife earlier on. The elders have the upper hand, but claim that they are often taken off their guard by the tough determination of some more agile women to hit back at them. The women relish the opportunity and no longer fear the sting of a whip (photograph Beckwith 1980:254–5). This episode has a parallel in the calf-of-the-threshold which normally follows for the oldest child soon after the father's Great Ox. By comparison the calf is a skinny animal with little rib-fat, but this fat even so is the prize of a boisterous tussle. This is between women who align themselves with their husbands' moieties, rather as moran were expected to divide between moieties in any squabble over the spoil after a raid. Of the two burlesques, that of the Great Ox recalls the violent friction of early marriage at a time when the wife is establishing a niche. So in the burlesque, the wives are finally entitled to capture the rib-fat. The calf-of-the-threshold burlesque plays on the rivalry between patrilineal groups over cattle and prestige. In these ways, two of the divisions of Matapato society that are relevant at the domestic level – between the sexes and between families – are enacted at a time when there is a ritual focus on the divide between generations. The father is raised to full elderhood as his first-born is poised for initiation.

The final act of the Great Ox takes place in the evening. It is again solemn as the celebrant shares the brisket-fat with his age partner in his own hut; and their firestick patrons bless them. They emphasise the extreme respect that they should show for each other in future, amounting almost to an avoidance, rather as they should respect their ritual leader or any distant age mate. It is respect for the age-set (12 and 13).

In these ways, those attending the Great Ox feast perform the occasion, by reading the left-hand column of Figure 14 downwards, as it were. However, their experience is coloured by the wider connotations, in effect reading the chart across at each stage. The feast is replete with metaphorical associations: initiation, death, the ceremonial development of the age-set through a succession of critical transitions, and so on. Having been involved in each of these other ceremonies on many occasions, all participants carry a repertoire of these vivid associations. The symbolism of the feast yields a panoramic representation of a whole system of collective representations.

PRINCIPLES OF ALLOCATING MEAT

A systematic analysis of all the cross-links between Matapato ceremonies is beyond the scope of this work, but the meat feast at least is an ideal topic to probe in this direction. It is a central feature in nearly every ceremony, each with its prescribed variations. Meat feasting is avidly discussed both in its major principles and with a loving attention to detail, and even in times of hunger. It is clear that it goes beyond the need for subsistence or the sheer enjoyment of good food and good company. It is a topic in its own right that appears to have its own inner logic, although this is never quite made explicit. One is led therefore to explore the implicit patterns as a further step towards interpreting ceremony.

The basic structure of any meat feast is most clear when an ox is slaughtered for its meat in a time of need. The prescribed cuts for different

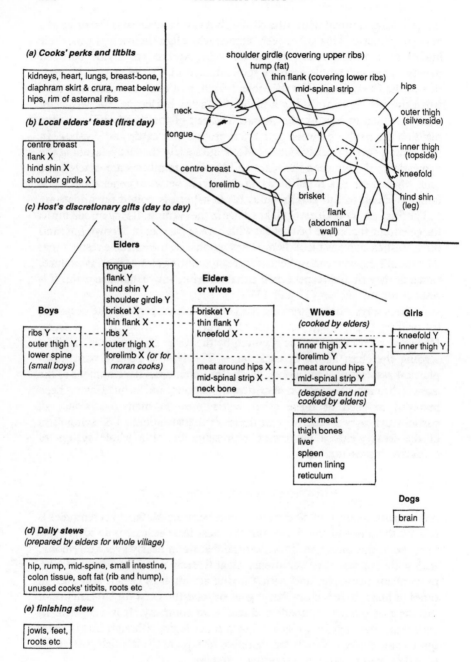

(a) Cooks' perks and titbits

kidneys, heart, lungs, breast-bone, diaphram skirt & crura, meat below hips, rim of asternal ribs

(b) Local elders' feast (first day)

centre breast
flank X
hind shin X
shoulder girdle X

(c) Host's discretionary gifts (day to day)

Elders

tongue
flank Y
hind shin Y
shoulder girdle Y
brisket X - - - - - -
thin flank X - - - -
ribs X
outer thigh X
forelimb X *(or for
     moran cooks)*

Boys

ribs Y - - - - -
outer thigh Y - - - -
lower spine
(small boys)

**Elders
or wives**

brisket Y
thin flank Y
kneefold X - - - - -
inner thigh X - - - - -
forelimb Y
meat around hips X - - - -
mid-spinal strip X - - - -
neck bone

Wives
(cooked by elders)

inner thigh X - - - - -
forelimb Y
meat around hips Y
mid-spinal strip Y

*(despised and not
cooked by elders)*

neck meat
thigh bones
liver
spleen
rumen lining
reticulum

Girls

kneefold Y
inner thigh Y

Dogs

brain

(d) Daily stews
(prepared by elders for whole village)

hip, rump, mid-spine, small intestine, colon tissue, soft fat (rib and hump), unused cooks' titbits, roots etc

(e) finishing stew

jowls, feet, roots etc

Figure 15 Distribution of cuts in a subsistence meat feast.

KEY

X	Paired
Y	cuts ↓
e	Elders
m	Moran
b	Boys
w	Wives
d	Dogs
mw	Choice of m or w etc ↓

1. Moran forest feasts (p. 123)
2. Ox-of-the-wooden-earplugs (p. 84)
3. *Eunoto* forest feasts (pp. 153, 162-3)
4. *Eunoto* sacrifices (pp.158-61)
5. Moran *esoogo* punishment (p. 211)
6. Boys' dancing festival (p. 70)
7. Initiation ox (for either sex - p. 59)
8. Death ox & Great Ox (pp. 240, 252-4)
9. Elders' *esoogo* punishment (p. 211)
10. Ox-that-smears-the-women (p. 202)
11. Women's festival (p. 222)
12. Calf-of-the-threshold (pp. 58, 63n, 269n)
13. Women's mobbing (actual - p. 205)
14. Women's mobbing (fantasy - p. 206)

CUTS	1	2	3	4	5	6	7	8	9	10	11	12	13	14	TASTE RATING	COMMENTS
Tongue	m	e	e	e	e	e	e	e	e	e	e	e	e	w	1	Very high status and tender
Centre breast	m	e	e	e	e	e	e	e	e	e	e	e	e	w	3	Very high status, but tough
Flank X	m	e	e	e	e	e	e	e	e	e	e	e	e	w	1	High status
															5	
Hind shin X	m	me	e	e	e	e	e	e	e	e	e	e	e	w	2	High status
Shoulder girdle X	m	me	me	me	e	e	e	e	e	e	e	e	e	w	3	m Given to ritual leader
Hind shin Y	m	m	me	me	me	b	e	e	e	e	e	e+w	ew	w	2	
															7	
Outer thigh X	m	m	m	m	me	be	e	e	e	e	e	e	ew	w	2	Outer thigh Y given to boys
Thin flank X	m	m	**m**	**m**	me	be	e	e	e	e	e	e	ew	w	3	m Given to ritual leader
Ribs X	m	m	m	me	m	be	e	e	e	e	e	w	e	w	2	Ribs Y given to boys
															7	
Flank Y	m	m	**m**	m	m	b	e	e	e	e	e	e+w	w	w	1	m Given to ritual leader or to a highly respected age mate
Brisket X	m	m	m	m	me	be	e	e	e	ew	ew	e	ew	w	4	
Shoulder girdle Y	m	m	m	m	m	b	●	e	e	e	e	e+w	w	w	3	e Given to the circumciser
															8	
Mid-spinal strip X	m	m	☆	☆	m	☆	e	e	e	ew	ew	e	w	w	4	☆ Included in the hump
Hip meat X	m	m	m	m	m	b	e	e	e	ew	ew	w	w	w	5	
Forelimb X	m	m	m	m	m	b	me	e	e	ew	w	w	w	w	2	m Given to moran if butcher/cooks to eat in the bush
															11	
Neck bone	m	m	m	m	m	b	e	e	e	ew	w	w	w	w	4	Very tough
Thin flank Y	m	m	m	m	m	b	e	ew	ew	w	w	e+w	w	w	3	Esp. owner's discretion
Brisket Y	m	m	m	m	m	b	ew	ew	ew	w	w	w	w	w	4	Esp. owner's discretion
															11	
Mid-spinal strip Y	m	m	☆	☆	m	☆	ew	ew	ew	w	w	w	w	w	4	☆ Included in the hump
Hip meat Y	m	mw	mw	mw	mw	bw	ew	ew	ew	w	w	w	w	w	5	Esp. determined by demand
Kneefold X	m	mw	mw	mw	mw	bw	ew	ew	ew	w	w	w	w	w	3	Kneefold Y given to girls
															12	
Inner thigh X	m	w	w	w	w	w	w	w	w	w	w	w	w	w	5	Inner thigh Y given to girls
Forelimb Y	m	w	w	w	w	w	w	w	w	w	w	w	w	w	2	
Neck meat	m	w	w	w	w	w	w	w	w	w	w	w	w	w	4	
															11	
Thigh bones	m	w	w	w	w	w	w	w	w	w	w	w	w	w	6	
Innards: liver	m	w	w	w	w	w	w	w	w	w	w	w	w	w	7	None of these parts
spleen	m	w	w	w	w	w	w	w	w	w	w	w	w	w	7	would be cooked by
															20	the elders for the
reticulum	m	w	w	w	w	w	w	w	w	w	w	w	w	w	7	women, even at
rumen	m	w	w	w	w	w	w	w	w	w	w	w	w	w	8	festivals
Brain	m	d	d	d	d	d	d	d	d	d	d	d	d	d	8	
	(a)					(b)			(c)						23	

(a) All firestick sacrifices follow an identical pattern to *eunoto*, with the firestick wards cast as 'moran' (m). In addition to the brisket and a flank, the moran wards are offered the inner chest (*enabooshoke*, ie. heart+lungs+breast-bone+diaphram) and inside meat of the upper forelimb. The firestick patrons have the hump including the mid-spinal strips.
(b) Moran may share with the elders at the feast of a death ox, but not at the Great Ox feast.
(c) Includes two unusual pairs: the backbone+hump (X and Y) and breastbone+brisket (X and Y). See p. 269 n3.

Figure 16 The ceremonial distribution of meat

categories of feaster on such an occasions are summarised in Figure 15.
Initially, there is a minor feast in the bush in which some choice cuts are
shared by any elders who happen to be in the area. Separating the animal
into its various cuts and preparing for this feast is an ideal job for moran.
They may nibble certain titbits, and be given a forelimb to share further
from the village when their task is done. The remaining cuts are stored
and cooked in the elders' mess near the host's village, and the feasting
continues as a village affair with an extended supply of roast meat and stew
for a week or so. Daily preparation is largely by men who maintain that
women are atrocious and dirty cooks. Within this broad structure, the
host has complete discretion to make the elders' local feast more of an
occasion by donating further cuts to it. Equally he may allocate particular
cuts to selected elders or wives or to the stew. It is his interpretation of his
obligations and of the needs of the occasion as well as the quality of the
beast that are the memorable aspects of the feast. They may even be
recited years later. Finally, when the supply of meat is ended, a finishing
stew is prepared to clear up any upset tummies.[1]

The subsistence feast provides a basic pattern for more ceremonial
occasions and is elaborated according to ritual context. This leaves less
discretion for the host and less food subsequently for the village.
Frequently, the elaborations focus on particular cuts of meat, but all cuts
have their prescribed use. The matrix shown in Figure 16 summarises the
allocations of twenty-nine cuts of meat in fourteen different ceremonial ox
feasts. The columns and rows in this matrix have been ordered so as to
group together categories of feaster, avoiding what would otherwise have
resembled a haphazard distribution. No other way of ordering the matrix
readily suggests itself. With this summary of the data, a number of
underlying principles can be explored.

(a) THE BALANCE OF SUPPLY WITH DEMAND

The grouping of categories of feaster in this way produces a gradation of
columns. On the extreme left, moran (M) at their remote forest feasts
demolish the entire beast, even the most despised parts. On the extreme
right, in the fantasy of a mobbing, women (W) are held to ravage the
carcase in their fury, and elders would not dare or even want to share in
this. Between these two extremes as one scans across the matrix, there is a
logical trend with elders (E) predominating in the central columns. The
broad profile of allocations reflects a basic principle of these feasts that the
supply of meat should match the demand. It is this principle that explains
the more flexible categories (such as M/E) where the numbers who happen
to be present will determine whether it is moran or elders who will be
given a particular cut. The basic rule is that guests should be feasted, and

this imposes certain pragmatic constraints on the discretion of the host.

(b) THE HIERARCHY OF TASTE

The ordering of the rows of Figure 16 implies a hierarchy of cuts. The most striking aspect of this hierarchy was discovered almost by chance after a wide-ranging search for basic structural principles had revealed very little. This new factor was the Matapato elders' perception of taste, which is popularly regarded as universal rather than acquired through their culture. Not only could informants compare the taste of different cuts of beef, but when asked, they were even able to rank them in order as an abstract exercise. This gave the elusiveness of taste an unexpectedly direct relevance. To remove some quite minor inconsistencies between informants, especially over cuts that were grouped closely together, their rankings were reduced to an eight-point scale, ranging from 'extremely sweet' (1) down to 'barely tolerable' (7) and 'distasteful' (8). A column towards the right in Figure 16 shows the taste-ratings of the various cuts according to this scale. The cuts have also been aggregated in groups of three to indicate more clearly the broad trend from the tastiest cuts at the top to the most degrading.

The allocation of the best cuts to the elders is axiomatic. They see themselves as the gourmets of Matapato, and in relegating the worst cuts to women, they argue that women are quite undiscriminating (or sometimes more honestly, that they cannot know the value of what they have never tasted). It is taste that is emphasised; and there is no notion, for instance, that the brain should be more respected as a cut because the head is revered in other contexts (pp. 105 and 176). In fact, the brain is considered quite revolting and fit only for dogs, who have even less taste sense than women. However, it is held that even dogs are part of the village community, scavenging by day and alert for intruders by night. They have a right to their cut like everyone else.

(c) DUAL OPPOSITIONS BETWEEN CUTS

We now turn from the broad principles to the finer logic in allocating specific cuts. The slaughter of an animal entails a transformation from a living whole owned by one man to an arrangement of pairs. Pairing is a recurrent feature of Maasai society with clans divided between two moieties, two opposed firestick alliances, and the division of age-groups and also wives between right-hand and left-hand. Similarly in ceremony there is a deliberate emphasis on the opposition of pairs, and pairs of pairs, whence the frequent occurrence of the numbers two, four and sometimes even eight.[2] The celebrant at the Great Ox is linked to a ritual

partner, and both together are opposed to the two firestick patrons who
bless them; there are four token whippings and four sorties by the women.
There are four cuts of meat at the subsistence feast for local elders. The
curse in Case 49 was by two pairs of elders; the outcome in Case 63 was
contrived to balance the marriages of two pairs of daughters; and so on.

It is therefore quite consistent that the allocation of cuts should make
use of the symmetry of the carcass. In Figures 15 and 16, X and Y refer to
paired cuts between the two sides, with no preference between right and
left in the course of allocation. It is the balanced pairing that counts.
Almost without exception, these pairs are divided between the representatives of separate social categories, drawing attention to the structural
opposition between them. Often this is prescribed, sometimes it is
adaptable at the host's discretion to demand, but always it is fully explicit.
Thus in Figure 15 one has:

ribs X : Y ::	elders : boys
outer thigh X : Y ::	elders : boys
inner thigh X : Y ::	wives : girls
kneefold X : Y ::	wives : girls *or* elders : girls
forelimb X : Y ::	elders : wives *or* moran : wives
hip meat X : Y ::	elders : wives *or* all wives
mid-spinal strip X : Y ::	elders : wives *or* all wives

Among elders, the host is expected to provide cuts for each age-set to
share in their own separate group. The principle of designated pairs is
extended to his own age-set as against his firestick patrons (or wards); and
to his own firestick alliance as against the opposed firestick alliance. This
leaves him with a certain discretion regarding a cut designated for, say, the
other firestick alliance. It could be given to either of the age-sets
representing this alliance, or it could be reserved for a particular elder.
The host could, for instance, save this cut for a senior kinsman or a
father-in-law, representing the designated age-set, to share in his own way
and his own time. Either way, it is the age-sets that are respected and again
the principle of binary opposition applies in the division:

flank X : Y ::	host's firestick patrons : respected age mate (host should abstain)
hind shin X : Y ::	other firestick alliance : host's firestick alliance
shoulder girdle X : Y ::	outsider/other age-set : host (for himself, his family or age mates)

This may be reduced to an implicit hierarchy of binary oppositions, as in
Figure 17.

The meat feast probably more than any other activity brings every
sector of Matapato society together, and this careful balance in the
allocation of cuts is noted. Due respect for status is discussed as though it

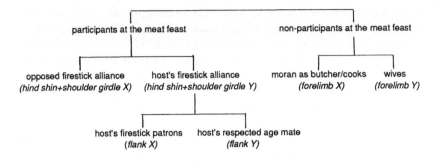

Figure 17   Pairing of cuts among feasters

is not just a matter of decorum but also of aesthetic principle. Regardless of the personalities who actually attend, every social category has its place in the scheme of things. This gives an unassailable organic unity to the meat feast that binds together the more intimate unity of the feasting circles that share each cut. In other contexts, these categories are opposed to one another by sex or age. By pairing them with paired cuts of meat they remain opposed and yet are uniquely united, and the feasting embraces the whole of Matapato society in a wholesome activity.[3]

(d)   THE UPPER AND LOWER INNARDS

At first sight, the priority given to the taste-buds in the allocation of cuts masks any association between parts of the animal's carcase and their counterparts in the feaster's own body. There is, even so, an explicit pattern in the allocation of some of the inner parts. Men's attitude towards their own inner workings is reflected in the roots that they put in their soups and notably the finishing stew. These aim to flush out their systems after the body has absorbed the goodness of the meat, leaving them generally fitter. Consistent with this distaste for the digestive tracts, it is held that bits of the stomach are inappropriate for elders, and this extends down to the inner thigh area. It is not just that they are distasteful to men, but by their very nature they are more appropriate for women. It is women that are felt to be more conscious of these vital but messy regions, with their intense concern over reproductive matters and disorders, and with their clothing infused by the smelly messes of their infants. The gluttony of ravenous moran at their forest feasts notwithstanding, these parts are generally felt to be unwholesome and on the whole unmanly.

The upper innards, on the other hand, are ideal for men. The chest regions have a special association with emotional power and the father (pp.

121 and 241). Heading the list is the tongue, which the host should give to his father or to some other very senior elders living locally, for it will not keep long. The tongue has a unique association with both the chest and the head. It is the only wholesome cut from the head, and by analogy it is associated with very senior elders whose heads embody their wisdom and authority, and whose mouths bless their dependants with spittle that comes up from the chest.

Despite its mediocre rating in the scale of taste, the centre breast ranks high in Figure 16, and is reserved for senior men with strong teeth. The heart, like the brain, is disqualified from the higher reaches because of its taste (rating 6) and is relegated to boys in other Maasai areas. However, in Matapato it is regarded as too important a part for the uninitiated. It has therefore been redesignated as a cook's titbit, effectively promoting it to join the lungs and breast-bone as a piece that only moran or elders should taste.

After a sacrifice, three of the four principal cuts that the firestick patrons offer their wards inside the ritual enclosure are from the chest region; and in the blessing that follows, it is the brisket-fat covering the chest that is used to anoint them. These parts would not normally be given to women except at their festival with the sacrifice of a pregnant heifer, and even then the brisket-fat is mixed with foetal fluid.

This provides a further dualism that translates Matapato ideas about the human body into the allocation of inner cuts.

chest/tongue : stomach parts :: ritual power : child-bearing :: elders : wives

(e) THE BROAD BACK, THE SOFT UNDERSIDE, AND THE SIGNIFICANCE OF FATS

The colour and markings of Matapato oxen have a ritual significance. Certain markings, for instance, are held to bring luck to the herd (*a-munyak*), and an ox with these would not be belled, slaughtered or given away, for this would end the luck. Certain other animals are thought to be especially propitious (*a-sunya*), and it is these that are ideal for sacrifice. In general, a propitious animal should have two colours, one of which is partly concealed. An ox with dark fur that conceals a lighter colour (*pukoti*) or a light dappled fur that conceals a darker colour (*sirua*), for instance, would be propitious. So would an ox that has a lighter underside and inner leg, but is predominantly brown or dappled around its back and outer parts (*laarus* and *warikuoi* respectively). This distinction between the well protected back and the less protected underparts appears to have a wider relevance, both in the allocation of the slaughtered fats and in attitudes towards the human body.

Type of fat	Communal sharing	Tracing (a-sir)	Smearing (a-el)	Object of play	Comments
	A	**B**	**C**	**D**	
Brisket-fat (underside)	Living father /owner	Age-set blessing	Father's death ox		**A** Normal use; must be shared with an age mate **B** To remove possible sorcery (*esoogo*, p. 211) **C** Corpse smeared by senior son (p. 240)
"	Great Ox blessing	*Eunoto* blessing			**A and B** Both administered by firestick patrons **B** Applies also to all firestick sacrifices (pp. 140, 264)
"	Calf-of-the threshold blessing	Women's heifer blessing			**A and B** Both administered by elders; and neither animal has much fat (p. 58) **B** Heifer's fat is mixed with foetal fluid (p. 223)
Scrotal-fat (underside)	Living mother /wife			Ox-of-the wooden- earplugs	**A** No prescription on sharing (p. 264) **D** Play between moran and mothers reported in some other Maasai sections (p. 84)
Rib-fat (outside)	Owner		Women's gathering blessing	Great Ox	**A** Normal use; can be shared with any elder **C** Terminates gathering; fat mixed with red ochre and rubbed around neck and shoulders (p. 202) **D** Whipping contest between sexes (p. 254)
"			Moran war blessing	Calf-of-the threshold	**C** Precedes raid; fat rubbed esp into hair (p. 127) **D** Vying between wives of moieties (pp. 58, 255)
Butter		Suitor's------------------------> gift of anointment			**D** Subject to play by wives on unsuspecting girl, who tries to rub it off immediately (p. 26)
Sheep fat			Bride's blessing		**C** Given by elders on leaving parental home, and bride reluctant to wash it off (p. 31)
"			Mother's death sheep		**C** Corpse smeared by a son (ideally the youngest)

Figure 18 The ceremonial uses of fats

The fats of any slaughtered animal have a special and sometimes colourful role, summarised in Figure 18. When the carcase of an ox is cut up, they are carefully separated from the meat and grouped into three types. The very hard white lumps of fat located in the stomach region and rump have no ritual uses and are regarded with distaste by the elders (taste rating 7 or 8). Like other stomach parts, they are relegated to the women, who may cook them with their own cereal foods. Fats covering the exposed outer parts of the body such as the rib-fat and hump and also by the heart are sweeter and softer (rating 2). They are retained as a relish by the owner, to be shared with any other elders. Softest and sweetest of all is the fat covering the underside (rating 1), which will keep almost indefinitely once the oil has been separated from the tissue. This is divided at about the level of the navel, again repeating the division between the sexes. The brisket-fat under the chest belongs to the owner's father so long as he lives, and is then smeared over his corpse when he dies. The cod-fat or scrotal-fat lower down and inside the thighs belongs to the mother for as long as she lives. Ideally, if he is within a day's journey by foot, the owner's father would also be given the hump-fat, tongue and perhaps the centre breast. But he *must* be given the brisket-fat sooner or later, and the mother must be given the scrotal-fat, no matter how far away they are. After his parent's death, the owner keeps the brisket-fat of each slaughter, and his wife has the scrotal-fat.

The brisket-fat towers above all other cuts in importance. Other cuts are shared among age mates as a matter of course at any meat feast, but there is a reverence about sharing the brisket-fat, as if it is the age-set itself and not just an age mate that is sharing. After ritual partners have shared it at the Great Ox festival, they use the word for brisket-fat, *enkiyu*, as a reciprocal term of address, expressing their deep respect for one another. On other occasions it must always be shared with an age mate. At sacrifices, oil extracted from this fat provides the ultimate blessing and protection from sorcery. It is traced down the body of each firestick ward in the patrons' blessing, and also in blessing an elder after an age-set punishment (*esoogo*). There is in these blessings an implicit association between the soft underside of the ox and the corresponding forefront of the wards or penitent. The oil is traced down the right-hand side of his face, neck, inside arm, and down the chest, stomach and inside thigh. A similar pattern is followed in the meat cuts that are ritually shared by wards before this blessing with a broadly similar sequence down the underside of the animal's body. These are the inner chest, the meat inside the upper forelimb, the brisket, and the flank. Each cut is traced four times down the brow of each ward and he is then offered it to taste. In other words, the transfer of protection from God to the feasters through the ox, noted previously in the analysis of sacrifice, appears to apply also to the blessing. There is a matching of the soft underside of the ox to the corresponding region of the participant's body.

There is a similar matching of cut to human surface in the ritual use of the rib-fat covering the outer back. This may be used in lesser blessings when the slaughtered animal is not actually sacrificed. For instance, it is used when women are blessed after their fertility gathering, and also in blessing moran before they set out on a raid in the past. On such occasions the rib-fat is mixed with red ochre and the participants smear it over their hair and shoulders (as opposed to its being traced down the front by those blessing them). This matching of the less sensitive areas of the body is repeated on two other occasions when the rib-fat – a men's portion – is the subject of horseplay involving women. The first is when they try to snatch it from elders at the Great Ox feast; and the other time is when they vie for it at the calf-of-the-threshold. Here, the rib-fat that covers the back is the trophy in these whipping games, and as with other beatings, the whipping should be confined to the back and limbs, avoiding the front (Cases 42c and 45). On each of these occasions, this violent play with the rib-fat contrasts almost pointedly with the ritual gravity of sharing the brisket-fat later in the day.[4]

The broad back and soft front are also symbolically contrasted in the context of moranhood. At *eunoto*, as in other firestick sacrifices, the soft underfat is used for blessing the wards. On these occasions, the broad back – or at least the hump with the midspinal strips – is allocated to the patrons, because, they say, they are like the elder who sits behind an initiate at circumcision and clutches his body from behind. This elder is typically a mother's-brother, but he may equally be a firestick patron in an avuncular role, and ideally he would be both. A striking feature of circumcision is the utter defencelessness of the initiate as a most vital part of his front is exposed to the ordeal. This is seen as a supreme test anticipating his moranhood when again if necessary he is expected to face any enemy frontally and not run away. The rib-fat blessing before a raid protected his shoulders and hair only; he had to risk and protect his front for himself. Moran do not have frontal brisket-fat blessings until *eunoto*, and this is then seen as the first significant step towards elderhood.

This suggests that one should examine the symbolic clues of the ritual use of fats in relation to the vulnerability of the individual in the course of ageing. Children are protected above all, for they are most vulnerable and the future of the family and society at large lies with them. When food is short, they are the first to be fed. However even in childhood, boys prime themselves for the exposure of moranhood as a coveted ambition. Through their meat feasts in the forest, moran aim to build up their physiques and prime themselves for fulfilment in battle. The symbolic exposedness of the moran is the protection of Matapato, rather as the inadequacy of the fence surrounding their manyata is intended to convey a defiant vigilance. Defending their society for a period is a prerequisite for elderhood. Their exposed position is progressively sanctified with age, and the brisket-fat, which belongs to the older men, is conferred as blessings on younger men in their ceremonial upgradings, as at *eunoto*, *olngesher*, and ultimately at the Great Ox when they return to the shelter of the village.

Taking this a step further, women are also circumcised and then have to face the frontal risks of child-birth. The parallel is most explicit in their urge for babies at their fertility gatherings. At this time, they compare themselves with diehards who have an urge for cattle, and they too are then blessed with rib-fat on their shoulders. This frontal exposure is *their* prerequisite for the security of motherhood, symbolised by the scrotal-fat that will be theirs. Unlike the moran whose ideology lingers from past warfare, the dangers facing women in natural child-birth are unabated and should not be underestimated. It is the younger people of both sexes that are expected to expose themselves to the greatest dangers in perpetuating their society. This is their traditional role, and the gift of the underfat to their surviving parents is an obligatory token of respect by the younger generation, whose very existence is owed entirely to the risks previously taken on their behalf. To deny their seniors this respect would automatically bring a death curse and would be inconceivable, except at a sacrifice where the fat is conferred downwards in blessing instead of upwards in respect. The gift symbolises the axiom that the lifestyle of the older generation must be protected through the respect of the young. Metaphorically, comparing the notion of propitiousness with the endurance of Matapato, it is as if the senior generation are rather like the vital underside of the propitious ox or the hidden colour in its fur. It is propitious for them to be ritually protected by their children, who now take their turn in exposing themselves outwardly to the risks of regeneration. It is propitious because it is proper.

CONCLUSION: THE CIRCLE OF THE FEAST

The opposition between the protective back and the soft underside is not woven into a coherent philosophy. It may be seen as an expression of vague feelings that can only be made explicit through symbols and metaphors. The belief in sorcery is a metaphor of the same general notion that when Matapato collective life is most festive, it is also particularly vulnerable.

This chapter has primarily concerned feasting among elders. It is important to stress that in reviving the ideals of manyata sharing, the elders are selecting just one aspect of moranhood, which is opposed to elderhood in other respects. In this context, it is intriguing to consider the diehard who is loyal to his brothers in battle and the sorcerer who is jealous of them at home. They are two quite different semi-mythical misanthropes in Matapato belief that reflect a transformation of the meat feast itself as moran are transformed into elderhood. The diehards are associated with the sombre fantasies of moran feasting in the forest, symbolising what the moran as committed warriors were to Matapato, and what the meat feast is to the moran. The diehard fantasy has no place in the manyata where there is a greater emphasis on comradeship and less on personal prowess. With elderhood and the easing of moran expectation, it is as if meat feasting itself moves from the forest into the manyata. It recaptures for the moment the close rapport between age mates. It is the sharing rather than the commitment to excel that prevails and the spectre of the diehard recedes. At the same time, the fundamental premise of their existence moves from the republican ideal of the manyata to the rudimentary capitalism of the elders' villages, and stimulates the one emotion that is anathema to moran: greed.

At their *eunoto*, moran take their first step towards elderhood. Standing in a circle facing inwards, two of their number are plucked from the circle and are taken outside to suffer the misfortune that would otherwise fall on their age-group. Then at the sacrifices as the moran 'pass through the ox' (*a-polos*) they again face inwards towards the centre (*em-polos*) of an exclusive circle bounded by their backs and beyond these by the ritual enclosure. It is the possibility of sorcery that is kept outside when they exclude other age-sets and non-Matapato from this enclosure. It is this more than the forest feasting of the moran that seems to provide a formalised model of any elders' meat feast. Here too there is an intricate division of cuts, and age mates gather into a loose group. Figuratively speaking, they face inwards as they share their allocated cut, pressing choice pieces on one another with warm insistence. While their fronts are turned figuratively towards one another in this grouping, their backs form an excluding boundary, turned towards the bush, and to other age-sets with their own cuts seated nearby. They are also turning their backs to the other side of their lives centred on their villages where they pursue their own private interests. The Great Ox feast breaks down some of this exclusiveness, dispensing with the division between age-sets, but here once again there is a special concern to exclude sorcerers from the feast enclosure.

Neither Matapato as a society nor their meat feasts are dominated by an excessive concern over sorcery; but in so far as it is always felt to be a remote possibility with its own cosmological niche, sorcery belongs to the area beyond the feasting circle. The belief in sorcery is an expression of a vague unease whose shadow is cast over feasts of celebration, and more especially when a feeling of general misfortune is the pretext for the sacrifice in the first place. The meat feast is felt to provide the most potent opportunity for some unseen malcontent, somewhere out there in the bush, waiting for his opportunity to contaminate the site or the meat itself. Unlike the stranger with 'eyes' who can be made welcome if he spits, the sorcerer is most definitely unwelcome. All that he stands for is opposed to the spirit of the meat feast, which is about transforming a private asset into a very public sharing. It overrides the petty jealousies that divide communities, and confers a general blessing on the feasters and on the host.

After a meat feast, elders may drink beer, or stew or tea without milk or just water. However, no-one who has tasted meat should touch any milk on that day, for the feaster is still in contact with the death of an ox from the herd. It is believed that if he breaks this rule, then the cattle would stop giving milk and the herd would die out. Children could be beaten for ignoring this. This avoidance neatly expresses the contradiction between a stock owner's investment in his living herd and the irreversible destruction of his capital through slaughter. Even the slaughter of an infertile ox is a capital loss, for the finer the animal, the more likely it is that it was obtained or could have been given in exchange for an immature female. The conflict between private ambition and public interest runs like a thread through this analysis. It is therefore not altogether surprising that the transformation from a living animal to a meat feast should reflect earlier points of discussion.

The meat feast provides a high point of collective life in Matapato. It is an alternative aspect to the dispersed pastoralism that provides their daily milk and investment for the future. In their age-sets, they are mobilised once again like moran, their backs turned against the possibility of selfishness and sorcery. In the calculated allocation of cuts between groups, there is a more inclusive organic unity, and a sense that Matapato society itself is involved and sanctions the purpose of the feast. As a topic for discussion, the meat feast provides an ethnographer's cue that can be developed in almost any direction. For it is a topic on which every elder considers himself an expert and its ramifications are a reflection of the fascination Matapato have in their own society.

NOTES

1   In a meat feast, according to availability and personal taste, the following could be added to the daily stews: (woods) *oltimigomi, olkiloriti, oloilalei*; (barks) *olkiloriti; esokonoi*; (roots) *olmangula, olkinyil*; (fruit) *loodua*. According to the desired purgative or emetic effect, the following could be added to the finishing stew: (roots) *enkokola, olkinyil, eremit, olmokotan*; (bark) *olkiloriti*.

2   In relation to a binary scale, Matapato explain the ritual significance of 5 and 9 in ceremonies for men as 4+1 and 8+1. Similarly, the recurrence of 49 is perceived as $(4 \times 10) + 8 + 1$. See Figure 9, and also *Models* (Chapter 4) for an elaboration of the ritual significance of numerical cycles.

3   The principle of binary opposition applies also to the feast of the calf-of-the-threshold, yielding the following pattern for the two principal feasts:

(flank + hind shin + shoulder girdle) X : elders' morning feast in the bush
(flank + hind shin + shoulder girdle) Y : evening feast for elders and wives

A calf does not lend itself to the same carving pattern as larger animals padded with meat and fat. However, its spine and breast bone can be more easily split lengthways, and this makes possible two unconventional pairs of cuts (*embaat*) that are also roast for selected participants:

(backbone + hump) X and (breastbone + brisket) X : two elders who lead the calf
(backbone + hump) Y and (breastbone + brisket) Y : two wives chosen by the mother

Altogether this ceremony is recognised as having a pattern of its own, but it is also claimed to be an ancient Maasai practice.

4   In a somewhat similar way, the teasing between moran and their mothers at the ox-of-the-wooden-earplugs in some other parts of Maasai, is sometimes said to involve the mothers' scrotal-fat, with moran even forcing the women to drink this on the spot. Elders in Matapato suggest that any such behaviour simply reflects the exuberant disrespect of novice moran and has no place in the standard routine of Matapato ritual.

CHAPTER 15

CONCLUSION: RITUALS OF REBELLION AND THE TRUSTEESHIP OF MAASAI CULTURE

Stratification by age entails a type of social organisation that was not considered in the classification of African political systems by Fortes and Evans-Pritchard (1940:5). As Frank Stewart (1977:2) has noted, age organisation is a topic that has frequently been omitted from general anthropological textbooks. Even in some influential ethnographic accounts, it has been largely ignored or relegated somewhat anomalously as a separate, self-contained and self-explanatory phenomenon.[1] Despite the fact of ageing in every society, age organisation generally has somehow evaded the attention of social theorists.

Yet an organisation of this sort was a central theme in Plato's *The Republic*, which was probably the earliest attempt at classifying political systems, and his analysis has a relevance for the present study. There is an intriguing complementarity between Plato's model and Freud's *Totem and Taboo*. Both writers made guesses about social evolution that are really metaphors of their insights into the process of ageing at different stages of life. Freud assumed a parallel between a child's emotional development, from self-centredness to group deference, and the evolution from pre-human primate to pristine society. Plato assumed a parallel between the loss of deference in middle-age and the loss of group integrity in the political devolution of society, his age graded Republic representing an earlier uncorrupted form. These successive aspects of ageing, one following logically after the other, provide a useful framework for recapitulating aspects of the argument of this volume. For a more comprehensive treatment, the reader is referred to the conclusions of each chapter. The Maasai have certain practices relating to the family that would have intrigued Freud, and an age organisation whose cumulative wisdom associated with the divisions of age resembles Plato's Divided Line. Family and age organisation are the two strands in this work. They are linked by various forms of ritual protest that reveal some of the fundamental strains of a system in motion, but also have a manifest role in controlling it.

THE FREUDIAN MODEL AND THE GENERATION OF THE PACT AMONG PEERS

Among the Matapato and other central and northern Maasai, the cyclical process of generating a new age-group every seven or eight years is focused on the formation of manyat, local warrior villages, throughout the region. This is pre-empted by a symbolic display of strength when a new age-group of moran assume the privileges of warriorhood and capture the popular limelight from their predecessors. Usually these privileges are reluctantly conceded to them sooner or later, but with the real possibility that they may be usurped by force if they are refused. In this transition, there is a fine dividing line between a ritualised display of power and true rebellion in which the coveted domain of moranhood is seized by those best fitted to take on its responsibilities.

Having assumed the prerequisites of full moranhood, there follows the most flamboyant episode of this sequence. This takes the form of raids on the villages of fathers of moran to abduct the mothers and cattle for the manyata. Maasai fathers have an exceptionally potent curse, but if the father protests on this occasion, other moran are ready to hold him down while the mother is snatched away. In this way, the manyata is founded out of a symbolic uprising against the patriarchal edifice of Maasai society. It may be seen as a ritual of rebellion in the sense that Max Gluckman coined the term (1955:109–136, 1971:259). It is conducted in the spirit of a protest that is felt to invigorate the established order. It is widely condoned, even by most fathers, and assumed to be good for the sons, good for the Maasai, and good for the defence of their herds. In a number of other respects the raid is more extreme than any of the examples cited by Gluckman. It is more than a temporary protest that symbolically enacts a social conflict, followed by a return to normal life: the sons do not return to their fathers' homes. Or more precisely, they only return when the manyata disperses and they are poised for elderhood. Moreover, it provides a clear exception to Gluckman's suggestion that ritual conflict is never carried into the elementary family since this would be too damaging for the most fundamental relationships of society. In the Maasai instance, the ritual of rebellion goes to the core of the family with sons snatching away their mothers and seceding from their fathers. Within the family, this entails a real shift in power rather than merely a protest against power.

In this challenge to the father's patriarchal hold, one is reminded of Freud's excursion into anthropological theorising. The scenario of his

Totem and Taboo was based on Darwin's notion that Man's primal ancestor herded as many wives as he could retain. Meanwhile, the younger males were obliged to wait until they were mature enough to dispose of the father and seize control of the women. The parallel in nature with the polygamous family among the Maasai is apt. It provides a metaphor that was once drawn for me by a Samburu when he used Maasai categories to point out the relationship between two herds of gazelle nearby. One herd, he explained, was the herd of the 'elder' and his 'wives'. The other was of 'moran', excluded from the parent herd by the 'elder' and frisking among themselves.[2] The Maasai father is a bull-like patriarch and his sons face a prolonged bachelorhood as moran because of the shortage of women. In *Totem and Taboo*, Freud developed this scenario into an oedipal theory of social evolution. He used his insight into the experience of becoming social for each individual as an analogy for the experience of becoming human among the species as a whole. This led him to suggest that the intense remorse among the sons at having killed their father and coveted their mothers and sisters, led them to a joint pact. They renounced their animal lusts and cultivated a morality associated with behaviour that was decisively human, including sexual avoidances, self-restraint, and the beginnings of communal sharing.

Details of this pact and notions of remorse hardly match the Maasai instance. Nevertheless, there are some intriguing parallels in other respects. Freud was delving into the emotional ambiguities and underlying problems of personality development in patriarchal families in Europe. Yet he happened to alight upon a scenario resembling the Maasai, albeit that this entails a switch from individual experience to the level of cultural expectation. Among the Maasai, the transition of power within each family, the pact among young peers, and the whole process of moranhood is also fraught with emotion and fantasy (Chapter 8). Both the Freudian and the Maasai models conceive of a superior constraining power that acts from within. In the Maasai instance the individual reaction to this is experienced as a consuming anger in the process of submitting to this power. In Freud's model this was seen as retrospective guilt at having defied such a power, even in fantasy. It is as if the uprising within the individual against his social conditioning is stifled at an earlier point in the Maasai model. Defiance is more unthinkable and to this extent the constraining forces of society are stronger. Yet at the level of shared ritual behaviour, a rebellion of sorts does take place.

In selecting which households they will raid for recruitment, the moran are indirectly mounting a boundary display of the territory that their manyata is pledged to defend. At a more metaphorical level, each stage that leads towards setting up the manyata takes the form of a boundary display against virtually every other sector of the community: against the previous age-group who have to concede the privileges, against their fathers by absconding with their mothers, and ultimately against the elders at large by establishing an independent manyata. In this way, the developmental cycle within individual families is geared to the developmental cycle of the sons' age-group. The thrust against the father's authority is just one aspect of a thrust against the established authority of all older men. This is more than a temporary ritual of rebellion that purges the system, a kind of symbolic sneeze. So far as the shift within the community is concerned, there is an element of true rebellion when the moran oust their predecessors, and not just a ritualised gesture. So far as the shift within family is concerned, this amounts almost to a ritual of revolution, discarding the patriarchal regime in favour of one based on the peer group. However, for the Maasai community at large, there is neither rebellion nor revolution, but the assurance of continuity. The moran are recognised as high-spirited at this time, almost to the point of being out of control. However, their behaviour is no more than a charade of rebellion, and the reputation of their age-group hinges on the aplomb with which they carry it off. This suggests an elaboration of Gluckman's notion that the participants in rituals of protest are acting the conflicts of principle within a wider social order (1971:259–60). In the Maasai instance, to borrow an analogy from Ricoeur (1971), these conflicts merely provide the text of the play that is acted. It is the manner of their interpretation that persuades the community at large how far the actors are worthy of their role. The new age-group build up their reputation and their future prospects by the stature of their performance. In this respect, the pact among the young men is the extent to which they adhere to the ideals of moranhood and enhance their reputation as a forceful and cohesive age-group.

It is within this wider established order that the moran require a recognition of their manyat. This is given by their firestick patrons, two age-sets senior to their own and many of them fathers of moran. The ceremony marking this point is conducted in the spirit of a ritual of counter-rebellion. The patrons demand conditions on their own terms and are poised to lash out with their whips at any moran on the slightest pretext. They in their turn have a role to play, and their control over the moran hinges on their ability to intimidate the moran through a convincing display of their superior moral power.

From this point the exact balance of power between the physical supremacy of the moran and the moral superiority of the elders is indeterminate. It is a matter of constant intrigue among all sectors of the community. Generally, the moran are expected to build up their reputation as a worthy and forceful group. When they are caught as individuals falling short of the ideal, as is bound to happen, then the initiative reverts again to the elders. It is a pretext for mounting a harangue, using the indiscretions of a few to humiliate the manyata as a whole rhetorically for their immature lack of respect and worthlessness. That the elders' control over the moran also hinges on the quality of their own performance is well illustrated by the failure of each official attempt to repress the moran by banning the manyata system. The elders have given such measures their formal support, but apparently without much conviction. In Kenya the irrepressibility of each new age-group of moran has outweighed the performance of their repressers, and the manyata system has survived.

Throughout the period of its existence – at one time until it was displaced by its successor – the manyata remains a symbol of insurgence. In the spirit in which it was formed, it represents a protest against the flaccid self-indulgence of elderhood that is associated with the village areas. The manyata embraces instead a group-indulgence towards the peer group with its own separate existence. To be a true moran is to remain without possessions and to share in all things with other moran. While the manyata lasts, the prospect of settling down as elders is anathema. To marry, to stay in the father's village, or to take up inheritance are all regarded as corruptions of moranhood; and elderhood in general is regarded as the corruption of an ideal. No moran should want to become an elder before being forced to do so. At the same time, the ritual of rebellion invokes the authority of a higher moral order, the communitas of Maasai society at large. What is liminal to the ultimate control of the elders is a central feature of Maasai identity. Symbolically the manyata is a microcosm of the Maasai ideal rising above neighbouring peoples and above the petty concerns of each family. In this sense, the community of interest within the manyata shared by all moran is a cultural heritage that is prized within Maasai society at large. It is this that enriches the pact of renunciation among peers. Instead of Freud's once-and-for-all generation of a cultural ideal arising out of and above patriarchal self-interest, one has the periodic regeneration of the ideal with each new age-group. It is an ideal that is culturally opposed to the private investment of self-interest within the patriarchal family.

This liminal position of the moran leads one to reconsider Van Gennep's analysis of Maasai initiations as a prime example of a rite of transition lasting several months and leading on to warriorhood. Bearing in mind his elaboration of rites within rites, Van Gennep could quite consistently have extrapolated the analysis to the manyata episode as an extended second phase. The moran live separately from their fathers and under ritualised restrictions that place them in a liminal position.[3] Founding the manyata and the whole manyata episode, bridging the transition from herdboy to elder, may be seen as an extended ritual of rebellion and at the same time as a rite of transition over a period of years and not just months.

THE PLATONIC MODEL AND THE DEGENERATION OF
THE PACT IN ELDERHOOD

For present purposes, Plato's *The Republic* may be regarded as taking over the argument where Freud's *Totem and Taboo* leaves off, with a complementary theory of ageing. Freud's is a progressive model of emotional development and the genesis of self-denial associated with a sense of personal and group integrity in early years. Plato's is a regressive model of the loss of self-denial and group integrity in later years.[4] Taken at a more inclusive level, the two models may be related to the ebb and flow of the Maasai age cycle. Each age-group rises to a climax after initiation and then dwindles into elderhood in later years as it is absorbed into an age-set.

The types of character and human weakness outlined by the Maasai in relation to facets of their society are recognisably similar to those expressed by Plato in his classification of political systems. Their caricature of a diehard among moran has the intellectual limitations of Plato's honour-bound timocratic man. Their caricature of a sorcerer has the underlying greed of an elder as he tends towards oligarchic man in middle-age. Their caricature of a wastrel who has gone adrift has the disorientation of Plato's democratic man. Their caricature of an elder who lives with his family alone has the unchecked power of Plato's tyrant. Plato's ideal was to achieve a fine and stable balance between such tendencies within the individual and within society at large, placing the most morally responsible type in control. Such a role in Maasai is idealised in the manyata spokesman, who is expected to cultivate the qualities of an ideal ruler with the guidance of his peers.

In his typology, Plato coined the term timocracy for the Spartan type of society where honour played an important part in its government. In his analysis, it was the strict hierarchy of age grading in the Spartan system that appears to have impressed him. It distinguished it decisively from the other forms of polity that he considered. In this respect, Lee (1974:22) has suggested that this is a type of society that has no real parallel in modern experience. However, this is to overlook such peoples as the Maasai, who can well be described as a timocracy in Plato's sense. Among the Maasai, as in Sparta, young men are expected to live and eat together as a way of inculcating them with the virtues of self-denial and respect for authority. Maasai warriors, like Spartans, also disclaim possessions, and those that have married can only steal furtive visits to their wives. Both societies have been admired by their more progressive neighbours for the vitality of their austere conservatism and self-regard (Bury 1967:123–34, Jones 1967: 34–9).

Plato's notion of an ideal state was modelled on that of Sparta, with similar age grading. The strict military discipline of youth would ideally be carried through to old age with the cultivation of higher moral qualities that still precluded personal possessions or marriage among those best suited to rule; wives and children would be held in common. Plato recognised that his ideal state was virtually unattainable, but institutions at least have been modelled on similar lines. Among the Maasai, the manyata is such an institution in a way that the patriarchal family certainly is not. It is established as a self-governing community that rejects any notion of private property or self-seeking. Together moran learn to develop a rapport in which the individual is both subservient to the collective will and has a role in shaping it. In the dialectic of debate or informal discourse, any moran can defend his self-interest, but he should not allow it to impede the progress towards consensus, which has the binding force of a unanimous decision. The charm of moranhood for Maasai is focused on the manyata and the integrity of a cultivated selflessness. Arguments over lionskin trophies and matters of personal honour are mere episodes subordinated to the general will.

In his scheme, Plato argued that timocracies such as Sparta were degenerate forms of this ideal, in that the military virtues instilled in youth no longer carried through to elderhood. The ideal became compromised by a desire to accumulate property in middle-age: egalitarianism in Sparta was only superficial and they were notorious for their avarice. This can be matched with the Maasai reputation in relation to accumulating cattle. Even moran betrayed self-interest when the sequel to a raid was a fight among themselves for a larger share of the spoil. It is in this context that Merker (1904:80–1, 97), one of the sincerest admirers of the Maasai, indirectly invoked Thrasymachus's argument in *The Republic* that 'Might is Right.' Or as the Maasai put it, 'Cattle have their own law.' However, moran at their worst are subject to manyata discipline, and in Maasai characterisation it is only elders who accumulate possessions and are prone to avarice, caricatured in its most pernicious form by the sorcerer.

When they settle to family life as elders, the idealisation of moranhood is edged to one side by the developing self-interest in their possessions, but it is not destroyed. As elders, they reinvoke the manyata ideal whenever they congregate as an age-set, whether in debate or at a meat feast, or by chance. When Maasai claim that the manyata alone cultivates a true sense of respect, they are acknowledging that the wisdom and responsibility accrued by older men are founded on the integrity of the manyata experience. It is in this sense that any gathering of the age-set espouses the Platonic ideal.

The thrust of the present work concerns the interplay between these two contradictory ideals: self-interest grounded in family possessions as against group dependence idealised in the age system. Neither can be considered in isolation. There is a natural drift towards private self-interest that is held in check by public obligation. When a Maasai elder slaughters an ox, it is transformed from a living animal that he covets into a feast in which he is the host and acts especially on behalf of his age-set. When he entertains a visiting age mate, they both share together as representatives of their age-set, and the hut and the wife of the host are transformed into the hut and the wife of the age-set. When age mates (or indeed clansmen) combine to check the excesses of an elder who has abused his power over his family, then he is transformed from a patriarchal tyrant to a member of the community, accountable to the wider public interest. These are public acts that raise the issue above self-interest and free choice. In other words, the element of self-interest, which Plato relegated to the governed classes beneath consideration, is relegated among Maasai to the flip-side of their existence: their alter persona in private life. The interplay between these two ideas in daily life entails a switch between private and public arenas and a transformation of meaning. When a matter becomes public, the individual is bound by his social role and the interpretation of this role is expressed symbolically, and in this sense it is ritualised behaviour.

Similarly, when a woman joins other wives in a dance, she is transformed from a dependent 'child' to a member of a collectivity that men must respect. The Maasai ideal loses sight of women, who normally have a subservient role as domestic commodities, rather as Plato's ideal loses sight of the subservient population. The critical position of women in relation to the domestication of moran into elderhood and the range of their collective behaviour are summarised in the conclusions to Chapters 10 and 11. Here, it must suffice to point out that when they gather as a punitive mob, it is in defence of a principle that is more fundamental than any for which elders or moran gather to admonish an age mate. This principle concerns the horror of incest between any elder and a 'daughter'. By transforming Lévi-Strauss's model of marriage alliance and social cohesion from the relationship between descent groups through their sisters/wives to the relationship between age-sets through their daughters/ wives, one arrives at the bedrock of morality in Maasai terms. It is this that is defended by married women above all. Their collective response is the most extreme form of ritual rebellion in Maasai society, and through it the women are underpinning a system that holds them in subservience.

Thus on the one hand, the hub of moran activity is the manyata, which represents at the same time a counter-culture and the highest ideal of Maasai existence. While on the other hand, the women's fertility dances and more especially their mobbing are both a counter-culture and the expression of a fundamental moral principle. In their public lives, the elders aim to live up to these ideals and to be the trustees of Maasai culture, setting the principles that they expect all other members of the community to observe. In their private lives they are accountable to one another to a considerable degree. However, beyond this in different ways, it is the moran at their manyat and women acting as a collectivity and parading themselves like diehards, who are the active trustees of the principles on which the culture is based.

The power emanating from rituals of rebellion among the Maasai, then, is not that they legitimise conflict within a wider order as Gluckman suggested. They are closer to true rebellion in the sense that he coined the term. They set the moral parameters within which a political order becomes possible. They represent the communitas of Maasai culture, rising above the elders, and displayed by those who as individuals are subservient, and yet as a collectivity can claim an inviolable tradition. It is the tradition of their identity and persistence as Maasai.

NOTES

1 Thus Evans-Pritchard (1940:249) appended his account of the Nuer age-set system as an unrelated afterthought to his classic study of holism. Similarly, in his study of Jie kinship and property rights, Gulliver (1955:11) excluded the complexities of the Jie age organisation as irrelevant to his work.
2 Spencer 1965:100–1, 305–6, Freud 1913:125, Darwin 1871:590, and see above p. 99.
3 Van Gennep 1960:84–7; Spencer 1965:259.
4 The relevant passages of *The Republic* in this section are principally taken from Lee 1974: 77–8, 163–5, 177–95, 344–405.

REFERENCES

Austin, H.H., 1903. *With MacDonald in Uganda*. Arnold, London.

Barth, F., 1964. 'Capital, investment and the social structure of a pastoral nomad group in South Persia', in Firth, R. and B.S. Yamey (eds.), *Capital, Saving and Credit in Peasant Societies*. Allen and Unwin, London.

Beckwith, C. and T. Ole Saitoti, 1980. *Maasai*. Elm Tree Books, London.

Bury, J.B., 1967. *A History of Greece*. Macmillan, London.

Dallas, D., 1931. 'The sacred tree of ol Donyesha'. *Man*, 31, pp. 39–41.

Darwin, C.R., 1871. *The Descent of Man, and Selection in Relation to Sex*. Murray, London.

Durkheim, E., 1933. *Division of Labour in Society*. (Orig. 1893, trans. G. Simpson), Macmillan, New York.

  1951. *Suicide*. (Orig. 1897, trans. J. Spaulding and G. Simpson), Free Press, New York.

Evans-Pritchard, E.E., 1940. *The Nuer*. Clarendon Press, Oxford.

Fadiman, J.A., 1982. *An Oral History of Tribal Warfare, the Meru of Mt. Kenya*. Ohio University Press, Ohio.

Fortes, M. and E.E. Evans-Pritchard (eds.), 1940. *African Political Systems*. Oxford University Press, London, for the International African Institute.

Fosbrooke, H.A., 1948. 'An administrative survey of the Masai social system'. *Tanganyika Notes and Records*, 26, pp. 1–50.

Fox, D.S., 1930. 'Further notes on the Masai of Kenya Colony'. *Journal of the Royal Anthropological Institute*, 60, pp. 447–65.

  1931. 'Notes on marriage customs among the Maasai'. *Journal of the East Africa and Uganda Natural History Society*, 42–3, pp. 183–91.

Frazer, J.G., 1922. *The Golden Bough*. Macmillan, London.

Freud, S., 1950. *Totem and Taboo*. (Orig. 1913, trans. J. Strachey), Routledge and Kegan Paul, London.

Gluckman, M., 1955. *Custom and Conflict in Africa*. Blackwell, Oxford.

  1963. 'Rituals of rebellion in South-East Africa', in Gluckman M., *Order and Rebellion in Tribal Africa*. (Orig. 1954), Cohen & West, London.

  1971. *Politics, Law and Ritual in Tribal Society*. Blackwell, Oxford.

Goldschmidt, W., 1976. *Culture and Behaviour of the Sebei*. University of California Press, Berkeley.

Gulliver, P.H., 1955. *The Family Herds*. Routledge & Kegan Paul, London.

  1963. *Social Control in an African Society: a study of the Arusha, agricultural Masai of northern Tanganyika*. Routledge and Kegan Paul, London.

Hamilton, C.D., 1963. 'The "e-unoto" ceremony of the Masai'. *Man* 63, pp. 107–9.

  nd. 'Masai'. (Ms. library of School of Oriental and African Studies, London, MS 297457).

Hinde, S.L. and H., 1901. *The Last of the Masai*. Heinemann, London.

Hobley, C.W., 1910. *Ethnology of the A-Kamba and Other East African Tribes*.

Cambridge University Press, Cambridge.

Höhnel, L. von., 1894. *The Discovery of Lakes Rudolf and Stefanie*. (Trans. Bell. N.), Longmans, Green, London.

Hollis, A.C., 1905. *The Masai: their language and folklore*. Clarendon, Oxford.

Huntingford, G.W.B., 1931. 'Masai water trees'. *Man*, 31, p. 143.

Jackson, F., 1930. *Early Days in East Africa*. Arnold, London.

Jacobs, A.H., 1965. 'The Traditional Political Organization of the Pastoral Masai'. Unpublished D. Phil. thesis, Oxford.

— 1971. 'The warrior village and ritual house of the pastoral Maasai'. *Plan East Africa, Journal of the Architectural Association of Kenya*, 2, pp. 19–42.

Jones, A.H.M., 1967. *Sparta*. Blackwell, Oxford.

Kenya, Ministry of Finance and Planning, 1965. *Kenya Population Census, 1962*. Nairobi.

Kenya, Republic of, 1980. *Statistical Abstract*. Central Bureau of Statistics, Nairobi.

Lambert, H.E., 1956. *Kikuyu Social and Political Institutions*. Oxford University Press, London, for the International African Institute.

Leach, E.R., 1954. *Political Systems of Highland Burma*. Athlone, London.

Leakey, L.S.B., 1930. 'Some notes on the Masai of Kenya Colony'. *Journal of the Royal Anthropological Institute*, 60, pp. 185–209.

Lee, D. (trans.), 1974. *Plato: The Republic*. Penguin Books, Harmondsworth.

Lévi-Strauss, C., 1969. *The Elementary Structures of Kinship*. (Orig. 1949, trans. Bell, J.H., J.R. von Sturmer and R. Needham), Eyre and Spottiswoode, London.

Lewis, I.M., 1975. 'The dynamics of nomadism: prospects for sedentarization and social change', in Monod, T. (ed.), *Pastoralism in Tropical Africa*. Oxford University Press, London, for the International African Institute.

Llewelyn-Davies, M., 1978. 'Two contexts of solidarity among pastoral Maasai women', in Caplan P. and J.M. Bujra (eds.), *Women United, Women Divided*. Tavistock, London.

MacDonald, J.R.L., 1897. *Soldiering and Surveying in British East Africa*. Arnold, London.

Malinowski, B., 1929. *The Sexual Life of Savages in North-Western Melanesia*. Routledge, London.

Merker, M., 1904. *Die Masai*. Dietrich Reimer, Berlin.

— 1910. *Die Masai*. (Revised edition, ms. trans. Buxton), Dietrich Reimer, Berlin.

Mol, F., 1978. *Maa: a dictionary of the Maasai language and folklore, English-Maasai*. Marketing & Publishing Ltd, Nairobi.

Moore, H.L., 1986. *Space, Text and Gender: an anthropological study of the Marakwet of Kenya*. Cambridge University Press, Cambridge.

Mpaayei, J. T. Ole., 1954. *Inkuti Pukunot oo Lmaasai*. Oxford University Press, London.

Orchardson, I.Q., 1961. *The Kipsigis*. East African Literature Bureau, Nairobi.

Orr, J.B. and J.L., Gilks, 1931. *Studies of Nutrition: the physique and health of two African tribes (Masai and Kikuyu)*. Medical Research Council, Special Report Series, no 155, London.

Paine, R., 1971. 'Animals as capital'. *Anthropological Quarterly*, 44, pp. 157–172.

Peristiany, J.G., 1939. *The Social Institutions of the Kipsigis*. Routledge and Kegan Paul, London.

Ricoeur, P., 1971. 'The model of the text: meaningful action considered as a text'. *Social Research*, 38.

Rigby, P., 1969. 'Some Gogo rituals of "purification", an essay on social and moral categories', in Leach E.R. (ed.), *Dialectic in Practical Religion*. Cambridge University Press, Cambridge.

Saberwal, S., 1970. *The Traditional Political System of the Embu of Central Kenya*. East African Publishing House, Nairobi.

Saitoti, T. Ole 1986. *The Worlds of a Maasai Warrior: an autobiography*. André Deutsch, London.

Sankan, S.S. Ole 1971. *The Maasai*. East African Literature Bureau, Nairobi.

Shelford, F., 1910. 'Notes on the Masai'. *Journal of the African Society*, 9, pp. 267–9.

Snell, G.S., 1954. *Nandi Customary Law*. East African Literature Bureau, Nairobi.

Spagnolo, L.M., 1960. *Bari English Italian Dictionary*, Museum Combonianum N. 9, Istituto Missioni Africane, Verona.

Spencer, P., 1959. 'Dynamics of Samburu Religion'. (Ms. East Africa Institute of Social Research conference paper).

    1965. *The Samburu: a study of gerontocracy in a nomadic tribe*. Routledge and Kegan Paul, London.

    1973. *Nomads in Alliance: symbiosis and growth among the Rendille and Samburu of Kenya*. Oxford University Press, London.

    1974. 'Drought and the commitment to growth'. *African Affairs*, 73, pp. 419–427.

    1976. 'Opposing streams and gerontocratic ladder: two models of age organisation in East Africa'. *Man* (N.S.) 11, pp. 153–75.

    1978a. 'Age organisation, family and property among the Maasai of East Africa'. Final Report to Social Science Research Council, London (ref. HR 4014).

    1978b. 'The Jie Generation Paradox', in Baxter, P.T.W. and U. Almagor (eds.), *Age, Generation and Time: some Features of East African age organisations*. Hurst, London.

    1980. 'Polygyny as a measure of social differentiation in Africa', in Mitchell, J.C. (ed.), *Numerical Techniques in Social Anthropology*. Institute for the Study of Human Issues, Philadelphia.

    1984. 'Pastoralists and the ghost of capitalism', *Production Pastorale et Société*, 15, pp. 61–76.

    nd. 'Models of the Maasai'. (Unpublished draft ms.).

Stewart, F.H., 1977. *Fundamentals of Age-Group Systems*. Academic Press, New York.

Thomson, J., 1885. *Through Masailand*. Cass, London.

Tucker, A.N. and J.T. Ole Mpaayei, 1955. *A Maasai Grammar*. Longmans, Green, London.

Tylor, E.B., 1889. 'On a method of investigating the development of institutions; applied to laws of marriage and descent'. *Journal of the Royal Anthropological Institute*, 18, pp. 245–69.

Van Gennep, A., 1960. *The Rites of Passage*. (Orig. 1909, trans. Vizedom, M.B. and G.L. Caffee), Routledge and Kegan Paul, London.

Waller, R., 1976. 'The Maasai and the British 1895–1905: the origins of an alliance'. *Journal of African History*, 17, pp. 529–553.

Warrington, J. (trans.), 1959. *Aristotle's Politics and The Athenian Constitution*. Dent, London.

Western, D., 1973. 'The Structure, Dynamics and Changes of the Amboseli Ecosystem'. Ph.D. thesis, University of Nairobi.

Whitehouse, L.E., 1933. 'Masai social customs'. *Journal of the East Africa and Uganda Natural History Society*, 47–8, pp. 146–53.

SUBJECT INDEX

MAASAI INDEX

Glossary of Maasai terms cited in the text. For pronunciation, see p xxi.
Prefixes. *a-*: infinitive; *e/em/en-*: feminine; *o/ol-*: masculine; *i/im/in-;i/il-*: corresponding plurals.

a-dumu: to lift, filch legitimately, 109
a-el: to smear (fat in a blessing), 263
a-gilaki; to raise a spear and grunt in a dance, 68
a-goro: to be angry, 121
a-ibelekenya: to change about, transform, 121
a-ibok: to contain, confine, corral, 14
a-ikirikira: to shiver, 120
a-imal: to make a gift of respect, to refer to this gift in address, 31, 82–3
a-ingoraki: to look towards, visit a festival with good-will, 140–1
a-ipak: to perform a dance associated with mustering for war, 70
a-iroishi: to be heavy, pregnant, 213
a-irrag: to lie down, retire, 186
a-irrita: to herd, look after, beat, 14
a-iseer: to yelp at night as moran, 68
a-ishirita: to weep, 121
a-ishiru; to cry to one another (in mounting anger), 120, 205
a-isul: to excel, 68
a-itore: to control, rule, 14, 84, 108, 234
a-lom: to be possessive over a wife or lover, 189
a-munyak: to bring luck, 262
a-or: to divide (a herd for a son to pre-inherit), 234
a-poshoo: to shake, 120

a-purr: to steal, 109
a-sai: to ask for (a girl in marriage), 33
a-sir: to trace (fat in a blessing), 263
a-sulari: to fall, lose status, 129, 182
a-sunya: to be propitious, 262
a-uno: to be erected, planked upright, 139

e-lukunya, pl. *i-lukuny*: head, spokesman, 104
e-manyata, pl. *i-manyat*: manyata, 5
e-masho oonkituak: women's festival, 221–2
em-boo, pl. *im-booitie*: elder's corral, whence *e-boo*, adj.: his personal herd and possessions, 12–3, 34, 239
e-modet: ritual mishandling, 140
e-mosiroi: ritualised dance, 147–8
em-pikas, pl. *im-pikasin*: posse, 86, 110, 116
em-polosata ol-kiteng: sacrifice (passing through an ox), 139
e-muro, pl. *i-muroishi*: hind leg, 111
e-murt, pl. *i-murto*: neck, spokesman's aides, 106
en-dungore: division ('cutting') between age-sets, 66
e-ngooki: unresolvable state of sin, 39, 220, 240
en-kai: God, sky, rain, 48

AUTHOR INDEX